SAGE was founded in 1965 by Sara Miller McCune to support the dissemination of usable knowledge by publishing innovative and high-quality research and teaching content. Today, we publish over 900 journals, including those of more than 400 learned societies, more than 800 new books per year, and a growing range of library products including archives, data, case studies, reports, and video. SAGE remains majority-owned by our founder, and after Sara's lifetime will become owned by a charitable trust that secures our continued independence.

Los Angeles | London | New Delhi | Singapore | Washington DC | Melbourne

Introduction to Social Work

Thank you for choosing a SAGE product!
If you have any comment, observation or feedback,
I would like to personally hear from you.

Please write to me at **contactceo@sagepub.in**

Vivek Mehra, Managing Director and CEO, SAGE India.

Bulk Sales

SAGE India offers special discounts
for bulk institutional purchases.

For queries/orders/inspection copy requests,
write to **textbooksales@sagepub.in**

Publishing

Would you like to publish a textbook with SAGE?
Please send your proposal to **publishtextbook@sagepub.in**

Subscribe to our mailing list

Write to **marketing@sagepub.in**

This book is also available as an e-book.

Introduction to Social Work

Edited by

Bishnu Mohan Dash

Faculty, Indira Gandhi National Open University (IGNOU), New Delhi

Los Angeles | London | New Delhi
Singapore | Washington DC | Melbourne

Copyright © Bishnu Mohan Dash, 2022

All rights reserved. No part of this book may be reproduced or utilized in any form or by any means, electronic or mechanical, including photocopying, recording or by any information storage or retrieval system, without permission in writing from the publisher.

First published in 2022 by

SAGE Publications India Pvt Ltd
B1/I-1 Mohan Cooperative Industrial Area
Mathura Road, New Delhi 110 044, India
www.sagepub.in

SAGE Publications Inc
2455 Teller Road
Thousand Oaks, California 91320, USA

SAGE Publications Ltd
1 Oliver's Yard, 55 City Road
London EC1Y 1SP, United Kingdom

SAGE Publications Asia-Pacific Pte Ltd
18 Cross Street #10-10/11/12
China Square Central
Singapore 048423

Published by Vivek Mehra for SAGE Publications India Pvt Ltd. Typeset in 10.5/12.5 pt Baskerville by AG Infographics, Delhi.

Library of Congress Cataloging-in-Publication Data

Names: Dash, Bishnu Mohan, editor.
Title: Introduction to social work / edited by Bishnu Mohan Dash.
Description: New Delhi, India; Thousand Oaks, California : SAGE, 2022. | Includes bibliographical references and index.
Identifiers: LCCN 2022016787 | ISBN 9789354795039 (paperback) | ISBN 9789354795046 (epub) | ISBN 9789354795053 (ebook)
Subjects: LCSH: Social service. | Social service—Practice.
Classification: LCC HV40 .I595 2022 | DDC 361.3/2–dc23/eng/20220411
LC record available at https://lccn.loc.gov/2022016787

ISBN: 978-93-5479-503-9 (PB)

SAGE Team: Amit Kumar, Ariba Zainab, Shipra Pant, Madhurima Thapa, Sonam Rana, Aishna Bhatt and Kanika Mathur

Contents

List of Illustrations — xv
List of Abbreviations — xvii
Preface — xix
About the Book — xxi
About the Editor and Contributors — xxiii

SECTION A. SOCIAL WORK: MEANING AND BASIC CONCEPTS

CHAPTER 1 Social Work: Meaning and Concept, Objectives and Functions — 3
Shahin Sultana

CHAPTER 2 History of Social Work in the USA, the UK and India — 15
Indrajit Goswami

CHAPTER 3 Social Reform Movements in India — 33
Akileswari S.

CHAPTER 4 Great Depression and the Growth of Social Work Education — 48
Supriya Rani

CHAPTER 5 Social Welfare — 60
Archana Kaushik

CHAPTER 6 Social Service — 75
Manisha Pal and Rakesh Choudhary

CHAPTER 7 Social Reform — 89
Lakshmana G

CHAPTER 8 Social Justice — 104
Avtar Singh

CHAPTER 9 Social Legislations — 119
Eshita Sharma

CHAPTER 10 Social Development — 134
Kislay Kumar Singh

CHAPTER 11 Social Security — 147
Sunil Prasad and Arul Actovin C.

SECTION B. SOCIAL WORK AS A PROFESSION: PRINCIPLES AND METHODS, SCOPE, THEORIES, MODELS AND PROFESSIONAL STATUS

CHAPTER 12 Professional Status of Social Work Profession in India 163
Bishnu Mohan Dash, Rajan Prakash and Sheeba Joseph

CHAPTER 13 Professional Social Work Associations in India 176
Ram Babu Botcha

CHAPTER 14 Scope and Fields of Social Work and Emerging Areas 190
Shashi Rani

CHAPTER 15 Principles and Methods of Social Work 206
Nita Kumari

CHAPTER 16 Models of Social Work 219
Sayantani Guin

CHAPTER 17 Theories in Social Work 231
Sonam Rohta

CHAPTER 18 Skills in Social Work 248
Rutwik Gandhe

SECTION C. PHILOSOPHY, VALUES AND ETHICS OF SOCIAL WORK

CHAPTER 19 Philosophy of Social Work 267
Nagalingam

CHAPTER 20 Social Work Values: Traditional and Emancipatory 282
Poonam Gulalia

CHAPTER 21 Social Work Ethics 297
K. Rajeshwari and Vijay Kumar Sharma

SECTION D. APPROACHES TO SOCIAL WORK

CHAPTER 22 Ideologies Background of Social Work 315
Saumya and Tushar Singh

CHAPTER 23 Modern Indian Thinkers and Their Relevance in Social Work 330
Chittaranjan Subudhi and J. Raja Meenakshi

CHAPTER 24 Radical Social Work 343
Binod Kumar

CHAPTER 25 Gandhian Social Work 353
Mithilesh Kumar and Rajan Prakash

CHAPTER 26 African Social Work 369
Safia Winifred Ahmadu

Index I–1

Detailed Contents

List of Illustrations — xv
List of Abbreviations — xvii
Preface — xix
About the Book — xxi
About the Editor and Contributors — xxiii

SECTION A. SOCIAL WORK: MEANING AND BASIC CONCEPTS

Chapter 1
Social Work: Meaning and Concept, Objectives and Functions — 3
Shahin Sultana

- Introduction — 3
- Social Work: Meaning and Definitions — 4
- Social Work: Concept and Scope — 6
- Social Work: Objective and Functions — 8
- Summary — 10

Chapter 2
History of Social Work in the USA, the UK and India — 15
Indrajit Goswami

- Introduction — 15
- History of Social Work in the UK — 16
- History of Social Work in the USA — 19
- History of Social Work in India — 21
- Summary — 28

Chapter 3
Social Reform Movements in India — 33
Akileswari S.

- Introduction — 33
- Brahmo Samaj: Raja Ram Mohan Roy (1772–1833) — 34
- Theosophical Society: Annie Besant (1847–1933) — 35
- Ramakrishna Mission: Swami Vivekananda (1863–1902) — 35
- Satyashodhak Samaj: Mahatma Jyotirao Govindrao Phule (1827–1890) — 36
- Prarthana Samaj: Dadoba Pandurang (1814–1882) and Role of Mahadev Govind Ranade (1842–1901) — 37
- Young Bengal Movement: Henry Louis Vivian Derozio (1809–1831) — 38
- Arya Samaj: Swami Dayanand Saraswati (1824–1883) — 38

Aligarh Movement: Sir Syed Ahmed Khan (1817–1898) — 39
Widow Remarriage Association: Vishnu Shastri Pandit (1827–1876) and Mahadev Govind Ranade (1842–1901) — 40
Deoband Movement: Muhammad Qasim Nanautawi (1833–1880) and Rashid Ahmad Gangohi (1826–1905) — 40
Other Social Reformers and Revivalists — 40
Social Reform Movements across Religions — 41
Women Reformers — 43
Summary — 44

Chapter 4
Great Depression and the Growth of Social Work Education — 48
Supriya Rani

Introduction — 48
Great Depression, the New Deal and Social Work — 49
Social Work Education Post the Great Depression — 52
The Great Depression and Social Work Education in India — 53
Summary — 55

Chapter 5
Social Welfare — 60
Archana Kaushik

Introduction — 60
Social Welfare: Concept, Scope and Definitions — 61
Philosophical Base of Social Welfare — 63
Social Welfare and Related Terms — 64
Historical to Current Features of Social Welfare and Social Work — 66
Social Welfare: Scope and Practice — 68
Summary — 70

Chapter 6
Social Service — 75
Manisha Pal and Rakesh Choudhary

Introduction — 75
Social Service: Concept, Meaning and Definitions — 76
Social Work and Social Services — 78
Summary — 84

Chapter 7
Social Reform — 89
Lakshmana G

Introduction — 89
Social Problems and Social Reform — 90
What Is Social Reform? — 90
Early Reformers in India — 91
Social Reform Movements in India in the 18th, 19th and 20th Centuries — 91

Discussion 94
Summary 99

Chapter 8
Social Justice — 104
Avtar Singh

Introduction 104
Social Justice: Concept and Definition 105
Important Theories of Social Justice 106
Social Justice under the Constitution of India 107
The Concept of Access to Justice 107
Barriers to Access to Justice 108
Historical Background of Social Justice in India 108
Social Justice to Vulnerable Groups 109
The Constitutional Perspective of Social Justice 110
Directive Principles of State Policy Bring Social Justice 111
The Role of Social Workers in Legal Assistance 112
Social Justice through Welfare Legislation 112
The Role of Judiciary as a Dispenser of Social Justice 113
Summary 113

Chapter 9
Social Legislations — 119
Eshita Sharma

Introduction 119
Social Legislation and Social Work: The Role of the Social Worker 120
Social Legislation and Social Change 122
Social Legislation and Social Justice 122
Addressing Social Problems through Legislative Means 123
Specific Social Legislation in the Country 123
Castes 128
Persons with Disabilities 128
Summary 129

Chapter 10
Social Development — 134
Kislay Kumar Singh

Introduction 134
Theoretical Debate: The Genesis of Social Development 135
The Aftermaths of Colonialism 137
Modernization Theory 137
Dependency Theory 138
A Theory of Urban Bias 138
Social Development: Nature, Concept and Definition 139
Social Development: A Unified Approach to Development 140
Relevance of Social Development in the Social Work Practice 141
Summary 142

Chapter 11
Social Security — 147
Sunil Prasad and Arul Actovin C.

Introduction	147
Concept and Definition	148
Need of Social Security	149
Types of Social Security	149
The Historical Development of Social Security	150
Historical Perspectives on Social Security Measures in India	150
Social Security Measures in India	151
Social Security and Social Work	153
The Social Worker's Role in Social Security	154
Summary	154

SECTION B. SOCIAL WORK AS A PROFESSION: PRINCIPLES AND METHODS, SCOPE, THEORIES, MODELS AND PROFESSIONAL STATUS

Chapter 12
Professional Status of Social Work Profession in India — 163
Bishnu Mohan Dash, Rajan Prakash and Sheeba Joseph

Introduction	163
The Concept of Profession	164
Social Work as a Profession in India	167
Summary	170

Chapter 13
Professional Social Work Associations in India — 176
Ram Babu Botcha

Introduction	176
National Association: Concept, Scope and Definition	177
Types/Categories of Professional Associations	177
Various National-level Associations in India	178
Need of National Associations in Social Work in India	181
Functions of National Associations in Social Work in India	182
Contribution of National Associations in Social Work in India	183
National Associations and Promotion of Core Values of Social Work	183
Role of National Associations in Strengthening Social Work Profession in India	184
Summary	185

Chapter 14
Scope and Fields of Social Work and Emerging Areas — 190
Shashi Rani

Introduction	190
Background of Social Work Education and Practice	191
Social Work Practice—Definition and Ethical Guiding Principles	194

Social Work Practice Areas and Scope	196
Summary	201

Chapter 15
Principles and Methods of Social Work — 206
Nita Kumari

Introduction	206
Principles of Social Work	207
Methods of Social Work	212
Summary	214

Chapter 16
Models of Social Work — 219
Sayantani Guin

Introduction	219
Social Work Models: Concept, Scope and Definitions	220
Charity Model of Social Work	220
Remedial Model of Social Work	222
Developmental Model of Social Work	224
Sustainable Model of Social Work	225
Summary	226

Chapter 17
Theories in Social Work — 231
Sonam Rohta

Introduction	231
The Significance of Theory in Social Work Practice	232
Ecological System Theory	233
The Ecological Perspective	233
The Psychodynamic Theory	235
The Diagnostic or Psychosocial School	235
The Functional School	236
The Problem-solving Model	236
Anti-oppressive Social Work	236
Strengths Perspective	238
Social Learning Theory	239
Applications for Social Work Intervention	240
Task-centred Approach	241
Gandhian Approach	243
Summary	244

Chapter 18
Skills in Social Work — 248
Rutwik Gandhe

Introduction	248
Formative Components of Skills in Social Work	249

Defining Skills in Social Work	250
Skills Required for Social Workers	251
Core Skills Required for Social Workers: The Splendid Seven	253
Prominent Subsidiary Skills Attached to the Splendid Seven	256
Classification of Social Work Skills	257
Summary	258

SECTION C. PHILOSOPHY, VALUES AND ETHICS OF SOCIAL WORK

Chapter 19
Philosophy of Social Work — 267
Nagalingam

Introduction	267
Philosophy of Social Work by Eduard and Herbert	268
The Contributions of *Panchatantra*	269
Arthashastra on Welfare State	270
Thirukkural and Its Relevance to Social Work	271
The Relevance of Preaching of Buddha and Mahavira towards Social Work	272
The Relevance of Preaching from Shri Shankaracharya	273
Bhakti Movement and Its Contribution	274
The Preaching of Sri Ramakrishna Paramahansa and Swami Vivekananda and Their Notable Contribution to Mankind	275
Sree Narayana Guru's Model on Social Upliftment of the Downtrodden	276
The Gandhian Philosophical Foundation to Social Work in India	276
Summary	277

Chapter 20
Social Work Values: Traditional and Emancipatory — 282
Poonam Gulalia

Introduction	282
Social Work Values: Concept, Scope and Definition	283
Skill Building in the Context of a Value Framework	284
How Do We Understand Values?	285
How Do Values Impact Us While Working with People?	286
Suffering and Approaching It within a Value Framework	286
Situational Learning and Daily Coping in Fieldwork	287
How Is the Self understood and Interpreted in the Context of Fieldwork?	288
How Does 'Traditional' Practice Fare in Terms of Newer Approaches?	289
On Creating a Social Work Identity	291
Summary	291

Chapter 21
Social Work Ethics — 297
K. Rajeshwari and Vijay Kumar Sharma

Introduction	297
Six Purposes of the Code	299

Major Points from the Social Work Code of Ethics	300
Values of Social Work Profession	303
Service	304
Social Justice	304
Dignity and Worth of the Person	305
Importance of Human Relationships	305
Integrity	305
Competence	305
Problems Faced by Social Workers in India with Regard to Social Work Ethics	306
Summary	308

SECTION D. APPROACHES TO SOCIAL WORK

Chapter 22
Ideologies Background of Social Work — 315
Saumya and Tushar Singh

Introduction	315
Ideology: Concept and Definitions	316
Humanism	316
Socialism	318
Liberalism	319
Utilitarianism	321
Feminism	323
Summary	325

Chapter 23
Modern Indian Thinkers and Their Relevance in Social Work — 330
Chittaranjan Subudhi and J. Raja Meenakshi

Introduction	330
Bhimrao Ramji Ambedkar (14 April 1891–6 December 1956)	331
Jyotirao Phule (11 April 1827–28 November 1890)	333
Rabindranath Tagore (7 May 1861–7 August 1941)	334
Periyar E. V. Ramasamy (17 September 1879–24 December 1973)	337
Relevance in Social Work	338
Summary	339

Chapter 24
Radical Social Work — 343
Binod Kumar

Introduction	343
Tracing Radical Social Work	345
Theoretical Foundations of Radical Social Work	346
Salient Features of Radical Social Work Practice	347
Contextualizing Radical Social Work Practice	347
Radical Social Work: An Indian Perspective	348

    Limits to Radical Social Work — 348
    Summary — 349

Chapter 25
Gandhian Social Work — 353
Mithilesh Kumar and Rajan Prakash

    Introduction — 353
    Foundation of Gandhian Thought — 354
    Dimensions of Gandhian Social Work — 356
    Ethics of Gandhian Social Work — 360
    Summary — 364

Chapter 26
African Social Work — 369
Safia Winifred Ahmadu

    Introduction — 369
    African Traditional Structures for Social Services — 370
    African Social Values — 371
    Summary — 377

Index — I–1

List of Illustrations

BOXES

1.1	Roles of Social Workers	8
4.1	Immediate Outcomes of the Great Depression	50
5.1	The 17 SDGs to Transform Our World	69
10.1	Indicators of Development	136
11.1	Past Studies/Commissions on Social Security	152
12.1	University Grants Commission Review Committees on Social Work Education	165
14.1	UNDP SDGs	195
15.1	Global Definition of Social Work	207
15.2	Skills Required by Professional Social Workers	208
18.1	Two Definitions that Are Most Pertinent to Skills in Context of Social Work	251
18.2	Twelve Skills Outlined by National Association of Social Workers, USA	252
18.3	Classification of Skills Pertaining to Social Work	258
22.1	A Summarized Structure of The Universal Declaration of Human Rights	321
25.1	Gandhi's Work in Timeline	359

FIGURES

6.1	Framework of Service Delivery Relationships	77
14.1	17 Goals to Transform Our World	195
17.1	Thompson's (2006) Personal, Cultural and Structural Analysis (PCS) Model	237
20.1	Core Values of Social Work Profession	284
21.1	Purpose of Social Work Code of Ethics	299
21.2	Philosophical Base of Social Work Practice	301

TABLES

5.1	Philosophical Base of Social Welfare	63
7.1	Social Problems Addressed by Social Reformers and Present Conditions	96
13.1	Categories of Professional Associations in Social Work	178
13.2	Prominent Social Work Associations in India	179
17.1	List of the Five Steps with the Three Main Sequences for Task-centred Practice	242

List of Abbreviations

AAOU	Asian Association of Open Universities
ASSWI	Association of Schools of Social Work in India
BSKP	Bharatiya Samaj Karya Parishad
COS	Charity Organization Society
CSWB	Central Social Welfare Board
DSSW	Delhi School of Social Work
GDP	Gross domestic product
IASSW	International Association of Schools of Social Work
IATSW	Indian Association of Trained Social Workers
ICSSR	Indian Council of Social Science Research
IFSW	International Federation of Social Workers
IGNOU	Indira Gandhi National Open University
ILO	International Labour Organization
INPSWA	India Network of Professional Social Workers' Associations
ISPSW	Indian Society of Professional Social Work
ISS	Indian Sociological Society
ISSA	Indian Social Science Association
JNU	Jawaharlal Nehru University
KST	Knowledge, skills and tools
MSW	Master of Social Work
NAPSWI	National Association of Professional Social Workers in India
NASW	National Association of Social Workers
NIPM	National Institute of Personnel Management
PAS	Person and situations
PCS	Personal, Cultural and Structural Analysis
PIE	Person in environment
SDGs	Sustainable Development Goals
SEWA	Self Employed Women's Association
TISS	Tata Institute of Social Sciences
TLA	Textile Labour Association
UDHR	Universal Declaration of Human Rights
UNDP	United Nations Development Programme
WB	World Bank

Preface

Social work is an academic discipline and also a professional course whose primary function is dealing with individuals, families, groups and communities to enhance social functioning and overall well-being by making use of social work knowledge, skills and techniques. The social work profession endeavours to promote social change, empowerment and liberation of people to ameliorate their social circumstances. The book introduces the readers with the basic concepts of social work, the objectives and functions of social work, history of social work, status of social work profession and the role of social work associations. It has also systematically presented the social work philosophy, values, ethics of social work and various approaches of social work.

The book is divided into 4 sections consisting of 26 chapters. The first section, comprising 11 chapters, has made a modest attempt in defining the basic concepts of social work, namely social welfare, social reform, social development, and social security and social legislations. It describes the concept, objectives and functions of social work. It specifically focuses on the evolution of the meaning of social work, the existing diverse concepts of social work, the primary objectives of the discipline, its functions and the anticipated outcomes. It further looks at the origin and historical trajectory of the growth and development of social work in the UK, the USA and India. It also attempts to trace the historical journey of professional social work education in the aftermath of the Great Depression and looks at how the various trends of social work education have evolved over the years in the Indian subcontinent. In addition to this, it also discusses the reform movements in India and how they have played a critical role in the growth of social work profession in India. The first section is unique in itself as it discusses the conceptualization, definitions and scope of certain terms such as *kalyan*, *mangal* and *yogkshem* that have origin in the Indian sociocultural panorama and have been clubbed under the gamut of 'social welfare'. Besides having a separate chapter on social welfare, the section has also introduced separate chapters on social service, social reform, social security and social development, social justice and social legislations to provide a better and clearer understanding of various social work concepts.

The second section consisting of seven chapters introduces the readers with the principles and methods of social work, scope of social work and emerging areas of social work practice. Besides, the relevant social work theories and models, and essential social work skills have been lucidly presented in a comprehensive manner. In addition to this, it has critically presented an overview of status of social work as a profession in India. As it is very important for social work trainees to understand the nature of work/services provided by the social workers in various settings, the section also provides knowledge on areas and scope of social practice at national and international levels and the use of relevant principles, skills, theories and models for successful fieldwork practice. Since social work associations play an important role in shaping the social work profession, the section has a separate chapter on professional social work associations, which seeks to explain the journey of professional associations at national level in India and also reflects the efforts of various national-level associations based on the available literature along with a set of suggestions to improvise the functioning of social work associations. Social work has an undefined area of practice furthering its scope day by day and venturing into each and every field. The lack of proper fieldwork manual and proper training in developing skills and competencies as professionals, absence of professional council of social work education, weak professional associations, lack of indigenous literature and absence of continuous training for faculty members pose major hindrances in the professionalization of social work education. The unsystematic fieldwork supervision, lack of seriousness in the evaluation of fieldwork reports and lack of linkages between theory teaching and realities in the fieldwork further obstruct the process of professionalization of social work education in India. The purpose of this section is to add to the understanding of the principles and methods of social work, as well as to look into the application of these principles, methods, skills, models and theories and their usage/practice in the fieldwork settings.

The third section consisting of three chapters has discussed the philosophy, values and ethics of social work. This section discusses the contributions of Indian philosophy to social work, particularly various Indian scriptures, and the relevance of preaching from Bhagwan Buddha, Lord Mahavira and Sri Shankaracharya towards the building of social work philosophy. Significantly, it also discusses how the Bhakti movement has given the message on equality. The preaching of Sri Ramakrishna Paramahansa and Swami Vivekananda and their notable contribution to social work philosophy are presented in this section. It also discusses the concept of values in social work and highlights both traditional and emancipatory values in social work. It highlights skill building in the context of a value framework, and how do values impact us while working with people. It discusses the purpose of code of ethics in social work practice. This section clearly specifies the use of code of ethics towards the clients, and responsibility of colleagues and employers to the social work profession. Besides, the problems faced by social workers in India with regard to social work ethics are also specially discussed.

The last section containing five chapters discusses various approaches to social work and the ideological background of social work. Social work profession has undergone a paradigm shift from charity to welfare to clinical to ecological, radical, progressive, and feminist approaches and so on. Behind each of this approach, there is an ideological underpinning which shapes the thoughts, beliefs and explanations or justifications for social work practice/intervention. In this section, the chapter on ideological background of social work has been included, which delves with deliberation into ideologies of social work that helps in deciding various approaches to social work which in turn contributes towards social change. It also discusses the nature, history and significance of some of the ideologies such as secular humanism and rationalism in terms of social work philosophy, polity, and national and international contexts in which the contemporary reality and social work approaches can be understood. This section throws light on the various approaches of social work, particularly, the radical and Gandhian approaches to social work and their relevance in social work education. It discusses Afrocentric social work and its generics as social work practice involving traditional methods of social work, which focus on reducing problems in human relationships and enriching individual's maximum life and way of living through improved human interaction. The revolutionary ideas of four modern Indian thinkers, namely Babasaheb Ambedkar, Mahatma Phule, Rabindranath Tagore and Periyar E. V. Ramasamy, and their importance in social work education have also been included.

The book has incorporated all the important fundamental concepts in social work and tries to provide a holistic understanding of the various social work concepts. It will be extremely helpful to the students of social work at the bachelor's and master's levels, as well as the teachers of social work. The book will also be an asset to the students preparing for UGC NET/JRF/civil services examination in social work.

About the Book

The book endeavours to introduce the basic and core concepts of social work to the students, teachers and social work professionals. It provides a clear understanding of various social work concepts: social reform, social justice, social security, social development, social legislations, social welfare and so on. It has covered the values, ethics, principles, scope and various approaches to social work, which are quite essential to understand the social work profession. It has also clearly presented the social work philosophy and ideological background in social work. The book has also made a modest attempt to examine professional status of social work in the Indian context as well as the role of national associations of social work in strengthening the social work profession. It has incorporated all the important basic concepts in social work and tries to provide a holistic understanding of the various concepts of social work. The book has been prepared keeping in mind the syllabus of various universities offering social work education. It will be an essential read for the students of social work at the bachelor's and master's levels in the various universities in India and abroad. It will be extremely helpful to the students preparing for UGC NET/JRF examination in social work.

About the Editor and Contributors

EDITOR

Bishnu Mohan Dash, Master of Social Work (MSW; Visva-Bharati), MPhil (University of Delhi), PhD (University of Delhi), Indian Council of Social Science Research (ICSSR) postdoctoral fellow, is presently working as Associate Professor in rural development, Indira Gandhi National Open University (IGNOU), New Delhi, and is also discipline coordinator and PhD programme coordinator in rural development. He is engaged in spearheading the movement towards Indianization of social work education. He was earlier associate professor, Department of Social Work, at Dr Bhim Rao Ambedkar College (University of Delhi) and has more than 15 years of teaching experience. He is the recipient of the *Best Teacher Award*, 2019–2020, from the Government of Delhi, and the prestigious *Delhi University Excellence Award for Teachers*, 2021. He is also an editorial board member/advisory member in several national and international journals including *Practice: Social Work in Action*, associate editor of *South Asian Journal of Participative Development* and member, editorial board of *BSSS Journal of Social Work*. He has authored/co-authored/edited 16 books. He has published more than 60 papers in various reputed national and international journals by SAGE Publications and so on, and has contributed chapters for postgraduate course in social work (MSW)/social work and counselling of IGNOU, New Delhi, and frequently contributes to leading national newspapers. He has presented papers and chaired sessions in various national/international conferences in Canada, Japan, Sri Lanka and so on, as well as has delivered invited lectures in various academic forums. Professor Dash was also member of the Expert Committee in the course revision; member, School Board, IGNOU, New Delhi; Odisha State Open University, Mahatma Gandhi Antarrashtriya Hindi Vishwavidyalaya, Maharashtra; BPS University, Sonipat; and member, Board of Studies in Social Work, Indore School of Social Work, Indore; and Academic Advisory Board, School of Social Sciences, Doon University and Member of National Curriculum Framework (NCF). He has completed a number of research projects sponsored by ICSSR and University Grants Commission and organized various workshops and seminars. His areas of interest are rural development, child welfare and social work education.

CONTRIBUTORS

Arul Actovin C. is currently pursuing his doctoral research as UGC Senior Research Fellow in Social Work, Pondicherry University. He has completed his master's in social work from Pondicherry University. He has published research articles in various national and international journals. His main areas of research interest are social work with tribal communities, rural community development, urban community development, human rights and indigenous social work practice.

Safia Winifred Ahmadu, Senior Lecturer, Federal Polytechnic, Department of Social Development, Kaduna, Nigeria. She has a postgraduate diploma certificate in child welfare and childhood studies from the University of Swansea, Wales, the UK, and master's in social policy and social work from Masaryk University, Brno, Czech Republic. She is a member of the Nigerian Council for Social Services, Nigeria Association of Social Workers, Association of Social Workers Educators of Nigeria and the African Network for the Prevention and Protection against Child Abuse and Neglect in Nigeria. She is also the founder of Community Empowerment and Development Initiative, which works for empowering people in difficult circumstances.

Ram Babu Botcha is an Assistant Professor in the Department of Social Work, Rajiv Gandhi National Institute of Youth Development, Sriperumbudur. He has received his MPhil and PhD in social work from IGNOU, New Delhi. Dr Botcha is the recipient of the Young Achievement Award in Social Work. He has presented numerous research papers in international and national conferences and seminars. Besides three books, he has several publications in Scopus indexed/peer-reviewed national/international journals/edited volumes to his credit. He has completed research projects funded by national and international agencies. He has visited China, Bangkok and Sri Lanka and represented India as an official nominated by the Ministry of Youth Affairs and Sports, Government of India.

Rakesh Choudhary is Assistant Professor, Department of Social Work, Aditi Mahavidyalaya, University of Delhi. He has teaching experience of more than six years at the University of Delhi. He has contributed several research papers in various national and international journals. He has also contributed chapters in edited books. He is engaged as a fellow editor in the *International Research Journal of Social Sciences and Humanities*. He has presented research papers in several international and national conferences in and outside India. Being a professional social worker, the author is also involved with many national and international non-governmental organizations working in the field of social and economic development of society.

Lakshmana G is an Assistant Professor in the Department of Social Work, School of Social and Behavioural Sciences at the Central University of Karnataka, Kalaburagi, Karnataka, India. He has done his graduation (BA) and postgraduation in social work (MSW) from Bangalore University, Bengaluru. He obtained his MPhil and PhD from the National Institute of Mental Health and Neurosciences, Bengaluru. In addition to his doctoral degree, he has PGDHRM to his academic credentials. He has published 35 articles in international and national journals including *Journal of Social Work Practice in the Addictions*, *Asian Social Work and Policy Review*, *Hong Kong Journal of Social Work*, *Indian Journal of Social Work*, *Epilepsy & Behavior*, *Frontiers in Psychology*, *Indian Journal of Psychological Medicine* and so on. He has written 15 chapters in books, edited 2 books, published 8 monographs (2 co-authored), and presented many papers in national and international conferences. He has completed seven research projects and three more projects are ongoing. He has written 18 e-content modules on social work education. He has visited Australia, China, Hong Kong, Sri Lanka, Indonesia and Nepal. He was an executive committee member of the Indian Society of Professional Social Work and Karnataka

About the Editor and Contributors

Association of Professional Social Workers and presently elected member at large of the International Consortium for Social Development. His research interests include addiction medicine, psychosocial intervention with families and children, community care and mental health, corporate social responsibility and vulnerable populations.

Rutwik Gandhe holds dual master's degrees in social work and management (HR). He has a doctorate from Pandit Deendayal Energy University, Gandhinagar, Gujarat. Dr Gandhe has worked for multiple civil society and research organizations before joining The Bhopal School of Social Sciences, where he is engaged in teaching and research for around a decade now. He has several research articles, book chapters and books to his credit. Presently, he is teaching subjects pertaining to social research, organizational behaviour and human resource development to students of social work at the graduate and postgraduate levels. Pro-social behaviour, voluntarism, correctional social work and organizational development are the areas of his research interest.

Indrajit Goswami is an MSW from Visva-Bharati Central University, Shantiniketan; an MBA from Indian Institute of Social Welfare and Business Management, Kolkata; has obtained his PhD in social work code of ethics and earned more than 30 certificates from Michigan University, Yale University, Northwestern University, Copenhagen Business School, University of Virginia and so on. Dr Goswami is also a certified international career coach. He has more than 26 years of experience in designing curriculum and course modules, postgraduate teaching, mentoring, consultancy, research and publication. He has taught courses on human values, corporate ethics, corporate social responsibility, human happiness, organizational development, talent retention, business communication, strategic management, research methods and so on. He serves as resource person for management development programme and faculty development programme, chairperson of technical sessions in seminar and conferences, member of editorial advisory boards and consultant to development organizations. He is currently a member of different professional bodies and associations such as Indian Social Science Association (ISSA), Indian Sociological Society (ISS), National Institute of Personnel Management (NIPM), Rashtriya Samaj Vigyan Parishad and U3A. Dr Goswami has made numerous presentations, published research papers, articles and reviews, and delivered technical sessions in UGC, Academic Staff Colleges, and several other training and development programmes.

Sayantani Guin is currently an Assistant Professor at the School of Social Work, IGNOU, New Delhi. She holds PhD and MPhil degrees in social sciences from Tata Institute of Social Sciences (TISS), Mumbai. Her master's degree is in social work with specialization in criminology and correctional administration. She has presented various academic and research papers at several international and national conferences. She publishes extensively in a wide range of international scholarly journals. Her academic and research interests include social work, criminology and correctional administration, and HIV/AIDS in prisons.

Poonam Gulalia is working as a Field Work Coordinator at School of Social Work in TISS, Mumbai. She also teaches a core paper, 'Social Case Work: Working with Individuals', at the School of Social Work. She has worked as an education social worker and community social worker with United Nations High Commissioner for Refugees, New Delhi, for over eight years. She also worked with Community Aid and Sponsorship Programme Plan, Nehru Yuva Kendra

Sangathan and Springdales School. Her more recent achievements include coordinating the development of various modules on field and field supervision along with her colleagues. This was an initiative of the Ministry of Human Resource Development, Government of India (INFLIBNET). She has extensive experience and has been working as a practising professional for over three decades. She has been contributing extensively to the profession through her academic writing work.

Sheeba Joseph works as an Associate Professor in the Department of Social Work, Bhopal School of Social Sciences, Bhopal. At present, along with teaching, she is serving the institute with the additional portfolio of Internal Quality Assurance Cell coordinator. She has published articles in refereed/Scopus indexed journals and also contributed chapters in edited books and has authored/edited books. She has organized various national seminars, conferences and workshops and was invited to deliver lectures in various training programmes and workshops. Her areas of interest include geriatric social work, children and adolescents, and social work education.

Archana Kaushik is a Professor at the Department of Social Work, University of Delhi, India. Her areas of specialization and research interest include gerontological social work, empowerment of marginalized communities, families and children, development administration, spiritual social work and HIV/AIDS. She has many books and research articles on varied issues in the journals of national and international repute to her credit. She has conducted several research studies on topics such as determinants of active ageing, elder abuse and social support for the aged, vulnerabilities and empowerment of the Dalits and forgiveness as a public health issue.

Binod Kumar, PhD, is currently working as Assistant Professor at the School of Social Work, IGNOU, New Delhi. He obtained MPhil and PhD from the Centre for the Study of Law and Governance, JNU, New Delhi. He did MSW from TISS, Mumbai, and holds BA LLB from Faculty of Law, Aligarh Muslim University, Aligarh, Uttar Pradesh. Previously, he worked as assistant professor (ad hoc), Department of Social Work, Dr Bhim Rao Ambedkar College, University of Delhi, for four years. He has publications in various journals and edited books. Dr Binod has also presented papers and chaired sessions in various seminars and conferences at national and international levels. His areas of interest are disaster management, law and social work, community development, social entrepreneurship, corporate social responsibility and social policy.

Mithilesh Kumar is working as a Senior Assistant Professor at Mahatma Gandhi Fuji Guruji Centre for Social Work, Mahatma Gandhi Antarrashtriya Hindi Vishwavidyalaya, Wardha. His areas of specialization are human rights, research methodology and Gandhian social work. He has written/edited 14 books including *Indian Social Work*, *Social Work in India: Indigenous Models and Approaches*, *Nanaji Deshmukh: An Epitome of Indian Social Work* and *New Frontier in Social Work Practice: Bhartiya Contexts, Perspectives and Experiences* and 21 research papers in reputed national/international journals. He is the recipient of the Social Work Education and Promotion Award by the International Association for World Peace (affiliated with the Economic and Social Council of the United Nations, Department of Public Information,

United Nations Children's Fund and United Nations Educational, Scientific and Cultural Organization). He is also working as Joint Secretary, Bharatiya Samaj Karya Parishad, a national-level professional social worker organization for the promotion of indigenous social work/Bhartiyakaran of social work.

Nita Kumari has done MA, MPhil and PhD in social work. She was a guest faculty at Dr Bhim Rao Ambedkar College, University of Delhi. She has also worked as a consultant and research and teaching assistant at the School of Social Work, IGNOU, New Delhi. She has been awarded Junior Research Fellowship by the University Grants Commission. She has contributed chapters in books and articles in refereed journals. She has also presented several papers in national and international seminars.

J. Raja Meenakshi, PhD, is an ICSSR Postdoctoral Fellow at the Central University of Tamil Nadu. She started her career as human resource coordinator at the Aravind Eye Care System and following her passion for teaching social work, she joined as assistant professor in the Department of Social Work, The American College, and later Fatima College, Madurai. She was part of the curriculum development team for the human resource and labour management specialization of MSW at the Central University of Tamil Nadu. Her areas of interest are human resource development, corporate social responsibility, occupational health of women and gerontology. She has authored articles and books.

Nagalingam, Assistant Professor, Department of Social Work, Indira Gandhi National Tribal University, Amarkantak. He has done MSW and PhD in social work with specialization in urban, rural and tribal community development, Department of Social Work, Bharathidasan University, Tamil Nadu. He has about 21 years of experience as social work practitioner, social work educator and social science researcher. He has presented many papers in reputed journals and in various seminars and conferences.

Manisha Pal is Assistant Professor, Department of Social Work, Aditi Mahavidyalaya, University of Delhi. She has teaching experience of more than eight years at the University of Delhi. She has contributed several research papers in various national and international journals. She has also contributed chapters in edited books. She has presented research papers in several international and national conferences and contributed to many research projects. Being a professional social worker, she is also involved with many national and international non-governmental organizations working in the field of social and economic development of society.

Rajan Prakash is presently pursuing PhD from the Department of Social Work, Jamia Millia Islamia, New Delhi. He cleared the UGC JRF in 2017. He has done his master's and MPhil in social work from Mahatma Gandhi Antarrashtriya Hindi Vishwavidyalaya, Wardha, Maharashtra. His research interests include community engagement in social work practices, medical social work and cultural competence in social work.

Sunil Prasad is presently working as Assistant Professor, Department of Social Work, School of Social and Behavioural Sciences, Amrita Vishwa Vidyapeetham, Kerala. He has graduated from Kirori Mal College, University of Delhi. He has completed his master's in social work from Delhi School of Social Work, University of Delhi. He cleared the UGC NET examination in the year 2016. Currently, he is pursuing his PhD from the Department of Social Work, Visva-Bharati University, which is a central university and an institution of national importance, and he has submitted his thesis. He also holds postgraduate diploma in sustainable rural development. He has published many articles in reputed Scopus listed journals, UGC listed journals and chapters in books by international and national publishers. His research interest is in the areas of rural and community development, sustainable livelihood and social work education. He is also the founder/director of Centre for Livelihood & Development Foundation.

Shashi Rani is Assistant Professor in the Department of Social Work, University of Delhi, India. She also taught at the Department of Social Work, BPS Women's University, Sonipat, Haryana. She has done MPhil and PhD from Centre of Social Medicine and Community Health, JNU, New Delhi. Her specialization is in industrial health services and occupational health. She did her master's in social work from Institute of Social Sciences, Dr Bhimrao Ambedkar University, Agra, Uttar Pradesh. She has 11 years of teaching and research experience at university level. Along with teaching, she has been actively engaged in research and training for more than 10 years on various issues including marginalization, inclusion, social justice, women and child development, quality health care, counselling and public–private partnership in health services. Also, she is associated with various research and developmental organizations (working at national–international level) in the area of social justice and development. She is also recognized as master trainer in HIV/AIDS under the Global Fund Project, Round 7, Department of Social Work, Jamia Millia Islamia (Central University), New Delhi. She has given her services and contributed to various committees on different issues. She is a member of various advisory, monitoring and supervision committees of the Government of National Capital Territory of Delhi.

Supriya Rani is a PhD scholar at the Department of Social Work, University of Delhi. She has a wide range of research interests. These range from pedagogy in education, mental health, gender to political and cultural ecology. She has published articles on topics such as non-formal education, student politics, and cultural and political ecology. Her PhD research revolves around assessing the level of subjective well-being among social work professionals in India. She has presented a number of research papers in various conferences.

K. Rajeshwari is presently working as an Assistant Professor, Department of Social Work, Telangana University, South Campus at Bhiknoor, Kamaredddy. She has an experience of two decades after completing her MSW in 1997 from Osmania University. She always desired for career in teaching, training, psychological counselling, social science research and HRM with growth-oriented organizations. Her career goals and her two decades of experience have helped her to carve a niche in writing her experiences in the form of research articles and this is the outcome of her dedication to professional social work. She has written several research articles for renowned national and international journal.

Sonam Rohta has been working since July 2021 in a social enterprise based in the UK which works with Public Health England in areas including mental health, learning disability, substance

About the Editor and Contributors

misuse and criminal justice system in more than 240 locations across England and Wales. She is part of the Children and Young People's Services. She worked as an assistant professor in the Department of Sociology and Social Work, Himachal Pradesh University, Shimla, from 2016 to 2021. She completed her master's and doctorate from Centre for Social Work, Panjab University, Chandigarh. She has experience in the field of corporate social responsibility with Talwandi Sabo Power Limited, Vedanta Group, Punjab. She is a keen researcher and social work practitioner. Her areas of specialization include children in care homes, child abuse, care leavers, substance misuse among young people, social work research and social work education.

Akileswari S. is an Assistant Professor in the Department of Social Work, Dwaraka Doss Goverdhan Doss Vaishnav College (Autonomous), Chennai, Tamil Nadu, India. Prior to joining this position, she was an assistant professor in the Department of Social Work, Loyola College, Chennai, for over 10 years. She holds a PhD in social work from the University of Madras. She was selected for the Social Work Education Research Student Award, in the memory of Jo Campling, a full monetary scholarship for the completion of her PhD, by the *Social Work Education: The International Journal*. She has over 16 years of teaching and research experience and has several publications to her credit. She is a peer reviewer for the *Social Work Education: The International Journal*. She has been involved in research activities related to areas such as rehabilitation of tsunami victims, marginalization of women, fieldwork practicum and supervision in social work education.

Saumya is working as an Assistant Professor, School of Social Work, IGNOU, New Delhi. She has received Asian Association of Open Universities (AAOU) Inter University Staff Exchange Fellowship at Open University of Sri Lanka, 2021, Visiting Fellowship to Shanghai Open University, China, in 2014 and Commonwealth Fellowship in 2018 and 2021. She has won the 2018 Young Innovator Award for her paper at the 32nd Annual Conference of AAOU. She has received a research project grant under the ICSSR IMPRESS (Impactful Policy Research in Social Science) Scheme for her research proposal on 'Impact of Swachh Bharat Abhiyan on Rural Health and Hygiene Practices', 2019–2021. She has written and edited books and published several articles in national and international journals. She has presented several papers in national and international seminars and webinars. She has been an invited speaker at several workshops and webinars. She coordinates the MSW programme at IGNOU, New Delhi. Her academic and research interests include fieldwork, social work education, open and distance education, tribal issues and community organization.

Eshita Sharma has completed her doctoral research in health communication from Centre of Social Medicine and Community Health, School of Social Sciences, Jawaharlal Nehru University (JNU). She has a master's degree in social work from the Department of Social Work, University of Delhi, and a postgraduate diploma in journalism from the Indian Institute of Mass Communication, New Delhi. She has taught BA (Hons) social work at University of Delhi and is currently working as a communication expert on health-related government projects and campaigns.

Vijay Kumar Sharma is presently working as an Associate Professor, Social Work, Mahatma Gandhi Central University, Motihari. He was formerly assistant professor, Department of Social

Work, Telangana University, South Campus at Bhiknoor, Telangana. He has 27 years of experience. He also has three master's degrees. He holds a doctorate degree in sociology and social work and a postdoctoral degree in sociology and DLitt from University of South America.

Avtar Singh did graduation in social work from Jamia Millia Islamia University and has master's in social work and PhD from Department of Social Work, University of Delhi. He did his LLB from Faculty of Law, University of Delhi. He also has postgraduate diploma in personnel management and industrial relation from Bhartiya Vidya Bhawan (Delhi). Currently, he is working as an associate professor in Social Work Department of Dr Bhim Rao Ambedkar College, University of Delhi. He has authored 3 books and published more than 20 research papers in professional reputed journals. He has presented many research papers in various national and international conferences and seminars in India and abroad. He is also life member of many professional institutions.

Kislay Kumar Singh is currently teaching at the Department of Social Work, Dr Bhim Rao Ambedkar College, University of Delhi. He has contributed many papers in reputed journals and presented papers in various seminars and conferences. His areas of interest include social development, social policy and migration studies.

Tushar Singh, PhD Scholar at School of Social Work, IGNOU, New Delhi. He has published several articles in national and international journals. He has presented several papers in national and international seminars and webinars.

Chittaranjan Subudhi, PhD, is working as an Assistant Professor, Department of Social Work, Central University of Tamil Nadu, India. He has completed his PhD in mental health from Department of Humanities and Social Sciences, National Institute of Technology Rourkela, India. He has conducted research in various areas such as health and mental health, medical anthropology, family and child welfare, disability studies and tribal health issues. He teaches psychiatric social work, working with individuals and communities, qualitative research, information and communications technologies in social development and health system management. He has published many book chapters including edited books and conference papers and published articles in national and international reputed peer-reviewed journals of Springer, SAGE, Routledge, Taylor & Francis, Bloomsbury, Web of Science and Scopus indexed journals.

Shahin Sultana is a Professor in the Department of Social Work, School of Social Sciences and International Studies, Pondicherry University. She teaches postgraduate students and guides PhD students. Her areas of work and research include medical and psychiatric social work, youth and women welfare, social work with families and children, early childhood care and development, social case work and counselling. Currently, she is teaching psychology for social work practice, medical social work, public health for social workers, social policy and social welfare administration.

SECTION A

Social Work: Meaning and Basic Concepts

Chapter 1   *Social Work: Meaning and Concept, Objectives and Functions*

Chapter 2   *History of Social Work in the USA, the UK and India*

Chapter 3   *Social Reform Movements in India*

Chapter 4   *Great Depression and the Growth of Social Work Education*

Chapter 5   *Social Welfare*

Chapter 6   *Social Service*

Chapter 7   *Social Reform*

Chapter 8   *Social Justice*

Chapter 9   *Social Legislations*

Chapter 10   *Social Development*

Chapter 11   *Social Security*

1

Social Work
Meaning and Concept, Objectives and Functions

Shahin Sultana

LEARNING OBJECTIVES

- To gain knowledge on meaning of social work as a profession
- To know the concepts related to social work
- To understand the objectives of social work and its relevance
- To learn the functions of social work as a profession

The happiest people I know are those who lose themselves in the service of others.

—Gordon B. Hinckley

INTRODUCTION

Social work is an academic discipline as well as a professional course whose primary function is to deal with individuals, families, groups and communities. The main goal of the discipline is to enhance social functioning and overall well-being. 'Social work is the art of bringing various resources bear on individual, group and community needs by the application of a scientific method of helping people to help themselves' (Stroup, 1960). It begins with attending to the needs of the individuals in crisis to promote better functioning not only at their level but also within their groups, families and communities. The process of development, industrialization and urbanization has evolved complex systems and relationships. Therefore, in this context, a revisit to the effectiveness of social work as a profession is very much necessary.

Social work is a helping profession. One of the major concerns of social work is ensuring social justice and improving the quality of life of all. Social work addresses social problems in relation to its impact on the lives of the individuals, groups, families and communities. It rests on the basic premise that everyone has a capacity for effective social functioning, and they need to be provided adequate opportunities for that. The social workers not only address social problems but also work with the concern that rights and needs are interrelated, which influences human well-being to a great extent. Social workers focus on helping the individuals to help themselves to live amicably in their social environment. They also believe that individual harmony influences social harmony and development. The social workers not only work with people in solving their problems but focus on preventing the problems so that they are able to continue with their social functioning for their well-being.

SOCIAL WORK: MEANING AND DEFINITIONS

Social work is a helping profession. It primarily aims at the welfare of the individuals, groups, families and communities. It is referred to as a practice-based profession. It aims at promoting social change, development, cohesion and the empowerment of people and communities. Social workers work towards the welfare of various stakeholders, thereby meeting their complex and basic needs at different stages of their developmental phase. They work with the basic instinct that all problems can have a solution, and they aim towards achieving them with the participation of the client in need. The fundamental base on which social work practice relies on is the understanding of human development, behaviour and the social, economic and cultural institutions and interactions. Social workers work on social work values and principles as well as the research which evolves out of the academic front that helps them shape their practice. Social work is both a taxing and a rewarding profession. The practice will depend on how best the social worker is able to empathize, listen, think critically and communicate effectively, and client–worker relationship, interpersonal skills and so on.

Some of the definitions of social work are as follows:

> 'Social work is the provision of service designed to aid individuals, singly or in groups in coping with present or future social problems and obstacles that prevent or are likely to prevent, full or effective participation in society.' (Fink, 1942)
>
> 'Social work is a professional service rendered to people for the purpose of assisting them, as individuals or in groups, to attain satisfying relationships and standard of life in accordance with their particular wishes and capacities and in harmony with those of the community.' (Anderson, 1943)
>
> 'Social work is a form of professional service comprising a composite of knowledge and skills, parts of which are and of which are not distinctive of social work, which attempts on one hand to help the individuals satisfy their need in the social milieu and on the other to remove as far as possible the barriers which obstruct people from achieving the best of which they are capable.' (Clarke, 1947)
>
> 'Social work seeks two things for people: economic well-being and the deeper source of happiness, that is self-realization; the stuff of concern is human behaviour and relationship.

Its focus of attention is the individual and his self-adjustment to a recognized reality.' (Youngdahl, 1949)

'Social work is a professional service, based on scientific knowledge and skill in human relations, which assist individuals, alone or in groups, to obtain social and personal satisfaction and independence.' (Friedlander, 1955)

'Social work seeks to enhance the social functioning of the individuals, singly and in groups, by activities focused upon their social relationships which constitute interaction between man and his environment. These activities can be grouped into three functions: restoration of impaired capacity, provision of individual and social resources and prevention of social dysfunctions.' (Boehm, 1959)

'Social work is a welfare activity based on humanitarian philosophy, scientific knowledge and technical skill for helping individuals or community, to live a rich and full life.' (Indian Conference of Social Work, 1957)

'Social work is the art of bringing various resources bear on individual, group and community need by the application of a scientific method of helping people to help themselves.' (Stroup, 1960)

'Social work is professional service based on knowledge of human relations and skill relationship and concerned with problem of intra-personal and or inter-personal adjustments resulting from unmet individual, group, or community need.' (Ahmed, 1969)

Did You Know?

'Social work is a practice-based profession and an academic discipline that promotes social change and development, social cohesion, and the empowerment and liberation of people. Principles of social justice, human rights, collective responsibility and respect for diversities are central to social work.' Underpinned by theories of social work, social sciences, humanities and indigenous knowledge, social work engages people and structures to address life challenges, and enhance well-being.

The above definition may be amplified at national and/or regional levels. It was approved by the International Federation of Social Workers General Meeting and the International Association of Schools of Social Work General Assembly in July 2014.

Based on the above-mentioned definitions, it is understood that social work is a helping profession which primarily aims to resolve the problems of the individuals at varied levels: individual, group, family and community. The process involves the practitioner, that is, the social worker who with their knowledge of the basic understanding of human behaviour and development, social environment and psychosocial wisdom envisages a road map to help the individual in crisis for effective social functioning, thereby capacitating one to adapt to their environment. The primary meaning of social work is 'helping one to help themselves' so that the person in need believes and has faith in one's own effort and determination in resolving the problem.

The above-mentioned definitions bring to the fore a basic understanding of the meaning and nature of social work as a profession. The definitions of social work across the years highlight social work as a helping profession targeted at the welfare of individuals, families, groups and communities. It aims at improving their lives through human intervention, thereby helping one to help themselves. The human behaviour is the primordial source of intervention in relation to the family and social environments. The profession rests on the fact that every problem has a solution and it can be worked out through proper study and assessment. Social work as profession is interdisciplinary in approach and it rests upon literature drawn from sociology, psychology, law, media, human rights, politics, women studies and anthropology to name a few. It has a great scope for intervention in the lives of individuals at both personal and professional levels. The client–worker interface is the base for social work intervention and this relationship facilitates the individuals back to normal social functioning with self-determination and self-realization.

SOCIAL WORK: CONCEPT AND SCOPE

Social work is a practice-based profession which believes in attending the problems of the clients in a phased manner through democratic decision-making. It might have borrowed literature form other disciplines, but it has a body of specialized knowledge and a set of related skills. Social workers can work in a multicultural context as they tend to gain knowledge in different places. The profession of social work is unique in itself where any learner can not only learn but also practice in different set-ups whether within their country or outside as the methods, skills and techniques are almost similar but the experiences are different. It works with a set of philosophical understanding that every individual is unique and they are dependent on others as human beings are considered to be social animals. All the needs, wants and desires are interconnected, and they depend on each other for their mutual well-being. In order to have peaceful coexistence and self-existence, they require what is known as professional intervention, which helps them overcome their constraints and challenges in life.

This profession is based on the humanitarian philosophy; when an individual confronts a problem, it is believed that a 'person in need' is to be attended by any other being in whatever way or form to help them adjust to their social environment. Social adjustment is the keyword and this influences the individuals to a greater extent. Praag (1957) informs that to understand individuals, groups and communities, we need the help of the behavioural sciences as without these sciences, a diagnosis cannot be made and without diagnosis, no effective and adequate help can be given. Social work is believed to work on individual and social problems by applying different methods and techniques and it is appreciative that the profession has been developing a set of knowledge with its own methods, skills and techniques to attend to the problems the individuals face. The motto of the profession so as to say is to make the individuals self-reliant so that they understand the background of their problem and they know that they have to work towards solution of the same. The other aspect of the profession is to coordinate and relate various resources and services and connect them with individuals, groups and communities to utilize them and see how they could come out of the problem to gain and restore normal and social functioning. In short, based on the experiences, it is said that social work has developed as a scientific process with the experiences the profession has gained over so many decades in different cultures and set-ups in dealing with human relationships.

The profession of social work has a vast scope when it comes to practice. Though it was said to have started with the concept of charity way back during the times of the World Wars, it is gradually moving towards a professional stance where the aim is to help individuals solve psychosocial problems through a scientific method. The fact that all human beings are unique when it comes to behaviour, attitude, maturity, personality and other attributes, all need to be attended to differently. The manner in which each individual is attended to has grown over so many decades and it is still growing leaps and bounds. To explain further, it can be said that no two children are the same even if they are within the same family of the same parents; as they are different identities, the intervention is also going to be certainly different. Different cultures, geographical locations, family types, thoughts and behaviours, all require varied levels of interventions and approaches. Thus, it is believed that social work has a vast scope to intervene in the lives of individuals to restore their social functioning.

The scope of social work profession is diverse and wide-ranging. There are many stakeholders with whom social workers have been working with such as (a) children, (b) adolescents, (c) youth, (d) adults, (e) women and (f) elderly and now this canvas is expanding even more with the new kinds of challenges coming up as developments over the years, be it the transgenders or any vulnerable group. The areas where social work intervenes to mention a few are: (a) health and mental health, (b) education, (c) social security, (d) social legislation, (e) social justice, (f) social policy, (g) disasters, (h) disability, (i) poverty, (j) unemployment, (k) social assistance, (l) migration, (m) marriage, (n) correctional services, (o) relief and rehabilitation, (p) climate change, (q) human rights, (r) sustainable development, (s) social protection, (t) trafficking, (u) social development, (v) substance abuse, (w) refugees and asylum seekers, (x) leadership and management, (y) family violence and (z) homelessness.

The means through which social workers have intervened are also wide-ranging such as the agencies, governmental and non-governmental organizations, international bodies, research institutes, educational institutions, private bodies, and charitable trusts and societies. The scope of social work has witnessed a sea change in its actual sense. Both academicians and practitioners have contributed a lot in their own ways to witness this expansion. Given its professional status, people from other disciplines have started shifting their attention towards this course and the number of learners has also increased. The professional associations are also rising region wise and country wise so that all can come under the ambit of social work as one family and exchange their ideas, opinions, practices and modes of operation to encourage and learn from each other's cultures and social environments.

Social workers work at various levels: grassroots, regional, national and international levels. The profession is very much value based and it aims at creating a just and humane society for all human beings to live amicably in a social environment. To make this happen, social workers work in the following settings:

1. Hospitals
2. Educational institutions
3. Disability set-ups
4. Community-based organizations
5. Corporate set-ups/industries
6. Charitable trusts/societies
7. Government departments
8. Non-governmental bodies
9. International bodies
10. Disaster settings

The above-mentioned are only a few, the scope is expanding like never before given the speed with which the world is changing and the kind of stress and vulnerability the human beings are experiencing in the given situation. Social workers are going to be in huge demand as it is being realized that inner peace and harmony are more important than material things and other accomplishments. People are now getting geared up setting aside the stigma associated with visiting a social worker to work on their problems to seek out solutions for their well-being.

SOCIAL WORK: OBJECTIVE AND FUNCTIONS

Social work as a profession is based on the values of services, dignity and worth of the person. Its objectives refer to a statement of what the profession is trying to do or is planning to achieve. One of the main objectives of this profession is to enhance human well-being for which a social worker plays many roles such as (a) broker, (b) advocate, (c) case manager, (d) educator, (e) facilitator, (f) organizer and (g) manager (Box 1.1). It is clearly established that research, knowledge and skills enhance social work practice.

The social workers mainly (a) identify individuals, groups, families and communities in need; (b) assess the needs of the clients, examine their situations, their strengths and weaknesses and identify support systems that can enhance their well-being; and (c) connect them to social support systems that can help them to enhance their well-being. They try to reduce the suffering of the human lives, help them in achieving social justice and improve their lives and of the people surrounding them. Social work is a noble profession in which the social worker tries to help people cope with physical and mental illness, disability, poverty, injustice, addiction, abuse, discrimination, inequality and many other social problems. This profession, though challenging, is highly rewarding.

In social work, the worker also gets directly involved in counselling of clients, groups, families and communities with a common goal to achieve a well-defined objective. Family discord, marital problems, family abuse and violence, and such other problems are very sensitive to deal with but the profession engages a certain sense of professional maturity. They also get involved in research, policy and advocacy to protect and promote the rights and entitlements of their clientele. The social workers are also bound to participate in administrative

Box 1.1 Roles of Social Workers

- Broker
- Advocate
- Case manager
- Educator
- Facilitator
- Organizer
- Manager
- Counsellor
- Mobilizer
- Therapist
- Researcher
- Community change agent

activities, if necessary, within the agency and also equipped to attend rehabilitative services along with trauma care and emergency services.

The primary objective of social work is helping one to help themselves. It also enables one to decide on their own, make the best decisions for their problems to move ahead. The voice of the clientele is encouraged to be heard and based on that adequate steps are taken to enhance their well-being. Follow-up and rehabilitation are also part of the objectives of the social work profession.

When it comes to the functions of the social work profession, they are (a) restoration, (b) provision of resources and (c) prevention. These three are critically important to facilitate the client for their social functioning.

Restoration further involves two aspects: (a) curative and (b) rehabilitative.

By curative, it means attempting to eliminate the factors which hamper the client to function normally in their social environment. The client is helped to identify the factors affecting them and help them in understanding their irrelevance and how they could be neglected for the client's better functioning. Once this is done, the client will have difficulties in adjusting to the new normal. In this case, the social worker plays a pivotal role to enable them to adapt to the changes and restore their normalcy for their personal and family well-being.

Provision of resources is further classified into (a) developmental and (b) educational. Developmental means the social structure, be it a family or workplace where there are chances of disagreement which hampers the functioning. A mutual understanding can be brought there through a social worker by mediating between both the parties. In this manner, the problem is resolved and the system is going to only improve. When it comes to educational, a session on mobile addiction and its challenges and how it impacts relationships or any other educative session for that matter, a social worker may influence individual well-being and restore individuals to their normalcy.

The third function is prevention, where the social workers have a more challenging role to play.

In this function, the social worker attempts at large to prevent the problem from happening in the first instance, then if it occurs, the other functions are put to use. Prevention minimizes the problems to a larger extent. For example, pre-marital counselling can be a wonderful preventive tool to minimize conflicts post-marriage, and it can help strengthen the bonding between the two partners. Sex education is another preventive mechanism wherein the young adults are oriented to their reproductive system and the hormonal changes it accompanies and the challenges associated with them. This can prepare the young adults to experience this transition phase cautiously and take decisions with diligence and care. It can prevent many mishaps leading to abuse, conflict, suicides, trafficking, addiction, violence and substance abuse.

To add on to this, Popple and Leighninger (2011) list seven core functions of the social workers which include: (a) engagement, (b) assessment, (c) planning, (d) implementation, (e) monitoring/evaluation, (f) supportive counselling and (g) graduated disengagement.

1. Engagement refers to the process in which the client–worker interface begins.
2. Assessment means identifying the client's needs and necessities which obstruct their social functioning.
3. Planning refers to the plan of action chalked out to work on the client's problem.

4. Implementation is the way the action plan is executed to attend to the person in problem and the social environment.
5. Monitoring/Evaluation is necessary and can also be carried out in a team to check if the process in which the problem has been implemented and carried out is fine or requires a review/reconsideration for better outcomes.
6. Supportive counselling refers to the additional feature rendered to the client along with the process of direct intervention which is a boost to the morale and the spirit of the client in need.
7. Graduated disengagement is the final step where the entire process is gradually disengaged where the client no longer depends on the worker but becomes self-reliant and strong to move on further without any direct support.

Thus, the above-mentioned functions determine the objectives of social work and how it is practised among varied settings catering to the needs of the clients which differ from one another, which is gauged accordingly by the social worker working with the client.

SUMMARY

Social work is an academic discipline as well as a professional course. It is referred to as a helping profession. It improves the quality of life and well-being of the individuals, groups, families and communities by direct practice. Social work begins with attending to the needs of the individual in crisis to promote better functioning not only at their level but also within their groups, families and communities. The fundamental base on which social work practice relies on is the understanding of human development, behaviour and the social, economic and cultural institutions and interactions. The human behaviour is the primordial source of intervention in relation to the family and social environment. The other aspect of the profession is to coordinate and relate various resources and services and connect them with individuals, groups and communities to utilize them and see how they could come out of the problem to gain and restore normal and social functioning. One of the main objectives of this profession is to enhance human well-being and it is clearly established that research, knowledge and skills enhance social work practice. The scope of social work profession is diverse and wide-ranging. The profession is very much value based, and it aims at creating a just and humane society for all human beings to live amicably in a social environment.

TOP 10 TAKEAWAYS/MAIN POINTS

1. Social work is a helping profession. It draws its knowledge and literature from other interrelated disciplines such as sociology, psychology, law, women studies, anthropology, human rights, politics and media.
2. The client comes with a problem to the social worker who works through a process to solve the problem together to restore social functioning.

3. Social work is a practice-based profession, and, hence, it involves working with individuals, groups, families and communities.
4. Its main objective is to work on the psychosocial problems of the clientele and facilitate their well-being.
5. It not only works on the problems but also helps in preventing the problems for individuals and groups at large.
6. Social work intervenes in the lives of the individuals to facilitate their effective participation in the development of the society.
7. Social work rests on the principle of acceptance wherein the clients are accepted as they are as it is considered that all individuals are unique.
8. Principle of self-determination is the heart and soul of the profession. It simply means that the client with the problem is enabled to decide on their own what suits them best, given the external support and guidance from the social worker.
9. Trust and confidentiality are the base on which the social work process rests upon.
10. Social work aims at influencing the lives of individuals for positive growth and development.

Keywords: Social work, social welfare, social justice, social development, social functioning, human behaviour, human intervention, human well-being

GLOSSARY

Empathy This is an act of perceiving, understanding, feeling or experiencing, and responding to the other person who is sharing their problem.

Human behaviour The diverse range of behaviour exhibited by individuals in their social environment due to varied psycho, socio and cultural influences.

Human intervention Intervention by individuals addressing the needs, services, rights and grievances of other individuals, groups, families and communities.

Human well-being The ability of individuals to lead a happy and better life encompassing many aspects of everyday life.

Rapport This is the preliminary step initiated towards the social work process where the client–worker interface happens, thereby building trust and confidentiality to work on the problem together.

Social development This implies the development of the society as a whole. It involves individuals, groups, families, communities and their socio-economic development. Political development also influences social development.

Social environment It is the locale, context, milieu, sociocultural set-up of an individual with their relationships, social structures, institutions and culture.

Social functioning The ability of an individual to perform their roles in the social environment effectively.

Social justice It is a means through which the rights, needs and entitlements of the poor, deprived, neglected, vulnerable and discriminated are achieved. It is a process aimed at ensuring human rights and entitlements.

Social service It means giving away something in charity. It can be in the form of food, clothes, medicines, financial assistance, books, furniture or even volunteering.

Social welfare   It is a means of helping, assisting, enabling any individual or group depending on their vulnerability in terms of caste, class, gender or income to improve their basic needs and necessities for their development.

Social work   It is a practice-based and a helping profession. Its aim is to help one to help themselves. This process takes place through a client–worker interface. The principle of confidentiality and self-determination of the client are crucial components of this profession.

MULTIPLE CHOICE QUESTIONS

1. Why is social work called a helping profession?
   a. **Helping one to help themselves**
   b. Helping one to help others
   c. Helping many to help themselves
   d. None of the above

2. Who is a professional social worker?
   a. One who has done social service
   b. **One who has a social work degree**
   c. One who has done both social work and social service
   d. One who has a social science degree

3. Which among these is referred to as a practice-based profession?
   a. Sociology
   b. Economics
   c. Anthropology
   d. **Social work**

4. ……… is the first step towards establishing a purposeful relationship.
   a. **Rapport**
   b. Contact
   c. Support
   d. Report

5. ……… is the base on which the relationship of a social worker and a client rests on.
   a. Empathy
   b. Sincerity
   c. **Confidentiality**
   d. Accountability

6. Which is one of the functions of social work practice?
   a. Termination
   b. Study
   c. Follow-up
   d. **Rehabilitation**

7. .... is an act of perceiving, understanding, feeling or experiencing, responding to the other person who is sharing their problem.
   a. **Empathy**
   b. Sympathy
   c. Mood disorder
   d. Attitude

8. One of the major concerns of social work is ....
   a. Providing referral
   b. Networking
   c. **Ensuring justice**
   d. To advocate

9. .... is a step towards ensuring client well-being.
   a. **Rehabilitation**
   b. Lobbying
   c. Adjustment
   d. Accommodation

10. .... of clientele is the objective of social work practice.
    a. Emotional well-being
    b. Economic well-being
    c. **Psychosocial being**
    d. Physical well-being

REVIEW QUESTIONS

1. Why is social work referred to as a 'helping profession'?
2. What is the basic premise the social workers work on?
3. What are the emerging fields of social work profession? Discuss.
4. Why do you think the scope of social work profession has been expanding in leaps and bounds?
5. What are the primary functions of the social work profession?
6. Write a short note on the objectives of social work profession?

REFERENCES

Ahmad, M. R. (1969). *Samaj karya-darshan evam pranaliya*. British Book Depot.

Anderson, J. P. (1943). Joseph P. Anderson (1910–1979)—Settlement worker, administrator and first executive director of the National Association of Social Workers (NASW). Social Welfare History Project. http://socialwelfare.library.vcu.edu/people/anderson-joseph-p/

Boehm, W. W. (1959). *Objectives of the social work curriculum of the future* (Vol. 1). Council on Social Work Education.

Chowdhry, P. (1992). *Introduction to social work*. Atma Ram and Sons.
Clarke, H. I. (1947). *Principles and practice of social work*. D. Appleton-Century Co.
Dasgupta, S. (1967). *Towards a philosophy of social work in India*. Popular Book Services.
Desai, M. (2002). *Ideologies and social work (historical and contemporary analysis)*. Rawat Publications.
Dubois, B., & Miley, K. K. (1999). *Social work: An empowering profession* (3rd ed.). Allyn and Bacon.
Fink, A. E. (1942). *The field of social work*. Henry Holt and Co.
Friedlander, W. A. (1955). *Introduction to social welfare*. Prentice Hall.
Friedlander, W. A. (1977). *Concepts and methods of social work*. Prentice Hall.
Indian Conference of Social Work. (1957). Associated Advertisers and Printers. Bombay.
Mirza, R. A. (1969). Social welfare policy in India. *Lucknow University Journal of Social Work, 4*.
Morales, A., & Bradford, S. (1989). *Social work: A profession of many faces* (5th ed.). Allyn & Bacon.
Nair, T. K. (1981). *Social work education and social work practice in India*. Association of School of Social Work in India.
Popple, P. R., & Leighninger, L. (2011). *Social work, social welfare, and American society*. Allyn & Bacon.
Praag P. H. V. (1957). Basic concepts of social work. *Social Service Review, 31*(2), 183–191.
Siddiqui, H. Y. (1984). *Social work and social action*. Harnam Publications.
Skidmore, R. A., Thackrey, M. G., & Farley, W. (1991). *Introduction to social work*. Prentice Hall.
Stroup, H. H. (1960). *Social work, an introduction to the field*. American Book Company.
Wadia, A. R. (1961). *History and philosophy of social work in India*. Allied Publishers.
Youngdahl, B. E. (1949). Social work as a profession. In M. B. Hodges (Ed.), *Social work year book*. Russell Sage.
Zastraw, H. C. (2003). *The practice of social work*. Thomson Learning Academic Centre.

RECOMMENDED READING

Batra, S., & Dash, B. M. (2021). *Fundamentals of social work*. Concept Publisher.

2

History of Social Work in the USA, the UK and India

Indrajit Goswami

LEARNING OBJECTIVES

- Understand the historical contexts through which social work emerged into its present form
- Identify different factors that determined the course of historical development of different forms of social activities dedicated to the needy and marginalized
- Critically analyse the purpose and motive of different personalities, institutions, organizations and agencies in their stakes during development process
- Understand the relevance of heritage and traditions, including religious approaches in shaping social movements and their destinies

Social work would embrace a growing world consciousness.

—Jane Addams

INTRODUCTION

Historically, the development of social service traditions had always been greatly influenced and guided by the Judaeo-Christian religious teachings. Likewise, in India, the social service traditions and the activities of the service providers have been influenced by several religions, including *Sanatana Dharma*, Christianity and Islam. The religious teachings and principles had substantial influence in generating the 'will' among their followers to help the weak and the suffering, the oppressed and the depressed through 'sacrifice' and 'selfless' services. While in the West, the quest for helping the needy emerged mainly through 'charity' and 'poor relief', in India, the doctrine of 'dharma' (duty) inspired and guided people, in general, and the rulers or kings, in particular, to serve the downtrodden and destitute people.

During the latter half of the 19th century, there was a growing realization to make the services more scientific, secular and humanitarian, especially for making the individuals 'self-reliant' and to create services to support people in distress. The author here makes an effort to revisit the history of social work in the UK, the USA and India to understand its evolution through different religious influences, social reform movements, governance mechanisms and politics.

HISTORY OF SOCIAL WORK IN THE UK

Inquiries regarding whether the onset of social work in the UK was a strategic move of Elizabethan politics, the government and churches to divert the attention of its people from the immoral colonial rule of the British (the East India Company) in the Indian Ocean region, Southeast Asia and Hong Kong and related assumptions or critical hypotheses have never been tested. Whatever evidences are available in the form of readable content directly relate the historical development of social work in the UK to some specific religious initiatives by the churches. It is believed that the folk (religious community) tradition influenced by religious faith was instrumental in sensitizing people about their obligation to the helpless and underprivileged for sympathetic care. Alms were collected in the parish and distributed by the priest and clergymen who used to identify the underprivileged individuals, especially poor. Perhaps the concern for care and service to poor emerged out of a perceived threat to the social order, peace and integrity. Later, the government took over the responsibility for relief, primarily through enacting the restrictive legislation forbidding begging and vagrancy.

It was between 1350 and 1530, a series of laws came into existence to exert legal pressure on the poor, especially the able-bodied persons, to opt for working for earning their livelihoods. The organized charities by the churches started witnessing diminishing popularity and gradually the legal and judicial systems posed a threat to centralized authorities of different churches. The law-led transformations in Britain shifted the welfare and other prominent public responsibilities to government authorities. Its impact was wider and, consequently, England witnessed the rise of series of measures which resulted in the Elizabethan Poor Law of 1601.

THE ELIZABETHAN POOR LAW, 1601

The Poor Law of 1601 continued to guide the governmental responsibility for about 300 years. The statute symbolizes the determination of the government to stabilize the effects of different church-led religious activities and economic changes through generations. The final form of the legislation categorically distinguished three classes of the poor:

1. The able-bodied beggars (sturdy beggars) were not allowed to survive on 'alms'. They were made to stay and work in designated correction centres.

2. The sick, the old, the blind, the deaf mute, the lame, the demented and mothers with young children were categorized as the *impotent persons*. They were kept in the almshouses and made to live within the limits of their capacities. Those who already had their own shelters were given 'outdoor relief' materials such as food, clothes and fuel.
3. The orphans and deserted children were referred to as 'dependent' and categorized as individuals who could not support themselves. Only the children of eight years and above were attached to townsmen for different domestic work.

Four Principles of the Elizabethan Poor Law

The Elizabethan Poor Law sustained as the most influential instrument and set of guidelines for more than three centuries in shaping welfare policies and social services. Following are the several important principles embedded in that Law and their major contributions:

1. The 'principle of state's responsibility' has made the most adorable and appreciable contribution through distinguishing state's moral responsibility from sporadic initiatives by churches.
2. The 'principle of local responsibility' echoed in the Poor Law for ensuring dignity and respect of the poor and their welfare.
3. The Law mooted another idea, that is, the principle of differential treatment, where the most marginalized and underprivileged such as children, the aged and the sick were considered to have greater claim on supportive services than the able-bodied poor. The Law entrusted the local communities to identify and help the most unfortunate.
4. It also redefined family responsibility for aiding dependents. The children, grandchildren, parents and grandparents were referred to as individuals having 'legally liable' relations with heads of families.

Changes through Amendments: 1834–1909

The Elizabethan Law underwent several revisions to incorporate changing aspirations and perspectives in the field of public welfare and social work. Based on recommendations of a Parliamentary Committee (1834), the following provisions were included in the legislation: (a) verification of eligibility of service seekers, (b) re-establishment of the workhouse test and (c) centralization of control. The recommendations facilitated the screening of eligible paupers, criteria to debar able-bodied poor from receiving any aid and consolidation of power of statutory commissioners. Through the above recommendations and necessary amendments, the administrative authority of the parishes has been completely dissolved.

The changes during this period brought into new provisions for services for dependent children in district schools and foster homes. For the insane and mentally challenged persons, provisions for specialized institutions were included. Later, the Poor Law Report (1909) advocated for curative treatment and rehabilitation rather than repression, and provision for all in the place of the selective workhouse test. It is observed that while the principles of 1834 provided a 'framework of repression', those of 1909 can be termed as the 'framework of prevention and cure'.

THE SPEENHAMLAND SYSTEM, 1795–1815

It was an amendment to the Elizabethan Poor Law and was devised by some local magistrates to alleviate the distress caused by a spike in grain prices as a result of poor harvest. The system institutionalized a provision for guaranteed minimum income for the poor. Families were paid extra wages beyond the already defined level, and that varied according to the number of children and the price of bread. Unfortunately, the system aggravated the underlying causes of poverty and that allowed employers to pay below subsistence wages because the parish would make up the difference. This resulted in the workers' low income to remain marginalized.

THE WILLIAM BEVERIDGE REPORT

In 1942, Sir William Beveridge, chairman of the Inter-departmental Committee on Social Insurance and Allied Services, submitted the report to the government. The report identified four major principles to make the public welfare programmes and services more inclusive by extending the opportunities beyond the conventional poor as had been defined in existing laws. The four major principles are as follows:

1. Coverage to all citizens
2. Adequately address through a single insurance the major risks of loss of income of people due to sickness, unemployment, accident, old age, widowhood, maternity and so on
3. Provision for a flat rate of contribution for public insurance regardless of the contributor's income
4. Provision for uniform rate of insurance benefit to all eligible persons irrespective of their income

The basic philosophy behind such recommendations was to secure all the British against undesirable incidents. Everyone was entitled to benefits related to maternity, sickness, loss of earning, industrial injury, retirement and grant for widows. Also, they were entitled to get benefits under different schemes such as family allowances, national health services and national assistance. The report had been considered as the foundation of the modern social welfare legislation in the UK.

THE CHARITY ORGANIZATION SOCIETY MOVEMENT AND ITS CONTRIBUTION

The Charity Organization Society (COS) movement in the beginning of the 17th century had endeavoured to provide help to the marginalized people. However, such 'organized' efforts never emerged naturally as a proactive plan to create greater impact but came into existence to delineate the sporadic, competing and mostly overlapping social services in Britain. A group of like-minded citizens founded the London Charity Organization Society in 1869. Octavia

Hill and Samuel Barnett were two pioneers. As a housing reformer, Octavia Hill introduced a system of 'friendly rent' as a method of improving slum housing. She introduced a system that 'each case and each situation must be individualized' and treated accordingly with due respect. Perhaps that initiative seeded the concept of 'individualization' and marked the beginning of practice of 'the value of dignity' in social work.

Samuel Augustus Barnett was the founder of Toynbee Hall, the first settlement house, in which wealthy Oxford students 'settled' in an attempt to improve the living conditions in the slums of Whitechapel. The basic idea was to bring the educated in contact with the marginalized for their mutual benefit and understand their real-life problems and sufferings.

> **Did You Know?**
>
> The *downward filtration theory*, adopted by the British colonial rule in India, purposively ignored the importance of vernacular language in education and extended the opportunities of modern education in English to the then small elite groups in urban areas. It facilitated the emergence of an education system that was elitist in nature and unfavourably led to the disappearance of indigenous system of learning and socialization, especially at the primary level.

HISTORY OF SOCIAL WORK IN THE USA

Historically, the emergence and development of modern social work in the USA was closely similar to that of UK. From an early part of the 17th century, the colonists from England and other countries brought with them the tradition of charity, voluntary action and organized efforts to initiate welfare activities. Obviously, the urge to help the marginalized emerged from religious desires of affluent sections of society but the motive behind such initiatives might be to ensure the social security of the helpers and protect their potential prospects in colonized settlements. The religious charity and philanthropic activities by both, the individuals and organized societies, attempted to meet the needs of the neighbourhoods, especially poor and needy people.

POOR RELIEF

The poor relief activities had been first initiated by the wealthy individuals and 'private charity associations' and later government public relief authorities came into existence to address issues, especially of the insane, feeble minded and law offenders. The private relief societies were usually associated with churches and played prominent roles in shaping social welfare programmes in the 19th century. They mooted the idea of segregation of children and other vulnerable groups from mixed almshouses to protect them from serious law offenders.

PRIVATE CHARITIES

The scope of intervention by the individual and private charity societies was mostly limited to aid for special local groups. The private charities realized the necessity to scientifically understand the causes of poverty and as a result, the New York Society for the Prevention of Pauperism was established in 1817. It started exploring constructive remedies for poverty and developing models for sustainable rehabilitation. The society engaged volunteers called 'visitors of the indigent' as its agents and established an employment bureau, a savings bank and pursued the foundation of mutual aid, mutual life insurance groups to protect the economically marginalized members.

CHARITY ORGANIZATION SOCIETIES

The first COS was established in 1877 in Buffalo, New York, by Stephen Humphreys Gurteen (1836–1898). In 1875, he was ordained as Episcopal priest and appointed assistant minister of St Paul's Church, Buffalo, New York. The Buffalo COS was launched in December 1877. The founders of those societies held individuals responsible for their poverty, but the friendly visitors hinted about different other factors that were responsible for their marginalization and misery. They assumed that it could be due to their unhealthy living and housing conditions, poor health and weak morals.

The COS gained momentum in promoting and enforcing social legislation for improvement of housing and slum clearance. The societies later inducted different initiatives such as loan disbursement, laundries, 'wayfarers' lodges, shelters, training centres and manufacturing workshops for the rehabilitation of the differently-abled persons. Gradually, the societies ventured into training for girls; running hospitals and dispensaries, and nurseries for young children; and recreation and summer camps for others.

SETTLEMENT HOUSE MOVEMENT

Along with the emergence of industries, there existed a severe shortage of accommodation facilities for individuals and families. The migrating masses of workers and their families were forced to live in overcrowded residential areas with inadequate sanitary facilities. In 1887, the Neighborhood Guild of New York City was founded based on the idea of Toynbee Hall in England. Soon Hull-house in Chicago, founded by Jane Addams and Ellen Gates Starr in 1889, gained popularity.

Hull-house Model

This model house was meant for promoting the educational, cultural and physical well-being of children and adults. Such houses had taken responsibilities to cater the needs of neighbouring beneficiaries. The model had been instrumental for school reforms in the USA (Friedlander & Apte, 1974, p. 112).

The legacy of social work from its ancient to present forms, evolved and developed out of a long religiously dominated tradition of charity, has been widely acknowledged by all Western chronicles who have written extremely on the history of social work, including Friedlander's *Introduction to Social Welfare* (Singh, 2000). Charity, especially in Western societies, had always been associated with religion. First, it acquired the sanction of religion and then became personal virtue, a religious duty and a social utility. Charity had been an overt expression of impulse of individuals towards sufferings of fellow citizens (Singh, 2000), but there had been no organized effort to examine the dormant motive behind such impulses. Whether the religious urge surfaced due to any perceived threat to the wealthy sections of society or was purely driven by self-less spiritual emancipation, the quest still remains unanswered. However, later, the secularization of professions has set free 'social work' from the strangulating church control (Prasad, 2003) and marked the beginning of a new era where rationality, scientific outlook, freedom, democratization and more so indigenization became the hallmark of any organized service.

HISTORY OF SOCIAL WORK IN INDIA

Wadia (1968) observed that modern social work existed in India since time immemorial in the form of tradition of social services. It is prominent in the Vedic literature that the basic philosophy of social service was seeded into the principles of *karuna* (compassion), *daya* (mercy), *maitree* (friendship), *prem* (love), *seva* (service) and mutual cooperation (Pandey, 2003). While revisiting the history of social work in India, Pathare (2010) observed that the spirit of serving fellow citizens and voluntarism had already existed as part of the quest for attaining cosmic consciousness and harmony with nature and communion with God. Canda (1998) observed the phenomenon as a common experience of people here in considering spirituality as the soulful awareness of interconnectedness and the realization that self and others are inseparable.

Unfortunately, a group of academicians in India always had been trying to equate spirituality-led social service traditions with sectarian religious beliefs and practices in the line of Christian or Jewish form. Unlike in the UK and the USA, social work in India in the form of social services continued and was inspired by selfless 'service' and 'sacrifice'. If we critically review the observations made by Moorthy (1989), we find that while the social service traditions in Europe, the UK and the USA have been wrongly metamorphosed into present form of professional social work, a similar attempt in India has almost failed to win confidence and endorsement by people and larger society in India. Moorthy (1989) concluded that 'whilst service is commendable and is not social work, social work includes social service'. Chronologically, social service preceded social work and has a long tradition in India.

ANCIENT INDIA

Social welfare in ancient India was considered as the 'dharma' (duty) of people, in general, and the rulers or kings, in particular. The doctrine of dharma had a very profound influence on setting the social dimension in general and politico-legal system by the kings. The greatest events of the ancient Indian history, as depicted in the epics of the Ramayana and the Mahabharata, are the two wars fought to uphold the dharma. It was considered both as an absolute and instrumental duty to protect the entire society and social system. Dharma was respected as law with an ultimate aim to remove the miseries of the people and to create conditions so that people may pursue the aims of life.

While the object of the (affluent and wealthy) people of Europe was to exterminate the poor and marginalized in order to secure their own life, the *Varnashrama dharma* in ancient India ensured welfare and peaceful living of all *varnas* (class of people based on occupations). The Aryans always wanted to raise all up to their levels. While the means of European civilization was the sword, the Aryans embraced the division of different *varnas*. That system of division or social order had been the stepping stone of civilization, enabling one to prosper and rise in proportion to one's learning, labour (hard work) and culture. While in Europe, it was victory of the strong, and death of the weak, in India, every social rule was directed towards the protection of the weak (Kumar, 2005).

The king assumed the position of *paterfamilias* par excellence, responsible for the protection of all. Although the care of the helpless was the spiritual and moral duty (dharma) of the concerned families, the local bodies stepped in when families failed and the king assumed responsibility if local bodies failed. The ancient Indian welfare process reveals a three-tier system: (a) the joint family at the primary level, (b) the local body (village or town) at the intermediary level and (c) the state at the secondary level (Moorthy, 1981). Helping fellow human beings as a 'dharma' and 'spiritual' act had been embraced by people as means to facilitate their souls for an upward journey towards realization of super consciousness (*moksha*).

The vast range of ancient Hindu literature—religious and philosophical, medical, psychological, sociological, yogic and poetic—has ample suggestions for building theories and practices of social work along what has been done in modern times. In ancient India, the social and individual problems were mostly not of such nature and dimensions as to attract special research and study. Instead, wisdom-led insights and projections played prominent roles in understanding and addressing common sufferings of people.

The Karma Yoga and Doctrine of Karma

Yogah Karmasu Kausalam (the Bhagavad Gita, 2.50)

The Bhagavad Gita has narrated *yoga* as an art of getting perfection (*kausalam*) in every work (*karmasu*) of life. This perfection comes in *karma* with the regular practice of devoting *karma* to others. The spiritual principle has been guiding the people in action since time immemorial. It provides two alternatives: (a) *karma* with ambition of results or fruits (*sakama karma*) and (b) *karma* without any desire or expectation of results (*nishkama karma*). Sakama karma creates egoism, hatred and jealousy in a person's heart consciously or unconsciously but *nishkama karma* is referred to as pure *karma* or *karma yoga*, where we have no intention of receiving anything in return of our services to people. Historically, the spiritual actions in the form of forgiveness, helping, loving and compassion to humanity existed as ideal examples of *nishkama karma* or selfless action.

> **Did You Know?**
>
> The Gandhian philosophy of *sarvodaya* (development and welfare of all) and *antyodaya* (development and welfare of the poorest or the weakest segments of society) was very much similar to the philosophy enunciated by John Ruskin. Gandhiji was very much influenced by Ruskin's classic *Unto This Last* (Kulkarni, 1993).

The Concept of 'Sadharana Dharma' (Universal Duties)

For nurturing of helping personality, the sage Manu prescribed five universal dharmas: (a) non-violence, (b) truth speaking, (c) non-stealing, (d) personal hygiene and (e) control of the senses (*Manusmriti*, X.63). Later, the scope of practising these five universal duties was expanded by taking inputs from the Vedic texts, which included *dana* (spontaneous offerings to the needy), *daya* (pity or compassion), *kshanti* (forgiveness) and *dama* (self-restraint or equanimity; *Yajnavalkya Smriti*, I. 122).

India, historically, directed and shaped its welfare activities through the guidelines that appear as: *lokah samasta sukhino bhavantu* ≈ *sarve janah sukhino bhavantu* ≈ *sarva jiva jantu sukhino bhavantu* (May the whole world be happy and peaceful ≈ May all the people in the world be happy and peaceful ≈ May all forms of life be happy and peaceful). The helping personality of an average individual, family, group or any association had been influenced and shaped by the teachings and wisdoms of ancient texts, including the Upanishads.

The Role of Upanishads

The Upanishadic teachings explained that behind the illusory plurality of selves, there exists one 'universal self', called *Paramatman* (or *Brahman*). It accepted the existence of one single conscious organic whole and so it universally declared the entire world as a single family *(Vasudhaiva Kutumbakam,* Maha Upanishad, VI-72). This perennial philosophy has provided the basis for the system of ethics to entire humanity, including different service professions (Ravindran, 2003).

Kautilya's Arthashastra

During Mauryan rule, Kautilya's *Arthashastra* (economics) laid the foundation of duties and responsibilities of the welfare state. He compiled the strategies and guidelines for the state of Magadha to take care of the state of economic affairs and welfare of people. He kept provisions of subsistence for helpless women and expecting mothers and their children, and employment for prostitutes. Also, it included provisions for public relief during flood and famine, and care for the aged and the poor (Pathak, 2012).

The Ashokan Empire and Social Welfare

The reign of Ashoka during the 3rd century BC is frequently referred to as the golden age of ancient Indian history. The Mauryan empire founded by Chandragupta Maurya reached its peak as an ideal welfare state during the reign of his grandson Ashoka. He introduced the practice of providing employment to the poor to establish social equity through redistribution of resources. There was a wide variety of taxes on actors and prostitutes to generate welfare fund to support the poor and needy. Ashoka introduced several welfare activities for women, rehabilitation for prisoners, free medical care, regulation of prostitution, building roads, rest houses for travellers, construction of wells and so on. He also established a comprehensive and well-organized public administration system. While he encouraged the propagation of Buddhism, he respected and allowed other religious practices including Brahmanism. He pioneered an administration which led the economy to create surplus economic wealth to cater the welfare needs of poor and needy and, thus, helped in maintaining social integration and social control (Pathak, 2012).

THE MEDIEVAL PERIOD (1206–1706)

It is universally recognized that religion has played an important role in the development of social work (Midgley & Sanzenbach, 1989), but the role that Christianity played in the upheavals of Eastern Europe, inter-religious (communalism) and intra-religious (caste based) conflicts in India cannot be ignored. Further, a call for vengeance in the name of Islamic *fatwa* and the expansion of Christianity and Islam through conversion of native Hindus in the subcontinent were indicative of understanding their hidden agenda, if any, and their role in driving communities and shaping sociopolitical milieu (Pathare, 2010). Until the arrival of Islam and Christianity, there was no dispute against the central role of spirituality in personal and public life (Bullis, 1996; Green, 1987) but the evolution of Western social work models through Judeo-Christian beliefs and later their import to India, projected social work as a secular profession and along with advocating religion as private affair, they purposefully added sectarian colour to spirituality too and disconnected it from the philosophy of universal soul or greater consciousness. The following section deals with the development of social welfare and other related traditions from the early 13th century to the beginning of the 18th century.

During Sultanate and Mughal regimes, imams were responsible for collecting charity tax (*zakat*) from the followers of Islam but for non-Muslims, especially Hindus, they imposed controversial special poll tax called *jizya*. While *zakat* was used for welfare of poor and needy Muslims, *jizya* was meant for religious protection for *dhimmis* (non-Muslim allies). Later, when Sufism came to India, the Sufi leaders, mostly from Iran and Arabia, promoted austerity, equality and public welfare, combined with deep mysticism and spirituality (Pathak, 2012).

The major social problems of this period were poverty, exploitation, alcoholism, gambling and prostitution. In the name of education, the state (kingdom) maintained theological schools, known as *madrasas*. Consequently, all the Mughal rulers established *madrasas* and increased their numbers but the expansion of such facility was limited to urban areas, especially Delhi. Likewise, the medical care centres were limited to only Delhi. During the regime of Sher Shah, every *serai* (rest houses) had a resident physician and Sher Shah constructed large number of *serais* for travellers.

Reforms during Akbar's Regime

Unlike other Muslim rulers, Akbar was praised as *insan-i-kamil* (perfect man) due to his policies and actions against Islamic orthodoxy. He abolished pilgrim's tax in 1563, *jizya* in 1564, slavery in 1583, and introduced reforms in the state grants for charities. He made the public administration impartial and made *madad-i-maash* (a type of state grant) liberal to benefit all, including Hindus, Jains, Parsees and so on. Akbar extended support to Hindus to promote the study of Sanskrit and other traditional Hindu systems of learning. Also, he initiated transformation in education system by incorporating subjects of practical importance such as mathematics, accounting, agriculture, physics, astronomy, history, logic and divinity. However, the health care facilities were mostly restricted to state capitals and prominent towns. The large mass of rural people was deprived of such facilities.

REFORM DURING COLONIAL PERIOD

It was in 1757, the Mughal rule ended after British army defeated them at the Battle of Plassey in Bengal. That was the beginning of colonial rule in India, and it lasted for two centuries after that war. The social reform movements of this period can be divided into three phases: (a) the first phase covers 1815–1860, (b) the second phase covers 1860–1920 and (c) the last phase encompasses the period of 1920–1948.

First Phase Reforms

During the 16th and the 17th centuries, the (undivided) Bengal was famous in the world for its fine muslin industry. The artisans and weavers experienced a huge setback and loss due to unfair competition created by colonial rule through industrialization. The British allowed trade of duty-free and mechanical textile products. By the second half of the 19th century, the muslin weavers were forced to live in extreme poverty and had been pushed out of industrial towns. This created undesirable tension and disharmony between the weavers and agricultural communities (Pathak, 2012).

In social and religious sectors, the Company was cautious and did not primarily allow setting up of Christian missions, and they protected existing religious and social practices. Later, they encouraged Christian missionaries to penetrate into different sectors, including education and health. Hidden behind the veil of their charity activities, the Christian missions started attacking native religious practices (idol worship) and indulged in religious conversion. They were also instrumental in the disappearance of indigenous education system by the end of the 19th century. The expansion of English education was limited to small groups of urban elites, which was otherwise responsible for creating disharmony between different social classes.

Despite some of their undesirable interventions in the then social and religious systems, the Christian missions made some contributions to social reform. They extended moral support to two prominent social reformers, Raja Ram Mohan Roy (1772–1833) and Ishwar Chandra Vidyasagar (1820–1891), in abolishing some of the social ills and bringing renaissance in society. Raja Ram Mohan Roy dedicated his life to the abolition of 'Sati', promotion of female education, widow remarriage and prohibition of polygamy. Later, Vidyasagar carried forward those reform activities. Due to their efforts, the Widow Remarriage Act was passed in 1856.

During that time in Eastern India, there existed some social organizations such as *Brahmo Sabha* and *Tattwabodhini Sabha*, and some Bengali journals (e.g., *Som Prakash*) and newspapers (e.g., *Tattwabodhini Patrika* and *Bombay Darpan*), which actively advocated and promoted social reform movements. Similarly, in the Western India, two prominent reformers, Gopal Hari Deshmukh and Jyotirao Phule, tirelessly worked for women's equality (widow remarriage), promotion of indigenous goods among people, establishment of dispensaries, maternity homes, orphanages and establishment of schools for girls and students from lower castes.

Reforms during Second Phase (1857–1920)

This was the time when the imperialism of British colonial rule came to surface and it was ruthless to traditional institutions and traditions (Pathak, 2012). The period was instrumental in the emergence and growth of new professions such as medicine, accountancy, teaching, law and journalism. While the British were very keen to export raw materials and other industrial produce from India to Britain, they grossly neglected the humanitarian and other needs of the native Indian labourers, who had been forced to live in overcrowded labour colonies without basic minimum facilities. The labourers, including women and children, were not only separated from their families, but they also received inhuman treatment from their employers. They were forced to work for longer hours and were paid paltry wages.

During famine (1870) in Bengal, Ishwar Chandra Vidyasagar and Brahmo Samaj worked hard and organized famine relief for the people. Another reformer, Sasipada Banerjee, made notable contribution to women's education, widow remarriage and labour welfare. Other notable reformers who contributed and continued their missions included Jyotirao Phule (established *Satyashodhak Samaj* in 1868 for socio-economic improvement of low-caste people), Debendranath Tagore (advocated to raise the age of marriage in 1871–1872) and Anant Shastri Dongre (established ashram schools for girls) among many. A few Muslim reformers such as Abdul Latif and Amir Ali from Bengal and Sir Syed Ahmed Khan from Uttar Pradesh were keen to promote English education among Muslims, and they were against the orthodoxy of *moulavis* in using Quran. However, they were British sympathizers, openly supported their rule when a sociopolitical movement against the British rule started in eastern and other parts of India. To counter the expansion of Christian mission in India, Brahmo Samaj, Prarthana Samaj and Arya Samaj started several charity activities and as a result, charity became increasingly a non-religious activity in most parts of India.

Reforms during Third Phase (1920–1948)

The socio-economic conditions of Indian labourers remained unchanged. The period witnessed the emergence of trade union movements against low wages, inhuman working and living conditions of labourers. Some distinguished trade union leaders and activists such as N. M. Joshi, N. G. Chandavarkar Rao and M. G. Ranade were active in organizing activities such as night classes, recreational programmes and mutual aid societies for the welfare of industrial labourers. The colonial rule overlooked the sufferings of industrial labourers and hardly did anything to protect the interests of agriculturalists and agricultural labourers after economic crises due to two World Wars.

M. K. Gandhi came back from Africa and initiated political movement against the British misrule. He favoured integration of social and political reforms to ensure eradication of social ills, especially the practice of untouchability. He opposed the idea of inter-caste marriage, showed reluctance for frontal attack on caste system and organized *satyagraha* on behalf of the untouchables. Natarajan (1962) observed Gandhi's initial response to ongoing social reform activities as ambiguous and conflicting to mainstream ideologies. Later, he believed that until there was a strong social bond, a united national movement against the British was not possible. It was during this time, Jyotirao Phule, Sasipada Banerjee and then Gandhiji established voluntary organizations to undertake different welfare activities and, undoubtedly, that was the beginning of exploration for an indigenous base for social work and welfare in India. Gandhi's philosophy as well as the plan was grounded on a broad strategy of total social development with a concentrated focus on community-oriented process of rural development. He advocated that social work should not only be meant for ameliorative activity but should also be geared to radical transformation for establishing an equitable social order (Ganguli, 1975). He imagined the role of *samagra grama sevak* as someone who would be a resident social worker and would be dedicated to *sarvodaya* (i.e., universal uplift or progress of all, a term first coined by Gandhi as the title of his 1908 translation of John Ruskin's tract on political economy, *Unto This Last*). His philosophy of social work differed to that of professional social work and it still exists as 'Gandhian social work' and inspires our practices in India.

DOES THE LEGACY CONTINUE?

Since ancient times, Indian civilization and its *Sanatana Dharma* have guided its people to take up social service activities as their 'duty' to humanity. However, it is evident from literature (Bingham, 2006; Lim, 2016; Putnam & Campbell, 2010) that followers of Christianity, both in the UK and the USA, confess that they remain associated with churches primarily to fulfil their own 'life satisfaction'. Does this mean that their activities in churches were just the medium to gain some narrow self-gain? Was it this motive which categorically turned churches into 'centre for poor relief' in those countries and later was brought to India?

To understand the historical implications of old legacies on modern social work, we need organized efforts in conducting research and different academic discourses, including conferences and seminars. Unfortunately, there had been no prominent effort in the past to incorporate the available Indic literature in this regard into our social work courses and syllabus. It is evident from history that the rich tradition of charity has been the bedrock for professional social work, but we never explored the motive behind such charity activities. An honest analysis of historical traditions of charity and philanthropic (religious) activities is very much needed to understand the merit of their contributions from the perspective of ideals of Upanishadic and Vedic Bharat (undivided India), a civilization that was already highly developed by the end of the 4th millennium BC. It is evident from the above historical accounts that while the Western and European social work emerged mainly through micro-level 'helping-a-poor' model, Indic social work approaches had been born through social reform movements in India. Those were directed towards establishing greater social equality, welfare of industrial labourers, education for the masses, including women, welfare of marginalized communities, total development of rural communities and so on. Historically and chronologically, in India, the concept and practices of social service preceded today's imported 'social work' models, and people here largely embraced and admired the service (*seva*) traditions. During the latter part of the second decade of the 20th century, the House of Tatas, a leading industry group in India, came to know about Dr Clifford Manshardt, who was visiting India to work with the American Marathi Mission for the welfare of the people of Nagappa neighbourhood, who were then suffering mainly from poverty, delinquency and prostitution. The Tatas invited Manshardt to set up a 'formal training centre' in Mumbai to train social service personnel, but Manshardt was not sure whether Western theories and models of social work would fit into the Indian context (Desai, 1985). There had been other indigenous forerunners such as 'Social Service League' and 'Servants of India Society' in Mumbai for the formalized process of training, and there was already a consensus for the requirement of an evidence-based learning system. But the history does not provide any scientific evidence about how a foreign curriculum (content) was implanted to subjugate an existing Indic tradition and its quest. The legacy was not only overlooked but purposively neglected while 'professional social work' was institutionalized in India.

SUMMARY

While the Elizabethan poor law, followed by the churches and COSs, had been instrumental behind the evolution of modern social work in the UK, in the USA, private charities in the beginning and later COSs and settlement house movement were prominent initiatives for the abolition of pauperism. Unlike in the UK and the USA, in India, the seed of modern social work was dormant inside the doctrine of *Sanatana Dharma*, which has been pivotal in inculcating the practice of 'duty' to humanity. Although the concept of charity was imported by Christian missionaries, the Indian social reformers during the 18th–20th centuries led social reform movements to uplift the poor and disadvantaged sections of society, including women and children, through the principle of *sarvodaya* and the establishment of dispensaries, maternity homes, orphanages and schools for girls and students from lower castes.

TOP 10 TAKEAWAYS/MAIN POINTS

1. The Elizabethan Poor Law, 1601, and poor laws of colonial America continued their influence for about 300 years in conceptualizing and framing of social welfare policies, both in the UK and colonial America.
2. Historically, women, children and labourers were the most vulnerable and marginalized groups in all the three countries.
3. Charities, especially in Western societies, had always been associated with religion.
4. While attainment of *moksha* (super consciousness) was the divine goal of every social service volunteer in India, 'self-satisfaction' was the strong desire of Christians to stay associated with church activities, including charity.
5. The Mauryan empire evolved as an ideal welfare state during the time of Ashoka.
6. To counter religious charity activities by Christian mission in India, Brahmo Samaj, Prarthana Samaj and Arya Samaj started several charity activities and as a result, charity became increasingly a non-religious activity in most parts of India.

7. The COS movement in the beginning of the 17th century had endeavoured to provide help to the marginalized people.
8. The Speenhamland System was an amendment to the Elizabethan Poor Law and was devised by some local magistrates to alleviate the distress caused by a spike in grain prices as a result of poor harvest.
9. The Upanishadic teachings explained that behind the illusory plurality of selves, there exists one 'universal self'.
10. Jyotirao Phule established *Satyashodhak Samaj* in 1868 for socio-economic improvement of low-caste people.

Keywords: Church, charity, charity organization, Elizabethan Law, sturdy beggars, marginalized, poverty, welfare, dharma, spirituality, consciousness, social service, selfless service, *moksha*, voluntarism, family system, colonization, settlement houses, social welfare, Vedic tradition, Upanishads, *karma yoga*, *sarvodaya*, Gandhian social work

GLOSSARY

***Arthashastra*:** Subject of economics as propounded by Kautilya during the Mauryan rule, which laid the foundation of duties and responsibilities of the welfare state.
Charity: Considered to be an overt expression of impulse of individuals towards sufferings of fellow citizens.
Dharma: Referred to the spiritual and moral duty of a Hindu and it was considered different to religious obligations.
Friendly rent: Introduced by Octavia Hill as a system and method of improving slum housing. It referred to a system where 'each case and each situation must be individualized' and treated accordingly with due respect.
Gandhian social work: An approach of social service inspired by the philosophy of *sarvodaya* and *antyodaya* as propounded by M. K. Gandhi.
Impotent: Referred to those categorized as the sick, old, blind, deaf mute, lame, demented and mothers with young children as per the Elizabethan Poor Law, 1601.
Karma yoga: Referred to *nishkama karma* as pure *karma* or *karma toga*, where we have no intention of receiving anything in return of our services to people.
Madrasa: A model of theological school brought in India by the Mughal rulers.
Spirituality: A principle that guided service personnel in India to realize and accept the interconnectedness (super consciousness) between the service providers and service recipients.
Sturdy beggars: Referred to able-bodied persons who were not allowed to survive on alms.

ANALYTICAL QUESTIONS

1. What could be the motives of different religions behind their welfare initiatives in the UK, the USA and India? Discuss.
2. Do you find any ideological differences between 'Christian mission' and 'Ramakrishna mission'? Explain.

MULTIPLE CHOICE QUESTIONS

1. Who according to COS was responsible for poverty?
   a. The greater society
   b. The government
   c. **The poor**
   d. The economy

2. Which of the following was instrumental for the provision of 'guaranteed minimum income' for the poor?
   a. COS
   b. **Speenhamland System**
   c. Settlement house
   d. Hull-house

3. Which of the following features was common to Brahmo Samaj, Prarthana Samaj and Arya Samaj?
   a. They were orthodox religious organizations
   b. All three were founded by the same person
   c. **They pioneered non-religious charity activity in India**
   d. Their activities were funded by the British

4. During pre-Independence India, the major reform initiatives about women were related to:
   a. Abolition of Sati
   b. Promotion of widow remarriage
   c. Education for women
   d. **All three**

5. Which one of the following was the best combination advocated by the Poor Law Report, 1909?
   a. Framework for repression and cure
   b. Framework for repression and rehabilitation
   c. Framework for prevention and repression
   d. **Framework for prevention and cure**

6. For which of the following reasons did Tatas invite Manshardt?
   a. To undertake a skill survey of Indian social service personnel
   b. **To set up a formal training centre in Mumbai to train social service personnel**
   c. To import Western models of social work to India
   d. For capacity building of 'Social Service League' and 'Servants of India Society' in Mumbai

7. Which of the following are the universal dharmas as prescribed by Manu?
   a. Non-violence
   b. Truth speaking
   c. Non-stealing
   d. **All of the above**

History of Social Work in the USA, the UK and India

8. When did Jyotirao Phule establish Satyashodhak Samaj for socio-economic improvement of low-caste people?
   a. **1868**
   b. 1869
   c. 1870
   d. 1871

9. When was the Widow Remarriage Act passed in India?
   a. 1851
   b. **1856**
   c. 1852
   d. 1852

10. Which Muslim ruler in India was praised as *insan-i-kamil*?
    a. Babur
    b. Humayun
    c. **Akbar**
    d. Jahangir

REVIEW QUESTIONS

1. What do you mean by the three-tier system of social welfare in ancient India?
2. What was the basic philosophy of 'Gandhian social work'?
3. Can you differentiate between *zakat* and *jizya*?
4. What was the significance of the Battle of Plassey in Bengal?
5. How would you identify Ram Mohan Roy, Vidyasagar and Jyotirao Phule as social reformers of India?
6. What are the major contributing principles of the Elizabethan Law?
7. What were the recommendations of the Parliamentary Committee (1834)?
8. Could you perceive any potential motive of wealthy individuals' association with churches in helping the needy?
9. What different types of activities were done by COS in the USA?
10. Why Hull-houses gained prominence over settlement houses?

REFERENCES

Bingham, J. (2006). Religion can make your life happier, official figures suggest. http://www.telegraph.co.uk
Bullis, R. (1996). *Spirituality in social work practice*. Taylor & Francis.
Canda, E. R. (1998). Afterword: Linking spirituality and social work—five themes for innovation. *Social Thought, 18*(2), 97–106.
Desai, A. S. (1985). The foundations of social work in India. *The Indian Journal of Social Work, 46*(1), 41–60.
Friedlander, W. A., & Apte, R. Z. (1974). *Introduction to social welfare*. Prentice Hall.

Ganguli, B. N. (1975). *Concept of equality: The nineteenth century Indian debate* (pp. 29–30). Indian Institute of Advanced Studies.

Green, A. (1987). Spirituality. In A. A. Cohen and P. Mendes-Flohr (Eds.), *Contemporary Jewish religious thought: original essays on critical concepts, movements and beliefs* (pp. 903–7). The Free Press.

Green, R. R. (1994). Human behaviour theory: A diversity framework. Aldine de Gruyer.

Kulkarni, P. D. (1993). The indigenous base of social work profession in India. *The Indian Journal of Social Work, 25*(4), 555–565.

Kumar, V. (2005). Social welfare in Hindu jurisprudence. *NALSAR Law Review, 2*(1), 154–160.

Lim, C. (2016). Religion and subjective well-being across religious traditions: Evidence from 1.3 million Americans. *Journal of the Scientific Study of Religion, 54*(4), 684–701.

Midgley, J., & Sanzenbach, P. (1989). Social work, religion and the global challenge of fundamentalism. *International Social Work, 32*, 273–287.

Moorthy, M. V. (1989). *Social work education in india: retrospect and prospect*. In Souvenir Published by the Department of Studies in Sociology and Social Work. University of Mysore.

Moorthy, M. V. (1981). Philosophy of social work in changing India. In T. Krishnan Nair (Ed.), *Social work education and social work practice in India* (pp. 26–51). ASSWI.

Natarajan, S. (1962). *A century of social reform in India* (pp. 152–161). Asia Publishing House.

Pandey, H. (2003, 13–15 November). *The form of service in Vedic literature* [Paper presentation]. National Seminar on Social Work: The Ethico-spiritual Paradigm, Jain Vishva Bharati Institute, Ladnun, Rajasthan, India.

Pathak, S. (2012). *Social work and social welfare*. Niruta.

Pathare, S. (2010). Christianity among dalits of maharashtra: a case of mahars of ahmednagar district. In Patil Ravi (Ed.), *Dalit Christians in India*. Indian Social Institute.

Prasad, R. (2003, 13–15 November). *Professions and society: A case of social work* [Paper presentation]. National Seminar on Social Work: The Ethico-spiritual Paradigm, Jain Vishva Bharati Institute, Ladnun, Rajasthan, India.

Putnam, R., & Campbell, D. (2010). *American grace: How religion divides and unites us*. Simon & Schuster.

Ravindran, K. (2003, 13–15 November). *Ethico-spiritual paradigm for social work praxiology* [Paper presentation]. National Seminar on Social Work: The Ethico-spiritual Paradigm, Jain Vishva Bharati Institute, Ladnun, Rajasthan, India.

Singh, R. K. (2000, October). The legacy of professional social work in India: Examining its implications. *Contemporary Social Work, XVII*, 29–40.

Wadia, A. R. (1968). Ethical and spiritual values in the practice of social work. In A. R. Wadia (Ed.), *History and philosophy of social work in India*. Allied.

RECOMMENDED READINGS

Axinn, J., & Stern, M. J. (2005). *Social welfare: A history of the American response to need*. Pearson.

Banerjee, G. R. (1972). *Social welfare in ancient India in papers on social work: An Indian perspective*. TISS.

Dasgupta, S. (1958, December). Ashoka's concept of social welfare. *The Indian Journal of Social Work, 19*(3), 197–201.

Gore, M. S. (1965). *Social work and social work education*. Asia Publishing House.

Gore, M. S. (1966, July). The cultural perspective of social work in India. *International Social Work, 9*, 6.

Sastri, R. R. (1966). *Social work tradition in India*. Welfare Forum and Research Organization.

Tice, C., & Perkins, K. (2002). *The faces of social policy: A strengths perspective*. Brooks/Cole.

Valentine, C. A. (1968). *Culture and poverty*. The University of Chicago Press.

Wilensky, H. S., & Lebeaux, C. N. (1965). *Industrial society and social welfare*. The Free Press.

3

Social Reform Movements in India
Akileswari S.

LEARNING OBJECTIVES

- To understand the beginning of social reform movements in Indian society
- To learn the path followed by the social reformers to attain their goal towards social reformation and revival
- To imbibe their teaching and methods in our contemporary society and inculcate them to build our nation

Social reforms are never carried out by the weakness of the strong; but always by the strength of the weak.

—Karl Marx

INTRODUCTION

In the beginning of the 19th century, Indian society witnessed with strong traditions, beliefs and practices which were caste driven with the threat of extirpation of humanitarian values. Such ideals were upheld in the name of religion and there was a strong need felt to bring about a change in the society. The entry of the British into India marked the beginning of Westernization, which sowed the seeds for liberty, social and economic equality, fraternity, democracy and social justice. The impact of British education in India manifested as a social awakening leading to several social changes in India. Many were agitated and had enlightened thoughts to eradicate or change the prevailing situation in the nation. Many Indians spearheaded several movements to bring about social reformation. These social reform movements were of two kinds: social reformist and social revivalist. The significant social reform movements were Brahmo Samaj led by Raja Ram Mohan Roy, Theosophical Society of Annie Besant, Ramakrishna Mission of Swami Vivekananda, Satyashodhak Samaj by

Jyotirao Govindrao Phule, Prarthana Samaj initiated by Dadoba Pandurang and propagated by Ranade, Young Bengal movement of Henry Louis Vivian Derozio, Arya Samaj led by Swami Dayanand Saraswati, Aligarh movement of Sir Syed Ahmed Khan, Widow Remarriage Association by Vishnu Shastri Pandit and Mahadev Govind Ranade, Deoband Movement by Muhammad Qasim Nanautawi and Rashid Ahmad Gangohi. Contributions to social reform and revival were also channelled by Sri Ramakrishna Paramahamsa, Debendranath Tagore, Keshab Chandra Sen and Ishwar Chandra Vidyasagar. The growth of social reform movements can also be studied as those that spread in Western India and South India, and also as developments in the form of Muslim reforms and reforms among the Parsis and Sikhs. The social reform movements also known as Renaissance, saw the imprints of women reformers such as Pandita Ramabai, Savitribai Phule and Sarojini Naidu.

BRAHMO SAMAJ: RAJA RAM MOHAN ROY (1772–1833)

Did You Know?

Raja Ram Mohan Roy is known as the first feminist of India. He was the pioneer of the social reform movements in India and was thereby called the 'Father of Indian Renaissance'.

Born on 22 May 1772 in an orthodox Bengali family, Roy's early education was in his village in Bengali and later moved to Patna to study Persian and Arabic. He educated himself in English language as well. Roy was a great scholar and had great flair for the religious studies and did an extensive study on Hinduism, Christianity, Islam and other religions and had made many translations of various religious scripts including Vedanta.

RAJA RAM MOHAN ROY'S IDEOLOGY FOR SOCIAL TRANSFORMATION

Raja Ram Mohan Roy had a modernized concept, especially during those ages when women rights were completely wrecked up. The idea to transform the society started with the Bengal traditions where he had witnessed the explicated rituals which exploited the society. Roy focused on women liberation and the snags they faced due to the religion and the society. He had always felt that religion had great influence on society and believed that changing one's thoughts on religion would change the entire society. He did a commendable work for the abolition of Sati system in which the wife was also thrown on the funeral pyre of her deceased husband. He went as an Indian ambassador along with Lord William Bentinck for the bill to be passed against the Sati system and the horrifying act be prohibited permanently. In addition, he also promoted widow remarriage and motivated women for educating themselves so that they can face the society. Hence, Roy's liberal reformism brought various changes and set a great milestone in the society.

BRAHMO SAMAJ

Roy established the Atmiya Sabha (1815), later named as Brahmo Sabha (1828) and further finally named as Brahmo Samaj, which struggled for one religion and to practice rationalism. The organization focused on one worship and opposed various rituals and superstitions amalgamated in it. The Sabha made a way for the social, religious and political movements in India. Brahmo Samaj was later split into Brahmo Samaj of India and Adi Brahmo Samaj led by Keshab Chandra Sen and Debendranath Tagore, respectively. They worked hard to abolish caste system, untouchability and various other dehumanizing beliefs in the society.

THEOSOPHICAL SOCIETY: ANNIE BESANT (1847–1933)

Born in London, Annie Besant, after taking over the presidentship of the Theosophical Society, moved to Adyar, India. She developed herself as a fervent reader and became a voracious publisher of more than 200 books. She was married to Frank Besant and soon had two children. However, it was not a compatible relationship and had a hard time; hence, they separated, but she remained as Mrs Besant during her lifetime. She emphasized on freedom of thought, workers' rights, secularism and birth control as she felt that children will decide what freedom they can have.

THEOSOPHICAL SOCIETY

Found in the year 1875 by H. P. Blavatsky and Col H. S. Olcott, the Theosophical Society was started in the USA, followed by their headquarters in Bombay, India, which later shifted to Adyar, India. After the death of Col H. S. Olcott, Annie Besant took over as president. Though the Society had no specific religion to be followed, Mrs Besant became popular by preaching the ideals of Krishna and the Bhagavad Gita. Hence, the word of the Society spread all over India. Moreover, it was also working for the development of youth and education. She established the Central Hindu School, which was later named as Central Hindu University by Madan Mohan Malviya. The Society opened schools for both boys and girls of the deprived communities. Mrs Besant worked hard in eradicating the social evils of child marriage and post-puberty marriage. The Society opened more than hundred branches all over India and did commendable work, especially in educating the children and youth. It respected the Indian values and self-respect movement, and hence, Annie Besant was very much respected during her lifetime in India.

RAMAKRISHNA MISSION: SWAMI VIVEKANANDA (1863–1902)

Originally named as Narendranath Dutta, Swami Vivekananda had a great interest in both reading and writing. Like many other youths of his times, Vivekananda was highly influenced by Keshab Chandra Sen and his preaching. Vivekananda's meeting with Ramakrishna completely changed his ideologies. Though Ramakrishna was not well educated, he had great wisdom and understanding of the scriptures, which influenced Swami Vivekananda to a great extent.

RAMAKRISHNA MISSION

Sri Ramakrishna Paramahamsa (1836–1886) was born in Bengal in a Brahmin family. Ramakrishna was a very pious person and focused on teaching the scriptures. He followed various faiths and was a strong devotee of Goddess Kali. Later, he was initiated into *Sanyasa* by Monk Totapuri. He became an expert in Advaita Vedanta and in the last stages of his life, he followed Islam and even Christianity where he professed the vision of Madonna and Child himself.

Sri Ramakrishna wanted to educate youth to continue his mission and so did Narendranath who became a follower of him and changed his name and is famously known as Vivekananda. Vivekananda started the Ramakrishna Math and then Ramakrishna Mission to teach and educate the youth and do social work along with them. Vivekananda became well known for propagating the Hindu religion in the world forum of religion and had introduced Hinduism in the Parliament of Masses. On knowing about the values of the Brahmo Samaj, Vivekananda reiterated that widow remarriage will not uplift the society but educating the women will uplift them. His teaching was that education will make women handle themselves in the right direction. He says, 'Educate your women first and leave them to themselves; then they will tell you what reforms are necessary for them. With such an education they will solve their own problems.' His teaching was very powerful and all the people in the Parliament of Religions always applauded his initiatives. He travelled around the world and continuously spread his knowledge on education and development. He mainly focused on spreading the Vedanta ideologies in the West. Vivekananda also emphasized on reformation in its own nature and not blindly accepting the Western ideas and following them. He also said that we must grow in our own culture and environment. He stated that there can be no upliftment leaving away the poor. Hence, reformation should be done for the benefit of all the people in the nation. Adding to it, he spoke about the evils practised in our society and the need for the nation to work on them rather than on Westernization.

SATYASHODHAK SAMAJ: MAHATMA JYOTIRAO GOVINDRAO PHULE (1827–1890)

Mahatma Jyotirao Govindrao Phule was born in Satara, Maharashtra. He was a school dropout as his parents were not able to pay for his studies due to poverty. However, some of his friends noticed his ability and sponsored his education and, hence, he was able to complete it. Later, he was married to Savitribai Phule at the age of 13. She was from the Mali caste, not educated and, hence, Jyotirao educated her at home. Jyotirao Govindrao Phule occupies a unique position among the social reformers of Maharashtra in the 19th century. While other reformers concentrated more on reforming the social institutions of family and marriage with special emphasis on the status and rights of women, Jyotirao Phule revolted against the unjust caste system under which millions of people had suffered for centuries (Dash, 2010).

SATYASHODHAK SAMAJ

> **Did You Know?**
>
> Way ahead of Mahatma Gandhi, Jyotirao Phule was given the title of Mahatma on 11 May 1888 by a Maharashtra activist, Vithalrao Krishnaji Vandekar.

He, along with his wife, became very prominent in the upliftment of women as he found them to be the most oppressed humans in the society. He worked for the lower caste people and farmers who suffered badly at that point of time. He was the pioneer in starting a school for girls for which he was asked to leave the house by his parents. He coined the word 'Dalit' which became famous later. He laid the foundation for women's education by opening schools and appointing women teachers for the same.

Savitribai Phule was the first woman teacher in the school and was also the first woman teacher in the whole India as discrimination against women was very high during those times and girls were not allowed to attend schools. She was a pillar of support for Jyotirao Phule in all his endeavours. Phule later opened a school for the untouchables and had a common bath place in front of his house to show unity of all castes. It could be accessed by anyone regardless of their caste. He and his wife together opened a centre for the pregnant rape victims. Mahila Seva Mandal was also started by Savitribai Phule to support women rights and freedom. Phule was the main reason for the government to pass the Agriculture Act, and after his death due to paralysis, the government also introduced a scheme, Mahatma Jyotirao Phule Jan Arogya Yojana, to provide free medical aid to the poor. Until his last breath, he strongly opposed Brahminism and their ritual ideologies, and strived hard for the liberation of the untouchables.

PRARTHANA SAMAJ: DADOBA PANDURANG (1814–1882) AND ROLE OF MAHADEV GOVIND RANADE (1842–1901)

The Prarthana Samaj, understood as the prayer house, was founded by Dadoba Pandurang (1814–1882) and his brother Atmaram Pandurang (1823–1898) in 1867 at Bombay with the objective of rational worship and social reform. The two great members of Prarthana Samaj were Mahadev Govind Ranade and R. G. Bhandarkar. M. G. Ranade was a high court judge in Bombay and R. G. Bhandarkar was a great scholar of the time. They followed the ideologies of the Brahmo Samaj and K. C. Sen, but they were unique in instilling Hindu thoughts and in working against the social evils such as polygamy, polyandry and child marriage. Prarthana Samaj, in contrary to the Brahmo Samaj, supported caste system, idol worship and Hindu rituals. They worked for Hinduism to regain its respect as they felt that the caste system was not the problem but oppressing the fellow human beings/or lower caste was the problem. He continuously fought for abolition of child marriage and to stop all unethical and non-meaningful practices.

Ranade devoted his entire life to Prarthana Samaj. He instituted the Widow Remarriage Association (1861) and Deccan Education Society. He secretly started the inter-caste dining method and later, it became more prominent in the society. He also promoted inter-caste marriage, widow remarriage and upliftment of women and depressed classes. He established the Poona Sarvajanik Sabha as well. To Ranade, religious reform was inseparable from social reform. He believed that the reformation comes through various movements and started night schools for the working class and instituted libraries. The Prarthana Samaj has highly influenced a positive approach and growth of life and all fellow human beings. Ranade was the leader of social reformation and cultural renaissance in Western India.

YOUNG BENGAL MOVEMENT: HENRY LOUIS VIVIAN DEROZIO (1809–1831)

Henry Louis Vivian Derozio was a Scottish man and he came to Calcutta to sell watches. Later, after observing the society, he went to teach in the Hindu College. He was able to capture the young minds by his liberal speeches and openly pointing out the problems and the needs to be foreseen. The followers were called Derozians and some of his famous followers were Rev. Krishnamohan Bandopadhyay, Pearychand Mitra, Ramtanu Lahiri and Tarachand Chakraborty who were great contributors to the movement. Derozio promoted radical ideas through his teaching and by organizing an association for debate and discussions on literature, philosophy, history and science. He inspired his followers and students to question all authority. Derozio and his famous followers, known as the Derozians and Young Bengal, were fiery patriots. They cherished the ideals of the French Revolution (1789 AD) and the liberal thinking of Britain.

Derozio was dismissed from his post at the college as his propaganda was going out of hands. Derozians were absolutely against many Hindu rituals such as polygamy, sati, child marriage, caste discrimination, dowry and pardah system. Hence, most of the followers of the movement were Christians, and they followed Western culture, dress, food and manners. Derozio died of cholera at the young age of 22. Though deprived of leadership, the members of this group continued preaching radical views through teaching and journalism. However, this movement lasted for a very short period.

ARYA SAMAJ: SWAMI DAYANAND SARASWATI (1824–1883)

Swami Dayanand Saraswati, earlier called Mool Shankar, was born in Gujarat and was brought up in a Brahmin family. They were strong believers of Lord Shiva and great followers of the Hindu religion. However, after his sister's death, he started questioning his being and about the life after death and so on. Being compelled for marriage, he left the house and wandered around and met many gurus and wanted to seek answers to his questions on life. Finally, he was enlightened by the teachings of Swami Virajananda. He insisted him to read the Vedas and miraculously, Mool Shankar was able to find all his answers in the same. He held that the Vedas contained all the knowledge imparted to man by God and essentials of modern science could also be traced in them. He was opposed to idolatry, ritual and priesthood, particularly, to the prevalent caste practices and popular Hinduism as preached by the Brahmins. He favoured the study of Western science. Later, he instituted the Arya Samaj.

ARYA SAMAJ

The Hindu reform movement, Arya Samaj, was founded on 11 April 1875. This movement wanted to revive the Hindu religion and its best practices. The movement completely opposed the Westernization of thoughts and wanted to live according to the culture and values of the nation. The main concept of the origin of Arya Samaj was to give Vedic education to all. Swami Dayanand Saraswati made the Vedas available to all the people and insisted them to read the same. The Samaj opposed the evil practices such as sati, pardah, child marriage and idol worship. In addition, it insisted that all acts should be done with a noble cause and we should be ready to denounce any evil practice. The Shuddi movement was one of the best revival measures started to bring back the Hindus who converted to Christianity and Islam. The Arya Samaj tried to inculcate the spirit of self-respect and self-reliance among the people of India. This promoted nationalism. It also instituted many schools and colleges including the very popular Dayanand Anglo Vedic (DAV) schools to understand the society and to spread national consciousness. Today, Arya Samaj is present all over the world and is involved in very prominent activities. Though Dayanand was not a freedom fighter, he has influenced Lala Lajpat Rai, Subhas Chandra Bose, Bhagat Singh, Madam Cama and Ram Prasad Bismil. He died a painful death, where a cook mixed a piece of glass in the milk, on the day of Diwali, 30 October 1883.

ALIGARH MOVEMENT: SIR SYED AHMED KHAN (1817–1898)

Sir Syed Ahmed Khan was a Muslim reformer born in 1817. He was a loyal judicial worker of the government till his retirement. By 1878, he joined the Imperial Legislative Council and later earned knighthood by 1888. He had a great pursuit in the development of Muslims as he saw them very much deprived of education and jobs. He encouraged his fellow religious mates to get educated to be on par with the fellow Hindus who were greatly empowered. He also stressed on English education as it would fetch lucrative jobs for the Muslims. He realized that unless the Muslims adapted themselves to the changed circumstances of the British rule, they would be deprived of all new opportunities for status and prosperity. He continuously focused on Muslim folks to get enlightened on the concepts of pardah, polygamy, child marriage, women education, slavery, divorce and so on. The orthodox Muslims opposed his ideologies, but he always convinced them and never let his vision in vain.

Syed Ahmed Khan rightly felt that isolation would harm the Muslim community and to prevent that, he did his best to create a link with the progressive cultural forces of the outside world. He worked hard to remove the hostility of the British rulers towards the Muslims whom they considered as their real enemies. His greatest achievement was the formation of

Muhammadan Anglo-Oriental College, later known as Aligarh Muslim University, in Aligarh in 1875. It was meant to be a centre for spreading Western sciences and culture. The university provided education in humanities and science and the medium of instruction was English. The British approved of the institution and provided teachers and administrative support.

The liberal, social and cultural movement started by Syed Ahmad Khan among the Muslims is known as the Aligarh movement as it originated in Aligarh. The Anglo-Oriental College was the centre of this movement. It aimed at promoting modern education among Muslims without weakening the ties with Islam. It became the central educational institution for Indian Muslims.

WIDOW REMARRIAGE ASSOCIATION: VISHNU SHASTRI PANDIT (1827–1876) AND MAHADEV GOVIND RANADE (1842–1901)

Widow Remarriage Association was founded by Vishnu Shastri Pandit and Mahadev Govind Ranade in Bombay in 1861. It promoted widow remarriage and campaigned against child marriage, the heavy cost of marriages and customs like the shaving of widow's head.

DEOBAND MOVEMENT: MUHAMMAD QASIM NANAUTAWI (1833–1880) AND RASHID AHMAD GANGOHI (1826–1905)

The Deoband movement was started in 1867 at Deoband, Saharanpur, Uttar Pradesh, by the theologians, Muhammad Qasim Nanautawi and Rashid Ahmad Gangohi. It was an anti-British movement that aimed at the upliftment of the Muslims through educational efforts. The two main objectives of Deoband movement were: (a) popularizing the teachings of the Quran and Hadith and (b) initiating jihad against foreign rule. They did not support Western education and culture. They advocated the unity of all religions.

OTHER SOCIAL REFORMERS AND REVIVALISTS

DEBENDRANATH TAGORE (1817–1905)

Debendranath Tagore founded the **Tattwabodhini Sabha** (1839) and also published *Tattwabodhini Patrika*. Tattwabodhini Sabha amalgamated with the Brahmo Samaj in 1859. He also compiled selected passages from the Upanishads, known as **Brahma Dharma**.

KESHAB CHANDRA SEN (1838–1884)

Keshab Chandra Sen joined the Brahmo Samaj in 1857 and assumed its leadership in 1861. He established the Sangat Sabha for discussing religious and moral questions. He was in favour of radical reforms which were not liked by the older sections of the Samaj. The younger section also opposed the wearing of Brahmanical thread. There was an open conflict between the older and the younger sections and as a result of such conflict, Keshab Chandra Sen broke away from the original Brahmo Samaj in 1866 and formed a new organization known as the Brahmo Samaj of India or Bharatiya Brahmo Samaj. The new organization of Keshab Chandra Sen adopted radical reforms such as abolition of pardah, caste system, child marriage and polygamy; and encouraged widow remarriage and inter-caste marriage. He was also a pioneer in starting the Depressed Class movement which is the precursor of the Harijan Movement of M. K. Gandhi. Along with his followers, he set up a number of educational institutions for female education.

ISHWAR CHANDRA VIDYASAGAR (1820–1891)

Ishwar Chandra Vidyasagar was born in Bengal on 26 September 1820. Owing to a great thirst for education, he studied Sanskrit and joined the Fort William College as the head of the department at the age of 21. He was also a philosopher, translator, philanthropist and entrepreneur. Ishwar introduced the concepts of admission and tuition fee and opened a teacher-training school which was used to train teachers to bring about unity and uniformity in their methods of teaching. He wanted the students to imbibe both the Western and Indian thoughts and to use the best practices for development. He was awarded the name 'Vidyasagar' for his knowledge.

A scholar of great depths, he dedicated himself to the cause of the emancipation of women. He specially objected the orthodox Hindu practices. For example, the widow women were supposed to shave their head and cover it. They were also denied the freedom of going out. Ishwar firmly held that when teenage girls or girls of even lesser age were married to much older men, they would become widows at an early age. Hence, he fought for women liberation and empowerment where he wanted them to marry at the right age and with a right aged person. It was due to his sincere efforts that obstacles to the marriage of widows were removed and the Hindu Widow Remarriage Act, 1856, was passed with the support of the British authorities. He made his son marry a widow. He played a leading role in promoting education of girls and started and helped in setting up a number of schools for girls. Vidyasagar did not concern himself much with religious questions. However, he was against all those who opposed reforms in the name of religion. He died due to ill health at the age of 70.

SOCIAL REFORM MOVEMENTS ACROSS RELIGIONS

REFORM MOVEMENTS AMONG MUSLIMS

As reformation took place within the Hindu religion, its practices and social institutions, a similar reform movement was also taking place within Islam. The Muslim upper classes had tended to avoid contact with Western education and culture and it was only after the revolt of 1857 that modern ideas of religious reform began to appear. The beginning was made by the Mohammedan Literary Society founded in Calcutta in 1863 by Nawab Abdul Latif (1828–1893).

It promoted discussion of religious, social and political questions in the light of modern ideas and encouraged upper- and middle-class Muslims to adopt Western education. It also played an important role in Muslim unity. The Muslim masses were also influenced by movements carried on by the Chishti Sufis who preached not only submission to God but also promoted the veneration of saints. Another movement is associated with Shah Waliullah in Delhi, who opposed the unorthodox religious practices and revived the Shia sect and strict monotheism. The philosophical and learned tradition of the Firangi Mahal in Lucknow was incorporated into the new educational syllabus and propagated throughout India during the 18th and the 19th centuries. Shariatullah of Bengal was the leader of the Faraizi movement which took up the cause of the peasants and even spoke against the caste system among the Muslims.

The most notable of the Muslim reformers was Syed Ahmed of Raebareli, in Uttar Pradesh, about whom it has been discussed earlier in this chapter. Syed Ahmed attracted the Muslim artisans of the declining weaving towns of Allahabad and Patna, finding a ready audience and giving the common people dignity and an identity through a common faith at a time of social dislocation. He felt that the religious and social life of the Muslims could be improved only with the help of modem Western scientific knowledge, culture and proper education. As an official, he founded schools at many places. He got many Western books translated into Urdu. The Aligarh movement started by him was largely responsible for the Muslim revival that followed. It provided a focal point for the scattered Muslim population in different parts of the country. Syed Ahmad's efforts extended to the social sphere as well. He worked for social reforms. He wanted women to be educated and advocated the removal of the pardah. He was also against polygamy.

There were several other socio-religious movements which in one way or the other helped the national awakening of the Muslims. Mirza Ghulam Ahmad had founded the Ahmadiyya movement in 1899. Under this movement, a number of schools and colleges were opened all over the country, imparting modern education. In the field of religion, the followers of this movement emphasized the universal and humanitarian character of Islam. They favoured the unity among Hindus and Muslims.

One of the greatest poets of modern India, Muhammad Iqbal (1877–1938), also profoundly influenced through his poetry the philosophical and religious outlook of the younger generation of Muslims as well as of Hindus. He urged the adoption of a dynamic outlook that would help change the world. He was basically a humanist.

REFORM MOVEMENTS AMONG PARSIS

Religious reform began among the Parsis in Mumbai in the middle of the 19th century. In 1851, the Rehnumai Maz'dayasan Sabha or Religious Reform Association was founded by Naoroji Furdunji, Dadabhai Naoroji, S. S. Bengalee and others. They started a journal, *Rast Goftar*, for the purpose of social-religious reforms among the Parsis. They also played an important role in the spread of education, especially among girls. They campaigned against the entrenched orthodoxy in the religious field and initiated the modernization of Parsi social customs regarding the education and marriage of girls and the social position of women in general. In the course of time, the Parsis became socially the most Westernized section of Indian society.

Social Reform Movements in India

RELIGIOUS REFORMS AMONG SIKHS

Religious reform among the Sikhs was started at the end of the 19th century when the Khalsa College started at Amritsar. Through the efforts of the Singh Sabhas (1870) and with British support, the Khalsa College was founded at Amritsar in 1892. This college and schools set up as a result of similar efforts, promoted Gurumukhi, Sikh learning and Punjabi literature as a whole.

After 1920, the Sikh reform gained momentum when the Akali movement rose in Punjab. The chief object of the Akalis was to improve the management of the gurdwaras or Sikh shrines that were under the control of priests or mahants who treated them as their private property. In 1925, a law was passed which gave the right of managing gurdwaras to the Shiromani Gurdwara Prabandhak Committee.

WOMEN REFORMERS

PANDITA RAMABAI (1858–1922)

Born in the year 1858, Ramabai was an eminent scholar of her time. At a young age, she had to face adverse conditions in her life; however, being a very strong woman, she started to teach and her knowledge in Sanskrit stunned everyone whom she spoke to. Hence, she was awarded the title of Pandita and Saraswati for her meticulous scholarship.

Pandita Ramabai was an educationist even before she had turned 20 and propagated the idea of women's education and empowerment. She started the Arya Mahila Samaj to show her commitment towards education and social transformation. One of her famous statements in her speech is, 'It is not strange, my countrymen, that my voice is small, for you have never given a woman the chance to make her voice strong!' She was invited to America by her cousin for her medical degree graduation and her speeches gained her many followers who later formed the American Ramabai Association which helped in collecting funds for widow education. She wrote a book *The High-caste Hindu Women*, which sold 10,000 copies.

In her later stages of life, she converted to Christianity which shocked India as she had strong foundations of Brahminism. She is the driving source for many women who are working for women empowerment and Dalit empowerment.

SAROJINI NAIDU (1879–1949)

As long as I have life, as long as blood flows through this arm of mine, I shall not leave the cause of freedom…I am only a woman, only a poet. But as a woman, I give to you the weapons of faith and courage and the shield of fortitude. And as a poet, I fling out the banner of song and sound, the bugle call to battle. How shall I kindle the flame which shall waken you men from slavery….

Born on 13 February 1879, in Hyderabad, Sarojini Naidu was the daughter of Aghorenath Chattopadhyay and Varada Sundari, and her father instituted the Hyderabad College, later known as the Nizam College. She was very intelligent and well versed in many languages at an early age. She was the first woman governor of India and the first woman president of the Indian National Congress. Her meeting with Gopal Krishna Gokhale introduced her to many freedom struggle activists such as Mahatma Gandhi, Rabindranath Tagore and Annie Besant. Gokhale stirred her thoughts by asking to use her knowledge to fight for the freedom of the country and not just for writing. She contributed mainly to Salt Satyagraha where she gathered all women for the protest. She fought against the British in Champaran for the rights of the farmers. She was also a leading freedom fighter and made her contributions in the Civil Disobedience movement and Quit India movement along with other leaders. Sarojini's focus on women empowerment is worth highlighting. She shaped the Indian Women's Association, 1917, along with Annie Besant and also fought for equal voting rights of women. Sarojini lives in many hearts for her selfless contribution to the society.

SUMMARY

It is a great privilege that India has had so many social reformative and revivalist movements under intellectual reformers who have worked in shaping the society. These reformers and their movements have greatly contributed to the development and upliftment of the poor and the downtrodden. It has to be understood that all the reformers had mainly used an important weapon, that is, education. They have also insisted on education of the masses to prevent various problems that will affect the growth of the nation.

TOP 10 TAKEAWAYS/MAIN POINTS

1. The impact of British rule in India led to a number of social and religious reforms.
2. Raja Ram Mohan Roy can be regarded as the central figure of India's awakening for championing the spread of modern education, science and technology and for his relentless fight against many social evils.
3. The Theosophical Society, under the guidance of Annie Besant, promoted studies of ancient Indian religions, philosophies and doctrines.
4. Swami Vivekananda, a great humanist, through his Ramakrishna Mission condemned religious narrow-mindedness, advocated free thinking and emphasized on service for the poor.
5. Jyotirao Phule and Savitribai Phule played a very prominent role in the upliftment of women as they found them to be the most oppressed humans in the society.
6. R. G. Bhandarkar and M. G. Ranade carried out their work of religious reforms in Maharashtra through the Prarthana Samaj by propagating inter-caste marriages, freedom from priestly domination and improvement of women.
7. Swami Dayanand Saraswati founded the Arya Samaj and pleaded for the right of individuals to study the Vedas and free themselves from the tyranny of priests. Besides all this, the organization fought against untouchability and caste rigidity as well as worked for promoting modern education.
8. Syed Ahmed Khan rightly felt that isolation would harm the Muslim community and to prevent that, he did his best to create a link with the progressive cultural forces of the outside world.

Social Reform Movements in India 45

9. Religious reforms among the Muslims, Parsis and Sikhs were also carried out to uplift the people of the respective religions.
10. Women reformers such as Pandita Ramabai and Sarojini Naidu worked for the upliftment and empowerment of women as they found it to be important for our nation.

Keywords: Social reformer, movements, society, enlightenment

GLOSSARY

Reform: The word reform or reformation means re (again) form (birth). This is used to stop any form of injustice that is happening.
Social reformer: Social reformer is a person who is working for change in the society. They can be an advocate, a teacher or a preacher who wants to bring a positive change in the society.

MULTIPLE CHOICE QUESTIONS

1. Which among the following movements objected idol worship and emphasized on self-repentance?
   a. **Arya Samaj**
   b. Brahmo Samaj
   c. Prarthana Samaj
   d. Aligarh movement

2. Who were the founders of the Theosophical Society?
   a. H. P. Blavatsky and Col H. S. Olcott
   b. **Annie Besant and Col H. S. Olcott**
   c. H. P. Blavatsky and Annie Besant
   d. Annie Besant and Pandita Ramabai

3. Match the following:
   a. Arya Samaj   Raja Ram Mohan Roy
   b. Brahmo Samaj   Sir Syed Ahmed Khan
   c. Prarthana Samaj   Swami Dayanand Saraswati
   d. Aligarh movement   Dadoba Pandurang
   Ans.
   a. Arya Samaj   Swami Dayanand Saraswati
   b. Brahmo Samaj   Raja Ram Mohan Roy
   c. Prarthana Samaj   Dadoba Pandurang
   d. Aligarh movement   Sir Syed Ahmed Khan

4. Which of the following is related with the Young Bengal movement?
   a. **Derozians**
   b. Arya Mahila Samaj
   c. Widow Remarriage Association
   d. Civil Disobedience

5. Who among the following reformers formed the Arya Mahila Samaj?
   a. **Pandita Ramabai**
   b. Sarojini Naidu
   c. K. C. Sen
   d. Debendranath Tagore

6. Why was the Mukti Mission started?
   a. To develop vocational training
   b. To support education of women
   c. **To help young widows from deserted and abused families**
   d. To help people below the poverty line

7. Who was given the title of Mahatma much before Mahatma Gandhi?
   a. Savitribai Phule
   b. Pandita Ramabai
   c. Swami Vivekananda
   d. **Jyotirao Phule**

8. Which woman reformer had a great contribution in Salt Satyagraha and Civil Disobedience movement?
   a. Annie Besant
   b. Barada Sundari
   c. Mahadev Govind Ranade
   d. **Sarojini Naidu**

9. Which of the following major Indian reformers was one of the reasons for abolishing Sati?
   a. **Raja Ram Mohan Roy**
   b. Swami Vivekananda
   c. Ishwar Chandra Vidyasagar
   d. Henry Vivian Derozio

10. Match the following:

a.	Brahmo Samaj	1875
b.	Arya Samaj	1828
c.	Satyashodhak Samaj	1892
d.	Young Bengal movement	1860s
e.	Aligarh movement	1820s
f.	Ramakrishna Mission	24 September 1873

    Ans.

a.	Brahmo Samaj	1828
b.	Arya Samaj	1875
c.	Satyashodhak Samaj	24 September 1873
d.	Young Bengal movement	1820s
e.	Aligarh movement	1860s
f.	Ramakrishna Mission	1892

REVIEW QUESTIONS

1. Write a note on one Muslim reform Movement and its contributions.
2. Describe the events where Sarojini Naidu has played an important role in the freedom struggle.
3. Write a note on Mrs Annie Besant as a woman reformer.
4. What is Brahmo Samaj and what were its major contributions?

REFERENCE

Dash, B. M. (2010). History of social work: Individual initiatives. In G. Thomas (Ed.), *Origin and development of social work in India* (pp. 55–57). Indira Gandhi National Open University.

RECOMMENDED READINGS

Cromwell, S. C. (1984). *Ram Mohan Roy: His era and ethics*. Arnold Heinemann Publishers.
Das, J. (1958). *Ram Mohan Roy: The modernizer* (pp. 2–13). Sadharan Brahmo Samaj.
Haldar, S. (1920). *Ram Mohan Roy and Hinduism: The Brahmo Samaj*. Victoria Press.
Krishnayya, G. S. (1969). *Raja Ram Mohan Roy: Pioneer of modern education*. National Council of Educational Research and Training.

4

Great Depression and the Growth of Social Work Education

Supriya Rani

> **LEARNING OBJECTIVES**
> - To understand the relevance of the Great Depression in the development of social work profession
> - To understand the impact of the New Deal on social work education and practice
> - To trace the historical trajectory of the development of professional social work education institutions in the aftermath of the Great Depression
> - To comprehend the influence of the Great Depression on the growth of professional social work education institutions in the Indian subcontinent

No one can possibly have lived through the Great Depression without being scarred by it. No amount of experience since the depression can convince someone who has lived through it that the world is safe economically.

—Isaac Asimov

INTRODUCTION

Social work as an academic discipline and profession has come a long way from its inception as a summer school in 'applied philanthropy' that took place in New York in 1898 to professional graduate programmes in the present-day postmodernist times. There are certain points in the world history that have pushed the development of a social work profession more than the others. One of such turning points is the Great Depression. The Great Depression was the historical phase that pushed the need to practice and develop social work as a professional and educational entity that goes beyond philanthropy. Owing to which it remains an essential incidence in the history and evolution of social work education and practice throughout the globe.

> ### Did You Know?
>
> The New York Charity Organization Society introduced the Summer School in Applied Philanthropy (a six-week course) in the year 1898, and it was the first ever professional setting where social work education was imparted. This was then transformed into the New York School of Philanthropy in 1904. This School of Philanthropy was renamed as the New York School of Social Work in the year 1919 and in 1940, it ended up becoming a part of Columbia University. In 1963, it was finally rechristened as what we today know as the Columbia University School of Social Work, one of the leading schools of social work in the world.

In October 1929, the world economy crashed and with this began the start of the Great Depression that lasted for a decade (1929–1939). As a result of the economic breakdown, a number of social issues such as unemployment, poverty and mental health problems escalated considerably during this period. This impelled the states in various parts of the globe to play an active role in the social welfare of their citizens and that brought social work professionals to the forefront. The Great Depression refocused on the professional roles of social workers and also increased their demand more than ever, which led to the proliferation of social work institutions throughout the globe. This chapter attempts to trace the historical trajectory of professional social work education institutions in the aftermath of the Great Depression. While doing so, it looks at the various trends that social work education has gone through since then and how it has evolved over the years. After critically analysing the events in the post-Great Depression phase and their impact on the growth of professional social work education institutions in the Western world, the chapter also looks at their influence on social work education in the Indian subcontinent.

GREAT DEPRESSION, THE NEW DEAL AND SOCIAL WORK

The stock market crash of 1929 that was followed by a decade of economic recession is known as the Great Depression; this created a major chaos in the American as well as the global society. The Great Depression originated in the USA in October 1929 and thereon it reached the other parts of the world. According to Crafts and Fearon (2010), the Great Depression completely deserves its given name as they argued that the economic disaster that started in 1929, eventually, had a negative impact on each and every manufacturing nation and on all the producers of food and raw material. Even renowned British economists like Keynes observed that during the depression, the entire world was in the midst of the ultimate economic tragedy of the contemporary world. He also indicated in his work that there is a great likelihood that

> **Box 4.1   Immediate Outcomes of the Great Depression**
>
> Some of the immediate social and economic outcomes of the Great Depression can be listed as follows:
>
> 1. Crash down of the economy
> 2. Failing of the banks
> 3. Unemployment
> 4. Mental health issues
> 5. Dwindling agriculture
> 6. Declining market demand globally due to the loss of consumption power
> 7. Hunger
> 8. Homelessness

when the future economic historians will look at this catastrophe, they will certainly mark it as one of the major tuning points in the world history (Keynes, 1931). And just as Keynes had foretold, the Great Depression is understood as the lengthiest and the most severe fall of the economy ever in the realm of economic history (Box 4.1).

In this phase of social history, it became more evident that present social service agencies were not prepared to deal with such a large-scale crisis. During this period, social workers found themselves to be unable to help out not just the poor and the needy but the members of the working class as well. In order to deal with the problems that were prevalent in this period, the social workers began to look at the issues faced by the individuals in a broader context of social and economic forces (Axinn & Stern, 1988). They began looking for the 'cause' behind the prevailing social and economic problems and began lobbying to the government to take on responsibility for the welfare of its subjects in this phase of extreme social and economic crisis (Trattner, 1999). Social workers were able to see the gravity of the Great Depression from its earlier days. They, in fact, sought to turn away from the individual centric approach that they had devised in the early days of social work practice and started looking at solutions which could cause reform in a broader sense. They had a work experience that provided them with a unique vantage point to look at this issue in a holistic manner. They, in fact, played a vital role in the formulation of policies that the governments launched as a response to the socio-economic havoc caused by the Great Depression. They lobbied for the adequate standards of living for everyone to be provided by the government in such an hour of need.

In 1932, when the Roosevelt government came into being, it introduced a federal relief programme to alleviate the issues faced by the poor and the needy. The Roosevelt government consisted of experienced social workers as its staff, such as Harry Hopkins and Frances Perkins. With the help of these minds, his government created various social welfare programmes. Harry Hopkins was appointed as the head of the Federal Emergency Relief Administration, which was a major large-scale relief programme.

Government welfare programmes started growing during the Roosevelt administration. The New Deal resulted in many social welfare acts such as the Social Security Act of 1935. The Social

Security Act of 1935 was the focal point of the New Deal. It aided in improving the standards of living throughout the communities and provided the beneficiaries with a sense of dignity and individual liberty. It expanded the scope of social welfare beyond financial assistance to the disadvantaged sections of society and went on to include issues related to housing, cultural events and so on. Social welfare programmes under the deal consisted of recreation, housing, cultural events, child welfare programmes and social insurance. The New Deal focused on public work projects such as dams but many of the construction site jobs created by the government to provide employment during the Great Depression were temporary in nature and the people would end up becoming unemployed again once the construction work was over. It also focused on financial reforms (such as social security system and unemployment insurance). The New Deal consisted of programmes, laws and governmental agencies that were formed to help the American society fight the challenges posed by the Great Depression. These laws were effective in placing rules and regulation on banks, stock market and industries or businesses in general. They dealt with providing immediate relief to the people suffering from the manifestations of the Great Depression while introducing measures to safeguard the economy in the long haul.

The New Deal produced a very comprehensive assortment of federal government programmes which were aimed to offer fiscal and social respite to the misery of the community and individuals, control private industry and develop the economy. The New Deal is frequently explained by using the 'three Rs' (Kantor et al., 2012).

- Relief (for the out-of-work people)
- Recovery (of the economy)
- Reform (of capitalism, by means of regulatory legislation and the creation of new social welfare programmes)

Under the New Deal, social work professionals were appointed to work at all ranks, ranging from administrators to investigators at the Federal Emergency Relief Association's Social Service Division, for executing the government's welfare programmes and communicating the welfare programmes to the community. Hopkins had once expressed, 'I want at least one competent social worker in every district office in America' (Kurzman, 1974, pp. 174–176). According to Kurzman (1974), between the years of 1930 and 1940, the strength of professional social workers almost doubled.

These reformative actions were applauded by the social work professionals and the Americans in general. The New Deal generated new job opportunities for social work professionals to help the government in executing its social welfare programmes. With the increasing demand of social workers to help the government in implementing its social welfare programmes, there emerged a need for more social work education and training institutes that could train them. This led to the expansion of social work education and training institutes. By looking at this backdrop, it can be said that the beginning of the Great Depression paved way for the expansion of social work education institutions and the making of new social work programmes like never before.

The new sociopolitical reforms under the Roosevelt government had a significant impact on the social work profession in multiple ways: first, it made the social work profession more visible than ever in the public eye. Second, it created important work opportunities for social work professionals within the government administration and enabled them to pursue their profession beyond the avenues of private agencies. Third, it made public welfare and policy integral parts of social work practice. Finally, it created so many more job opportunities for social work professional not just in urban areas but also in the rural areas. All these factors put together led to better jobs and working conditions for social work professionals with improved salaries and enhanced education and training.

SOCIAL WORK EDUCATION POST THE GREAT DEPRESSION

To deal with the disruptions caused by the Great Depression (such as unemployment, hunger and poverty), which were then followed by the Second World War (which left a further dent in the social and economic institutions), there developed an urgency to do something or rather anything to deal with the troubling social and psychological unrest that was haunting not just the American society but the global society ever since the start of the Great Depression. The state governments in various parts of the globe began responding to the need of the hour by introducing various social welfare policies and became more proactive in their efforts to alleviate the problems that were prevalent during the Great Depression. For the execution of these welfare programmes, they needed professionals that could work both with the government and the people, and also possessed the skills and know-how for dealing with the individuals in the challenging circumstances. Up until this point of time, there was no 'fundamental' curriculum that was being taught to the social work professionals. Also, not many people then looked at social work as a legitimate profession. But this was all about to change with the increasing demand of social work professionals.

This increase in demand for social work professionals as mentioned in the above section led to the proliferation of social work education institutions. These social work education institutions imparted education on the theory and practices of social work. Over time, with the fading away of the dawn of the Great Depression, the discussions began became more centred on as to what all should be included in the curriculum for the educational programme for social work professionals. During the 1930s, social workers began to develop new theories and methods of social work practice. Among social casework practitioners, new methods that were heavily influenced by the works of psychiatrists such as Otto Rank and Sigmund Freud emerged. At the National Conference of Social Work in 1935 and 1939, respectively, group workers and community organization workers endeavoured to conceptualize their practice methods. Group work sessions at the National Conference of Social Work held in 1935 resulted in the creation of Association for the Study of Group Work, while the community organization sessions of 1939 led to the formation of Association for the Study of Community Organization (Stuart, 2013).

Ernest Hollis and Alice Taylor (who were both senior administrators in the Federal Security Agency) in a study conducted under their guidance in 1948 had recommended that the social work education should be a two-year graduate programme and there should be a social work education curriculum that has a basic or so to say a 'generic' curriculum that is adaptable to various potential arenas of social work practice ranging from correctional settings to public health to welfare activities of labour unions. This study also reflected on how once social work enters the traditional academia, it is going to be compared with the already established social science disciplines. This led to the enrolment of social work professional in doctoral programmes at various social sciences departments and then they opened doctoral programmes in their own social work department or schools (Hollis & Taylor, 1951). This study can be seen as a major milestone in the field of social work education research. It was also an important stepping stone in 'professionalizing' the field of social work. Earlier, social work was seen as predominantly a female vocation owing to the charitable works done by the missionary nuns over the years. The recommendations of this study expanded the scope of social work as a profession appropriate to both males and females while also giving it a credible look of a 'real profession' that could be taught as well as practised in an organized set-up. The association between the recommendation of creating a two-year graduate programme and making social work a 'true profession' in the public eye was seen as an essential part of the 'professionalization' of the vocation of social work (Austin, 1997).

During the Second World War, many social work professionals were given war-related jobs to cultivate services for all the individuals and communities that were getting affected by the war. Social work professionals on these jobs were given tasks to help the soldiers and their loved ones to deal with physical injuries, mental traumas and other problems. From this particular kind of engagement of social work professionals in the war period, a special category of social work professionals took birth, it was called military social workers. After the conclusion of the Second World War, efforts to improve the professional status of social work profession were made. In 1952, the Council on Social Work Education was formed. In the USA, the National Association of Social Workers (NASW) was established in 1955 to strengthen the social standing of professional social work. Many other social work organizations came together to merge with the NASW (Ingaro, 2014).

In the 1960s, there was a significant growth of social work education institutions among many public universities. Around 16 of the 19 social work education programmes that were launched in the 1960s were introduced in public universities (Austin, 1997). In the 1970s, there were some encouraging changes in the field of social work education. Many universities and colleges established Bachelor of Social Work as an entrance-level degree programme. Many social work practitioners began to work in private sector during this phase with more autonomy and legitimacy as a working professional. The development in the sum of both graduate and undergraduate programmes had carried on into the mid-1990s. In the 1990s, social work education institutes began focusing on doing research in the fields of mental health, aging, child welfare and domestic violence. In the 2000s, it was seen that social workers were mainly practising in the family services and the mental health settings (Ingaro, 2014).

THE GREAT DEPRESSION AND SOCIAL WORK EDUCATION IN INDIA

The Great Depression had its impact not just on the Western world but also on South Asian countries like India. The Great Depression had mixed impact on Indian economy and society. While the Indian trade and agriculture suffered massively, the Indian independence movement was strengthened during this time. The Civil Disobedience movement was launched during this time and the idea of complete independence for India was now seen as a possible outcome of the movement. Around the same time, professional social work education also made its debut in India. It started with the establishment of Sir Dorabji Tata Graduate School of Social Work (now Tata Institute of Social Sciences [TISS]) in 1936 under the guidance of Clifford Manshardt. Dr Manshardt was an American missionary who came to India in 1925 and was working with the American Marathi Mission, a Christian charity organization (Mukhopadyay, 2005). The syllabus that was taught at TISS was heavily influenced by the syllabus taught at the Western (specifically American) social work education institutions. Subjects such as social casework, research and administration were introduced initially. Not only the curriculum that was taught in the earlier social work education institutions in India was borrowed from the West, in fact, a lot of the early social work educators in India were trained and educated in the West. For instance, Dr Manshardt who was the founding director of TISS was an American missionary and J. M. Kumarappa who was appointed as a lecturer was educated at Columbia University in New York (Pathak, 1975).

> **Did You Know?**
>
> The Dorabji Tata Graduate School of Social Work was established for the education and training of professional social work in India in the year 1936. At first, it was started in Nagpada Neighbourhood House with Dr Clifford Manshardt as its first director. Even though initially it was just a diploma course, in its very first year of launch itself, the programme had more than 400 applicants just for 20 available seats in the course. It was renamed the Tata Institute of Social Sciences in 1944.

In the context of India, community organization method of social work practice developed as one of the dominant methods of practice along with social casework method. This is in clear contrast to the Western social work practice, where social casework has continuously remained the core method of practice. By comparing the individualism-oriented culture of the West with the cultural orientation of Indian society that has been mainly grounded on community living, it can be explained why the practice and training of community organization method acquired very timely importance in India. Though in the last one decade, with the continuous changes due to globalization and increased access to technology, social casework seems to be gaining prominence in the Indian context as well.

After the establishment of TISS in 1936, in the late 1940s, a number of new social work institutions emerged in India such as the Delhi School of Social Work, the Madras School of Social Work and the Baroda School of Social Work. A couple of social work departments also emerged in various universities around India such as Kashi Vidyapith, Gujarat Vidyapith and the University of Lucknow (Dash, 2017). The number of social work education imparting institutes has risen considerably since then with the presence of 350 schools of social work throughout the country (Botcha, 2012). While the number of schools of social work has risen, the substandard quality of education and fieldwork mentoring that is provided in these institutions is upsetting. A few scholars (like Singh, 2005) have pointed out that the lack of engagement by the professional social work organizations of the country have also contributed towards the continuously declining standard of social work education in the country. Scholars like Nandkarni and Desai (2012) have expressed their concern regarding the increasing commercialization of social work education over the decades, which is against the very heart and soul of social work practice. Thus, it seems that the journey of social work education in India has been mixed in nature as far as its accomplishments and drawbacks are concerned.

In the last eight and half decades of professional social work education in India, the social work education has witnessed a rapid growth. Unfortunately, this growth has given birth to certain issues in social work education. Fortunately, this growth has made social work education more popular and accessible that might help in 'professionalizing' social work in the Indian context. There have also been continuous attempts to develop social work education in India beyond the borrowed American theories and models of social work practice, which is a good sign as it prompts debates and discussions among the members of social work sorority in India.

SUMMARY

In this chapter, we looked at a major period of the world history, the Great Depression. This great historical event made people across the globe realize that poverty or human deprivation is not necessarily a result of personal failures but is very often a result of socio-economic set-up. It changed the way the world had been looking at human sufferings so far. The Great Depression and its catastrophic outcomes had a profound impact on various social and economic policies in the times yet to come. While looking at this major historical phase, a dissection was done of various occurrences during and after this period that led to the development of professional social work education throughout the world. Some of such incidences can be the introduction of the New Deal by the Roosevelt government, the fact that some of the staff members of Roosevelt were prominent social work professionals like Hopkins, creation of job profiles for social work professionals within the federal system to provide relief services to the individuals and community through the federal relief programmes, and, eventually, the formation of professional social work organizations/associations and establishment of more and more social work education institutions throughout the world, including the Third-World countries like India. The chapter has also looked at how in 1936, during the Great Depression, the first school of social work was established in India and the evolution of social work education in the Indian subcontinent thereafter. Essentially, this chapter shows us how the Great Depression created a platform for the governmental agencies to look at social work professionals beyond the 'voluntary charity workers' and as the allies of the government that could assist the government in taking the society forward in a more inclusive manner.

TOP 10 TAKEAWAYS/MAIN POINTS

1. The Great Depression was one of the most significant turning points in the historical trajectory of professional social work.
2. The need to deal with the social and economic challenges posed by the Depression created an encouraging space for social work to expand as a profession.
3. The three Rs of Roosevelt government's New Deal were: relief, regulation and reform. After the introduction of the New Deal, the demand for social work professionals increased and a lot of job profiles were created for them within and outside the federal system.
4. The increase in job profiles and opportunities in the great economic crisis led to the reality of social work professionals being recognized as 'real' professionals.
5. One of the major outcomes of the turmoil caused by the Great Depression was that the governments across the globe had the realization that free market economy can lead to a colossal disaster.
6. The crisis encouraged the governments to take charge of trade policies and put regulations in place that will not let such a disaster occur again.
7. The governments also realized that they need to undertake more proactive role in the social welfare of their people and it just cannot be left to the charity organizations alone. Rather, it was better for the well-being of society if they walked hand in hand.
8. The Great Depression further led to the flourishing of social work education and profession in the other parts of the world as well.
9. The after events of the economic depression have had a great impact on social work education and profession in the Indian subcontinent. In fact, the Western models of social work education and practice continue to influence the social work practice in the subcontinent.
10. If it was not for the Great Depression and the after conditions posed by it, the journey of social work education and profession and the humanitarian values on which it stands today would have been somewhat different.

Keywords: Great Depression, social work education, professional social work, social work education institutions

GLOSSARY

Great Depression: The Great Depression can be defined as the decade of economic slowdown that began in 1929 and ended in 1939. This phase had a great impact on global economy and society which led to the formation of rules and regulation that were meant to protect the society from the ill effects of economic slowdown.

Professional social work: 'Social work is a practice-based profession and an academic discipline that promotes social change and development, social cohesion, and the empowerment and liberation of people. Principles of social justice, human rights, collective responsibility and respect for diversities are central to social work. Underpinned by theories of social work, social sciences, humanities and indigenous knowledge, social work engages people and structures to address life challenges and enhance wellbeing. The above definition may be amplified at national and/or regional levels' (IASSW, 2014).

Social work education: Social work education entails the know-how of integrating the theories, values and skills of the social work and other allied disciplines such as sociology, psychology and law in order to ensure competent and ethical social work practice.

Social work education institutions: Social work education institutions refer to those education institutes (colleges, universities and so on) that impart theoretical as well as practice-based social work education at bachelor's or higher degree levels like master's or doctorate.

ANALYTICAL QUESTIONS

1. Analyse and assess the global impact of the Great Depression on the social work education institutes in the various parts of the world.
2. The Great Depression paved way for a more homogenous and Eurocentric social work education pedagogy throughout the world while sidelining the cultural and social diversity of its educators, practitioners as well as its beneficiaries. Discuss.

MULTIPLE CHOICE QUESTIONS

1. When did the Great Depression begin?
   a. October 1920
   b. October 1930
   c. **October 1929**
   d. October 1939

2. Which of the following were the social and economic outcomes of the Great Depression?
   a. Hunger
   b. Unemployment
   c. Crash down of the economy
   d. **All of the above**

3. When and where did the first professional course for social work take place?
   a. **Columbia University, 1898**
   b. New York University, 1879
   c. Boston University, 1879
   d. MIT, 1898

4. Which of the following was the first school of social work in India?
   a. Delhi School of Social Work
   b. Madras School of Social Work
   c. **Sir Dorabji Tata Graduate School of Social Work**
   d. Faculty of Social Work, Baroda University

5. What was the impact of the Great Depression on social work education institutions?
   a. **More demand/need for social work education institutions was created**
   b. Closing down of social work education institutions
   c. There was no impact whatsoever
   d. Lesser demand/need for social work education institutions was created
6. What was the impact of the Great Depression on social work professionals?
   a. More job profiles were created for the social work professionals within the government set-up
   b. There was an increase in the demand for social work professionals
   c. Social work was beginning to be seen as a 'real profession'
   d. **All of the above**
7. Who was the founding member of Sir Dorabji Tata Graduate School of Social Work?
   a. **Clifford Manshardt**
   b. Dorothy Moses
   c. Emilia Clarke
   d. J. M. Kumarappa
8. How many methods of social work practice are there?
   a. Two
   b. Four
   c. **Six**
   d. Eight
9. Which of the following is not a social work practice method?
   a. Social casework
   b. Social group work
   c. Community organization
   d. **Community group work**
10. Which of the following two psychiatrists had major influence on social casework practitioners during the 1930s?
    a. **Otto Rank and Sigmund Freud**
    b. Carl Jung and Otto Rank
    c. Sigmund Freud and Carl Jung
    d. Carl Rogers and Carl Jung

REVIEW QUESTIONS

1. What were the various social and economic problems that were prevalent during the Great Depression?
2. How did the Great Depression pave way for the expansion of social work education and practice?

REFERENCES

Austin, D. M. (1997). The institutional development of social work education. *Journal of Social Work Education, 33*(3), 599–612.

Axinn, J., & Stern, M. J. (1988). *Dependency and poverty: Old problems in a new world.* Lexington Books.

Botcha, R. (2012). Retrospect and prospect of professional social work education in India: A critical review. *Perspectives in Social Work, 25*(2), 14–28.

Crafts, N., & Fearon, P. (2010). Lessons from the 1930s Great Depression. *Oxford Review of Economic Policy, 26*(3), 285–317.

Dash, B. M. (2017). Revisiting eight decades of social work education in India. *Asian Social Work and Policy Review, 11,* 66–75.

Hollis, E. V., & Taylor, A. L. (1951). *Social work education in United States.* Columbia University Press.

IASSW. (2014). Global definition of social work. https://www.iassw-aiets.org/global-definition-of-social-work-review-of-the-global-definition/

Ingaro, C. (2014). The evolution of social work: Historical milestones. https://socialwork.simmons.edu/evolution-social-work-historical-milestones/

Kantor, S., Fishback, P. V., & Wallis, J. J. (2012). *Did the new deal solidify the 1932 democratic realignment?* (Working Paper No. 18500). National Bureau of Economic Research.

Keynes, J. M. (1931). An economic analysis of unemployment. In Q. Wright (Ed.), *Unemployment as a world problem.* University of Chicago Press.

Kurzman, P. A. (1974). *Harry Hopkins and the new deal.* R. E. Burdick Publishers.

Mukhopadyay, K. K. (2005). Professional social work and social realities. In S. Singh (Ed.), *Teaching and practice of social work in India* (pp. 19–41). New Royal Book Company.

Nadkarni, V. V., & Desai, K. T. (2012). *Report of the national consultation on national network of schools of social work for quality enhancement of social work education in India.* Tata Institute of Social Sciences.

Pathak, S. H. (1975). A quarter century of professional social work in India. In S. D. Gokhale (Ed.), *Social welfare: Legend and legacy* (pp. 193–203). Popular Prakashan.

Singh, S. (2005). Social work education in India: Major issues and strategies required. In S. Singh (Ed.), *Teaching and practice of social work in India* (pp. 1–18). New Royal Book Company.

Stuart, P. H. (2013). Social work profession: History. *Encyclopedia of Social Work.* https://doi.org/10.1093/acrefore/9780199975839.013.623

Trattner, W. I. (1999). *From poor law to welfare state* (6th ed.). Free Press.

5

Social Welfare

Archana Kaushik

LEARNING OBJECTIVES

- To understand the concept, nature and meaning of social welfare
- To examine the historical evolution of the term and contextual realities
- To note the current trends of social welfare and related notions
- To describe the scope of social welfare and its relevance in social work

Power has only one duty—to secure the social welfare of the people.

—Benjamin Disraeli

INTRODUCTION

Since time immemorial, humans have faced challenges, problems, inequalities, injustice, disadvantages and distress. Equally old are the feelings of compassion, kindness, care, sympathy and empathy. In response to the social problems and with the inherent human values of compassion, empathy, fair play, justice and such others emerged the urge among humans to help their fellow beings and that was the beginning of the concept of social work. Gradually, with the evolution of societies, the nature, scope, approaches and modalities of social work changed. However, social welfare has remained the backbone of social work.

Social welfare is a broad concept which aims to achieve a state of collective well-being. It can be defined as a system of partnership between economic, political and social institutions as well as an overall effort for ensuring interests and well-being of a large segment of population where the term well-being covers physical, social, emotional, mental, economic and spiritual dimensions.

The chapter discusses the conceptualization, definitions and scope of social welfare and related terms such as social service, *kalyan*, *mangal* and *yogkshem*. It also chalks out the historical contours signifying origin of the terms, especially in the Indian sociocultural panorama. It describes the widening space of social welfare both as a system or institution and as efforts or measures in the present times. The chapter delineates the scope of social welfare services and its relevance in social work teaching and practice.

SOCIAL WELFARE: CONCEPT, SCOPE AND DEFINITIONS

According to the *Webster's Encyclopedic Unabridged Dictionary*, the term 'welfare' means 'the state or condition with regard to good, fortune, health, happiness, prosperity, etc' (Advantage Publishers Group & Thunder Bay Press, 1996, p. 1619). Social welfare has been defined as the various social services provided by a state for the benefits of its citizens. Dasgupta (1976, p. 27) has stated, 'by welfare we refer to the entire package of services, social and economic, that deal with income support, welfare provisions and social security, on the one hand, and view the whole range of social services, on the other'.

It implies that social welfare is the people's well-being promoted by society through a wide variety of ways and means. According to Friedlander (1963, p. 4),

> Social welfare is the organized system of social services and institutions, designed to aid individuals and groups to attain satisfying standards of life and health, and personal and social relationships which permit them to develop their full capacities and to promote their well-being in harmony with the needs of their families and the community.

It entails the institutional initiatives meant to ensure holistic well-being of members of a society or citizens of a nation.

Wilensky and Lebeaux (1958, p. 17) have defined social welfare as those formally organized and socially sponsored institutions, agencies and programmes that function to maintain or improve the economic conditions, health or interpersonal competence of some parts or all of the population. Wilensky and Lebeaux in 1965 have opined that two conceptions of social welfare seem to be dominant today: the residual and the institutional. The residual approach propounds that social welfare institutions should come into play only when the normal structures of supply, the family and market break down. In contrast, the second one, the institutional approach, views the welfare services as normal, 'first-line' functions of modern industrial society. The major traits which distinguish social welfare structure are as follows:

1. Formal organization
2. Social sponsorship and accountability
3. Absence of profit motive as dominant programme purpose
4. Functional generalization—integrative, rather than segmental, view of human needs
5. Direct focus on human consumption needs

As defined by Skidmore et al. (1991, pp. 3–4), 'Social welfare, in a broad sense, encompasses the well-being and interests of large numbers of people, including their physical, mental, emotional, spiritual and economic needs.' Zastrow (1978, p. 3) has defined the aim of social welfare as 'to fulfill the social, financial, health and recreational requirements of all individuals in a society'. He further adds,

> Social welfare seeks to enhance the social functioning of all age groups, both rich and poor. When other institutions in our society such as the market economy and the family, fail at times to meet the basic needs of individuals or groups of people, then social services are needed and demanded.

Social welfare has been conceptualized in a broad all-encompassing sense as well-being of all. However, some scholars have provided a narrower scope of social welfare, especially in the light of the administrative and programmatic feasibility. In a limited but practical perspective, social welfare is the welfare of society, especially of those segments of society which are underprivileged or disadvantaged because of poverty, poor education, unemployment and so on. Even the eminent personality and the first chairperson of Central Social Welfare Board (CSWB), Mrs Durgabai Deshmukh (1960, p. VII), has stated,

> The concept of social welfare is distinct from that of general social services like education, health, etc. Social welfare is specialized work for the benefit of the weaker and more vulnerable sections of the population and would include social services for the benefit of women, children, the physically handicapped, the mentally retarded and socially handicapped in various ways.

From the above discussion, it may be implied that social welfare can be conceptualized and defined in the following ways.

Social welfare as an ultimate goal: As Skidmore and others have defined it, social welfare is holistic (social, economic, psychological and spiritual) well-being of all the citizens, which is the ultimate aim of any government or society. This aim guides the social planners and policymakers to design interventions, schemes and programmes in various facets of life.

Social welfare as a mission: It is a gamut of specifically developed system of services and institutions meant to protect and promote well-being of the people. As given in certain definitions mentioned earlier, social welfare is an effort, an intervention to achieve the goal of well-being of all.

Social welfare as a value: It is a principle or an inherent quality or an ideology that is characterized by empathy, compassion, interdependence, care, justice and fair play which act as a driving force in ameliorating pain and sufferings of fellow beings, especially those who are poor, weak and marginalized.

Social welfare as a programme initiative: As a starting point, social welfare services and institutions aim to cater to the varied kinds of needs of the weaker and vulnerable sections of society. These initiatives aim at protecting and promoting the well-being of marginalized and disadvantaged sections of the society as mentioned by Mrs Deshmukh in her definition of social welfare. It may be noted that the weakness and vulnerability of these downtrodden sections are not a fallout of their personal fault but are a result of certain structural factors or various kinds of physical, mental and social barriers that adversely affect them. It is important to work for the weaker, and vulnerable sections of society who, on their own, may not be able to maximally develop and effectively compete to enter the mainstream society and live with liberty, decency and dignity. Thus, programmatically, the aim of social welfare is to protect and promote the interests of these sections to enable them to optimally realize whatever potentials, talents, abilities they may have to carve out a dignified place for themselves in society and to effectively discharge the duties and responsibilities of positions which they happen to occupy.

PHILOSOPHICAL BASE OF SOCIAL WELFARE

With the growth of human civilization, societies and nations have developed rules, norms, systems and modalities so as to enable their members to lead a decent, dignified life that is free from ailments, pains, sufferings and disadvantages so that everyone realizes their true potential. For optimum growth and development of citizens, provisions of different kinds of services such as health, education, housing and recreation are needed, which become the scope of social welfare.

Gauging the philosophical base of social welfare, doctrines of humanism, existentialism, idealism, religion and spiritualism intersect to propagate that the highest values among humans are based on the furtherance of well-being of self, significant others and the entire humankind. In India, sages have prayed and longed for the well-being of one and all. *Vasudhaiva Kutumbakam* is a Sanskrit phrase that is found in Hindu scriptures like the *Mahanarayana Upanishad* and it means 'the world is one family'. Helping fellow beings, interdependence and shared living are celebrated as virtues in religious texts and transmitted in sociocultural traditions and norms.

Since ancient times, sages in India have prayed and longed for the well-being for all, which is the philosophical foundation of social welfare, aptly denoted by the following prayer derived from the *Brihadaranyaka Upanishad* (Table 5.1).

In India, the sages and saints have chanted this universal prayer which depicts the quest for happiness and well-being of all living beings. This prayer is not only for humans but for 'all', which include everything—humans, animals, plants, atoms, energy, quanta and everything the universe is composed of. The basic premise is the fact that beyond our disguised individualistic identities, we all are one. Due to our false identification with body–mind, we are unable to see

TABLE 5.1 Philosophical Base of Social Welfare

Sanskrit	English	Meaning
ॐ सर्वे भवन्तु सुखिनः	Om sarve bhavantu sukhinah	Om, May all be happy
सर्वे सन्तु निरामयाः।	Sarve santu niraamayaah	May all be free from illness
सर्वे भद्राणि पश्यन्तु	Sarve bhadraanni pashyantu	May all see what is auspicious
मा कश्चिद्‌दुःखभाग्भवेत्‌।	Maa kashcid-duhkha-bhaag-bhavet		May no one suffer
ॐ शान्तिः शान्तिः शान्तिः॥	Om shaantih shaantih shaantih			Om peace, peace, peace

objective reality other than what our senses portray to us. We see ourselves separate from the world. This perception of separateness is the source of suffering. Sages and saints know the reality that the entire universe is one entity and all living beings and non-living things are manifestation of one consciousness.

As illustrated in the universal prayer, we all are one and we are praying for the welfare of the entire universe, with no demarcation between 'we' and 'them', 'us' and 'others'. The prayer is a reminder of our real self, that is, universal self. When we pray for all, we pray for ourselves too, and we begin to heal and become well. This prayer is really a reminder of our universal self: to *know* that we are no different from the universe even though our way of seeing the world does not usually feel that way. We pray so we may be joined in with the whole again.

Since we all are one interdependent entity, analogous to a human body, anyone else's suffering would make us suffer too, just as pain in any part of the body affects the whole body. This universal oneness is the crux of philosophical base of social welfare. Inherent empathy and the sense of oneness are the driving force for social welfare.

SOCIAL WELFARE AND RELATED TERMS

Certain related terms intersecting with concept and definitions of social welfare may be discussed in this section.

Moorthy and Rao (1970) have stated, 'social work is help rendered to any person or group, who is suffering from any disability, mental, physical, emotional or moral, so that the individual or group so helped is enabled is enabled to help himself or itself'.

According to Indian Conference of Social Work (1957), social work is a welfare activity based on humanitarian philosophy, scientific knowledge and technical skill for helping individuals or community to live a rich and full life.

National Association of Social Workers has defined social work as:

> the professional activity of helping individuals, groups, or communities enhance or restore their capacity for social functioning and creating societal conditions favourable to this goal. Social Work practice consists of the professional application of Social Work values, principles, and techniques to one or more of the following ends: helping people obtain tangible services; counselling and psychotherapy with individuals, families, and groups; helping communities or groups provide or improve processes. The practice of Social Work requires knowledge of human development and behaviour; of social, economic, and cultural institutions; and of the interactions of all these factors.

International Federation of Social Workers (2014) provides the following definition of the term: 'Social work is a practice-based profession and an academic discipline that promotes social change and development, social cohesion, and the empowerment and liberation of people. Principles of social justice, human rights, collective responsibility and respect for diversities are central to social work. Underpinned by theories of social work, social sciences, humanities and indigenous knowledge, social work engages people and structures to address life's challenges and enhance well-being'.

Social Welfare

Social work and social welfare are intertwined. Social work is a field that seeks to achieve justice and social welfare for the whole population. It is a profession trying to impact social welfare.

Another related term is social service. To a lay person, 'helping the helpless' is social service. H. M. Cassidy (1943, p. 13) states that social services are those organized activities that are primarily and directly concerned with the conservation, the protection and the improvement of human resources.

Social services cover a range of services meant for general public that are provided by the government and civil society organizations. Thus, social services mean the collective of those services which are provided on an extensive scale to the general population; they serve to meet the basic needs of the people and include services such as health, education and housing. These public services aim to create more effective organizations, build stronger communities and promote equality and opportunity.

There are strong common grounds of aim, scope, approach and modalities between social welfare and social services, especially when social welfare is seen from a broad perspective—holistic development and well-being of the entire population. Even if social welfare is viewed in a narrower outlook, services provided for the weaker and vulnerable sections of the society become a stepping stone to achieve well-being of the whole population.

Social security: Security means freedom from risk or danger. It is identified as a basic human need. Everyone wants to be protected against any kind of unforeseen conditions that can endanger their safety and threaten continuity of their income. There are certain contingent factors such as sickness, accident, disability and death in life that make certain vulnerable sections of society more prone to risks and destitution than others. Under these circumstances, individuals with certain vulnerabilities or small means meet basic needs by their own abilities alone. Initially, this security is provided to the individual through the institution of family, especially the joint family system. Caste or *biradari* would take over if and when the family fails to provide security to its members. In due course, such informal systems start to disintegrate and then social security is an effort on the part of the state or the employer or other related agency to provide protection and help.

It was for the first time in 1935 in England that a pioneer, Sir William Beveridge, came forward with the idea of 'social security' as means of freedom against five great giants: want, disease, ignorance, idleness and squalor. Since then the notion of social security became popular. Sir William Beveridge (1942, p. 120) stated,

> the term 'social security' is used to denote the security of an income to take the place of earnings when they are interrupted by unemployment, sickness or accident, to provide loss of support by the death of another person, and to meet exceptional expenditures, such as those concerned with birth, death and marriage.

The International Labour Organization (1942, p. 80) has defined social security as 'the security that society furnishes through appropriate organization, against certain risks to which its members are exposed'. Likewise, according to Friedlander (1963, p. 5),

> by social security we understand a programme of protection provided by society against those contingencies of modem life-sickness, unemployment, old age, dependence, industrial

accidents and invalidism—against which the individual cannot be expected to protect himself and his family by his own ability or foresight.

Social security services are of two types: social insurance and social assistance, where the former is contributory and the latter is non-contributory. The role of the government is crucial in administering social assistance programmes such as old-age pension, disability scholarships and widow pension.

Social security is an integral part of social welfare. Though social security focuses on protection against contingent conditions in life, its aim is social welfare or ensuring well-being of all the citizens of a country.

A few interrelated terms from the indigenous literature may be looked into. The first term is *kalyan*, which means welfare. And welfare is comprised of 'well' meaning healthy—physically, mentally, socially and spiritually—while 'fare' is understood as a journey or arrival. Though the term welfare in social work literature is understood since the 20th century as a provision of services and resources to the disadvantaged section of society for their upliftment, historically, it is related to happiness, prosperity and well-being.

Next is *mangal*, which means benediction, blessings, prayers for well-being, blessedness, grace and dedication. In contrast to the Western literature on social work where the rights-based approach dominates, the Indian indigenous literature talks about the 'dharma' or duty towards one's fellow beings to ensure their *mangal*. It denotes a sentiment, 'may all be well and blissful'.

The third term is *yogkshem*, which has a wider connotation. Technically, it is defined as 'making efforts to get the things needed for one's well-being (*yog*) and protecting the things that one has acquired (*kshem*)'. It implies acquiring things/services to fulfil one's needs and protecting and preserving them so that they can be utilized in the future too. Some scholars have connoted things in terms of body, its health and fitness, which in future would ensure adequate social functioning, while some others have denoted things as financial resources. Another meaning of the term is the state's administrative system that aims to ensure well-being of its citizens.

HISTORICAL TO CURRENT FEATURES OF SOCIAL WELFARE AND SOCIAL WORK

A look into the historical terrains of social welfare and social work would be beneficial in understanding their current trends in a better way. Directed by compassion, empathy and the desire to help one's fellow beings—the values that are universally present—individuals would provide need-based care, help and support to their community people. These efforts were based on an individual's benevolent nature. Gradually, religious and spiritual texts, sociocultural norms and guidelines of the then rulers dominated the social welfare and social work activities. Indian traditional view of social welfare is based on the concepts of *daya* (mercy), *daan* (charity), *dakshina* (donation), *bhiksha* (alms), *samya-bhavna* (equanimity), *swadharma* (self-righteousness) and *tyaga* (sacrifice), the essence of which are self-discipline, self-sacrifice and consideration for others. All religions have urged upon their followers to put aside a portion of their income for charity, which will provide them happiness in this world and salvation in the next world. The kings and royal families of earlier days extended help to the affected population during emergencies such as floods, earthquakes, fires, droughts and other natural calamities.

With the advent of political reforms and change in approaches of governance from autocracy to democracy, industrialization, urbanization, modernization and now liberalization, privatization and globalization, scope and contours, approaches and modalities of social work and social welfare have also changed. In the post-modern era, we observe activities of varied nature being carried out in the gamut of social welfare and social work, which range from charity and mutual help to the rights-based approach and emancipatory social work. A synoptic overview of history of execution of social welfare services in the Indian context is provided as follows.

The British government established an administrative set-up, though the intended purpose was mainly maintaining law and order and not social welfare of the people. Sporadic instances of some social reform measures were seen such as banning of sati custom and permitting widow remarriage through legislations passed in 1829 and 1856, respectively.

After Independence, in 1947, the new political set-up was geared for addressing several social evils that existed at that time. In the field of social welfare, during the First Five-year Plan, the Government of India entrusted voluntary organizations to manage the enormous range of social problems across the country through the financial assistance from the government. In this regard, the government created unique administrative machinery consisting of an autonomous board named Central Social Welfare Board in August 1953. Additionally, social welfare advisory boards were established at the state level. The main purpose of the CSWB has been to provide financial and technical assistance to voluntary organizations working in the field of social welfare.

Before 1964, social welfare programmes were being managed by different ministries such as education, health, labour, home and industries. The Renuka Ray Committee in its report submitted in 1960 recommended the establishment of the Department of Social Security. Under the leadership of the then prime minister, Sh. Lal Bahadur Shastri, a social security department was established and located under the Ministry of Law on 14 June 1964. Subjects, namely social security, social welfare, backward classes, and Khadi and handicrafts were allocated to this department. In 1966, it was renamed as Social Welfare Department. It was located under the Ministry of Education and Social Welfare created in 1971. Its status was raised to a ministry in 1979. Its name was further changed to the Ministry of Social and Women Welfare in 1984. With the creation of a separate Department of Women and Child Development in the Ministry of Human Resource Development, its name was changed to Ministry of Welfare in 1985 and subsequently, it was renamed as the Ministry of Social Justice and Empowerment. Through the ministry and its various autonomous bodies, a varied range of social welfare programmes is executed covering women, children in need and care, elderly, destitute and homeless and such others.

Let us look at the trends in social welfare in the present world, which are definitely not uniform across the globe, but in different nations, their presence can be seen.

The **conservatives** among the various political theorists have advocated for the free-market economy and limited involvement of the government. The role of government is to maintain social order and defend private property. In their view, social welfare is the domain of philanthropic and community-based institutions and government's role is minimalistic in this regard. The propagators of the conservative approach maintain that forces of competition, consumption and demand and supply would naturally nullify the monopoly of the market. Competition would ensure quality control and cost-effective supply of demands. For those who are vulnerable, religious and philanthropic organizations would provide social welfare services.

Next, the **liberals** asserted for regulation of the market and the state taking up a proactive role in providing services under the domain of social welfare. They urged the governments to step in and rectify the wrongdoings of the free-market approach and unjust sociocultural practices that are reflected in racism, caste conflicts, gender discrimination, class inequalities, labour rights, environmental degradation and such others. In liberal political economy, government facilitates and ensures delivery of social welfare services through certain regulations on the market and business firms and takes up measures for social justice for disadvantaged sections of the population.

The **radical leftist approach** provides democracy in business and the government provides social welfare for all. It is characterized by reorganization of institutions, government-planned economy and well-designed and widely applicable social welfare measures for the citizens.

Finally, in **capitalism**, characterized by private property ownership, government adopts a laissez-faire approach where it has minimal interference and market driven by its profit-making approach dominates. It is based on the premise that competition would allow for demand and supply to work out at lowest possible price. Here, administrators are paid well and unskilled workers get minimum wages causing wide wage gap. There is a wide need and scope of social welfare services but the state has limited say in their execution.

SOCIAL WELFARE: SCOPE AND PRACTICE

Social welfare is the lifeline of social work, both in teaching and practice. It provides direction for a utopian social order, an ultimate goal for social work to strive for. Goals of social welfare are reflected in the five-year plans, Millennium Development Goals and now the Sustainable Development Goals (SDGs). All these goals are the details and expressions of the goal of social welfare—ensuring well-being of all. The 17 SDGs are comprehensive, holistic and all-encompassing (see Box 5.1).

Certain values of social welfare which are considered core values imbibed by social workers are given as follows. These values are an integral part of social work education, training and practice.

The first one is conviction in the inherent worth and dignity of the individual. This is in sync with the philosophical base of social welfare. This value is manifested in the behaviour of social worker as they are able to provide unconditional positive regard to the client, who might not be having positive self-worth.

The second value is belief in democratic functioning. Social work relies on the democratic process while dealing with the client system. This implies that decisions are taken through consensus and nothing is imposed on the client. The worker, the client and others are all involved in the decision-making process. While doing so, the right of the client system in choosing the solution is given utmost importance.

The third value is the firm belief in equal opportunity for all, limited only by the individual's capacities (Friedlander, 1977). This value expresses the need for social justice. Social work fights against social injustices meted out to the disadvantaged and vulnerable sections of society.

> **Box 5.1   The 17 SDGs to Transform Our World**
>
> Goal 1: No poverty
> Goal 2: Zero hunger
> Goal 3: Good health and well-being
> Goal 4: Quality education
> Goal 5: Gender equality
> Goal 6: Clean water and sanitation
> Goal 7: Affordable and clean energy
> Goal 8: Decent work and economic growth
> Goal 9: Industry, innovation and infrastructure
> Goal 10: Reduced inequality
> Goal 11: Sustainable cities and communities
> Goal 12: Responsible consumption and production
> Goal 13: Climate action
> Goal 14: Life below water
> Goal 15: Life on land
> Goal 16: Peace and justice strong institutions
> Goal 17: Partnerships to achieve the goals

Irrespective of caste, religion, economic status, intelligence and so on, everyone must have equal access to societal resources.

The fourth value is social worker's social responsibility towards themself, their family and the society (Friedlander, 1977). As relation with the 'self' is the base of relation with others, it is imperative that if social workers fail to perform their responsibilities towards themselves and their families, then they may fail to perform their social responsibilities towards clients and colleagues.

The fifth value is to transmit knowledge and skills to others (Morales & Sheafor, 1989). This value instructs social workers to provide the information that they have, which would enable their clients to take care of themselves in case the client faces similar problems in the future. This is to avoid psychological dependence of clients on social workers. Further, sharing of information and skills among the co-professionals goes a long way in promoting the competence of the professional practice.

The sixth value is separating personal feelings from professional relationships (Morales & Sheafor, 1989) so that personal feelings, prejudices and biases do not intrude in a professional relationship with the client.

The seventh value assumes high standards of personal and professional conduct (Morales & Sheafor, 1989). It emphasizes that the conduct of the social worker should be exemplary at both personal and professional levels. As a professional, the code of ethics outlined for social work practitioners should be followed. In social work practice situations, clients come with a number of fears, hesitations and doubts regarding their problems and expect interventions. They may confess confidential and emotional information with high trust on social workers. Divulging the confidential information carelessly or making fun of the clients' plight or looking down upon the clients does great harm. Therefore, it is essential that a social worker be a person of high integrity and of high ethical conduct.

> **Did You Know?**
>
> Social sector development is a crucial component for the development of a country. It has direct implications on strengthening of human resource of a country, which, in turn, plays a vital role in national growth and development. Therefore, budgetary allocation on social sector is a critical variable to be studied.
>
> Social sector expenditure, as per the data of 2018, is highest in France, 32 per cent of its gross domestic product (GDP). The USA is the second highest with 30 per cent of its GDP. Austria, Finland, Sweden, Belgium, Denmark, Italy and Germany also spend more than 25 per cent of their GDP on social sector. In contrast, India's social sector expenditure was merely 7.7 per cent of the GDP for the year 2019–2020. It may be noted that the social sector encompasses important domains such as public health, education and labour welfare (United Nations, 2018).

It is now a well-accepted fact that social welfare programmes play a vital role in the overall development of a society or a country. Even in practice, when social welfare is viewed in a narrower sense, it is complementing the overall goal of well-being of all. Thus, social welfare services may intend to cater to the special needs of a person and groups who, by reason of some handicap, social, economic, physical or mental, are unable to avail themselves of, or are traditionally denied, the amenities and services provided by the community. In the long run, these services contribute to the ultimate broad goal of social welfare.

The scope of social welfare services is very vast and expanding day by day. It aims to bring out political, social, economic and cultural changes through proper planning and programme implementation, ensuring people's participation and distributive justice. Social welfare services cover a wide spectrum of programmes and schemes for varied groups of people and communities, which includes industrial and infrastructural programmes and those relating to development of agriculture, health, education, family planning, communication, social services and social reconstruction like rural–urban community development. Thus, social welfare services, in broad sense, comprise a whole gamut of the multifaceted developmental programmes.

SUMMARY

In this chapter, the concept and definitions of social welfare are provided. Social welfare is the crux of social work and in the literature, it has been conceptualized in two main ways: broadly, it means holistic well-being of all the members of a society and in a limited way, it means provision of services to the disadvantaged sections of the society, those who are marginalized and excluded from the mainstream.

As its philosophical base, social welfare draws from the spiritual notion of oneness of the universe, the existential approach that relies on the inherent divinity of one and all.

Social Welfare

The term social welfare shares its scope, contours and dimensions with other related terms such as social work, social service, social security, *kalyan*, *mangal* and *yogkshem*. These terms have been explained depicting their relation with social welfare.

The historical evolution of social welfare and trends in the present times are discussed. In ancient times, beginning with mutual aid and charity, social welfare services got diversified and became multifarious in the present era as responses to newer social problems and challenges. In the post-Independence India, social welfare began with establishment of CSWB and gradually turned into the full-fledged Ministry of Social Justice and Empowerment. Fate of social welfare services in different political economies is also discussed in the chapter.

Finally, scope of social welfare services is mentioned in terms of goals, values and programme implementation. Role of social welfare in social work teaching and practice is also mentioned.

TOP 10 TAKEAWAYS/MAIN POINTS

1. Social welfare, broadly, means physical, social, mental, economic and spiritual well-being of all the members of a society.
2. In a limited way, social welfare entails the services for the weaker, disadvantaged and marginalized sections of the population.
3. Universal oneness of the consciousness or soul as against the false identification of separate body–mind entities forms the philosophical base of social welfare.
4. Social work is a professional practice that aims to ensure well-being of all (social welfare) through well-defined values, ethics, principles, models, methods and techniques.
5. Social security encompasses social insurance (contributory) and social assistance (non-contributory) services against the contingent conditions in life such as unemployment, old age, accident and disability to compensate loss of income.
6. Social service covers a range of interventions in the areas of health, education, sanitation, housing and civic amenities for the optimum growth and development of the general public.
7. Three indigenous terms related to social welfare are *kalyan* (welfare and well-being), *mangal* (blessedness) and *yogkshem* (acquiring and protecting things for well-being; administrative system for social welfare).
8. Social welfare began with charity and mutual aid, remained dependent on kindness of rulers, was confined to voluntary organizations with financial assistance from the government and gradually the government expanded its role by establishing a ministry to deliver services.
9. Government intervention in ensuring social welfare in the four political economy approaches range from lowest in conservatives followed by capitalists, then liberals and highest in radical leftists.
10. The scope of practising social welfare is vast, covering industrial and infrastructural programmes, agriculture, health, education, family planning, communication, social services and social reconstruction like rural–urban community development.

Keywords: Social welfare, social security, social service, *kalyan*, *mangal*

GLOSSARY

Kalyan: It means welfare and entails services and resources to ensure health (physical, mental, social and spiritual).

Mangal: It means benediction, blessings and prayers for well-being, blessedness, grace and dedication.

Social security: It comprises making and implementing effective social assistance and social insurance provisions. It aims to compensate for the loss of income due to unemployment, disability or death caused by accident and old age through social insurance and social assistance.

Social service: These are a wide range of services in the areas of health, education, sanitation, livelihood, housing, recreation, electricity, water, transportation, communication and other civic amenities, which are meant for the optimum growth and development of the general population.

Social welfare: It aims at providing services to weaker sections of the population who because of various handicaps such as physical, mental, economic and social are unable to make use of social services provided. It includes the services for disadvantaged sections of society such as children, women, aged, the Scheduled Castes, the Scheduled Tribes, the Other Backward Classes, minorities, disabled, drug addicts and economically underprivileged such as destitute and unemployed.

Broadly, social welfare means physical, mental, social and spiritual well-being of all the members of a society or citizens of a nation.

Social work: 'Social work is professional service based on knowledge of human relations and skill relationship and concerned with problem of intra-personal and or inter-personal adjustments resulting from unmet individual, group, or community need' (Ahmed, 1969 in Social Work Nepal, 2020).

Yogkshem: It is defined as 'making efforts to get the things needed for one's well-being (*yog*) and protecting the things that one has acquired (*kshem*)'. It also means state's administrative system to ensure well-being of its citizens.

MULTIPLE CHOICE QUESTIONS

1. Which of the following is the apt meaning of *kalyan*?
   a. Administrative system of welfare
   b. Blessedness and dedication
   c. **Services and resources to ensure holistic well-being**
   d. Protecting one's belongingness

2. Services that aim to compensate for the loss of income due to unemployment, disability and so on are called:
   a. **Social security**
   b. *Yogkshem*
   c. Social service
   d. Social welfare

3. The professional activity of helping individuals, groups or communities to enhance or restore their capacity for social functioning is called:
   a. Social welfare
   b. **Social work**
   c. Social security
   d. Social service

4. Which of the following ministries deals with the subject matters of social welfare?
   a. Ministry of Welfare
   b. **Ministry of Social Justice and Empowerment**
   c. Ministry of Human Resource Development
   d. Ministry of Women and Child Development

5. Which of the following statements best depict the philosophical base of social welfare?
   a. Human beings are morally responsible for well-being of everyone
   b. Humans are empathetic, and they are moved by the plight of others
   c. All organisms are housed on planet Earth as members of one family
   d. **All living beings and non-living things are manifestation of one consciousness**

6. *Yogkshem* means:
   a. Administrative system of welfare
   b. Making efforts to get things needed for one's well-being and protecting them
   c. **Both a and b**
   d. None of the above

7. Which of the following political economy approaches is most apt for social welfare services?
   a. Liberals
   b. Conservatives
   c. Capitalists
   d. **Radical leftist**

8. Which of the following is not a Sustainable Development Goal?
   a. Gender equality
   b. **Capacity building**
   c. Quality education
   d. Zero hunger

9. Which of the following is not a field of practice of social welfare?
   a. Infrastructure and industrial development
   b. Curtailing abuse and exploitation
   c. Health and hygiene
   d. **Profit-making and property ownership**

10. Social welfare in a broad sense means:
    a. **Holistic well-being of all**
    b. Social assistance programme to the vulnerable population
    c. Services for the optimum development of general population
    d. Services for the disadvantaged, downtrodden and marginalized social groups

REVIEW QUESTIONS

1. Define social welfare in your own words.
2. Write a short note on philosophical base of social welfare.
3. Provide the relation between social welfare and social work.
4. Examine certain indigenous terms related to social welfare.
5. Compare the conceptualization of social welfare in the radical leftist and capitalist approaches.
6. Enlist some of the practice fields of social welfare.

REFERENCES

Advantage Publishers Group & Thunder Bay Press. (1996). *Webster's encyclopedic unabridged dictionary of the English language*. Thunder Bay Press.
Beveridge, W. (1942). *Social insurance and allied services*. HMSO.
Cassidy, H. M. (1943). *Social security and reconstruction in Canada*. Humphries.
Dasgupta, S. (1976). Social action. In Ministry of Social Welfare, Government of India (Ed.), *Encyclopaedia of social work in India* (Vol. 3). Publications Division, Government of India.
Deshmukh, D. (1960). Preface. In The Planning Commission, Government of India (Ed.), *Social welfare in India*. Publications Division, Government of India.
Friedlander, W. A. (1963). *Introduction to social welfare* (3rd ed.). Prentice Hall.
Friedlander, W. A. (1976). *Concepts and methods of social work*. Englewood cliffs, NJ: Prentice Hall (p. 212).
Friedlander, W. A. (1977). *Concepts and methods of social work*. Prentice Hall.
International Federation of Social Workers. (2014). *Global definition of social work*. Retrieved from https://www.ifsw.org/what-is-social-work/global-definition-of-social-work/_(accessed on 25 May 2022).
International Labour Organization. (1942). *Approaches to social security: An International Survey*. Author.
Moorthy, S., & Rao, S. N. (1970). *Field work in social work*. Waltair.
Morales. A., & Sheafor B. W. (1989). *Social work: A profession with many faces*. Allyn & Bacon.
NASW. (n.d.). *Social work practice*. Retrieved from https://www.socialworkers.org/Practice#:~:text=Social%20work%20practice%20consists%20of,provide%20or%20improve%20social%20and_(accessed on 25 May 2022).
Skidmore, R. A., Thackeray, M. G., & Farley, O. W. (1991). *Introduction to social work*. Prentice Hall.
Social Work Nepal. (2020, 12 September). What is social work? https://swnepal.blogspot.com/2020/09/what-is-social-work_12.html
United Nations. (2018). Department of Economic and Social Affairs, Sustainable Development. Retrieved from https://sdgs.un.org/goals
Wilensky H. L., & Lebeaux, C. N. (1958). *Industrial society and social welfare*. Russell Sage Foundation.
Wilensky, H. L., & Lebeaux, C. N. (1965). *Industrial society and social welfare*. New York: The Free Press.
Zastrow, C. (1978). *Introduction to social welfare institutions: Social problems, services and current issues*. The Dorsey Press.

RECOMMENDED READINGS

Adema, W., & Ladaique, M. (2005). *Net social expenditure, 2005 edition: More comprehensive measures of social support* (OECD Social Employment and Migration Paper 29). OECD.
Ayala, J. S. (2009). Blended learning as a new approach to social work education. *Journal of Social Work Education*, *45*(2), 277–287.
Bodhi, S. R. (2011), Professional social work education in India: a critical view from the periphery. *The Indian Journal of Social Work*, *72*(2), 289–300.
Burchardt, T. (2006). Happiness and social policy: Barking up the right tree in the wrong neck of the woods. *Social Policy Review*, *18*, 145–164.
Cutler, T., and Waine, B. (2001). Social insecurity and the retreat from social democracy: Occupational welfare in the long boom and financialization. *Review of International Political Economy*, *8*(1), 96–118.
Dash, B. M., Kumar, M., Singh, D. P., & Shukla, S. (2020). *Indian social work*. Routledge.
Dixon, J. (2000). A global ranking of national social security systems. *International Social Security Review*, *53*(1), 109–122.
Greve, B. (2008). What is welfare? *Central European Journal of Public Policy*, *2*(1), 50–73.

6

Social Service

Manisha Pal and Rakesh Choudhary

LEARNING OBJECTIVES

- To understand the concept and meaning of social service
- To describe the interrelationship between social service and social work practice
- To know about the historical development of social services

---

The best way to find yourself is to lose yourself in the service of others.

—Mahatma Gandhi

INTRODUCTION

The term 'social service' is used to denote help given by a volunteer to an individual or group at the time of need. Social service does not attempt at the study of needs and resources nor is it an activity to help the individual to help themselves. It is the kind of services provided to any person on the basis of desire to serve which is inspired by the feeling of helping others. It does not need any trained personnel or techniques. The main aim of social services is the enhancement of social competence. For example, changes in the individuals are not brought directly to modify their behaviour but through modification in their social environment. The chapter discusses the conceptualization, definitions and scope of social service and related terms like social work. The chapter also incorporates historical development of social service from premodern era to modern era. It has also discussed the interrelationship between the related terms like social work.

SOCIAL SERVICE: CONCEPT, MEANING AND DEFINITIONS

Social services are those organized activities that are primarily and directly concerned with the conservation, the protection and the improvement of human resources. It is the efforts to restore, maintain and enhance the social functioning of individuals and families through enabling social resources and process that enhance the capacity of individuals and families to cope with stress and with the normal demands of social life. These services are essentially 'people changing' institutions (developmental, remedial, supportive or substitutive). Its main aim is to equip individuals with the competence and resources essential for effective social participation.

R. H. Value Publishing (1996, p. 1304) described that

> every civilized society, in order to enable its members to lead a emancipated, respectful, decent and dignified life and for that to promote proper personality development through optimum realization of their potentials such as talents and abilities, makes provision for varied kinds of services like health, housing, education, recreation, etc. broadly defining, the term service means 'an act of helpful activity, help'.

The term 'social service' refers to the variety of programmes made available by public or private agencies to individuals and families who need special assistance. Prior to the 1920s, Americans referred to these services as charity or relief, but they covered a wide range of services, including legal aid, immigrant assistance and travellers' aid. The new terminology corresponded to changes in the philosophy, approach and organization of social work.

In other words, social services are those services, which are provided by the society to its people for their needs and desires and for protection and development of human resources. These services are organized efforts to advance human welfare (services such as free school lunches provided by the government for its disadvantaged citizens). Also, government provides benefits and facilities to the community such as education, medical care, food subsidies and subsidized housing to improve the life and living conditions of the children, disabled, the elderly and the poor in the national community.

Social services in areas such as education, health, water and sanitation can enhance individual well-being, raise productivity and contribute to the overall quality of life. These social services can enable families to care for and sustain their members and reduce both the costs and time involved in work and other daily activities. They increase the chances that individuals and their families can lift themselves out of poverty and live dignified and productive lives. Individuals' well-being can be measured by the types, quantity and quality of services they receive; poverty can be perceived as a failure to achieve certain basic capabilities arising in part from the absence of social services. Social services can bring a better change in the society in terms of development. There should be a universal approach for the provision of social services. It is essential to realize their full potential as a component of transformative social policy. The social services not only aim to improve the well-being of the society but also to enhance productivity and earnings of the society (Figure 6.1).

The broad long-term relationship of accountability connects policymakers to organizational providers. An explicit enforceable contract can be one form of a compact.

FIGURE 6.1 Framework of Service Delivery Relationships

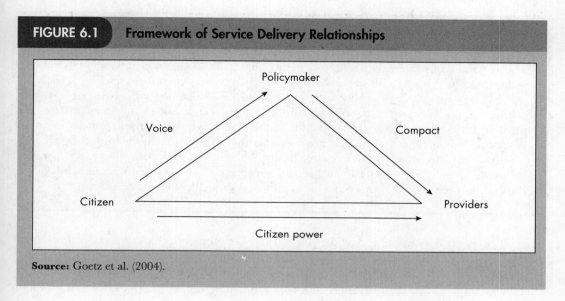

Source: Goetz et al. (2004).

According to Harry M. Cassidy, social services are 'those organized activities that are primarily and directly concerned with the conservation, protection and the improvement of human resources'. Social services also include social assistance, social insurance, child welfare, mental hygiene, public health, education, recreation, labour protection and housing.

'Helping the helpless' is social service. It is service rendered to any person on the basis of desire to serve which is inspired by the feeling of helping others. Thus, the term 'social service' is used to denote help given by a volunteer to an individual or group at the time of need or to enhance the welfare of individual or the community through personal efforts or by collective action. Social service does not require training in social work or skill in professional techniques. In the Indian context, social services are those services which are provided on an extensive scale to the needy population; they serve to meet the basic needs of the people and include services such as health, education and housing.

According to the Planning Commission of India, the term 'social services' denotes the services that cater to the special needs of individuals and groups who have a handicap—social, economic, physical or mental—and are thus unable to use or are traditionally denied the amenities and services provided by the community.

According to the *Collins Dictionary of Sociology*, the term *social services* refers to 'any state provided services which have a bearing on the quality of life of all citizens'. Social services are designated to provide meaningful opportunities for socio-economic growth of the disadvantaged section of the population in order to develop them into productive and self-reliant citizens and promote social equity. It is an activity designed to promote the social well-being of specifically disabled or disadvantaged. Social service providers may serve the needs of the children and families, the poor or homeless, immigrants, the mentally ill, handicapped and so on. It also includes child welfare, public health, education, housing, social assistance, social insurance and so on.

> **Did You Know?**
>
> The worthiness of social service is deeply engraved in India's social consciousness; individual and unorganized giving has existed in various forms from ancient times. The concepts of *daan* (giving) and *dakshina* (alms) in Hinduism, *bhiksha* (alms) in Buddhism and *zakat* (prescribed offerings) and *sadaqaat* (voluntary offerings) in Islam have been a part of Indian culture for many centuries. It was, however, with Buddhism, through the order of monks (sanghs) and later with Christianity that serving the needy first became an organized institutional concern. The gospel of service was preached through the establishment of schools, hospitals, leper homes and homes for the aged and the needy. The concept of social service is not new. It has existed from the the time of the Vedas to the present (Viswanath & Dadrawala, 2004).

Service delivery is conceptualized as the relationship between policymakers, service providers and poor people. It encompasses services and their supporting systems that are typically regarded as a state responsibility. These include social services (primary education and basic health services), infrastructure (water and sanitation, roads and bridges) and services that promote personal security (justice and police; Berry et al., 2004).

In general context, we can say that these services are public services that are provided by the government and non-governmental organizations. Their aims to create more effective organizations and build developed communities also promote equality and opportunity for people from low socio-economic backgrounds. Inclusive growth also demands that all social groups have equal access to the services provided by the state and equal opportunity for upward economic and social mobility.

SOCIAL WORK AND SOCIAL SERVICES

The primary function of social work however is to help the people of community to make effective use of social services so that they may achieve a minimum desirable standard of social and economic well-being. It means that mere rendering health services or organizing educational programmes for the economically backward as such is not social work.

Social work tries to fulfil the objectives of social services, for example, there are a few programmes of social services such as the following:

- Educational services
- Health services
- National employment services (placement services and assistance to physically handicapped people)

Social work

1. Is a professional service which includes specialized knowledge and skills for dealing with human behaviour.
2. Lays emphasis on the analysis and synthesis of human behaviour.

3. Applies different methods and techniques to solve individual and social problems.
4. Gives much emphasis on adjustment.
5. Makes individual self-dependent.
6. Also integrates and coordinates means and resources of social development.
7. Not only solves the problems but also prevents its occurring.
8. Believes in democratic values.

Social work includes all voluntary attempts to extend benefits in response to needs which are concerned with social relationships and which avail themselves of scientific knowledge methods (Alice, 1926).

Social work is the provision of services designed to aid individuals, singly or in groups, in coping with present or future social and psychological obstacles that prevent or are likely to prevent full or effective participation in society (Fink, 1942).

Social work is professional service rendered to people for the purpose of assisting them as individuals or in groups to attain satisfying relationship and standards of life in accordance with their particular wishes and capacities and in harmony with those of the community (Anderson, 1945).

Social work is an entity representing three clearly distinguished but interrelated parts: a network of social services, carefully developed methods and process, and social policy expressed through social institutions and individuals. All three are based on a view of human being, their interrelationships and the ethical demand made on them (Konopka, 1958).

The social work profession receives its sanction from public and private auspices and is the primary profession in the development, provision and evaluation of social services. Professional social workers are leaders in a variety of organizational settings and service delivery systems within a global context. The profession of social work is based on the values of service, social and economic justice, dignity and worth of the person, importance of human relationships, and integrity and competence in practice (Council on Social Work Education, 2004, p. 5)

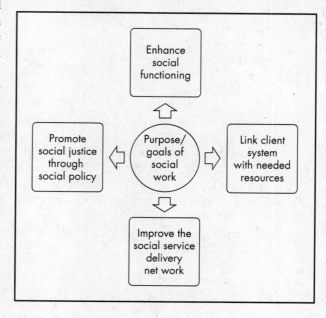

Generic objectives of social work are as follows:

1. To solve psycho-social problems
2. To fulfil humanitarian needs such as love, affection and care
3. To solve adjustment problems
4. To create self-sufficiency

5. To make and strengthen harmonious social relations
6. To make provision of corrective and recreational services
7. To develop democratic values among people
8. To provide opportunities for development and social progress
9. To conscientize the community
10. To change the environment in favour of individual's growth and development
11. To bring change in the defective social system for social development
12. To provide socio-legal aid to the needy who cannot afford to meet them

However, social services in different areas such as health, education, care, water and sanitation can enhance individual well-being, raise productivity and contribute to overall quality of life (UNRISD, 2010).

Characteristic of social services are as follows:

1. Social/public services are visualized and organized by society/state.
2. These services directly benefit all sections of society.
3. These services have a very wide scope including everything that has a direct bearing on the quality of life of people.
4. These services aim at promoting human and social development, protecting human rights of people and creating a sense of duty among them towards society.

Values of social service are as follows:

1. Service to humanity
2. Integrity
3. Competence

Social services are relevant to social work as mentioned below.

1. Social work is concerned with promoting human and social development.
2. Social work seeks to enhance effective social functioning and to create new social institutions that are required to modify existing institutions so that people can optimally realize their potentials and effectively contribute to the proper functioning of society.
3. Social work aims at promoting 'sustainable' development by conserving and developing environment so that enough resources may be left for future generations also to enable them to lead proper life.

One of the values of social work is service.
The ethical principles of service are as follows:

- Social worker's primary goal is to help people in need and to address social problems.
- Social workers elevate service to other above self-interest.
- Social workers use their knowledge, value and skill to help people in need and to address social problems.
- Social workers are encouraged to volunteer some of their professional skills with no expectation of significant financial return.

Social work and social services have an important role in helping the people. Social worker with the help of social services tries to provide the benefit to the poor, disadvantaged section of the society. Both are interrelated terms, and the aim of the social work and social services are interconnected. They try to improve the quality of life of the people by providing services and create the opportunities for people for their growth and development. Social services are also a type of public service in which social workers try to help and support the disadvantaged people, and social workers also try to achieve the objectives of social services.

HISTORICAL BACKGROUND OF SOCIAL SERVICE

To understand any concept deeply, it is important to know the root or origin of those concepts. For exploring the origin of social service, there are three categories which describe the existence of social service.

Premodern Era

Before the rise of modern European states, the church was providing social services. By 580 AD, the church had a system for circulating consumables to the poor; associated with each Parish was a Diaconium or office of the deacon. Monasteries also often served as comprehensive social service agencies, acting as hospitals, homes for the aged, orphanages and travellers' aid stations.

During the Middle Ages

The Christian church had a vast influence on the European society, and charity was considered to be a responsibility and a sign of one's pity. This charity was in the form of direct relief (e.g., giving money, food or other material goods to alleviate a particular need), as opposed to trying to change the root causes of poverty. As there was no effective bureaucracy below city government that was capable of large-scale charitable activities, the clergy carried out this role until the early modern period.

During the Modern Era

It was not until the emergence of industrialization and urbanization that the informal helping systems of the Church and family began to be replaced by social welfare services. The practice and profession of social work have a relatively modern and scientific origin and are generally considered to have developed out of three strands. The first was individual casework, a strategy pioneered by the Charity Organization Society in the mid-19th century. The second was social administration, which included various forms of poverty relief. State-wide poverty relief could be said to have its roots in the English Poor Laws of the 17th century but was first systematized through the efforts of the Charity Organization Society.

The social services have flourished in the 20th century as ideas of social responsibility have developed and spread. The basic concerns of social welfare: poverty, disability and disease, the dependent young and elderly are as old as society itself (Pinker, 1984).

- The laws of survival once severely limited the means by which these concerns could be addressed; to share another's burden meant to weaken one's own standing in the fierce struggle of daily existence. As societies developed, however, with their patterns of dependence between members, there arose more systematic responses to the factors that rendered individuals, and thus society at large, vulnerable. Religion and philosophy have tended to provide frameworks for the conduct of social welfare.
- The edicts of the Buddhist emperor Asoka in India, the sociopolitical doctrines of ancient Greece and Rome, and the simple rules of the early Christian communities are only a few examples of systems that addressed social needs.
- The Elizabethan Poor Laws in England, which sought relief of paupers through care services and workhouses administered at the Parish level, provided precedents for many modern legislative responses to poverty.
- In Victorian times, a more stringent legal view of poverty as a moral failing was met with the rise of humanitarianism and a proliferation of social reformers. The social charities and philanthropic societies founded by these pioneers formed the basis for many of today's welfare services.
- Perceived needs and the ability to address them determine each society's range of welfare services; there exists no universal vocabulary of social welfare. In some countries, a distinction is drawn between 'social services', denoting programmes, such as healthcare and education, which serve the general population, and 'welfare services', denoting aid directed to vulnerable groups, such as the poor, the disabled or the delinquent.
- According to another classification, remedial services address the basic needs of individuals in acute or chronic distress; preventive services seek to reduce the pressures and obstacles that cause such distress and supportive services attempt, through educational, health, employment and other programmes, to maintain and improve the functioning of individuals in society.
- Social welfare services originated as emergency measures that were to be applied when all else failed. However, they are now generally regarded as a necessary function in any society and a means not only of rescuing the endangered but also of fostering a society's ongoing, corporate well-being.
- The majority of personal social services are rendered on an individual basis to people who are unable, whether temporarily or permanently, to cope with the problems of everyday living. Recipients include families faced with loss of income, desertion or illness; children and youths whose physical or moral welfare is at risk; the sick; the disabled; the frail elderly and the unemployed. When possible, services are also directed towards preventing threats to personal or family independence.
- Social services generally place a high value on keeping families together in their local communities, organizing support from friends or neighbours when kinship ties are weak. Where necessary, the services provide substitute forms of home life or residential care and play a key role in the care and control of juvenile delinquents and other socially deviant groups, such as drug and alcohol abusers.

Indeed, services such as road, hospital and schools are critically important. These provide people with a progressive basis to change and develop, and to improve their quality of life. Sociopolitical history of India speaks volumes about the contribution of Islam rulers to socio-economic and cultural development of the society in terms of social services. Quite a few Muslim rulers have devoted attention and resources to infrastructural development in the land. Emperor Firoz Tughlaq (1309–1388) organized Diwan-e-Khairat which also supported facilities for the treatment of the sick and the afflicted. In this connection, one name that readily comes to mind is that of Sher Shah Suri (1472–1545) who ruled a large part of North India. He was a visionary ruler and introduced many military, civil and social reforms. He coined and introduced terms such as *rupayya* (rupee coin), *pargana* (district or subdivision) and munsif or magistrate. These terms are in currency even now. In his empire, he built a network of roads, with *sarais* (inns) at regular intervals where wayfarers and their steed could rest and recoup. Some of these facilities survive even to this day. Several rulers also paid attention to healthcare. Sher Shah Suri is reported to have posted hakims (practitioners of Unani medicine) at many *sarais* to provide healthcare for wayfarers as well as for general public. Alauddin Khilji, early in the 14th century, exercised social control over essential commodities, regulating supply and prices—a measure which greatly helped lower class and lower middle-class people. However, a more substantial contribution to healthcare and treatment of diseases came from hakims engaged in private practice. While they were patronized and recompensed by kings, nawabs and rajas, they would treat ailing public free of cost.

Gopal Krishna Gokhale, who had deep interest in the work of social services, established the Servants of India Society and undertook many social service activities for the well-being of people.

Did You Know?

The Bombay Social Service League was the first to start. The idea of social service was very much in the air among the educated classes of Indians. All over the country, social service leagues were springing up. In these leagues, Hindus, Mohammedans and Indian Christians united together. The Bombay Social Service League started a large and different programme, including night schools, cooperative societies and a travelling circulating library system. Another one was the Madras Social Service League, which formed a group and chose a district to attack the evils of debt, dirt, drink and ignorance. After some time, they also established small cooperative societies. Similarly, many service leagues were formed in different states to provide social services (Charity Organisation Review, 1961).

There are various government services which are provided for the benefits of the community such as education, medical care, subsidized housing, food subsidies and healthcare to improve the life and living standards of the community people, whereas social work involves the work that you do for people in need of service. Social welfare is the services that are offered to help people live a better quality of life. It was created to address poverty and health. This goes along with social policies that govern the process. The examples of those social services are as follows.

1. *Education:* It is the process of receiving or giving systematic instruction, especially at a school or university.
2. *Food subsidy:* It is the financial assistance given by the government to the poor to make low-cost food available to the poor.

3. *Healthcare:* Healthcare is an organized provision of medical care to individuals or a community.
4. *Subsidized housing:* It is government-sponsored economic assistance programme aimed towards alleviating housing costs and expenses for people in need with low to moderate incomes.

> **Did You Know?**
>
> There are different types of social services.
> - *Administration and management*: Social work administrators are proactive leaders in public and private agencies that provide services to clients.
> - Advocacy and community organization
> - Ageing
> - Child welfare
> - Developmental disabilities
> - Healthcare

Social service, also called welfare service or social work, refers to any of numerous publicly or privately provided services intended to aid disadvantaged, distressed or vulnerable persons or groups. The term *social service* also denotes the profession engaged in rendering such services.

Social work is an entity representing three clearly distinguished but interrelated parts: a network of social services, carefully developed methods and processes, and social policy expressed through social institutions and individuals. Social work is that process which deals directly and differentially with persons who have problems relating primarily to their social situation and which endeavours individual to individual to understand what help is needed and to assist the individual to find and utilize the help indicated. Thus, helping the helpless in social service, helping the helpless to help themselves is social work. Social services are essentially 'people changing' institutions (developmental, remedial, supportive or substitutive). Their main aim is to equip individuals with the competence and resources essential for effective social participation. Social work fulfils the objectives of social services (Misra, 1994).

SUMMARY

In this chapter, the concept and definitions of social service are described. For understanding the social work, it is important to learn about the social service. Social work fulfils the objectives of social service, whereas social services are services which the society provides to its members for the protection and development of human resources. Social services include health services, education, housing and so on. The primary function of social work, however, is to help the members of community to make effective use of social services so that they may achieve a minimum desirable standard of social and economic well-being. It is thus clear that rendering health services or organizing educational programmes for the poor people is not social work.

Social Service

Historical development of social service is mentioned and discussed here from premodern age to modern era. In ancient times, beginning with charity and alms, the church was providing social services. By 580 AD, the Church had a system for circulating consumables to the poor; associated with each Parish was a Diaconium or office of the deacon. Monasteries also often served as comprehensive social service agencies. During the modern era, it converted into the informal helping systems of the Church and family began to be replaced by social welfare services. Lastly, the chapter has discussed how social service is interlinked with social work profession and practice in different ways.

TOP 10 TAKEAWAYS/MAIN POINTS

1. Social services in areas such as health, education, care, water and sanitation can enhance individual well-being, raise productivity and contribute to overall quality of life. So there is focus on universal provision of social services for reduction of poverty.
2. Health and education are key goals in MDGs, and social service is trying to provide health and education to the disadvantaged section of the society, and social workers are trying to fulfil these objectives.
3. Social services improve the quality of life by creating, protecting and sustaining human capabilities.
4. Social work is a profession, which is based on the scientific knowledge that includes values, ethics, principles, models, methods and technique for helping the clients.
5. Social service is helping others directly on humanitarian philosophy, whereas social work tries to help people to help themselves.
6. 'Social services' is one interrelated term or part of social work. Social work encompasses many areas such as social welfare and social services (i.e., child protective services, foster care, family services, women welfare services), and includes programmes such as health, welfare and education.
7. The concept of social service is somewhere very old in Indian culture and tradition, however. Charity and philanthropy have been in the ethos of the Indian traditions. Individuals and religious institutions have been contributing to the welfare of the poor since premodern ages like the concept of *daan*, dharma, alms giving and giving zakat and so on.
8. The existence of social work, social welfare and social service since the birth of the civilization can be supported by the fact that early men took initiatives and made efforts to support and protect the weak in times of danger and need.
9. 'Social services', denoting programmes such as healthcare and education that benefit the general population, and 'welfare services', denoting aid directed to vulnerable groups such as the poor, the disabled or the delinquent.
10. The Tenth Five-Year Plan identified and focused on the strengthening of social service delivery as one of its most important tasks. It has clearly proposed 80 per cent increase in public social spending during this period, along with improved governance to ensure the more decentralized and improved delivery of pro-poor public services (Government of India, 2002).

Keywords: Social service, social work, social welfare, *daan*

GLOSSARY

Daan: It is understood as charity in the form of alms giving to the deserving.

Social service: 'Social service' is used to denote help given by a volunteer to an individual or group at the time of need. Social service is not a study of needs and resources, nor is it an activity to help the individual to help himself. It is a service rendered to any person on the basis of desire to serve which is inspired by the feeling of helping others. It neither involves any trained person nor professional techniques.

Social welfare: In its narrowest sense, social welfare includes those non-profit functions of society, public or voluntary, which are clearly aimed at alleviating distress and poverty or at ameliorating the conditions of causalities of society (Dolgoff & Feldstein, 1980).

Social work: Social work is the process which deals directly and differentially with persons who have problems relating primarily to their social situation and which endeavours, from individual to individual, to understand what help is needed and to assist the individual to find and utilize the help indicated (Friedlander, 1977).

MULTIPLE CHOICE QUESTIONS

1. The term 'social service' is used
   a. **To denote help given by a volunteer to an individual or group at the time of need**
   b. To provide help
   c. To maintain social policy
   d. To organize effort to provide human welfare

2. Social service refers to *any state providing services which have a bearing on the quality of life of all citizens.* This definition is given by
   a. A. M. Goetz
   b. Harry M. Cassidy
   c. ***Collins Dictionary of Sociology***
   d. A. K. Joshi

3. Social service includes
   a. Child welfare
   b. Public health
   c. Education and housing
   d. **All of the above**

4. What is social work?
   a. Giving charity
   b. Helping poor people and giving them alms
   c. **Professional services based on the scientific knowledge**
   d. Provide services to the community

5. Premodern era of social service was
   a. Charity Organization Society in the mid-19th century
   b. The Christian church had vast influence on European society

c. **Before the rise of modern European states (By 580 AD)**
   d. Charity was considered to be a responsibility and a sign of one's pity
6. 'Helping the helpless to help themselves' is
   a. Social service
   b. **Social work**
   c. Social welfare
   d. Social development
7. Values of social service are
   a. Social service is a service to humanity
   b. Integrity
   c. Competence
   d. **All of the above**
8. Generic objectives of social work are
   a. To solve psycho-social problems
   b. To fulfil humanitarian needs such as love, affection and care
   c. To solve adjustment problems
   d. **All of the above**
9. 'Helping the helpless' is
   a. Social service
   b. **Social work**
   c. Social welfare
   d. Social development
10. Types of social services are
    a. Ageing and healthcare
    b. Child welfare
    c. Developmental disabilities
    d. **All of the above**

REVIEW QUESTIONS

1. Define the term *social service*.
2. Write a short note on the origin of social service from Indian context.
3. Describe the relationship between social work and social service.
4. Write a short note on historical development of social service.

REFERENCES

Anderson, J. P. (1945). *Social work yearbook*. New York: Russel Sage Foundation (chapter: Social work as a profession).

Berry, C., Forder, A., Sultan, S., & Moreno-Torres, M. (2004). *Approaches to improving the delivery of social services in difficult environments*. Poverty Reduction in Difficult Environments Team, Policy Division, UK Department for International Development.

Charity Organisation Review. (1961). Social service in India. *New Series, 39*(231), 133–135. https://www.jstor.org/stable/43789642

Cheyney, A. (1926). *Nature and scope of social work*. American Association of Social Workers.

Council on Social Work Education. (2004). *Educational policy and accreditation standards*. The author.

Dolgoff, R. & Feldstein, D. (1980). *Understanding social welfare*. Harper and Row.

Fink, A. E. (1942). *The field of social work.* Henry Holt Co.
Friedlander, W. A. (1977). *Concepts and methods of social work.* Prentice Hall of India Pvt. Ltd.
Goetz, A. M., Joshi, A., & Moore, M. (2004). *Diversity, accountabilities and service delivery.* Institute of Development Studies. http://www.ids.ac.uk/ids/news/Archive/WDRjoshi.html
Government of India. (2002). *National human development report.* The author.
Konopka, G. (1958). *Social work philosophy.* Minneapolis. The University of Minnesota Press.
Misra, P. D. (1994). *Social work—Philosophy and method.* Inter-India Publications.
Pinker, R. (2012). The idea of welfare and the study of social policy: On unitarism and pluralism. *Journal of Social Policy, 41*(3).
Pinker, R. A. (1984). Populism and the social services. *Social Policy and Administration, 18*(1), 89–98.
R. H. Value Publishing. (1996). *Webster's encyclopedic unabridged dictionary* (2nd ed.). Gramercy.
UNRISD. (2010). Universal provision of social service (Chapter 6). In *Combating poverty and inequality.* http://www.unrisd.org/unrisd/website/document.nsf/(httpAuxPages)/5998EC 3397D55DE1C 12577890034B2E1?OpenDocument&panel=additional
Viswanath, P., & Dadrawala, N. (2004). *Philanthropy and equity: The case of India.* Global Equity Initiative, Harvard University.

RECOMMENDED READINGS

Desai, M. (2005). *Ideologies and social work: Historical and contemporary analysis.* Rawat Publication.
Higham, P. (2004). *Social work: Introducing professional practice.* SAGE.
Kumar, H. (1994). *Social work: An experience and experiment in India.* Gitanjali Publishing House.
Morales, A. T., Sheafor, B. W., & Scott, M. (2010). *Social work: A profession of many faces.* Allyn and Bacon.
Pathak, S. H. (1981). *Social welfare: An evolutionary and development perspectives.* Macmillan.
Wadia, A. R. (Ed.). (1961). *History and philosophy of social work in India.* Allied Publishers.

Social Reform
Lakshmana G

> **LEARNING OBJECTIVES**
>
> The chapter gives a glimpse of how social workers can draw lessons from the social reform movement and their contributions in the 21st century.
>
> - To understand the major social reform movements that have taken place in India and their contribution.
> - To examine the major social problems at present in India
> - To critically analyse social problems and the need for the active role of professional social workers

Each nation has its own peculiar method of work. Some work through politics, some through social reforms, and some through other lines. With us, religion is the only ground along which we can move.

—Swami Vivekananda

INTRODUCTION

Social work is a by-product of the changes taking place in society as a whole. Industrialization led to massive urbanization, which created a new order in society. Traditional family systems and society each had their own way of providing social security and social welfare. These institutions are forced to change their roles to suit the needs of individuals. Industrialization forced these institutions across the globe to change and adapt to the new changes. As a result, these social institutions reduced their social security and welfare roles. Hence, there were significant changes in the social structure and needs of the people. All these changes contributed to the emergence of modern social work in the West.

There was social reform by reformers in the 14th and 15th centuries, along with industrialization and urbanization. This social reform has happened in various spheres of life, that is, marriage, child labour, caste system, literature, race discrimination, bonded labour, devadasi system, education, equality and so on. The Indian society suffered from various social evils such as the caste system, female feticide, poor conditions for widow and women, landlessness and denial of education, all of which hampered the quality of life and well-being, deprivation and progress of sizeable sections of the society. Social reform was concerned with these sections of society and advocated for change in society. Social reform brings changes in social institutions, emphasizes the need for equality and advocates for justice, equal opportunities and favourable conditions for all, including all the people in the process.

SOCIAL PROBLEMS AND SOCIAL REFORM

The social problems that contributed to the reform movements. A social problem has been defined as 'a situation confronting a group or a section of society which inflicts injurious consequences that can be handled only collectively'. The definition implies that the entire society is responsible for the appearance of a socially problematic situation. Some of the problems have existed for many centuries and have shaken the social fabric of society. There were few voices against oppression, exploitation and discrimination. They were humanitarian in their approach and tried to reform society. These efforts can be seen across the globe in different periods. In India, these efforts were made by many social reformers.

WHAT IS SOCIAL REFORM?

Social reform aims to root out social evils or injustices prevalent in society at a given point of time by bringing radical changes in society for the better, in social affairs. Some practices, habits, customs, laws and other beliefs that are harmful or unjust are made based on the values held by social reformers. The means and methods for implementing their programmes have been adopted to follow the above values in the light of existing conditions in society. 'The reforms tried to change or replace the institutions, which have become totally or partly functionally irrelevant to the contemporary social order and were responsible for the low quality of life, deprivations, unrest and misery to the sizeable sections of the society' (Prasad, 1990).

Prasad (1990) defined 'etymologically, reform means forming again, reconstruct, which can be done only when a system is first demolished; but social reform envisages amendment, improvement and so on, thus entailing peaceful crusading, use of non-violent means for change and change in slow speed'.

According to Heimsath (1964),

In India, social reform did not ordinarily mean a reorganization of the structuring of society at large, as it did in the West, but for the benefit of underprivileged social and economic classes. Instead, it meant the infusion into the existing social structure of the new ways of life and thought; the society would be preserved, while its members would be transformed.

Ancient Indian society was completely dependent on religious aspects, and religion defined every aspect of human life. The Dharmaśāstra, Manusmṛiti and Upanishads were the basic books that regulated the lives of Indians, especially Hindus. Although considered more rigid, the Hindu religion was more flexible when it came to making changes. Using this flexibility, many social reformers emerged and questioned the discriminatory practices and order of society (Divekar, 1992; Jones, 1989).

EARLY REFORMERS IN INDIA

The early reformer in India, according to the available literature, was Buddha. He revolted against the social stratification based on the caste system, the excessive nature of rituals, the poor status of women and the exploitation of human beings on various other parameters. His followers established a separate religion, and it became known as Buddha dharma. Mahavir was the contemporary of Buddha, and he also advocated for change and rejuvenated Jainism. Mahatma Basaveshwara followed him in the 12th century. Mahatma Basavanna started a revolution against the practice of the caste system and started a new rational social order, which was later known as the 'Sharana movement'. Through *vachanas* (poetry), he spread social awareness. He created Anubhava Mantapa, which was like a model Parliament. In this, equal representation was given to men and women, and they had representatives from different socio-economic backgrounds. Other saints tried to eliminate the discriminatory practices of the Hindu religion, such as Kabir Das, Dnyaneshwar and Tukaram.

SOCIAL REFORM MOVEMENTS IN INDIA IN THE 18TH, 19TH AND 20TH CENTURIES

MAJOR REFORMERS AND THEIR CONTRIBUTIONS

Although there were many earlier efforts at social reform, they were more religious oriented, and major social reform started in the 18th century. Literature reports that British rule in India allowed Indians to learn about Western knowledge and their liberal ideals, the dignity of man and so on. Those who got a Western education got the opportunity to experience liberal ideals, social structure, religious practices and other ideals. They started comparing it with the Indian rigid social structure and understood the need for change in the Indian system.

Raja Ram Mohan Roy (1774–1833) was the pioneer of the social reform movement in modern India, known as the 'Father of the Indian Renaissance'. He started 'Brahmo Samaj' in 1928 and advocated for the abolition of *sati* (immolation of widows), the abolition of the caste system, child sacrifice and education for all. He advocated for free speech and expression and fought for the rights of the vernacular press.

> **Did You Know?**
>
> Social reform is 'a situation confronting a group or a section of society that inflicts injurious consequences that can be handled only collectively'.
> Ancient social and religious social reformers include Bhagwan Buddha, Mahaveer, Basaveshwara, Kabir Das, Dnyaneshwar and Tukaram.

Swami Dayanand Saraswati (1824–1883) was a reformer and believed in pragmatism. He formed 'Arya Samaj' in 1875. Through his teachings and Arya Samaj, he opposed many rituals of the Hindu religion, such as caste by birth, animal sacrifices, the idea of heaven and untouchability. He advocated for equal rights for men and women, marriageable age and opposed restrictions on women from reading Vedas. He emphasized removing illiteracy, imparting modern education and so on.

Dhondo Keshav Karve (1858–1962) advocated for reform in various sectors of society. Child marriage was widely prevalent, and many young girls were widowed. Their condition was pathetic, and society mistreated them. He established numerous institutions dedicated to pulling women from darkness, such as 'Mahila Vidyalaya', an educational organization for women, which was the first women's university in Pune, India, in the year 1916, and a training college for primary school teachers.

Jyotirao Phule (1827–1890) formed the Satyashodhak Samaj (Society of Seekers of Truth) to liberate the people of lower castes from suppression in 1873. He worked for the enlightenment of women and the lower caste people to combat the social evils. He established a girls' school and asked his wife to teach girls in the school. Later, he opened two more schools for girls, an indigenous school for the lower castes and established an orphanage.

Annie Besant was a Christian nun who worked for equality, the eradication of untouchability, freedom of thought, women's rights, secularism, birth control, workers' rights, poverty eradication and other social evils in India. Her contribution to women's education and health service is commendable. She was also a freedom fighter.

Ishwar Chandra Bandyopadhyay (1820–1891) was a well-known writer, intellectual and, above all, a staunch follower of humanity and is considered one of Bengal's pillars in the renaissance. He brought a revolution to the education system of Bengal and made it accessible to society's common strata. His major works include widow remarriage, the abolition of child marriage and polygamy and the opening of the doors of colleges and other educational institutions to lower caste students.

Atmaram Pandurang (1823–1898) established 'Prarthana Samaj' in 1867. He took an active role in social reform and emphasized universal brotherhood and equality of all castes. He said, 'The change we should all seek is a change from constraints to freedom, from credulity to faith, from status to contract, from authority to reason, from blind fatalism to human dignity.'

Mahadev Govind Ranade (1842–1901) helped to establish 'Poona Sarvajanik Sabha' and the 'Prarthana Samaj' and was actively involved in social and religious reform. His work involved reform against child marriage and the shaving of widows' heads, reducing the cost of weddings and social functions, caste restrictions on travelling abroad and advocating widow remarriage and female education.

King Shahu Chhatrapati (1874–1922) ruled the Kolhapur province in Maharashtra and was a precious gem in Kolhapur's history. He was considered a true democrat and a social reformer. Shahu was associated with many progressive activities, including education for women, free education for oppressed children, restricting child marriage, supporting inter-caste marriage and widow remarriage and working to provide education and employment to all.

Bankim Chandra Chatterjee (1838–1894) was one of the most celebrated novelists and poets of India. He challenged social evils, blind beliefs and injustice to the poor and downtrodden. He advocated remedial measures for the eradication of all evils and equality between the rich and the poor.

Rabindranath Tagore (1861–1941) and an agricultural economist, Leonard Elmhirst, set up the 'Institute for Rural Reconstruction' in 1921, later renamed 'Shriniketan' or 'Abode of Welfare' in Surul, a village near the ashram. He strived to provide inclusive education for all, challenging the 'abnormal caste consciousness' and untouchability.

Sri Ramakrishna Paramahamsa (1836–1886) advocated for women's rights, education, equality, the eradication of caste discrimination and simple living. He regarded every woman in society, including his wife, Sarada, as a holy mother.

Swami Vivekananda (1863–1902) founded the Ramakrishna Math and Ramakrishna Mission for the spread of education, uplift of the poor masses, women and the eradication of social evils. This organization is dedicated to people's causes.

There are other reformers who have contributed to social reform in Indian Hindu society.

SOCIAL REFORM AMONG JAINS

The existence of the Jain religion dates back to ancient India. This religion also has various sects and sub-sects. There were efforts made for religious reform by many people. Among them, the Das movement by Pandit Gopaldasji Baraiya of Banaras spearheaded the movement to allow the *dasas* to worship. The second movement was the printing of religious texts and allowing the public to use them in the 20th century, which is known as 'Shatra-mudrana Virodhi Andolan'. Another important movement among Śvetāmbara Mūrtipūjaka Jains, was 'Bala-diksha Pratibandha Andolana,' that is, 'Prevention of Initiation of Children's Movement'.

The social reform movement was undertaken in the early 20th century by many intellectuals and social workers among the Jains. Major reforms focused on age at marriage, preliminaries to marriage, selection of marriage partners and celebration of the marriage ceremony, widow remarriage and the elimination of bride price, dowry and the spread of education. Jains had no preference for girls, no female infanticide and no neglect of girls, no *sati* system and so on (Sangave, 1987).

SOCIAL REFORM IN ISLAM

Writing about the conditions of Muslims in India after the 1857 rebellion, the well-known Urdu poet Maulana Altaf Hussain Hali (1837–1914) said,

> We [Muslims] are not trusted by the government, nor are we among the prominent courtiers or the ruler neither are we among the educated elite. We have no share in the

trade or the industry, nor do you find [sic] us in the civil services or among the businesses.

Muslims were slow to adapt to the changes taking place in the country. The first significant social reform movement in India among Muslims was led by Sayyid Ahmed of Raebareli (1786–1831). The movement advocated overcoming superstitions and economically harmful practices. The movement also launched a successful campaign against objections to widow remarriages. Sir Sayyid Ahmad Khan interpreted that in Islam, polygamy was not permissible unless the husband was capable and willing to do equal justice to his co-wives. He also advocated for modern education. There were efforts to address the status of Muslim women (Mohsini, 1987).

THE NATURE OF SOCIAL REFORM IN INDIA

When we see social reform movements in India, it is like a spring, and many eminent personalities emerged in the 18th and 19th centuries. The prevailing socio-economic conditions were not conducive to any kind of reform. Nonetheless, the reformers made remarkable efforts and were successful in their efforts. It was not just one personality; it was a group of people across the country. This is an interesting fact in human history. Most of them were western educated or had imbibed western ideas directly or indirectly. Throughout the second half of the 19th century, they discussed social issues and often appealed to the government for executive action (Kulkarni, 1993; Wadia, 1968).

The reform movement among Hindus focused majorly on the abolition of the *sati* system, widow remarriage, opposed child marriage and advocated for fixing the marriage age. They strived to eradicate untouchability, uplift the untouchables, depressed classes and tribal people, land rights for women, inter-caste marriage and universalization of education irrespective of caste, creed and other social issues.

There were many resolutions to remove these social evils legally before independence and after independence. After independence, these reforms have taken a fast face. The Constitution of India aims at an equal and secular society. However, despite the legislation and constitutional provisions, many social evils survived. It is observed that, though the intensity of these evils has decreased, in rural and remote areas, they continue to be practised.

DISCUSSION

India has an ancient tradition of social service. Serving the needy is greatly valued in Indian culture. In the ancient and medieval periods, assistance was provided primarily in the form of charity. These efforts were centred on religious institutions, such as temples, *maths* (holy places where one can stay) and *dharamshala* (places to stay that are free; Kulkarni, 1993). In the villages, the joint family, caste system and the panchayat (the committee which looks after the affairs of a village) catered to the basic needs of the poor, disabled, ill, aged and all those in distress.

During the British period (1658–1947), social work activities were greatly influenced by the political and social conditions of the times and mostly concentrated on colonialist social reform (Wadia, 1968).

Karma is a spiritual philosophy embedded in Asian cultures that holds that people's inner character is the driving force behind their behaviour and consequences. The 'law of harvest' refers to the belief that people 'reap what they sow'. In other words, positive actions in the world generate positive life situations, whereas negative behaviours bring about adverse outcomes. The caseworkers used these concepts to encourage young people to think about the values they wanted their character to reflect and how their choices about alcohol and drug use could impact their moral character positively or negatively. Thus, the goal of the Western model is to help them understand the consequences of high-risk behaviours, which were discussed within the context of karma and their impact on their moral character (Kulkarni, 1993; Wadia, 1968).

It was observed that the young Indian men who graduated from English-education institutions, which constituted about 1 percent of the total Indian population as late as 1900, were part of this social reform. This elite group dominated the Indian religious, social and political movements throughout the late 18th, 19th and 20th centuries. They agitated for widow remarriage, opposed child marriage and advocated for women's literacy and education (Wadia, 1968).

Social reform is concerned with creating favourable conditions for social progress for those who are suffering from social discrimination, social neglect or being cornered due to the system and want to bring structural changes in society. Their struggle is evident in many fundamental changes that have happened in Indian society. Due to their efforts, Indian society has acquired a progressive outlook, and the depressed sections and other sections of the society have understood the need for change. The principles of social reform are very effective and imbibed in modern social work practice. The changing socio-economic, political, educational, religious and other aspects have helped the emergence of modern social work. There is a need to adopt the reformist nature of work by professional social workers in the changed scenario.

Many social reformers have emerged and done excellent work. Let us assess the present social problems and other emerging issues.

The author made an effort to review the major social issues the reformers addressed in the 18th and 19th centuries and their present status. It can be inferred from Table 7.1 that the reformers addressed many social problems. The prevailing socio-economic conditions would not have allowed discussion of some of the issues at that time. But still, these reformers were able to address them and faced the wrath of society. In human history, these reforms have far-reaching implications. Even after 2,400 years of Bhagwan Buddha, the caste system survives and still influences people's customs, ways of life, marriage choices, social life, political affiliation and so on. This shows that these social problems were extremely strong, and they took a while to address. Although legally, widow remarriage is allowed, it is not highly practised and still stigmatized.

Along with those age-old problems, new problems have also emerged as social problems that require intervention. To address these issues, dedicated and committed professionals are

TABLE 7.1 Social Problems Addressed by Social Reformers and Present Conditions

S. No.	Social Problem	Addressed by the Social Reformers	Present Status	Measures
1.	*Sati* system	Successfully combated	Completely eradicated	Through legislative measures
2.	Widow remarriage	Reformers were able to penetrate the scientific temper and bring about behaviour change in society	Widow remarriage is well accepted but still needs to work in society	Through social movement and legislative measures
3.	Child marriage	Reformers could influence society and bring significant changes	It is still practised in the community, but the intensity is reduced	Through legislation and awareness
4.	Eradication of untouchability	Social reformers successfully brought behaviour change in society	There are still reports of people practising this evil	Through legislation, changes have been brought
5.	Land rights to women	Reformers addressed the issue and advocated for land rights for women	As per the law, women have rights	Through legislation, changes have been made
6.	Universalization of education irrespective of caste, creed and other social issues	Reformers advocated for equal opportunity for all	It is available to everyone	Through legislation and awareness
7.	Inter-caste marriage	Reformers advocated for equality and inter-caste marriage	Although inter-caste marriages are taking place, it is still not widely practicable and accepted in all religions	Legislation provision of equal opportunities
8.	Slavery and bonded labour	Reformers advocated eliminating this inhuman practice	Although successfully eradicated, few cases were reported	Through legislative measures, education and welfare provisions
9.	Political participation	Reformers advocated for the involvement of all groups in society	The constitution provides equality, and everybody is free to participate. But in some places, restrictions and denials are reported	Through legislative measures

S. No.	Social Problem	Addressed by the Social Reformers	Present Status	Measures
10.	Poverty eradication	Many reformers advocated the same	Although poverty has been reduced, it is prevalent	Many government programs have been brought
11.	Land rights	Addressed by reformers	Still, it is a major issue	Many attempts have been made
12.	Beggary	Not a major focus	It is a social issue	Government has enacted laws
13.	Gender discrimination in religious places	Advocated for equality	Certain religious places are out of reach in most of the religions	Constitution provides equality
14.	Female infanticide	Addressed by the reformers	It is still a major social problem and requires attention	Through legislation, efforts are being made
15.	Child labour	Not a major concern	Attempts were made, and still, it is reported	Legislation has been enacted
16.	Dowry	Addressed by the reformers	A significant reduction is seen. Still, it is prevalent in society	Law prohibits the dowry
17.	Juvenile delinquency	Not a major concern	It is becoming a social problem, and close attention has been paid to it	Legislation has been enacted to address the issue
18.	Substance abuse including alcohol and other drugs	It was not a major issue, but reformers advocated for a healthy lifestyle	It has become a major social problem in the country	Many efforts have been made legally and through many programmes
19.	Prostitution	Reformers addressed the issue, but it was not a major concern	It has become a social problem that requires active intervention at the policy level	There are many efforts to eradicate it
20.	Unemployment	Not a major concern among reformers	It has become a major social problem and requires government intervention	Many attempts have been made
21.	Corruption	Not an issue for reformers	At present, this is a major issue, and it is shaking the pillars of the government	Many acts and polices have been brought to curb

(Table 7.1 Continued)

(Table 7.1 Continued)

S. No.	Social Problem	Addressed by the Social Reformers	Present Status	Measures
22.	Political participation and representation	This was an issue and reformers did demand this	It has been provided to all citizens. But some areas and sections require empowerment	Constitutionally, everybody has an opportunity to participate
23.	Health-related problems	Not a major concern but was addressed by a few reformers	Health has become a human right and requires many reforms	Many legislations and laws have been enacted to provide the health
24.	Gambling	Was not a major issue	It has become a social problem	Many policies at various levels of intervention have been brought
25.	Population explosion	Was not a major issue at that time	It has become a social problem	The government has brought legislative measures and family planning programmes
26.	Communalism	Was a major issue but not in the forefront	It has become a social problem	The government has brought legislative measures
27.	Youth unrest and agitation	Not a major problem	It is increasing	The government is trying to address youth issues through various measures
28.	Child abuse	Was not a major issue at that time	It has become an issue	The government has a clear policy for this
29.	Violence against women and sexual abuse	It was present and addressed by the reformers	It is present, and attention has been paid	The government has a clear policy to prevent violence and punish the perpetrators
30.	Terrorism	Was not an issue	It has become a social problem	The government has a clear policy
31.	Crime and criminals	Reformers did address this, but it was not a major agenda	Criminal reform is a major issue and a challenge	Policies have been brought in and refined over a period of time
32.	Black money	Did not address	It has become an issue	A law has been enacted to address the issue

needed. The prevailing socio-economic, political and religious conditions require professionals and a cadre of trained people to meet the needs of the hour.

Social work is a practice-based profession that professes non-discrimination, equality, multiculturalism, individual dignity and other ideals. The social work philosophy and ideals are reformist in nature. Through its principles and models, it tries to reform the individual, society and communities. Although it does not try to uproot the traditional values of institutions and systems, it tries to bring new values, patterns of life, imbibe new thoughts and bring new changes to the doorsteps of the people. These activities would help to bring about macro-level changes. Through their work, social workers influence the government in policy formulation and enlighten the people, policymakers, significant others, and other stakeholders. These activities contribute to the macro-level changes.

In the 21st century, there is a need to have convergence at the micro, miso and macro-level to bring about changes in the social structure and lives of the people. The aim of social work in the present context is to counteract the effects of oppression, help people understand their oppression, alienation and obstacles to utilizing the opportunities and build their self-esteem. Although many reformers are emerging, the present problems require all levels of intervention. Through social work methods, social workers can bring the necessary changes in the lives of people. For this, convergence with all the other systems is also required. Social workers are change agents who could work in this direction.

The strategies used, efforts made, organizational skills, tolerance to the obstructions to their work, sacrifice and ignorance by some people and so on are the guiding forces for modern social workers in India. Through these techniques, we can understand the dynamics of our society, people and other aspects. Definitely, this would help the social workers be more compact and people-oriented. The social work profession has imbibed all these strategies and theoretical knowledge in its body of knowledge and is trying to build on them.

The social reformers gave a road map for modern social workers. For example, to address the issues of women, we need to create women's associations, and to address youth issues, we need to create youth groups and guide them. These associations must be locally trained and blended with national interests.

SUMMARY

Social reform shows that problems will not be eliminated easily in society. But sustained efforts to bring about changes are required, which must be multifaceted. As social change theory says, the change is imminent, but it is a slow and steady process. Social work, being a helping profession, needs to keep the ideals of social reform and prepare its cadres to address this. Students often come with a lack of motivation, saying that whatever they try, they are not ready to change their learned behaviours, attitudes, practices and other aspects of life. The ideals of social reformers, their efforts and their paths have brought about changes in society as a result of their sustained efforts, which could open society's eyes. If they had not tried, the condition of the oppressed groups would also have been pathetic. This insight would bring motivation and rejuvenate social workers to work for a change. Even small changes observed need to be appreciated for this.

Did You Know?

- The ancient social and religious reformers were Bhagwan Buddha and Mahaveer. Before 2,500 years ago, they advocated for equality, the eradication of the caste system, untouchability, women's rights, simple living and so on.
- The only religion that was born in India and has spread across many countries is Buddhism. But the religion is extinguished in India.
- As per the 2011 census, there were 4,451,753 Jains in India. The majority of them live in Maharashtra, Rajasthan, Gujarat and Madhya Pradesh. The founder of the Maurya Empire, Chandragupta Maurya, embraced Jainism.
- The first people's parliament was run by Allama Prabhu under the leadership of Basavanna in the 12th century in Karnataka. Basavanna created the 'Anubhava Mantapa', which is a model Parliament.

TOP 10 TAKEAWAYS/MAIN POINTS

1. Social problems have existed since time immemorial, and entire society is responsible for the appearance of a socially problematic situation.
2. Social reform aims to root out social evils or injustices prevalent in society at a given point of time by bringing radical changes in society for the better in social affairs.
3. In ancient India, the Dharmaśāstra, Manusmṛiti and Upanishads were the basic books that regulated the lives of Indians, especially Hindus.
4. Although considered more rigid, the Hindu religion was more flexible when it came to making changes. Using this flexibility, many social reformers emerged and questioned the discriminatory practices and order of society.
5. The reformation has taken place in various aspects of social life, not only limited to religion.
6. Ancient social and religious reformers travelled to many parts of the country and advocated for reforms.
7. The social reform movements of the 18th and 19th centuries were massive in nature, and many reformers emerged.
8. Reform has taken place in all the major religions of India.
9. One of the interesting facts is that most reformers in the 18th and 19th centuries were Western educated or had imbibed Western ideas directly or indirectly.
10. The aim of social work in the present context is to counteract the effects of oppression, help people understand their oppression, alienation and obstacles to utilizing opportunities and build their self-esteem.

Keywords: Social reform, social work, industrialization, urbanization, social evils

Social Reform

GLOSSARY

Hindu: A person whose religion is Hinduism.
***Sati* system:** 'It is a practice among Hindu communities where a recently widowed woman, either voluntarily or by force, immolates herself on her deceased husband's pyre.'
Social reform: The act of improving or changing customs, practices and norms has become irrelevant over time. Social reform is 'a situation confronting a group or a section of society that inflicts injurious consequences that can be handled only collectively'.
Social reformer: A person who works to achieve political, social or religious change.
Social work: It is a professional activity that works for the betterment of people, society and community.
Untouchable: A member of a Hindu social caste that is considered by other castes to be the lowest.

ANALYTICAL QUESTIONS

1. Briefly explain the contributions of any five social reformers in India.
2. What were the major areas/issues the social reformers took up in the 18th and 19th centuries in India?

MULTIPLE CHOICE QUESTIONS

1. Who is called the 'Father of the Indian Renaissance'?
   a. **Raja Ram Mohan Roy**
   b. Kabir
   c. Basavanna
   d. Ashoka

2. Who founded the Arya Samaj?
   a. Buddha
   b. Vivekananda
   c. **Swami Dayanand Saraswati**
   d. Ambedkar

3. Who founded the Ramakrishna Mission?
   a. Jyotibha Phule
   b. Raja Ram Mohan Roy
   c. M. K. Gandhi
   d. **Swami Vivekananda**

4. Which organization was established by Atmaram Pandurang?
   a. **Prarthana Samaj**
   b. Harijan
   c. Advaith
   d. Annihilation of castes

5. Which is not a current social problem?
   a. Child labour
   b. Widow remarriage
   c. Poverty
   d. ***Sati* system**

6. Which was not a social evil in the 18th and 19th centuries in India?
   a. Caste system
   b. *Sati* system
   c. **Terrorism**
   d. Widow remarriage

7. Who created the 'Anubhava Mantapa', which is a model Parliament?
   a. **Basavanna**
   b. Kabir Das
   c. Sharanas
   d. M. K. Gandhi

8. Who were the ancient social and religious reformers?
   a. R. K. Narayan
   b. Raja Ram Mohan Roy
   c. **Bhagwan Buddha and Mahaveer**
   d. Swami Vivekananda

9. Under whose leadership was the first significant social reform movement in India among Muslims started?
   a. **Sayyid Ahmed of Raebareli**
   b. Maulana Altaf Hussain Hali
   c. Shamsur Rahman Mohsini
   d. A. R. Wadia

10. Who started the Das movement among Jains?
    a. Vilas Adinath Sangave
    b. **Pandit Gopaldasji Baraiya**
    c. Bankim Chandra Chatterjee
    d. Basavanna

REVIEW QUESTIONS

1. What is social reform? Explain.
2. What are the present social problems? How can social workers address them?
3. List out the ancient social reformers in India.
4. Write a note on the social reform movement among Jains.

REFERENCES

Divekar, V. D. (Ed.). (1992). Social reform movements in India: A historical perspective. Popular Prakashan.
Heimsath, C. H. (1964). *Indian nationalism and Hindu social reform.* Oxford University Press.
Jones, K. W. (1989). *Socio-religious reform movements in British India, The New Cambridge History of India*, Vol. 1, pt. 3. Cambridge University Press.
Kulkarni, P. D. (1993). The indigenous-base of social work profession in India. *Indian Journal of Social Work, 54*(4), 555–565.
Mohsini, S. R. (1987). *History of social reform among Muslims.* In *Encyclopedia of social work in India* (Vol. 2). Ministry of Welfare, Government of India.
Prasad, R. (ed.). (1990). *Social reform: An analysis of Indian society.* Y. K. Publishers, p. xiii.
Sangave, V. A. (1987). *History of social reform among Jains.* In *Encyclopedia of social work in India* (Vol. 2). Ministry of Welfare, Government of India.
Wadia, A. R. (1968). *History of social work in India 1818–1947.* In *Encyclopedia of social work in India* (pp. 393–400). Planning Commission of India.

RECOMMENDED READINGS

Dash, B. M. (2010). History of social work: Individual initiatives. In G. Thomas (Ed.), *Origin and development of social work in India* (pp. 55–76). Indira Gandhi National Open University.
Dash, B. M. (2010). History of social work: Initiatives through social movements. In G. Thomas (Ed.), *Origin and development of social work in India* (pp. 77–105). Indira Gandhi National Open University.

8
Social Justice
Avtar Singh

LEARNING OBJECTIVES
* Describe the legal provisions for Scheduled Caste and Tribes
* Understand the concept of social justice and social inequality
* Describe the legal remedies available to vulnerable sections in terms of social justice
* Analyse the relationship between social justice and social work
* Delineate the role of professional social workers in social justice and social advocacy

A just society is that society in which ascending sense of reverence and descending sense of contempt is dissolved into the creation of a compassionate society.

—B. R. Ambedkar

Justice is happiness and injustice misery.

—Plato

Nothing rankles more in the human heart than a brooding sense of injustice. Illness or adversity one can put up with but injustice makes us want to put thing down.

—Jude Brennan

INTRODUCTION

The French Revolution came up with the principles of liberty, equality and fraternity to create a just social order. Thus, social justice is inextricably related to social order/social structure and therefore a multi-dimensional concept that has to be understood in various ways. The basic aim of social justice is to create a just social order in society. The concept of social justice first surfaced in the wake of the Industrial Revolution and the development of socialist doctrine. The United Nations (2006) document, *Social Justice in an Open World: The Role of the United Nations*, states that 'social justice may be broadly understood as the fair and compassionate fruit of economic growth'.

'Justice as fairness' is an idea that was fully developed and presented in book form in 1971 by John Rawls. The idea simply proposes that the most reasonable principles of justice are those that can be agreed upon by mutual consent of individuals under fair conditions. John Rawls started working on the idea of 'justice as fairness' in 1957 when he published his nine-page article in the *Journal of Philosophy* on 'Justice as Fairness'. The book attracted wide publicity because of its novelty of idea and lucid presentation and was generally accepted to have revived normative political theory after a gap of almost 100 years. Rawls did not stop there; beginning in 1971, he continued to add to and spread his idea of justice as fairness until his death in 2002. However, the main idea remained intact (Dadhich, 2017).

The concept of social justice is replete with multifarious connotations. It is equated with a welfare state. It is considered to be analogous to a truly egalitarian society. It is treated as an incident of the rule of law. It is co-extensive with social welfare. Because social justice is supposed to dwell mainly in the abolition of all sorts of inequalities, which are the concomitants of all sorts of inequalities of wealth and opportunity, race, caste, religion, distinction and title. The US Declaration of Independence in 1776 discovered the individual's inalienable rights of equality, life and liberty. The French Declaration of Rights of Man in 1789 discovered the natural, imprescriptibly and inalienable rights of an individual. Such rights are regarded as natural because all individuals are equally endowed with rights by equal war (Chaturvedi, 1975).

SOCIAL JUSTICE: CONCEPT AND DEFINITION

'Justice', which has been equated with 'dharma' in our Shastra, is the basis of the entire universe. In every system of law, it has been given the supreme place. In fact, it is the fundamental law that governs our lives, and whenever there is any deviation from this basic law, there is a likelihood of crisis.

Today, all civilized societies are engaged in joint endeavours to secure justice as there are countless injustices done from individual to individual. Much thinking is done over problems related to this area. In spite of best thinking and best efforts to secure justice, the common individual is not getting their due. This problem has increased with growing complexities of society. But with the growing complexities of society, the desire for justice has become stronger and the quest for it has become more intense.

'What is justice?' The concept is very difficult to define. Many attempts to define it are either thwarted or failed. Justice changes with the advancement of society. Today, individuals want justice not only against one another but against the community and against the state. So many factors combine to make its composition. Many evils that at one time have been part of Indian life for centuries have become crimes, for example, untouchability, bonded labour, dowry practice and so on (Rahman, 1996).

This is evident from the way various thinkers and philosopher conceived the notion of justice. John Rawls conceptualizes justice as fairness. For William Frankena (1962), the concept of a just society should place emphasis on the principle and practice aspects of it. Justice is the notion of allotment of something to a person, in other word, distributive justice that involves comparative allotment. Each theorist therefore defends their own definition, and therefore, it has become problematic to define social justice (Miller, 1976). But each conceptualization is concerned with the distributive character of imparting justice. He further gives three different and conflicting meanings and interpretations of justice as three principles of justice, that is, to each according to his rights, to each according to his deserts, and to each according to his needs (Jogdand et al., 2008).

IMPORTANT THEORIES OF SOCIAL JUSTICE

There are numerous theories of justice and equality. Each theory has a specific target to achieve on the basis of which it is a theory. They have to take into account all the complex conditions. To found a just society, you need the conception of justice. Indian/Hindu conceptions of justice are found in Manusmṛiti and Dharmaśāstra. However, the concept or theory of social justice in the modern sense is probably missing in our ancient texts. But, in the occidental world, the concept and theories of social justice have been found since the days of Socrates and Plato. Socrates' disciples, Thrasymachus and Polemarchus, argued that justice was the 'justice of the strong and wealthy'; Socrates dissented and asserted that justice was based on knowledge for 'knowledge is virtue' and vice versa. Inspired by the teaching of his mentor, Socrates, Plato enunciated a class-based theory of social justice.

The utilitarian theory of justice comes from the ideas and works for social reform introduced by Jeremy Bentham, John Stuart Mill and their followers. Utilitarianism, as a doctrine, argues that the rightness of actions is to be judged by the overall amount of happiness they produce. David Miller distinguishes between four types of utilitarian theories: act utilitarianism, utilitarian generalization, actual-rule utilitarianism and ideal-rule utilitarianism, which try to produce a general amount of happiness in society (Miller, 1976).

Another important theory is propounded by John Rawls (1921–2002). His watershed publication, *A Theory of Justice* (1971), came at a time when serious questions were raised about the future of liberal political theory, especially in his own country, the USA, in the context of the ongoing furious debate over the Vietnam War, raging racial inequality and large-scale unemployment. Rawls, in his theory of justice, seeks to unite the libertarians' ideal of liberalism with economic egalitarianism into a single theoretical structure. He seeks to redefine the relationship between liberty, equality and fraternity. He rejects meritocracy and advocates fair equality of opportunity in order to correct morally arbitrary inequality in society. He is uncompromising on the primacy of liberty but wants society to endeavour to equalize economic wealth, social status and political power (Mukhopadhyay, 2017).

> ### Did You Know?
>
> **The Nozick Theory of Justice**
>
> In opposition to Rawls' theory of justice, Robert Nozick has formulated the idea of social justice as an entitlement. He regards any distribution of resources as just as long as it comes about in accordance with the following three principles.
> - **Justice in acquisition:** The appropriate of unowned things as long as enough is left over for others.
> - **Justice in transfer:** The acquisition of a holding from someone who is entitled to that holding.
> - **Rectification:** Any unjust transfers are to be rectified by compensation. According to Nozick, individuals have a right to own property and have self-ownership, which gives them the freedom to determine what to do. The role of the state is that of a right watchman, whose property is to protect rights. Nozick regards any attempt by the state to redistribute resources, for example, through taxation, as unjust.

SOCIAL JUSTICE UNDER THE CONSTITUTION OF INDIA

A picture of the constitution will give us the right perspective to appreciate the scope and place of social justice as an aspiration of the nation. The former Chief Justice of India, P. N. Bhagwati, inter alia, observed: 'Today a vast social revolution is taking place in the judicial process; the law is fast changing and the problems of the poor are coming to the forefront. The court has to invent new methods and devise new strategies for providing access to justice to large masses of people who are denied their basic human rights and to whom freedom and liberty have no meaning.'

Social justice is the foundation stone of the Indian Constitution. It is found useful for everyone in its kind and flexible form. Although it is not defined anywhere in the Constitution, it is an ideal element of feeling, which is the goal of the Constitution. Social justice is a relative concept that is always changeable according to the circumstances, needs and ambitions of people. However, in our Constitution, it is used in a very broad sense, which includes both social and economic justice. According to the former Chief Justice of India, P. B. Gajendragadkar, 'In this sense social Justice hold the aims of equal opportunity to every citizen in the matter of social and economical activities and to prevent inequalities (Sahay, 1996).'

THE CONCEPT OF ACCESS TO JUSTICE

Social justice concepts and theories have evolved in the 18th–20th centuries as an integral part of the growth of liberal democracies in the West. Access to justice refers, in the words of Professor Upendra Baxi, 'is the availability of effective means to seek justice by which one can participate in the judicial process' (Chitkara, 2000).

It is to be noted that access to justice is not only critical in the enforcement of other substantive rights but it is also a human right in and of itself. One of the fundamental duties of the state in a welfare state is to make justice-delivery mechanisms available to its citizens. Failure to make the necessary means and mechanisms available is tantamount to the denial of justice. In the absence of justice-delivery mechanisms, an individual whose rights have been violated is unable to effectively vindicate those rights. In other situations, although means and mechanisms may be available, citizens may find themselves deprived of justice as the latter may be inaccessible to them. This situation may arise as result of the existence of various impediments that prevent a justice-seeker from gaining effective access (Couto, 2015).

BARRIERS TO ACCESS TO JUSTICE

What are the impediments that may generally hinder citizens from having effective access to justice? Broadly speaking, there are operational barriers and structural barriers to access to justice. Operational barriers are those that are related to the administration of the justice system. Undue delay in the disposal of cases, high costs of litigation, procedural technicalities, unfilled vacancies in judges' posts, poor ration of judges to population and backlog of cases are some of the operational barriers that disallow effective access to justice. While structural barriers reflect problems that have to do with the various basic forms of societal organizations, they are inherently linked to the administration of justice, inadequate laws, lack of legal aid and legal representation, lack of legal awareness, socio-economic inequalities and other factors that compose the structure barriers.

HISTORICAL BACKGROUND OF SOCIAL JUSTICE IN INDIA

In India, the urge for democratic socialism to have a just order has come from Marxist socialist tradition with influence of Marx and Gandhi, Jawaharlal Nehru, Jayaprakash Narayan, Acharya Narendra Deva, Ram Manohar Lohia, Ashok Mehta and Minoo Masani were all influenced by democratic socialism and strove hard for the dissemination and inculcation of those values.

Ambedkarian approach is relevant in Indian context as it goes beyond the different traditions of social justice in India. Thorat (1998) has emphasized the importance of Ambedkarian perspective for social development in India. Ambedkar has presented a radical alternative for social development in India as 'state socialism' in his states and minorities. His social development agenda was different from Nehru and Gandhi is clear when Ambedkar responded to the resolution of Nehru on aims and objectives of future Constitution on 13 December 1946 in the Constituent Assembly.

Ambedkar said,

> I must confess that coming as the resolution does from Pandit Jawaharlal Nehru who is reputed to be a Socialist, this resolution, although non-controversial, is to my mind very disappointment. I should have expected him to go much further than he has done.... There are certain provisions which speak of justice, economic, social and political. I should have expected some provisions whereby it would have been possible for the state to make economic, social and political justice

a reality and I should have from that view expected the Resolution to state in most explicit terms that in order that there may be social and economic justice in the country. (LSS, 2014)

'... Political reforms ... cannot ignore the problem arising out of the prevailing social order' (Ambedkar, 1990).

The Ambedkarian perspective of a just society cannot be confined to his initiatives for the social liberation of Dalits (by annihilation of caste) by framing the Constitution and making provisions for Scheduled Castes/Scheduled Tribes in terms of protective discrimination policy and special measures and safeguards for these groups, though it is extremely important. Ambedkar has provided an alternative to social order in India, which could be free of hegemony, exploitation and oppression based on caste, class, ethnic group, sex and so on (Massey, 2003).

For instance, the position of social justice in ancient times was a sociological jurisprudence in its Indian perspective. It would be necessary to survey the present as well as pre-independence Indian law. The law during the British colonial rule in India was coercive, suppressive and insensitive to the sentiments and needs of the Indian people. The British rulers paralyzed the peace and prosperity of Indians by dividing them on the basis of caste, creed, religion, language and occupation so as to cause conflicts between different communities to meet their selfish ends (Paranjape, 2019).

A large number of Acts were passed related to the issues, namely the abolition of slavery, the prevention of the exploitation of women and children, labour relations, agrarian reforms, the humanization of intuition of marriage and so on, during this period. While making these Acts, the British adhered to a 'caution approach', because they did not want to hurt the sentiments of the Indian people. Apparently, they did not seek public consent on the issues that were likely to shock the public conscience. This cautious approach of the British can be seen in the case of the obnoxious practice of *sati*.

If we look at the position of social justice in medieval times, we find that in 1564, Akbar abolished *jizya* (a type of tax imposed on non-Muslim subjects who lived in a state governed by Islamic law) and began to charge a uniform trade tax on all. This tax was particularly hated by the Hindus as it was a symbol of their inferiority and involved quite a lot of humiliation. The abolition of the *jizya* tax meant that both Hindus and Muslims came to be considered equal citizens of the state. The offices of the state were open to all on merit and without distinction of caste or religion. Akbar noticed many social evils prevailing in society for which both the Hindus and Muslims were responsible. He now embarked upon social reforms which touched both the communities, whether it was child marriage, *sati* practice or encouraging widow remarriage among the Hindus. In 1562, he stopped the practice of converting prisoners of war to Islam. He also abolished the slave trade (Srinivas, 1985).

After independence, social legislation gained a new impetus. The rule of law and the legal system were strengthened considerably. The Constitution of India became the main inspiration for making a variety of laws.

SOCIAL JUSTICE TO VULNERABLE GROUPS

Social groups such as Scheduled Castes, Scheduled Tribes, Other Backward Classes, women, children, minorities and people with disabilities need special focus and attention. According to Article 46, the welfare measures that are directed to the state for the weaker section include promoting with special care their economic and educational interests and protecting them from social injustice and all forms of exploitation.

Although women are an important segment of the human family, they often do not get their due. They undergo pain and suffering of the crime committed against them. There is a need to take a fresh look at the laws and understand why they have failed so miserably. The Criminal Law (Amendment) Act, 2013, was enacted in order to amend the Indian Penal Code, 1860; the Criminal Procedure Code, 1973; the Indian Evidence Act, 1872, and the Protection of Children from Sexual Offences Act, 2012. But even after the amendment, there is no sign of a decline in crime against women (Ahmed, 2018).

India is a welfare state with a constitutional mandate and democratic obligations to ensure the social inclusion of all its citizens, with a special focus on the vulnerable, disadvantaged and weaker sections of society. Empowering them at par with the rest of society as part of social inclusion and inclusive development is the commitment of successive governments to the people of the country. Some of the important measures and interventions can be classified as educational, social, economic, political, employable and affirmative action, that is, reservation in employment, education, political representation and so on (Muniraju, 2019).

THE CONSTITUTIONAL PERSPECTIVE OF SOCIAL JUSTICE

The framers of the Constitution realized that unless unequal people were treated unequally, the socio-economic, political, regional and gender gaps could not be bridged. The compelling social situation led to the creation of special provisions in the Constitution for the advancement of socially and economically backward classes of citizens. Positive discrimination was thought of as a policy mechanism to realize the social goals set before the nation and as a means by which backward citizens could reach the mainstream to achieve social justice (Narayana, 1998).

The Constitution of India has solemnly promised to all its citizens justices: social, economic and political; liberty of thought, expression, belief, faith and worship; equality of status and opportunity, and to promote among all fraternity, assuring the dignity of the individual and the unity of the nation. The Constitution has attempted to attune the apparently conflicting claims of socio-economic justice and of individual liberty and fundamental rights by including some relevant provisions.

Did You Know?

The Constitution as a Living Ideal

The right to life is a fundamental right that the Constitution guarantees to all citizens of this country. As you have read in this book, over the years, this right, or Article 21, has been used by ordinary citizens to include issues to make this right more meaningful and substantial. So, for example, you have read about how the case of the injured farmer, Hakim Sheikh, established the right to health as part of the right to life. Similarly, you read how the case of the slum dwellers being evicted from Mumbai established the right to livelihood as part of the right to life. In this chapter, you have read about how the court ruled in favour of a person's right to the 'enjoyment of pollution-free water and air for the full enjoyment of life' as part of the right to life. In addition to these cases, the courts have also ruled to include the right to education and the right to shelter within this expanded understanding of Article 21.

The above expanded understanding of the Right to Life was achieved through the efforts of ordinary citizens to get justice from the courts when they believed that their Fundamental Rights were being violated. As you read in several instances in this book, these Fundamental Rights have also served time and again as the basis for the making of new laws and establishing certain policies to protect all citizens. All of this is possible because our Constitution contains certain constitutive rules that work towards protecting the dignity and self-respect of all citizens of India and guard against all forms of possible violations. What these should include is spelt out in the various provisions on Fundamental Rights and the rule of law.

DIRECTIVE PRINCIPLES OF STATE POLICY BRING SOCIAL JUSTICE

The Directive Principles of State Policy lay the foundations for a 'welfare state' which needs to work for the weaker sections of society. Accordingly, there is a need to identify specific groups among Scheduled Castes, Scheduled Tribes and Other Backward Classes for whom specific welfare measures could be designed and ensured.

It was also observed that ordinary and indigent people could not pay court fees for seeking justice in the court of law. The existing provision for exemption from court fee for paupers applies only to extremely poor people and is of no use to the ordinary poor litigants who may be able to pay some money but not the entire cost. It has been, therefore, rightly mentioned that the doors of the temple of justice are open with a golden key. It must also be remembered that the mandate of *Article 38 of our Constitution, which reads as follows:* 'The State shall strive to promote the welfare of the people by securing and protecting as effectively as it may a social order in which justice—social, economic and political, shall inform all the institutions of the national life' (Bakshi, 2011).

In India, all states secure economic justice through Article 39, which specifically contains a broader perspective on social justice. Article 39(a) states men and women equally to have the right to adequate means of livelihood; Article 39(b) states the distribution of ownership and control of the material resources of the community to the common good; Article 39(c) ensures the economy does not result in the concentration of wealth and means of production to the detriment of common good; Article 39(d) states that equal pay for equal work to both men and women; Article 39(e) speaks of health and strength of workers, men and women and the measures to prevent exploitation of children, and Article 39(f) directs that children be given opportunity and facilities to develop in a healthy manner and in conditions of freedom and dignity.

THE ROLE OF SOCIAL WORKERS IN LEGAL ASSISTANCE

A wide range of tasks may be allocated to the social work profession in the context of the justice system. There is also every advantage in inviting the social work profession, in keeping with its potential mandate, to contribute to developing relevant policies, legislation and programmes. The justice system is either equipped or mandated to fulfil this role alone and needs to work hard in hand with the social sector towards this end.

The concept of legal aid Article 39 is embodied in our Constitution. It would be apt to quote Justice Bhagwati on legal aid, who can truly be considered the father of public interest litigation in India. His views are especially relevant for social workers. According to him, a legal service programme should have a dynamic and activist content, and it must play many roles and perform diverse functions in the socio-legal system. Legal aid and advice would also improve the quality of justice and equalize the protection of the laws (Singh, 2017). Social workers, by combining their social work skills with para-legal skills, can make a lot of difference to the existing legal aid and assistance services and make them a potent instrument of social change as envisaged by Justice Bhagwati. Professional social workers have to assume a greater responsibility, along with the members of the legal profession, to promote and encourage social advocacy and social action litigation.

We believe that the role of trained social workers in legal aid and assistance programmes is a crucial one, which has not been given the attention it deserves. Recent years have seen an escalation in the awareness of one's rights. Social workers can play a significant role in improving the understanding and interpretation of the economic, social and cultural rights of the poor and vulnerable. Social workers can play the role of an enabler, activist, change agent, counsellor or advisor, depending on the issues and the needs of the clientele.

Social workers respect the distinct systems of beliefs and lifestyles of individuals, families, group's communities and nations without prejudice. Social workers, in particular, do not tolerate discrimination on the basis of age, abilities, ethnic background, gender, language, marital status, national ancestry, political affiliation, race, religion, sexual orientation or socio-economic status.

SOCIAL JUSTICE THROUGH WELFARE LEGISLATION

The welfare legislations was enacted during the post-independence era. The establishment of the human rights commission, women's commission, family courts, industrial tribunals, administrative tribunals, ombudsman, Panchayati Raj, Lok Adalat and so on are only a few illustrations to suggest that the sole objective is to make justice available to the common individual and ameliorate the sufferings of the masses, including women, children and other neglected and weaker sections of society. The laws relating to consumers protection, dowry prohibition, abolition of bonded labour, control of environmental pollution and so on have been enacted to provide social justice. As of January 2017, there were about *1,248 laws*. However, since there are central as well as state laws, it is difficult to ascertain their exact numbers on a given date, and the best way to find the central laws in India is from the official websites.

THE ROLE OF JUDICIARY AS A DISPENSER OF SOCIAL JUSTICE

It may be emphasized once again that expecting judiciary alone to provide a complete answer to the miseries of millions is an illusion. It is necessary that the two other organs of state, that is, the governors and the administration, should make it a common cause by joining hands with the judiciary on the principle of cooperation, mutual respect and good will. A hostile attitude on the part of the governors and bureaucrats, can thwart all the attempts of the judiciary in this direction to a very large extent.

Although the concept of social justice has no definite and fixed meaning, the Supreme Court in *D. S. Nakara & Others v. Union of India* has observed that the principal aim of socialism is to eliminate inequality in income, status and standard of life and to provide a decent standard of life to the working people. The expression 'social and economic justice' involves the concept of 'distributive justice', which can be defined as the removal of economic inequalities and the rectifying of injustice resulting from dealings or transactions between the unequal in society. Giving debt relief or regulation of contractual relations, social justice, therefore, encompasses more than the lessening of inequalities by differential fixation.

In the *Kesavananda Bharti case*, the Supreme Court declared that India is a welfare state as the basic structure in a parliamentary democracy. Further lead was taken in Minerva Mill's case, and the Supreme Court put on firm hold that the directive principles and fundamental rights should be harmoniously interpreted as two wheels of the chariot to establish an egalitarian social order. After the *Champakam Dorairajan case* (1951), the state should protect them from social injustice and all forms of exploitation. The *Rangachari* (1962) and *Thomas* (1976) case declared that reservation in promotions is a part of equality in Article 16(1), which was reiterated in the *Indira Sawhney case* (1993), that Article 16(4) is facet of Article 16(1) itself. Social justice for Scheduled Castes and Scheduled Tribes for socio-economic equality in results on par with other social group citizens has constitutionally been guaranteed to them. Protection of the minorities in Articles 29 and 30 is a facet of the right to social justice and prohibition on grounds of religion is outlawed by guaranteeing freedom of religion, the right to practice their choice and the right to manage their institutions subject to social welfare of their constituents.

The apex court in *Ashok Kumar Gupta v. State of UP* (1997) 5 SCC 201 (Para 26) held that the term 'social justice' is a fundamental right. In Ajaib *Singh v. Sirhind Cooperative Marketing-cum-Processing Service Society Ltd* (1999) 6 SCC 82 (Para 5), the court observed that in dealing with industrial disputes, the courts should keep in mind the doctrine of social justice. The Supreme Court in *Municipal Corporation of Delhi v. Female Workers (Muster Roll)* (2000), 3 SCC 224 (Para 32 and 33): AIR 2000 SC 1274), held that the provision entitling maternity leave under the Maternity Benefit Act, 1961, even to women engaged on a casual basis or on a muster roll basis on daily wage and not only to those in regular employment, is in consonance with the doctrine of social justice and any contention against it is contrary.

SUMMARY

In spite of the tremendous progress in almost all areas, especially in the economy, science and technology and infrastructure development, the gap between the poor and the rich is increasing day by day. In India, courts have played a great role in making the social justice successful. In the field of distributive justice, both the legislature and judiciary play a great role, but the courts play more powerful role in delivering compensatory or corrective justice. These principles are regarded as mutually relative, not mutually opposite. Ideals and goals are to deliver social justice.

> In keeping silent about evil, in burying it so deep within us that no sign of it appears on the surface, we are implanting it, and it will rise up a thousand fold in the future. When we neither punish nor reproach evil doers, we are not simply protecting their trivial old age, we are thereby ripping the foundation of Justice from beneath new generations. (Sharma, 2017)

TOP 10 TAKEAWAYS/MAIN POINTS

1. Justice as fairness is the idea that was fully developed and presented in book form in 1971 by John Rawls.
2. Social justice refers to people's ability to achieve their full potential in the society in which they live.
3. Justice, especially corrective justice or distributive justice, refers to ensuring that individuals both fulfil their duties and receive what they are due based on interactions with other people.
4. Social legislation is the laws that generally protect and assist the weaker member of society by promoting the common good.
5. A concept based upon the belief that each individual and group within a given society has a right to civil liberties, equal opportunity, fairness and participation in the educational, economic, institutional, social and moral freedoms and responsibilities valued by the community in social justice.
6. There has been a striving for holistic empowerment of women and children through laws, policies, programmes, capacity-building, training and awareness-creation.
7. There are differences between affirmative action programmes employed in the West and reservation policies in India. Yet considering that both aim at remedying existing inequalities, this chapter does not foreground their differences but treats them as an endeavour towards social and political justice.
8. Article 38 of our Constitution states that 'the State shall strive to promote the welfare of the people by securing and protecting as effectively as it may a social order in which justice—social, economic and political, shall inform all the institutions of the national life'.
9. The utilitarian theory of justice comes from the ideas and works for social reform introduced by Jeremy Bentham, John Stuart Mill and their followers.
10. David Miller distinguishes between four types of utilitarian theories: act utilitarianism, utilitarian generalization, actual-rule utilitarianism and ideal-rule utilitarianism, which try to produce a general amount of happiness in society.

Keywords: Judicial activism, social justice, social work, public interest litigation, legal aid

GLOSSARY

Judicial activism: Judicial activism is a way of exercising judicial power that motivates judges to depart from their normally practised strict adherence to judicial precedent in favour of progressive and new social policies. It is commonly marked by a decision calling for social engineering and, occasionally, its philosophy holds that the courts can and should go beyond the applicable law to consider broader societal implications of their decisions. It is sometimes used as an antonym for judicial restraint.

Legal aid: Legal aid is the provision of assistance to people, particularly to working classes, women, Scheduled Castes and Scheduled Tribes and other weaker sections who are unable to afford legal representation and access to the court system. Legal aid is regarded as central to providing access to justice by ensuring equality before the law, the right to counsel and the right to a fair trial.

Public interest litigation: It is the use of the legal system to advance human rights and equality or to raise issues of broad public concern. It helps advance the cause of minority or disadvantaged groups or individuals. Public interest causes may arise from both public and private law matters. It is the power given to the public by the courts through judicial activism.

Social justice: It is a social work principle that involves ensuring everyone has the same basic rights, protections and opportunities and addressing inequalities and injustice in order to eliminate oppression and unequal treatment. It is understood as the right of the weak, aged, destitute, poor, women, children and other underprivileged persons.

Social work: Social work is a practice-based profession and an academic discipline that promotes social change and development, social cohesion, and the empowerment and liberation of people. Principles of social justice, human rights, collective responsibility, and respect for diversities are central to social work. Underpinned by theories of social work, social sciences, humanities and indigenous knowledge, social work engages people and structures to address life challenges and enhance wellbeing. The above definition may be amplified at national and/or regional levels (IFSW, 2014).

ANALYTICAL QUESTIONS

1. Write a paragraph on the various measures of social justice in the constitution to protect the vulnerable sections of society.
2. How was social justice treated earlier? What has been the change in perception? Discuss.

MULTIPLE CHOICE QUESTIONS

1. The right to equality, one of the fundamental rights, is enunciated in the constitution under Part III, Article _____.
   a. 12
   b. 13
   c. **14**
   d. 15

2. Social legislation acts as an instrument of _____.
   a. Social justice
   b. Social development
   c. Social action
   d. **Social change**

3. Social justice is _____.
   a. Reformative in character
   b. Collectivist in nature
   c. Legal justice
   d. Preferential treatment in favour of the weaker section
   Find out the correct combination.
   i. **a, b and c**
   ii. a, b and d
   iii. b, c and d
   iv. b and c only

4. Certain human rights which cannot be limited or suspended under any circumstances are best called _____.
   a. Derogable rights
   b. **Non-derogable rights**
   c. Negative rights
   d. Positive rights

5. Assertion (A): Social justice does not mean equality.
   Reason (R): Social justice demands reverse discrimination in favour of the worst off.
   a. Both (A) and (R) are true, but (R) is not the correct explanation of (A).
   b. (A) is true, and (R) is false.
   c. **(C) (A) is false but (R) is true.**
   d. (D) Both (A) and (R) are true, and (R) is the correct explanation of (A).

6. Social justice is the balance between_____.
   a. **Individual's rights and social control**
   b. Society and individual
   c. Fundamental rights and judicial system
   d. Individual and family

7. The concept of social justice have emerged out of a process of _____.
   a. Individual rights
   b. Social practices
   c. **Social norms, order, law and morality**
   d. Religion, caste and community

8. Who was a pioneer of the movement for social justice in India?
   a. **M. K. Gandhi**
   b. J. Nehru
   c. Dr B. R. Ambedkar
   d. L. B. Shastri

9. Who is regarded as the 'Champion of Social Justice' in India?
   a. M. K. Gandhi
   b. **Dr B. R. Ambedkar**
   c. Dr Rajendra Prasad
   d. Jyotiba Phule

10. Which article of the Indian Constitution provides for the abolition of untouchability?
    a. Article 15
    b. Article 16
    c. **Article 17**
    d. Article 18

REVIEW QUESTION

1. What do you mean by the concept of social justice?

REFERENCES

Ahmed, I. (2018). Gender justice in India: Laws and the society. *Legal News & View, 32*(1), 2–4.

Agarwal, B., Humphries, J., & Robeyns, I. (2006), *Capabilities, freedom, and equality: Amartya Sen's work from a gender perspective.* Oxford University Press.

Bakshi, P. M. (2011). *The Constitution of India* (11th ed.). Universal Law Publishing.

Chaturvedi, R. G. (1975). *Natural and social justice.* Law Book Company, p. 469.

Chitkara, M. G. (2000). Accessibility of justice. *Nyaya Path, 4*(4), 81.

Couto, K. R. (2015). Overcoming impediments to access to justice. *Legal News and View, 29*(12).

Dadhich, N. (ed.). (2017). *The idea of 'justice as fairness'.* Rawat Publication.

Frankena, W. (1962). The concept of social justice. In B. Richard (Ed.), *Social justice.* Prentice-Hall.

IFSW. (2014). *Global Definition of the Social Work Profession.* https://www.ifsw.org/what-is-social-work/global-definition-of-social-work/

Jogdand, P. G., Bansode, P., Meshram, N. G. (Eds). (2008). *Globalization and social justice: Perspective, challenges and praxis.* Rawat Publications.

LSS. (2014). *Constituent Assembly Debates.* Official report. https://eparlib.nic.in/bitstream/123456789/762978/1/cad_09-12-1946.pdf

Mukhopadhyay, A. (2017). Rawls's theory of justice. In M.P. Dube (Ed.), *Social justice: Distributive principles and beyond.* Rawat Publication.

Muniraju, S. B. (2019). Social inclusion: Strategies and way forward. *Yojana, 63.*

Massey, J. (2003). *Dr B. R. Ambedkar: A study in just society.* Manohar Publications.

Miller, D. (1976). *Social justice.* Oxford University Press.

Narayana, K. S. (1998). Redefined goals of positive discrimination. *Deccan Herald,* p. 54.

Paranjape, V. N. (2019). *Jurisprudence and legal theory.* Central Law Agency.

Rahman, I. (1996). Search of justice: Problems and prospects. In D. R. Saxena (Ed.), *Law, justice and social change.* Deep and Deep Publication.

S.P. Gupta v. Union of India, AIR 1982 SC 49 C198, Writ Petition case No. 19 of 1981 Petitioner: S.P Gupta. Respondents: Union of India decided on 30.12.1981.

Sahay, S. (1996). *Social Justice' Judicial Training & Research Institute (JTRI) Journal* (4 &5), Lucknow, Uttar Pradesh, India.

Sharma, M. (2017). Constitution of India and social justice. *International Journal of Scientific Development & Research (IJSDR), Chhattisgarh, India, 2*(5). Retrieved from www.ijsdr.org (accessed on 25 May 2022).

Singh, V. (2017). Role of Justice P.N. Bhagwati in shaping up legal aid in India. *International Journal of Advanced Research (IJAR),* 5(7). Retrieved from www. journal ijar.com.

Srinivas, H. V. (1985). *History of India* (2nd ed.). Eastern Book Company, p. 254.

Thorat, S. (1998). *Ambedkar's role in economic planning and water policy.* Shipra Publications.

RECOMMENDED READINGS

Capeheart, L., & Milovanovic, D. (2018). *Social justice: Theories, issues and movements*. Rawat Publication.
Cybil, K. V. (Ed.). (2020). *Social justice: Interdisciplinary inquiries from India*. Routledge.
Margaret, A. (2019). *Sociologist and social justice*. SAGE Publications.

9
Social Legislations
Eshita Sharma

LEARNING OBJECTIVES
- To understand the concept of social legislation
- To examine its relationship with social work
- To trace its historical roots in the country
- To list and briefly discuss the various social legislations in the country

Legislation alone cannot by itself solve deep rooted social problems. One has to approach them in other ways too, but legislation is necessary and essential, so that it may give that push and have that educative factor as well as legal sanctions behind it, which will help public opinion to be given a certain shape.

—Jawaharlal Nehru

INTRODUCTION

Social legislation is defined as that branch of the law which is an aggregate of the laws relating to the various socio-economic conditions of the people. These laws are enacted keeping in mind the 'needs of the time, the circumstances of the nation and its socio-political ideals'.

Social legislation encompasses addressing social problems through 'legislative means'. The importance of social legislation, in general, and with regard to social work, in particular, could be gauged from the fact that it has been referred to as laws 'designed to improve and protect the economic and social position of those groups in society which, because of age, sex, race, physical or mental defect or lack of economic power, cannot achieve healthy and decent living standards for themselves' (Fairchild, cited in Sehgal, 2017 p. 35).

Hence, social legislation has become important to safeguard social justice, facilitate social reform and usher in desired social change. It also plays an instrumental role in promoting social welfare and protecting and promoting the rights of socio-economically disadvantaged groups in society.

Because social workers work in various settings and organizations, knowledge of the law and its application becomes very significant for social workers. There are a large number of laws covering various settings, which include mental health, children and adolescents, street children, families and the law, education, care and protection of children, adoption, domestic violence and legal issues in healthcare and mental health. The social worker needs to be aware of the rights and responsibilities, duties and infringements of the law of/by their clients. It is noteworthy that mere knowledge of such laws would not serve the aims of social workers; they need to understand the implications of the application of such laws.

Further, the role of social legislation in social work becomes important as it plays a pertinent role in ensuring social justice. It also plays a critical role in ensuring the fundamental rights of citizens across class, caste and gender. Further, the role of social legislation comes in handy here in providing 'proper formalized legal framework to achieve these goals'. The country, with several kinds of deprivations, needs such a framework to ensure social justice and promote social change in the desired direction. The role of social legislation then becomes significant in addressing the current social needs and problems. As one of the authors rightly suggests, social legislation 'aims to address social problems through legislative means and initiates a process of social reform and social change based on sound social rules'.

Some of the other definitions of social legislation are as follows.

According to *Merriam-Webster's Advanced Learner's English Dictionary*, social legislation is the exercise of the power and function of making rules that have the force of authority by virtue of their promulgation by an official organ of the state. Gangrade (1978) asserts that social legislations 'involves an active process of remedy by preventing or changing the wrong course of society or by selecting among the courses that are proved to be right'.

Saxena (1965) defines social legislation as 'any act passed by the legislature or a decree issued by the government for the removal of certain social evils or for the improvement of social conditions or with the aim of bringing about social reform'. Sehgal (2017) defines it as special laws which are passed for the special purposes of improving the socio-economic position of specific groups such as women, children, elderly, scheduled castes, scheduled tribes, physically and mentally challenged, unorganized workers, agricultural and landless labourers and other such vulnerable groups.

SOCIAL LEGISLATION AND SOCIAL WORK: THE ROLE OF THE SOCIAL WORKER

The importance of social legislation in social work cannot be undermined. The knowledge of the legal framework and the provision of clients belonging to certain sections becomes instrumental in making the tasks of social workers more effective. Since social legislation is geared towards achieving social justice, it assists social workers in achieving justice pertaining to individual/respective situations and contexts of their clients/target population. If a social worker is placed in an agency providing counselling services to women in distress, then their comprehensive knowledge of various legislation for protection and promotion of women's rights will ensure that the intervention is effective.

HELPING THE CLIENT CHOOSE THE BEST ALTERNATIVE AVAILABLE

It is only when they are aware of the rights and rules and various provisions of the law related to dowry, marriage, divorce, property rights, inheritance, maternity benefits and other basic rights guaranteed through the Constitution, that they will be able to help their clients to help themselves. This will come in handy in ensuring that they are aware of the best alternatives available to them under the law and make an informed choice with the guidance of the social worker. The social worker, aware of the various provisions of legislation against domestic violence, will be able to inform their client who is suffering any form of domestic violence at home about the various options available to them under the law, thereby helping the client exercise the right to self-determination by choosing from the alternatives available to them through the provisions of the law.

AWARENESS GENERATION

The social workers could also play a very crucial role in terms of generating awareness about various social legislations to the target population. Owing to their lack of education and access to resources, a large section of vulnerable population for whom the legislations have been made, would be unaware about existence of such legislations. Even if they have heard about it, they would not know the procedure of how to avail the benefits ensured thorough various provisions of legislations. The complex legal language could deter few (who are aware) to avail the provisions. Hence, the role of the Social Worker is integral here.

Years of negative gender norms have left many women bereft of self respect, dignity and self belief. Interventions need to be planned to address this and bring positive behaviour change lest the awareness of these laws by them will be ineffective. Hence awareness generation needs to be planned alongside behaviour change activities. The social worker plays a critical role by tying up with various media planners and influencers to come up with interventions that will address this factor.

ADVOCACY

The social worker will be aware of what legal provisions are available to address the current problems and situations and will be able to advocate for change in the existing law (modification of a clause), repeal of certain existing laws acting as impediments to the progress of certain sections (Section 377, before the landmark ruling repealing it) and inclusion of certain provisions in the law for the promotion of certain sections. For instance, the provisions under the Maternity Benefit Act are available to certain sections of female staff. There is a need for advocacy to make its provisions available/applicable to women working across sectors, regardless of the nature of their job (permanent/contractual/ad hoc). The social worker can play an instrumental role in this regard.

SOCIAL LEGISLATION AND SOCIAL CHANGE

Social legislation helps in facilitating the process of the welfare of certain 'vulnerable' sections of society. It helps them exercise and realize the rights guaranteed in the constitution. It assists in the process of bringing in and maintaining social change. A series of laws related to women, children, the elderly and particular castes have been instrumental in providing a legal framework for improving the conditions of these sections. Although there are still many impediments to ensuring complete social justice in these sections, social legislation has been instrumental in ushering in a certain level of change. Social legislation related to women has ensured that they have the same basic rights as men, such as equal pay for equal work and right to inherit and succeed. Certain laws have ensured social ills such as dowry and domestic violence have a mechanism to be dealt with and have secured basic rights of dignity for women. Likewise, legislation related to certain sections has made discrimination practised against those sections punishable by law, thus attempting to improve their status in society.

Social legislation ensures that the status and conditions of certain vulnerable sections improve, thereby contributing to social change. The patriarchal nature of society makes women live in pathetic and vulnerable conditions where they are denied even their basic rights of equality and living with dignity. The same is true with people belonging to certain 'backward' castes. This sort of discrimination has been rooted in social customs and norms, and certain social legislation in this regard has helped usher in some social change and attempted to bring about a change in the status and conditions of these vulnerable sections. Although it is far from satisfactory, it is much better than what it used to be when people belonging to certain castes were denied even the basic rights of taking water from community wells, going to temples, using other public facilities, such as roads and transport, and where women suffered harassment due to customs of dowry or domestic violence. This change has been ensured by a set of legislation attempting to address the discrimination suffered by these sections and improve their status and conditions. Hence, social legislation plays a crucial role in ensuring and maintaining social change.

SOCIAL LEGISLATION AND SOCIAL JUSTICE

A very important part of social work is making the clients aware about their rights. This includes making them aware of the remedies with which they have to exercise these rights. The legal language and system could be complicated for some clients, and it would be difficult for them to apply it in their own context. The social worker's role here is to make them aware of the options available to the clients based on legal provisions and help them understand those options (provisions) in their respective context. Hence, when clients are not aware of their basic rights or their other rights are being infringed upon, the knowledge and awareness of various aspects of social legislation by social workers comes in handy.

Only when the social worker knows about the legal provisions related to the clients they are working with, will they be able to help the clients address the issue in the best manner possible. For instance, if a social worker is working with a woman who has been facing harassment from her in-laws because of 'dowry', then for the social worker, knowledge about the various

Social Legislations

provisions of the Dowry Prohibition Act, 1961, becomes highly imperative. Only by making them aware of such a law and its provisions, will the rights of the woman be effectively protected and social justice ensured. Hence, in that sense, social workers become facilitators to ensure application of various aspects of social legislation and thereby ensure social justice for their clients/target population.

ADDRESSING SOCIAL PROBLEMS THROUGH LEGISLATIVE MEANS

Immoral trafficking, child labour, child marriage, juvenile justice and practices arising from low status accorded to women in the country are some of the social problems that could be dealt with effectively using social legislation. These issues are rooted in societal structure and are quite difficult to address without a proper legal framework. Hence, laws addressing these conditions are quite critical in the context of social work.

> ### Did You Know?
>
> **Legislation Related to Women**
>
> - The Immoral Traffic (Prevention) Act, 1956
> - The Dowry Prohibition Act, 1961 (28 of 1961; amended in 1986)
> - The Indecent Representation of Women (Prohibition) Act, 1986
> - The Commission of Sati (Prevention) Act, 1987 (3 of 1988)
> - The Protection of Women from Domestic Violence Act, 2005
> - The Sexual Harassment of Women at Workplace (Prevention, Prohibition and Redressal) Act, 2013
> - The Criminal Law (Amendment) Act, 2013
> - The Maternity Benefit Amendment Act, 2017
> - The Indian Penal Code, 1860
> - The Indian Evidence Act, 1872

SPECIFIC SOCIAL LEGISLATION IN THE COUNTRY

The legislation in the country has attempted to address the social problems arising from certain customs and norms that deny women their basic rights to live with dignity and equality. Although some were initiated by the British and followed ardently by Indian social reformers to bring about the change in the status of women, many others have been introduced and attempt to safeguard their rights, promote their welfare and protect women from the repercussions of certain customs. The legislation protects them against the ill effects of dowry and makes it punishable by law, sexual harassment at the workplace, domestic violence and ensures equal pay for equal work and maternity benefits.

It is noteworthy that the introduction and passing of this legislation has been only part of the struggle to bring about change in the position and status of women in the country. The patriarchal structure is so deeply rooted that, despite established laws, people find their way out of it. In some cases, they do not fear punishment owing to the social influence they have and feel they can be above the law, while in other cases, the loopholes in the laws allow easy escape for offenders. Further, the lack of knowledge of women about their rights also becomes a lacunae. Hence, many experts feel that a very intricate part of social legislation is to have strict provisions with no room for loopholes. This holds true, especially with regard to those related to women. Positive gender norms and values need to be promoted alongside the introduction of stricter legislation. Only the introduction of legislation without attempts to address the patriarchal attitude will be ineffective.

This is one of the reasons that despite the banning of act of sati by the British government, the practice has been prevalent. A major ceremony was performed, defying the rule of the law in 1986. Roop Kunwar, an 18-year-old woman, performed sati by burning herself alive along with funeral pyre of her husband. This was decades after the practice was legally banned, and to the shock of many, it was conducted as a public ceremony with many attendees. The news of this heinous and inhuman practice, conducted in a glorified manner, led to a huge public outrage which led to the Sati (Prevention) Act, 1987.

The practice is still performed in some parts of the country. In fact, that such a practice, which perceives the identity of a woman only in relation to her living husband, still thrives in parts of the country, calls for more stringent measures of social legislation for women in the country. However, this should be coupled with efforts to change the thinking of society by promoting positive gender norms and values. Further, the social legislation would be effective only if was strong both in terms of its provisions and implementation.

The loopholes are there and it takes time, but the fact remains that the legislation is in place and it is owing to these that certain practices have been controlled if not abolished. This is no reason to celebrate, since the stricter implementation of law is the need of the hour. However, with the introduction of legislation, the first step has been taken in the direction of protecting women from the excesses of patriarchal society.

Domestic violence is one such menace that makes their lives miserable on a day-to-day basis. Owing to the patriarchal set-up, a large number of women suffer and live in abysmal conditions on a day-to-day basis. Hence, the importance of the *Protection of Women from Domestic Violence Act, 2005*, in the context of safeguarding the rights of women to live with dignity and improving the conditions of women cannot be undermined as it has 'civil remedies with criminal procedures to ensure effective protection and immediate relief to victims of violence of any kind occurring within the family'. This becomes all the more important when keeping in view the prevalent issue of domestic violence in the country.

Studies reflect that one of the deterrents for self-reporting in domestic violence is fear of how society will perceive such women who defy social norms. Further, in many cases, women are financially dependent on male members and worry that any voice raised in the matter of violence they suffer will lead to their future being insecure. Hence, the role of the social worker here becomes to lay the background and create an environment conducive to the utilization of legal provisions. They counsel women that such behaviour needs to be reported and is punishable by law; it is their right to report such cases and raise their voice against such i treatment. Efforts need to be made to change the attitude of women towards their status in family and society, as well as to boost their self-esteem. This is in addition to making women aware of various provisions of the law.

Yet another crime that is committed against women and has its roots in perverse patriarchal norms is dowry. It is yet another social malpractice that has played a pertinent role in maintaining the 'low status' accorded to women at the household and societal level in the country. The practice of giving gifts to the groom's family during the marriage of the daughter has led to the perception of daughters as 'burdens' on their parents. This is intricately linked to other grave social issues plaguing the nation, especially female feticide and female infanticide, malnutrition, discrimination against children, low status of women, violence and dowry-related physical and mental torture.

The Dowry Prohibition Act, 1961 (28 of 1961; amended in 1986) attempts to address these issues by making the exchange of dowry punishable by law. The amendment was made to the Criminal Procedure Code in 1983, which made cruelty to and harassment of a woman by her dowry-seeking husband or his relatives punishable by law. This was followed by a further amendment of the Act in 1984 that made both 'giving and receiving dowry cognizable offences'. Yet another crucial amendment was passed in 1986. It defined 'dowry death and made it compulsory to conduct post-mortem of a woman who had committed suicide or died in suspicious circumstances within seven years of her marriage' (Ministry of Women and Child Development, 2019a).

Despite this law, the menace continues to grow, even amongst the 'educated' families. Critiques feel the dowry-related law has several loopholes which need to be strengthened. This is especially with regard to conviction cases. Few, however, also believes that this law has resulted in misutilization of provisions of law sometimes by women to falsely accuse their husbands and thus advocate for the inclusion of provisions to address this aspect.

In addition to the routine challenges women face in the workplace owing to gender discrimination in certain matters, this discrimination becomes manifold when they have to take a leave of absence from work owing to the condition of pregnancy. To ensure that the condition of pregnancy does not affect their professional goals and due to commitment to professional goals, they do not force themselves to work during critical periods of pregnancy and child birth, *the Maternity Amendment Act, 2017*, was passed with the objective of protecting and empowering women as workers. Further, it was amended in 1995 to protect the dignity of motherhood. The act was further amended in 2017 and safeguards the employment of women during maternity and ensures she is guaranteed 'maternity benefit', which is 'full paid absence from work to take care of her child' for a period of 26 weeks (Ministry of Women and Child Development, 2019b).

The legislation, a much needed intervention, has been welcomed and has provided respite to many women. However, the benefits of such legal protection are not enjoyed by women in the informal sector. The fact that women in the informal sector 'constitute 93 per cent of India's workforce' becomes all the more important. Thus, this crucial period for women working in the informal sector becomes physically and mentally strenuous. Many are either forced to quit their jobs after pregnancy/delivery or are forced to rejoin their work immediately after delivery. In many sectors, women working in contractual and ad hoc jobs go through mental and physical discomfort and agony since the provisions of the law do not extend to their jobs. Thus, for such women, the critical period during pregnancy and after delivery becomes more stressful owing to the insecure nature of their jobs and lack of maternity benefits and protection.

Yet legislation exists to ensure a just environment in the workplace and allow them to work with dignity. The Sexual Harassment of Women at Workplace (Prevention, Prohibition and Redressal) Act, 2013, includes provisions to protect (prevent, prohibit and redress) women from workplace harassment. The role of social workers has become more pertinent in such work environments. They engage in generating awareness amongst employees about the law and assisting in the facilitation of cases filed by the employees.

THE CRIMINAL LAW (AMENDMENT) ACT, 2013

One of the most prevalent, under-reported and heinous crimes against women in the country is sexual violence. Rooted deeply in the patriarchal values that perceive women as 'properties' to be exploited by men are the various forms of sexual violence that are committed in many parts of the country, differences in education, class and regions notwithstanding. Despite more than half a century of independence, the country's capital city was rocked by one of the most inhuman crimes; the gang rape of a female student on 16 December 2012 in the capital of the country. The crime was met with huge public outrage and mass protests across the country and the world. The inhuman incident was condemned by civil society, public figures, political heads and organizations across the globe. The United Nations Entity for Gender Equality and the Empowerment of Women expressly asked the Government of India to 'do everything in their power to take up radical reforms, ensure justice and reach out with robust public services to make women's lives more safe and secure'. The outrage and attention to the case led to the government forming a committee (Justice Verma Committee; 22 December 2012) within 6 days of the heinous incident to suggest amendments to various provisions of the criminal law. The committee received a huge number of suggestions and petitions in this regard and submitted a report within a month.

The report categorically stated 'failures on the part of the government and police were the root cause of crimes against women'.

The ordinance was passed within a month and later a bill was passed by the Lok Sabha on 19 March 2013. The law, though increased the punishment and also the scope of what constitutes a sexual offence, has been criticized by various groups. Many feel it is heavily gender-biased. Also, it has been criticized strongly for turning a blind eye to many critical suggestions recommended by the report of the Justice Verma Committee. These include marital rape, reducing the age of consent and amending Armed Forces (Special Powers) Act so that no sanction is needed when prosecuting an armed force personnel accused of a crime against a woman. Although the act in itself and its provisions were applauded and welcomed, experts are concerned about the loopholes that are still there in the law.

The fact that a woman had to go through this perverse form of violence for act to gain more teeth is one of the most unfortunate truths that will continue to rock the nation's conscience for ages to come. Despite this, sexual violence against women continues to prevail. At the heart of it is a lack of effective implementation and low conviction rates, along with an improvement in the status of women. The scope of intervention by social work increases manifold in the context of such offences. By working efficiently, the social workers may prove to be an effective link in the context of improving the situation.

Despite stringent laws, crimes against women show no signs of stopping and, in some instances, are 'deprived of basic freedom and thereby exposed to easy exploitation by the male-dominated society'. Even when the culprits are booked and the case registered against them under the existing legislation, the case drags on for years, and the victim and her family 'suffer' through these years and keep on their struggle for justice.

The length of time the case is dragged in court is one of the impediments to conviction for crimes/injustice against women. Many do not have the energy or the time to put up with these delayed hearings and finally give up. This is also one of the major deterrents for women and their family members not filing cases against crimes committed against them. In the meantime, if the case has not garnered media attention, then victims and/or witnesses' families are coerced and tortured by the alleged criminals' side to give up the case. Weak witness protection programmes thus act as a deterrent.

Perverse forms of violence are accepted by women and have been promoted for generations due to archaic and patriarchal norms and values that govern social life in the country. Women become objects of physical and emotional violence across regions and classes. The understanding of the prevalence of such practices becomes significant if one has to address them. Although legislation alone will not help to counter the forces that prevent women from living a life of equality and dignity, it is one of the fundamental requirements. Further, the need for change in the attitude of society towards women and the position it accords them cannot be overemphasized.

Did You Know?

Children Welfare

- Juvenile Justice (Care and Protection of Children) Act, 2015
- The Prohibition of Child Marriage Act, 2006
- The Protection of Children From Sexual Offences (Amendment) Act, 2019
- The Child Labour (Prohibition and Regulation) Act, 1986

The legislation (*the Juvenile Justice [Care and Protection of Children] Act, 2015*) related to child welfare has two sections: selling alcohol or drugs to a child punishable by law and the trading of children as slaves strictly punishable by law. The legislation also makes the adoption process of 'orphaned, abandoned and surrendered children' less complicated. The Juvenile Justice Act of 2000 was amended in 2015 with a provision allowing for Children in Conflict with Law to be tried as adults under certain circumstances. The other section of the law deals with providing care and protection for children who have been separated from their guardians. The law has provisions related to the procedure to be followed for the protection and care of children who have been separated from their guardians. The role of the child welfare committee and of the social worker in terms of providing protection and care to the children becomes prominent (Save the Children, 2018).

The Prohibition of Child Marriage Act, 2006, secures child rights by criminalizing child marriage and prohibiting the 'engagement of children in certain employments and regulating the conditions of work or children in certain other employments'. Legislation is also in place for the protection of children from offences of sexual assault, sexual harassment and pornography (the Protection of Children from Sexual Offences [Amendment] Act, 2019) and attempts 'to safeguard the interests of the child at every stage of the judicial process' (Child Marriage Restraint Act, 2019).

CASTES

In a caste-ridden society like India, people belonging to certain castes have suffered discrimination and have been denied the right to live a life of dignity for a long time. They had suffered discrimination in terms of the utilization of resources and facilities, including education, job opportunities and public facilities (roads, temples, wells, schools and utensils). Despite more than six decades of independence, this sort of discrimination is still practised in many parts of the country. This practice violates the fundamental principle of social justice and has been addressed through the Scheduled Castes and Tribes (Prevention of Atrocities) Act, 1989. Along with safeguarding them against all forms of discrimination, the Act has many provisions to ensure the overall development of people belonging to certain castes.

PERSONS WITH DISABILITIES

The country is home to a significant number of persons with disabilities. Their population is larger than the total population of many countries in the world, and India is one of the countries having the highest numbers of people with disabilities globally (Jha, 2017). However, despite being in large numbers, they face impediments to leading a life of dignity. They face certain discrimination and prejudice owing to certain preconceived notions about their abilities. To ensure this and safeguard their rights and to ensure their overall development and provide them with equal opportunities, legislation has been introduced. The Persons with Disabilities (Equal Opportunities, Protection of Rights and Full Participation) Act, 1995, ensures:

> Both the preventive and promotional aspects of rehabilitation like education, employment and vocational training, reservation, research and manpower development, creation of barrier-free environment, rehabilitation of persons with disability, unemployment allowance for the disabled, special insurance scheme for the disabled employees and establishment of homes for persons with severe disability etc. (Think Change, 2016)

Mental health legislation is essential for protecting the rights and dignity of persons with mental disorders and for developing accessible and effective mental health services. Hence, the importance of the Mental Health Act of 1987. The Rehabilitation Council of India Act, 1992, has provisions to regulate 'the training of rehabilitation professionals and to maintain a Central Rehabilitation Register to certify rehabilitation professionals' (indiankanoon.org, 2018).

SUMMARY

Social legislation plays a key role in ensuring social justice and promoting social change. They are formulated keeping in mind the needs of the citizens and the nation. Its importance in a country like India becomes manifold, keeping in view the many social problems leading to (or being led by) exploitation and unequal treatment of certain vulnerable sections.

Social legislation addresses various social problems through 'legislative means'. Its relationship with social work could be realized by the fact that these laws are formulated to safeguard the socio-economic position of certain vulnerable groups. Hence, social legislation has become important to safeguard social justice, facilitate social reform and usher in desired social change. It also plays an instrumental role in promoting social welfare and protecting and promoting the rights of socio-economically disadvantaged groups in society.

The following are the roles of a social worker:

1. **Generating awareness about their rights of women and laws that are there to protect them:** The scope of these campaigns needs to be extended beyond urban areas. However, there is a significant population that needs to be made aware of their rights and legislation for them. The role of the social worker becomes quite pivotal here. First, they have to discuss the provisions of the law in layman's language. Efforts need to be made to make sure that they understand the provisions and rights in their informal day-to-day language. The legal and formal language could be didactic for many women who are not aware of the formal jargons and language. Another important role of the social worker in this regard relates to encouraging women to welcome these rights and fostering an attitude amongst them that makes them look at injustices done in the name of gender norms and values. They need to be made aware that the injustices they experience at various levels—at home, public places, workplace and society—are not to be borne with silence and that it is not nature's law to treat women like this; rather, it is the archaic patriarchal principles and values that need to be fought. Years of negative gender norms have deprived many women of self-respect and dignity and self-belief. Interventions need to be planned to address this and bring positive behaviour change, lest the awareness of these laws by them will be ineffective. Hence, the awareness generation needs to be planned alongside behaviour change activities. Hence the role of the social worker.

    Tying up with various media planners and influencers to come up with interventions that will address this factor.

2. **Counselling and guidance:** The social worker can act as a facilitator, providing them with the support to register a case and carry on by helping them get legal representation.

3. **Advocacy:** Advocating to strengthen the existing laws and work on the loopholes which contribute to the country still being one of the most unsafe places for women in the world.

    As has been highlighted throughout the chapter, an essential element for the social worker in the context of social legislation is awareness that their role is not limited to merely generating awareness among the population about the provisions of laws that are meant to safeguard their rights in different circumstances. Efforts to make people realize that the ill-treatment they are being subjected to is not natural and unjust, and that by resorting to legal provisions, they are resorting to rights guaranteed to them by virtue of being human beings.

TOP 10 TAKEAWAYS/MAIN POINTS

1. Social legislation plays a critical role in social work.
2. Social legislation safeguards social justice by providing a framework for ensuring the basic rights of certain vulnerable sections are ensured.
3. It also facilitates social change by promoting the interests of certain vulnerable sections of society.
4. Social legislation provides a framework within which social workers can work towards ensuring social justice and social change in an effective manner.
5. The laws that are formulated keep in view the current needs and social problems of the nation.
6. The role of a social worker in the context of social legislation pertains to generating awareness about various aspects of social legislation affecting the target population, advocacy and helping the client choose the best available legal option.
7. The history of the country's social legislation can be traced back to the colonial era.
8. The country has social legislation related to women, which aims to safeguard their rights in both personal and professional spaces.
9. Specific legislation also exists which aims to protect the rights of people belonging to particular castes and tribes in the country.
10. There is legislation to safeguard the rights of and promote the overall development of people with disabilities in the country.

Keywords: Legislation, social work, women's rights, child rights

GLOSSARY

Social change: 'Social changes are variations from the accepted mode of life, whether due to alteration in geographical condition, in cultural equipment, composition of the population or ideologies & whether brought about by diffusion or inventions within the group' (Gillin & Gillin, 2017).

Social Justice: The concept

Takes within its sweep the objective of removing all inequalities and affording equal opportunities to all citizens in social affairs as well as economic activities. The term 'Justice without doubt means Justice to the deprived and weaker sections of society bringing an egalitarian order under which opportunities are afforded to the weaker sections of society. (Gupta, 1983, p. 390)

Social work:

It is a practice-based profession and an academic discipline that promotes social change and development, social cohesion, and the empowerment and liberation of people. Principles of social justice, human rights, collective responsibility and respect for diversities are central to social work. Underpinned by theories of social work, social sciences,

Social Legislations

humanities and indigenous knowledge, social work engages people and structures to address life challenges and enhance wellbeing. The above definition may be amplified at national and/or regional levels.

ANALYTICAL QUESTIONS

1. Analyse the role played by social legislation in the field of social work. Explain using examples.
2. Social legislation in India has played a critical role in attempting to improve the conditions of women across class, caste and religion. Comment on this statement using examples.

MULTIPLE CHOICE QUESTIONS

1. The Act dealing with domestic violence committed against women is called _____.
   a. The Mental Health Act, 1987
   b. The Indecent Representation of Women (Prohibition) Act, 1986
   c. The Immoral Traffic (Prevention) Act, 1956
   d. **The Protection of Women from Domestic Violence Act, 2005**

2. Social legislation ensures _____.
   a. Social exclusion
   b. Conflict
   c. **Social justice**
   d. Discrimination

3. The legislation that is part of the protection of child welfare is _____.
   a. The Rehabilitation Council of India Act, 1992
   b. The Criminal Law (Amendment) Act, 2013
   c. The Scheduled Castes and Tribes (Prevention of Atrocities) Act, 1989
   d. **The Juvenile Justice (Care and Protection of Children) Act, 2015**

4. The role of a social worker in the context of social legislation is _____.
   a. **Awareness generation to target population**
   b. Recorder
   c. Client
   d. Risk manager

5. The legislation, which has many provisions to ensure the overall development of people belonging to certain 'backward' castes, is _____.
   a. The Indecent Representation of Women (Prohibition) Act, 1986
   b. The Commission of Sati (Prevention) Act, 1987 (3 of 1988)
   c. **The Scheduled Castes and Tribes (Prevention of Atrocities) Act, 1989**
   d. The Mental Health Act, 1987

6. The legislation related to child welfare makes selling alcohol or drugs to a child punishable by law is _____.
   a. **The Juvenile Justice (Care and Protection of Children Act) 2015**
   b. The Prohibition of Child Marriage Act, 2006
   c. The Protection of Children from Sexual Offences (Amendment) Act, 2019
   d. Child Labour (Prohibition and Regulation) Act, 1986

7. Social legislation ensures that the status and conditions of certain vulnerable sections improve, thereby contributing to _____.
   a. **Social change**
   b. Policymaking
   c. Oppression
   d. Social action

8. The Act which banned the practice of burning a wife on the funeral pyre of the husband is _____.
   a. **The Commission of Sati (Prevention) Act, 1987 (3 of 1988)**
   b. The Mental Health Act, 1987
   c. The Rehabilitation Council of India Act, 1992
   d. The Criminal Law (Amendment) Act, 2013

9. _____ was further amended in 2017 and safeguards the employment of women during maternity and ensures she is guaranteed 'maternity benefit'.
   a. **The Maternity Benefit Amendment Act, 2017**
   b. The Criminal Law (Amendment) Act, 2013
   c. The Immoral Traffic (Prevention) Act, 1956
   d. The Dowry Prohibition Act, 1961

10. The act under which the exchange of dowry is punishable by law is _____.
    a. **The Dowry Prohibition Act, 1961**
    b. The Dowry Prevention Act, 1961
    c. The Dowry Punishment Act, 1961
    d. The Dowry Act, 1961

REVIEW QUESTIONS

1. Explain the concept of social legislation.
2. Write a short note on the role of social legislation in social work.
3. Explain the relationship between social legislation and social justice.
4. Write a short note on the role of social legislation in facilitating social change.
5. Discuss briefly the social legislation related to the protection of women in the country.
6. Write a short note on the legislation related to child welfare in India.

REFERENCES

Child Marriage Restraint Act. (2019). https://en.wikipedia.org/wiki/Child_Marriage_Restraint_Act
Gangrade, K. D. (1978). *Social legislation in India*. Concept Publishing House.
Gillin ann Gillin. (2017). Social Welfare Administration in India (p. 20). Lulu Press.
Gupta, S. K. K. (1983). Minimum bonus: A search for social justice. *Journal of Indian Law Institute, 25*, 390.
International Federation of social Workers (IFSW). (2020). Definition of social work. Retrieved from https://www.ifsw.org/what-is-social-work/global-definition-of-social-work/ (accessed on 30 August 2019).
Jha, M. (2017). India has a long road ahead to combat challenges faced by personas with disabilities. *The Wire*. Retrieved from https://thewire.in/health/persons-with-disabilities-challenges-india (accessed on 28 August 2019).
Ministry of Women & Child Development. (2019a). The Commission of Sati Prevention Act and Rules. https://wcd.nic.in/act/commission-sati-prevention-act-and-rules
Ministry of Women & Child Development. (2019b). Child related legislation. https://wcd.nic.in/act/2315
Save the Children. (2018). A brief on child protection policies in India. https://www.savethechildren.in/resource-centre/articles/a-brief-on-child-protection-policies-in-india
Saxena, R. N. (1965). Social Research and Social Policy in India (p. 51). Orient Longman.
Sehgal, R. (2017). Social legislation and role of social worker in legal assistance. Block-6 Basics of legal literacy, 1–79. http://ignou.ac.in/upload/bswe-02-block6-unit-31-small%20size.pdf
The Mental Health Act. (1987). Central Government Act. https://indiankanoon.org/doc/185191195/
The mental healthcare bill. (2016). https://prsindia.org/files/bills_acts/bills_parliament/2013/Bill%20as%20passed%20by%20RS.pdf
Think Change. (2016). The Persons with Disabilities Act Simplified, 1995. Retrieved from https://yourstory.com/2016/05/disabilities-act-simplified/amp%20(accessed%20on%2012 (accessed on 12 September 2019).
World Bank. (1997). *Social development and results on the Ground: Task group report*. World Bank.

RECOMMENDED READINGS

Agnes, F., Chandra, S., & Basu, M. (2016). *Women and law in India*. Oxford University Press.
Bajpai, A. (2003). *Child rights in India: Law, policy, and practice*. Oxford University Press.
Myeni, S. R. (2003). *Women and law*. Asia Law House.

10
Social Development
Kislay Kumar Singh

LEARNING OBJECTIVES
- To understand the concepts, nature and definitions of social development
- To examine the leading concepts that are identified as crucial to the process of social development
- To comprehend the relevant theories related to social development
- To outline the social development approaches and their relevance in the social work profession

People are the ends and the means of development, and the impact of development on people and their societies is the measure of its success.

INTRODUCTION

In the history of mankind, there have been some fundamental needs—water, shelter, food and sanitation—which are foundational to human existence. As described in Maslow's theory of need, these things enable people to simply survive (Hölscher, 2008). It is very hard for an individual to focus on achieving higher levels of achievement in their life if these basic needs are not met adequately. As societies advanced from pre-industrial civilizations to modern industrial civilizations, the problems of people fulfilling their basic needs such as shelter, access to drinking water and food remained the same. The concept of social development has evolved from this realization that change in political structure or the economy does not necessarily mean improvement in people's lives (Green, 2002). In other words, we may assume that development occurs in a society only when we see tangible shifts in the living standards of its people.

> **Did You Know?**
>
> The idea of social development paved the way for the creation of more extensive government social programmes, including social security, housing and comprehensive health care. The first modern-day social security programmes were established in Germany in the 1880s by the Chancellor, Count Otto von Bismarck. Later, such measures were introduced in other industrial countries.

The notion of such development emerged mainly from the two historical incidences. First was the recovery of war-torn countries in Europe and Japan after the Second World War. This was made possible due to the Marshall Plan (officially the European Recovery Program) initiated by the USA and the determination of war-torn countries' leaders to rebuild and strengthen their economies. Such an incident sets an example that constant and rapid development is possible. The second was the beginning of the decolonization process all over the world. This led to a redefined perspective of newly independent countries and the need to provide a better life to all citizens in all aspects, that is, politically, socially, economically and technologically, which are considered fundamental to the development of an individual, family, society or country as a whole. Thus, social development is regarded as a unified process that includes both social and economic elements for the well-being of people. Social development cannot take place without economic development and economic development is meaningless if it is not accompanied by improvements in social welfare for the whole population. Therefore, it is not a natural process of change but a deliberate human action that requires organized intervention.

Social development provides a new approach to development by linking well-being measures directly with economic development policies and programmes. This assumption has been broadly drawn from the performance of developing countries or Third-World countries where the need for social measures which are very much compatible with economic development is paramount. However, problems such as unemployment, poverty, recessions and other economic adversities remain today in many parts of the world. However, social development as an approach attracts widespread support. As it actively promotes development along with an emphasis on social intervention, that is relevant in all societies. Social development also advocates for how society and its institutions function so that they can contribute towards the betterment of people.

THEORETICAL DEBATE: THE GENESIS OF SOCIAL DEVELOPMENT

People generally understand development as a process of economic progress. The term 'development' refers to changes in the lifestyle brought about by urbanization, adoption of new attitudes and social progress in the overall well-beings. Development has a welfare connotation as it improves people's educational levels, boosts their incomes, housing conditions and overall status. However, the concept of development is frequently associated with economic development. The adoption of economic development has produced unprecedented

> **Box 10.1 Indicators of Development**
>
> In order to assess how well a country is developing, social indicators are outlined. Social indicators are numerical measures that are used to describe and evaluate community well-being. Thus, it is one way to find out what is happening with an individual, community or society as a whole within a state. The following are a few examples of social indicators:
>
> 1. Poverty rate
> 2. Employment rate
> 3. Educational attainment
> 4. Inequality rate
> 5. Life expectancy
> 6. Health expenditure
> 7. Life satisfaction
> 8. Fertility rate

growth rates along with a significant increase in the level of social welfare in most countries. However, many millions of people in Asia, Africa and Latin America are left behind by such development. An appreciation of theoretical debates in development is needed in order to understand the nature of social development aptly. We must see these debates with respect to the 'developed', 'underdeveloped' or 'developing' countries since all countries, one way or another, are in the process of development (Paiva, 1977). As each society or country moves with different pace of growth and progress, change is common characteristics to all countries. Thus, the theory of development must explain both the positive and negative aspects of changes that are taking place in societies. However, due to the differences in societies, each society will display its own unique development features and differences. Hence, it is important for social scientists to provide an analysis of the pre-existing social conditions that seek to change, suggest the processes of development and put forward the end goal that the development process seeks to attain.

Social scientists broadly connote underdevelopment as the initial social situation of a region or country that is socially and economically backward. It has been used to denote the deprived regions or whole regions of the country or group of countries. However, social workers or social planners see underdevelopment in terms of poor health facilities, low life expectancy, poverty, inadequate housing and low educational attainment. During the 1950s and 1960s, the term 'underdevelopment' occupied a central place in the development debate (Midgley, 2014). To find the reasons for underdevelopment all over the Third World, underdevelopment theories were developed mostly by Latin American scholars. These theories were drawn from the ideas of the economic system of capitalism, propounded by Karl Marx. The underdevelopment theories explain how the Third-World countries have been subjugated and forced to be underdeveloped in a systemic colonial exploitation regime or in the name of integrating into the global economic system. These theories also provide a structural perspective to the development.

THE AFTERMATHS OF COLONIALISM

The colonial expansion started way back in the 16th century and reached its peak during the late 19th century. Powerful countries at the time, such as England, Spain, France, Dutch and Portugal, went on to conquest, both militarily and politically, concealing land in Asia, Africa and Latin America, and establishing their colonies. Today, these colonies that gained independence during the mid-20th century are recognized as the Third World. They were systematically exploited and marginalized in all aspects—social, economic and political—by their colonial rulers. Thus, the impact of colonial rule on these countries is seen in their continued underdevelopment. These colonies served as suppliers of raw materials as well as consumers of finished goods for their colonial masters. For example, the industrial revolution in Britain was fostered by the deindustrialization of India (presently, India, Pakistan and Bangladesh). Raw materials, such as cotton and jute, cheap labour and capital in various forms were supplied from India to boost industrialization in Britain. Further, the finished products were sold at low prices in India while imposing heavy taxes on the goods produced by local artisans or cottage industries. Commercialization of agriculture and concentration of lands in the hands of a few (landlords) replaced food crops with non-food crops, such as rubber, indigo, sugarcane, tobacco, tea and coffee, that further led to famine in India between 1870 and 1900. Subjugation of the Third-World countries through suppressive policies adopted by their colonial rulers brought poverty, hunger, diseases and unemployment to a large mass of the population.

Most of the Third-World countries gained independence in the mid-20th century from their colonial rulers. Even after gaining freedom, their socio-economic decisions, political affairs, foreign policies, trades and so on are directed from outside. This is what has been termed 'neo-colonialism', where the internal policies and sovereignty of newly independent nations or developing states are compromised. The socio-economic dominance of developed countries in Third-World countries leads to a trapping of their economic system and their exploitation. As a result, Third-World countries remain underdeveloped.

MODERNIZATION THEORY

The modernization theory emerged between the 1950s and 1960s to offer an economic solution to come out of the state of underdevelopment. It was then generally accepted that underdevelopment was a natural and original state of economic and social backwardness. Earlier proponents such as Daniel Lerner, William Goode and Everett Hagan claimed that traditionalism kept people backward and restricted them from initiating any process of change that may have improved their situations. In order to take any initiative for the well-being of an individual, family or community, it should have the conformity of a family as well as fall under the purview of traditional beliefs. Ragnar Nurkse (1953), an earlier proponent, argued that underdevelopment exists because people in certain societies are too poor to escape poverty, destitution and disease without outside support. He believed that introducing capital in the form of investment from outside or other sources was the only solution to take society on the path of progress and development. Thus, if situations of economic and social backwardness in societies are to be eradicated, traditional beliefs must be altered.

However, the belief that underdevelopment is the original state of a society was later challenged by Frank, Rodney and other dependency theorists.

DEPENDENCY THEORY

This theory emerged during the 1960s and 1970s as an explanation for the conditions of the Latin American countries. Andre Gunder Frank and Walter Rodney were the leading proponents of this view who argued that continued exploitation of the developing or underdeveloped countries (also known as Third-World) like Argentina, Chile, Brazil or Peru by the rich industrial nations (developed countries) caused developing or underdeveloped regions to experience more underdevelopment and poverty. They further claimed that the poor conditions of Third-World countries made them dependent on being satellites of the metropolis of the world economic system, where resources from rural areas are transferred to urban areas of their own countries and then transported to developed countries. This process of transferring wealth and surplus from the Third-World countries (periphery) in a chain to the developed countries (centre) causes the exploitation of resources and marginalization of the people of the Third-World countries. In simple words, the development of advanced countries implied a simultaneous underdevelopment of Third-World countries.

However, this claim was challenged by development experts of widely opposite political views in the 1970s. Based on significant empirical evidence, they claimed that the economies of many developing countries were growing at a significant rate and the social conditions of the masses were also improving simultaneously. However, this was not true for all the Third-World countries; many were experiencing underdevelopment.

A THEORY OF URBAN BIAS

This theory was propounded in 1977 to explain the urban-rural imbalance in Third-World countries. Apart from accepting earlier underdevelopment theories and the history of colonialism in perpetuating Third-World underdevelopment, he believed that economic and social progress in developing countries was not occurring uniformly. Urban areas were developing faster than rural areas, and some rural areas were growing faster than others. Despite the difficulties that developing countries face, some of their urban areas have been able to provide unmatched income opportunities or access to services in comparison to their rural areas. As a result, uneven patterns of development began to rise in various parts of the developing countries. During the 1980s, many developing countries' economies were growing at a high rate, but they were also accompanied by poverty, denial of opportunities and services, squalor and other problems. This problem was severe in Latin America.

Social Development

> **Did You Know?**
>
> After India gained independence, Mahatma Gandhi urged the development of villages as an economy that could produce enough to meet the village's demand, create job opportunities and, simultaneously, build a better balance between man and nature. However, this approach to development was largely considered impractical and thus was not given serious attention at that time.

These events fostered the notion of distorted development that stands to connote economic development without the elements of social development. This further creates severe disparities between economic and social prosperity within societies. Today, the problem in most developing countries is not that their economies are not developing, but rather that such developments are not accompanied by enhancements in the social well-being of the whole population.

SOCIAL DEVELOPMENT: NATURE, CONCEPT AND DEFINITION

Today, we are all familiar with the term 'social development'. The meaning of this term is diverse and varied. Earlier, it was often understood as the socio-psychological growth of an individual in the family or the surroundings in which they lived. However, at present, social development globally extends the focus and puts individuals at the centre of development processes at all levels—within and between countries, especially in terms of economic welfare (Paiva, 1977). This suggests that the development processes should benefit individuals. Besides, it should also recognize the ways individuals interact in groups or societies and the principles that guide such interactions and shape the development processes. In short, we may say that social development is the development of individuals, institutions and their surroundings.

Alterations in social institutions or structures that push societies towards an inclusive development, guarantees social cohesion and accountability and institutional reforms for the betterment of individuals, communities or of the surroundings are also included in the concept of social development (Davis, 2004). For example, people must treat each other equally in their daily spheres. This will further enhance social cohesion where peaceful and healthy surroundings are created within communities or societies. People must have the freedom to express themselves freely and their voices should be heard by the concerned authorities. The provision for the protection of enshrined rights, ensuring the maximum participation of citizens in governance or better law enforcement, signifies the space for the institutional reforms that can be achieved. Hence, the primary goal of developmental processes should be the development of people.

Social workers acknowledge that there is a lack of an agreed definition of social development among them. However, Midgley (2014, pp. 13–17) defined this term by providing the following eight elements that are integral to practice.

- **A dynamic process:** It comprises the elements of change and growth simultaneously. It goes beyond a static posture by actively promoting a developmental process.

- **Progressive in nature:** It advocates for positive improvements in social conditions and restores faith in the prospect of human betterment.
- **Multifaceted:** By integrating social, cultural, economic, political, environmental and other aspects into its approach, it offers a better way to analyse and deal with the social problems that promote social well-being.
- **Interventionist:** It suggests that organized efforts in the form of various policies, legislative measures, projects, programmes and plans are needed to accomplish the goals of development.
- **Productivist:** Along with economic development, it also contributes towards the development of individuals, families or whole societies.
- **Comprehensive and universalistic:** It redresses target groups or disadvantages people at large within the community and also not only caters to the needs of individuals but seeks to focus on the well-being of whole populations.
- **Spatial focus:** At the practice level, it emphasizes within specific spatial settings such as slums, rural communities, cities, regions or the whole country.
- **Promoting social welfare:** It upholds the value of promoting people's social well-being through various mechanisms or institutions.

This provides a framework for addressing the needs and problems of all beings and engaging in actions to provide solutions at both micro and macro levels. Apart from this, the will and the ideology of a state must be committed towards social justice, the distribution of resources among all people and development, especially for the well-being of disadvantaged people. This further adds meaning to the concept of social development, where human needs, aspirations and relationships are valued for the betterment of social order.

SOCIAL DEVELOPMENT: A UNIFIED APPROACH TO DEVELOPMENT

As we discussed the concepts, meanings and relevant theories related to social development in the above sections, we can say that social development as an approach offers an effective response to the current social and economic problems. By linking social policies with a variety of strategies and measures, it promotes social welfare and overall development. In the process of providing a human touch to development prospects, it tends to integrate both social and economic components as essential facets in the process of development (Hugman, 2016). This attempt to integrate social and economic elements through policies and programmes in order to enhance the standard of living of the whole community or society distinguishes social development from the other approaches.

Generally, social philanthropy, social work and social administration are considered approaches to promoting social welfare. But these approaches do not address the social and economic issues together in the comprehensive process of growth and change (Midgley, 2014). Social philanthropy relies mainly on religious charity, private donations and voluntary efforts. It deals with disadvantaged people either by providing goods and services to them or by catering to their needs. While social work relies on professional trainees to achieve welfare goals in society by working with individuals, groups or communities. And social administration depends on government intervention by adopting various social services and schemes for target groups. This approach is also known as the social service or social policy approach. However, all three approaches have been widely practised all over the world, but they differ from social development approach. The key differences between social development and other approaches are as follows:

- Unlike other approaches that focus on catering to the needs of individuals, social development focuses on the social well-being of society as a whole in the process of growth and change.
- Unlike other approaches that are mainly concerned with maintaining a certain level of welfare, social development goes beyond this static posture by linking social policies and programmes directly to the development process.
- Social development aims to make structural changes in societies that allow all sections of the population to freely participate in the process of development.
- Social development seeks to harmonize social interventions with economic development efforts in a dynamic way.

The primary goal of all these approaches is to promote social welfare (or social well-being) in society at large. Thus, it is important to understand how social problems are addressed, to what extent their needs are met, and what possible opportunities are provided for the betterment of individuals, groups, communities or even whole societies. Today, it is widely accepted that access to an adequate level of food, shelter, drinking water, sanitation, health, education and security are the necessities for a community or society. Societies that provide these necessities and create social opportunities for their people to realize their potential are experiencing a high degree of social well-being. Societies that are unable to provide these necessities to their people are considered ineffective in achieving a satisfactory level of welfare. In this regard, social development has emerged as a unified approach that explicitly suggests how to deal with these issues.

Social development is, therefore, inclusive in nature. It emphasizes the progress of society in its totality that is, in its social, economic, political and cultural aspects. Broadly, it refers to all aspects of development that are comprehensive and collective in nature (Gore, 2003). Human welfare is the primary objective of social development. It seeks to improve the physical quality of life and demands an equitable distribution of material and cultural goods.

RELEVANCE OF SOCIAL DEVELOPMENT IN THE SOCIAL WORK PRACTICE

Since the inception of the social work profession, the primary function of social work has been to deal with the problems of society and bring changes, particularly at individual or institutional levels (Lee, 1937). However, to what extent these functions are carried out by social work professionals remains a matter of continuous contemplation. The problems dealt with by social work professionals are diverse, complex and multidimensional in nature and do not exist in isolation. In fact, most of the social problems are the result of development, underdevelopment or distorted development, and this indicates the utmost requirement for significant improvement in professional practice. As a result, social work professionals recognized the need to look beyond the conventional approach of interventions and emphasize the need to integrate various underlying concepts to identify the root causes of social problems and suggests specific methods for the social betterment of individuals. Spergel (1978) argued that the residual model of social work is a weak approach towards dealing with the welfare of the poor as it often diagnoses the personal and interpersonal problems of an individual within an existing institutional framework without considering the bigger picture of social reality. In order to ensure the overall well-being of the marginalized section of any society, there is a dire need to intervene not just at the micro but also at the macro level. Thus, the social development approach to social work practice denotes this very shift from micro to macro level practice among social work professionals and also a departure from the residual model of social work practice.

The primary objective of social work is to prevent social problems and help individuals fulfil their needs. While social development focuses on the creation of effective institutional structures of social provision, social control, social protection and social rehabilitation, these may contribute to the personal growth of an individual (Hugman, 2016). If existing institutional structures are failing to meet desired needs and require social adjustment, social development advocates for institutional reforms. Thus, the term 'social development' has been used to define 'macro-structural' practice. It may be considered a basic perspective of social work, as both are similar in terms of individual welfare and personal and social improvement (Spergel, 1978). Integrating these two concepts of practice provides a sense of general mission and recognizes new and changing areas of individual or institutional practices. These conceptions demand improvement in professional practices, role preparation and sometimes generate practice innovations. The principles of social development are also similar to the principles of social work in that they both have one single concern, which is to improve the well-being of human beings (Hugman, 2016). In trying to do so, both social development and social work strive to ensure the protection of human rights of all sections of society with a special focus on the marginalized sections of society. Thus, both social development and social work strive to empower all human beings by challenging the existing social relations and changing the distribution of power and resources.

The social development approach strengthens the role of social work professionals both as facilitators of social change and as someone who empowers individuals by helping them to realize their full potential. The implementation of the social development approach to social work revolves around developing policies that revolve around improving the lives of the marginalized sections of society. Social development can be seen as a principle concept or approach that is dedicated towards the upliftment and betterment of society. It is, in its very essence, compatible with the value base of social work education and practice. Just like social work, the fundamental value of social development is guided by the conviction that every human being has worth and dignity. Due to this, it believes that every individual should therefore be able to access equal opportunities in order to realize their optimum potential. Social development as a developmental model strives to ensure social justice in society and the fruits or outcomes of all the 'developmental' activities must be equally distributed.

SUMMARY

Social development emphasizes the well-being of individuals in society such that their socio-economic barriers are removed to help them reach their highest potential. Individuals are viewed as the basic units of social development who contribute to the growth of the entire society. Social development requires economic, social and cultural progress in a way that individuals explore the maximum opportunities to grow, sharpen their skills and contribute back to their families and communities\. Social development thereby advocates for an integrated and inclusive approach to development, which cannot take place without an enhancement in social welfare for the entire society. The concept of social development serves as the backbone of the discipline of social work as it focuses on the amelioration of social problems such as education, unemployment, poverty and ill-health, among others, through social reforms and legislation. In a nutshell, social development is essential for the prevalence of social justice and the overall upliftment of all.

TOP 10 TAKEAWAYS/MAIN POINTS

1. Water, shelter, food and sanitation are some of the fundamental needs that are foundational to human existence. If these basic needs are not fulfilled adequately, it is very hard for an individual to focus on higher levels of achievements in their life.
2. Earlier, social development was often understood as the socio-psychological growth of an individual in their family or the surroundings in which they lived.
3. The concept of social development has evolved from this realization that change in political structure or the economy does not necessarily mean improvements in people's lives. In other words, we may assume that development occurs in a society only when we see tangible shifts in the living standards of its people.
4. Today, social development globally extends the focus and puts individuals at the centre of development processes at all levels—within and between countries, especially in terms of economic welfare.
5. Social development cannot take place without economic development and economic development is meaningless if it is not accompanied by improvements in social welfare for the whole population.
6. Midgley (2014) defined the term 'social development' by providing eight elements that are integral to practice. This provides a framework for addressing the needs and problems of all beings and engaging in actions to provide solutions at both micro and macro levels.
7. The concept of social development suggests that the will and ideology of a state must be committed towards social justice, the distribution of resources among all people and development, especially for the well-being of disadvantaged people.
8. Underdevelopment is the initial social situation of a region or country that is socially and economically backward. During the 1950s and 1960s, the term 'underdevelopment' occupied a central place in the development debate.
9. Underdevelopment theories explain how Third-World countries have been subjugated and forced to be underdeveloped in a systemic colonial exploitation regime or in the name of integrating into the global economic system.
10. Just like social work, the fundamental value of social development is guided by the conviction that every human being has worth and dignity.

Keywords: Development, Social Development, Theory, social work

GLOSSARY

Development: It can be defined as the process or act of bringing about social change that must allow people to achieve their human potential.

Theory: Theory is a set of assumptions, patterns, or accepted facts that attempt to give a rational explanation of relationships among a group of observed phenomena.

Social development: The term 'social development', in general, can be defined as the process of organizing available resources and guiding human interactions to create opportunities for all people to develop themselves individually as well as collectively. It is very difficult to define the term 'social development' accurately. Thus, concepts such as socio-economic integration, structural change, institutional development and its reform are identified as chief key features to define social development.

Social work: It is a practice-based profession and an academic discipline that promotes social change and development, social cohesion, and the empowerment and liberation of people. Principles of social justice, human rights, collective responsibility and respect for diversities are central to social work. Underpinned by theories of social work, social sciences, humanities and indigenous knowledge, social work engages people and structures to address life challenges and enhance wellbeing. (IFSW, 2014)

ANALYTICAL QUESTIONS

1. Distinguish between the concepts of social development and economic development?
2. Delineate the various theories of development and analyse the theory that defines the model of development in India?

MULTIPLE CHOICE QUESTIONS

1. What are the fundamental needs of human existence?
   a. Food
   b. Shelter
   c. Water
   d. **All of the above**

2. The Marshall Plan, officially known as the European Recovery Program, was initiated by _____.
   a. Britain
   b. **The USA**
   c. Australia
   d. None of the above

Social Development

3. Which one of the following is not a Millennium Development Goal?
   a. Eradicate extreme poverty and hunger
   b. Achieve universal primary education
   c. **Increase sex ratio**
   d. Promote gender equality and empower women

4. The concept of social development implies _____.
   a. Alterations in social institutions or structures
   b. Guarantees social cohesion and accountability
   c. Institutional reforms for the betterment
   d. **All of the above**

5. Midgley (2014) defined the term 'social development' by providing _____ elements that are integral to practice.
   a. Nine
   b. Seven
   c. **Eight**
   d. Ten

6. Andre Gunder Frank and Walter Rodney are the leading proponents of _____.
   a. Modernization theory
   b. **Dependency theory**
   c. Theory of urban bias
   d. None of the above

7. Social development refers to integrating both the _____ and the _____ components as the essential facets in the process of development.
   a. Social and political
   b. Economic and political
   c. **Social and economic**
   d. None of the above

8. The fundamental values of social work and social development are guided by a belief in _____.
   a. The worth and dignity of every human being
   b. The upliftment and betterment of society
   c. The equal distribution of resources
   d. **All of the above**

9. Which one of the following is not a social indicator?
   a. Poverty rate
   b. Employment rate
   c. **Gross domestic product**
   d. Educational attainment

10. Social development can be seen as a principle concept or approach that is dedicated towards _____.
    a. Industrial growth
    b. **The upliftment and betterment of society**
    c. Reduce poverty
    d. None of the above

REVIEW QUESTIONS

1. How do the notions of social development emerge worldwide?
2. Discuss the core components of social development?

REFERENCES

Davis, G. (2004). *A history of the social development network in the World Bank*. The World Bank, Social Development, Paper No. 56. http://web.worldbank.org/archive/website00522/WEB/PDF/HISTORY_.PDF

International Federation of Social Workers (IFSW). (2014). *Global definition of social work*. https://www.ifsw.org/global-definition-of-social-work/

Green, M. (2002). Social development: Issues and approaches. In U. Kothari & M. Minogue (Eds.), *Development theory and practice: Critical perspectives*. Palgrave Macmillan.

Gore, M. S. (2003). *Social development: Challenges faced in an unequal and plural society*. Rawat Publications.

Hölscher, D. (2008). The emperor's new clothes: South Africa's attempted transition to developmental social welfare and social work. *International Journal of Social Welfare, 17*(2), 114–123.

Hugman, R. (2016). *Social development in social work: Practices and principles*. Routledge.

Lee, P. R. (1937). *Social work as cause and function, and other papers*. Columbia University Press.

Midgley, J. (2014). *Social development: Theory and practice*. SAGE Publications.

Nurkse, R. (1953). *Problems of capital formation in underdeveloped countries*. Oxford University Press.

Paiva, J. F. X. (1977). A conception of social development. *Social Service Review, 51*(2), 327–336.

Spergel, I. A. (1978). Social development and social work. *Administration in Social Work, 1*(3), 221–233. http://dx.doi.org/10.1300/J147v01n03_01

RECOMMENDED READINGS

Black, J. K. (1991). *Development in theory and practice: Bridging the gap*. Westview Press.
Booth, D. (1994). *Rethinking social development: Theory, research and practice*. Orient Longman.
Chakravarty, S. (1987). *Development planning: An Indian experience*. Clarendon Press.
Dreze, J., Sen, A. (1997). *Indian development: Selected regional perspective*. Oxford University Press.
Harrison, D. (1988). *The sociology of modernization and development*. Routledge.
Webster, A. (1990). *Introduction to the sociology of development*. Humanities Press.

Social Security
Sunil Prasad and Arul Actovin C.

LEARNING OBJECTIVES

- To learn about social security and its importance
- To know about the historical development of social security
- To acquire knowledge on social security policy issues from an international perspective
- To understand the current national social protection systems
- To know the connection between the social work profession and social security

---

If a free society cannot help the many who are poor, it cannot save the few who are rich.

—John F. Kennedy

INTRODUCTION

The human being is the core participant and beneficiary of development and the essential focus of the progress process (United Nations, 1986). Social security is protected in the Universal Declaration of Human Rights and in the agreement of social, cultural and economic rights. States have an obligation to provide all people with a minimum standard of well-being and social security.

Theoretically, social security aims to create positive collective outcomes by protecting persons against financial scarcities. In general, social security means granting rights or entitlements (e.g., benefits on economic aid from others) and imposing duties, such as a compulsion to pay taxes and donations or to provide care (Vrooman, 2009, p. 126). The social work profession realizes energy of social protection to take on changes in democracy and address economic disparities by focusing on conserving culture and social relationships, making relationships among people and promoting social integration as harmonious as possible. This section emphasizes social security's origin, development at international and national levels, measures in India as well as social work perspectives on social security and the role of social workers in social security.

CONCEPT AND DEFINITION

> **Did You Know?**
>
> Everyone, as a member of society, has the right to social security and is entitled to realization, through national effort and international co-operation and in accordance with the organization and resources of each State, of the economic, social and cultural rights indispensable for his dignity and the free development of his personality. (Article 22 of Universal Declaration of Human Rights)

The notion of social security has been established in different periods of time. In the ancient societies, humans fought against insecurity to save themselves from the notions of natural surroundings and search for elementary requirements of life. Then community living originated into a presence that carried the household to give sufficient social provisions for the needy. Social security is defined by various persons and organizations throughout the world. Therefore, the notion of social security has no universally recognized definition of the term. Consequently, an endeavour has been prepared in this part to examine the notion and definitions of social security.

Social security has been defined by Sir William Beveridge

> As want disease, ignorance, squalor, and idleness he subsequently clarified the meaning of the term social security as the securing of an income to the place of earning when they are interrupted by unemployment, sickness on accident to provide for retirement benefits during old age, to provide against loss of support by the death of another person, and to meet exceptional expenditure such as those connected with birth, death and marriage. (Beveridge, 1942)

According to W. A. Robson,

> Social Security is a way of ensuring freedom from want of or poverty which is one of the formidable obstacles in the way of progress social security implies insurance against those misfortunes to which an individual remains exposed even which the condition of society as whole improves. (Robson, 1945)

The *Encyclopædia Britannica* (1963) defines social security as 'the main purpose of any plan for social security in insurance against interruption and destruction of earning power and or special expenditure arising at birth, marriage or death'.

According to V. V. Giri,

> Social security is one of the dynamic concepts of the modern age which is influencing social as well as economic police and is the security that the state furnishes against the risks which an individual of small means cannot, today, stand up to by himself or even on private combination with his fellow countrymen. (Giri, 1972)

NEED OF SOCIAL SECURITY

> **Did You Know?**
>
> Social security protects people against a variety of risks to ensure them a basic floor of income in old age and to enable many people who have struggled all their lives to look forward to a decent standard of comfort and dignity when they retire. It would be a crime to take that away from them.
>
> —Paul Starr

Through the intensive hard work of the most suitable organizations, social security is one of the important requirements of the current human community to give other sources of revenue to the workforce at the time of opportunity. According to the Universal Declaration on Human Rights Article 25,

Everyone has the right to a standard of living adequate for the health and well-being of himself and of his family, including food, clothing, and housing and medical care and necessary social services, and the right to social security in the event of unemployment, sickness, disability, widowhood, old age or other lack of livelihood in circumstances beyond his control. Motherhood and childhood are entitled to special care and assistance. All children, whether born in or out of wedlock, shall enjoy the same social protection.

Without any doubt, everybody needs social security in one form or another, whether they are rich or poor. The difference is that the richer pay high premium on their own and protect themselves for everything: accident, medical, loss of baggage, houses, theft, loss of property, damage, pensions and so on. On the other hand, middle-class families and the poor, who are engaged in informal activities, have limited choices and an inability to pay to secure themselves under social security schemes.

TYPES OF SOCIAL SECURITY

There are two types of social security.

1. **Social assistance:** It is a method to provide benefits to people, usually for the vulnerable groups in a community (children, mothers, disabled, elderly people and so on) from general revenues of the state. It is non-contributory.
2. **Social insurance:** A method is to provide benefits to individuals through the contributions of beneficiaries, with contributions or subsidies from employer and the state.

THE HISTORICAL DEVELOPMENT OF SOCIAL SECURITY

In the course of historical development, the notion of social security has evolved because, as life becomes increasingly complex owing to industrial and scientific development, the dangers of life have multiplied. Through the instrumentality of social justice, the departure from laissez-faire philosophy to the concept of the welfare state gave rise to the new principles of social welfare and the common good, and the state was no longer content with playing the passive part of the spectator. Since the late 19th century, industrial jurisprudence has been born and recognized with social justice; almost every nation thought it was necessary to create a social security system to safeguard workers from the risks or contingencies of working life as a matter of right for employees. Each state had to actively participate in the development of human society in order to pursue a wide range of social and economic policies to guarantee human dignity in order to achieve the goal of freedom from want. As Grigson and Gibbs Smith argued, laissez-faire is the doctrine that the government should not interfere with the natural functioning of a nation's economy. It is that financial forces alone operating through private people should shape financial welfare. This died in the late 19th century and was buried in the 20th century (Chandra, 1976).

Therefore, modern society has assumed the obligation to implement social security measures to protect industrial workers from disease, old age, disability, unemployment and so on.

Although the wide system of social assurance was shaped by the Government of Germany, the term 'social security' was formally recognized and authoritatively used in the USA in 1935. The impact of the International Labour Organization also laid the basis for social security actions for labourers to implement the values of safe collective peace based on social justice. The Declaration of Philadelphia (1944) restated, in particular, that labour is not a product and that paucity wherever it exists is a threat to universal prosperity, with a vision to the rise of well-being.

HISTORICAL PERSPECTIVES ON SOCIAL SECURITY MEASURES IN INDIA

Did You Know?

The National Commission on Labour of India has defined social security as:

> Social security envisages that the members of the community shall be protected by collective action against social risks causing undue hardship and privation to individuals whose primary resources can seldom be adequate to meet them. The concept of social security is based on ideals of human dignity and social justice. The under lying ideal behind social security measure is that a citizen who has contributed or is likely to contribute to his country's welfare should be given protection against certain hazards or as consequence of it. (Government of India, 1969)

Ancient views on labour jurisprudence disclose that social security is not an unfamiliar concept and was present in family or religious social institutions in India. The impact of industrial development and, consequently, the recent approach to social security moved gradually to India. The development was step by step. In the pre-independence period, the enactments relating to social security were prepared for a particular section of labour alone. While preparing the constitution, the provisions related to social security were given more importance to labour. Later, in all policies of the governance of the state, social security for workers was a concern of the government.

A joint family was the unit of a social institution in ancient India, and it was the main guard for security, similar to the other social institutions. In social insurance, generation solidarity represented the reciprocal responsibilities of the parents to help the child in infancy and the son to help the parents in their old age was represented in social insurance.

In his works, Kautilya also referred to a number of pension systems, such as education pensions and public poor relief. He says that 'state itself should provide support to poor, pregnant women, to their new born offspring, to orphans, to the aged, the infirm, the afflicted and the helpless'. Since times immemorial, a social security system has existed in India. In the beginning, economic security was given mainly by individual efforts for the needy. Gradually, organized methods were developed to deal with the problems of insecurity in order to meet contingencies. Social security was given in the early days when human demands were restricted and survival was mainly based on farming, joint families, craft guilds, churches, charitable philanthropy and other religious organizations.

A fast decline in Indian industry happened during the Mughal period owing to frequent warfare. The effect of Muslim culture and thought on India gave the charity and social service concept a fresh depth. Islam imposes on its followers five significant responsibilities, one of which is *zakat*, which means charity. The Mughals had a unique government department to oversee charity and endowment administration (Jagdish, 2004). New trends began in technological innovations and industrialization during the British period, which led to the establishment in the community of employers and employees of two separate groups. In order to enhance their living circumstances, the joint family system lost its validity as a means of providing safety against certain socio-economic contingencies as labour was drawn into the plant. In India, there was hardly any land law governing labour matters.

SOCIAL SECURITY MEASURES IN INDIA

CONSTITUTIONAL SOCIAL SECURITY MEASURES

Concurrent List

Social security and labour welfare falls under Concurrent List. It means both union and state government can make laws regarding these topics.

The following are the items on the List-III in the Seventh Schedule of the Constitution of India.

Item No. 23: Social security and insurance; employment and unemployment.
Item No. 24: Welfare of labour including conditions of work, provident funds, employers' liability, workmen's compensation, invalidity and old age pension and maternity benefits.

Articles of Indian Constitution

The Indian Constitution contains all the ingredients obliging the state to move towards the realization of socio-economic rights under Articles 41, 42, 43 and 43A.

Article 41: Right to work, to education and to public assistance in certain cases and the State shall, within the limits of its economic capacity and development, make effective provision for securing the right to work, to education and to public assistance in cases of unemployment, old age, sickness and disablement, and in other cases of undeserved want.

Article 42: Provision for just and humane conditions of work and maternity relief and the State shall make provision for securing just and humane conditions of work and for maternity relief.

Article 43: Living wage, etc, for workers. The State shall endeavour to secure, by suitable legislation or economic organization or in any other way, to all workers, agricultural, industrial or otherwise, work, a living wage, conditions of work ensuring a decent standard of life and full enjoyment of leisure and social and cultural opportunities and, in particular, the State shall endeavour to promote cottage industries on an individual or cooperative basis in rural areas.

Article 43A: The State shall take steps, by suitable legislation or in any other way, to secure the participation of workers in the management of undertakings, establishments or other organizations engaged in any industry.

Box 11.1 Past Studies/Commissions on Social Security

- Royal Commission on Labour, 1931
- National Commission on Labour, 1969
- National Commission on Self-employed Women and Women in Unorganized Sector, 1989
- National Commission for Rural Labour, 1991
- Second National Commission on Labour, 2002
- National Commission for Enterprises in Unorganized Sector, 2008
- Social Protection for a Changing India—World Bank, 2011
- Social Protection Floor for India—International Labour Organization, 2013
- Social Security Reform in India—draft framework—International Labour Organization, 2016

Various Social Security Acts in India

The Employees' State Insurance Act, 1948: This act covers factories and establishments with ten or more employees and provides medical care to employees and their families. It provides cash benefits during sickness and maternity as well as a monthly pension after death or permanent disability.

The Workmen's Compensation Act, 1923: This act requires payment of compensation to the workman or his family in cases of employment-related injuries resulting in death or disability.

The Employees' Provident Funds Act, 1952: This act applies to specific scheduled factories and establishments employing twenty or more employees and ensures terminal benefits for the provident fund, superannuation pension, and family pension in case of death during service.

The Maternity Benefit Act, 1961: This act provides for 12 weeks of wages during maternity as well as paid leave in certain other related contingencies.

The Payment of Gratuity Act, 1972: This act provides 15 days' wages for each year of service to employees who have worked for five years or more in establishments with a minimum of 10 workers.

SOCIAL SECURITY AND SOCIAL WORK

Modern social work is a professional service based on scientific knowledge and skills. Social security, on the other hand, can be understood as the security that society provides against certain risks through appropriate organizations. In other words, social security is society's protection against certain life possibilities, that is, accidents, elderly people, disability, unemployment, sickness and so on. Social workers involve numerous actions such as enhancing people's solidarity, encouraging people to care for others, engaging individuals to respect others' rights and reinforcing solidarity within a family, community, and society. Social security should be intended, in the view of social work, to illuminate the sustainability and well-being of people as absolutely required.

The social work profession encourages social security systems as organizations specializing in building harmony among communities and between communities for social alteration. In addition, as a social work profession, democratic participation is encouraged and voices are strengthened in a broader community. In addition to financial advantages, social protection built on community engagement and human rights will also benefit. It will result in sustainability and safety. The theoretical and practical understandings of the social work profession are entrenched in the fact that human beings cannot live sustainable, fulfilled lives unless they are interdependently connected in a social context. Thus, an essential objective of the occupation is to decorate social security structures so that individuals can live confidently, safely, with dignity and with a complete appreciation of their freedoms in social environments.

This strategy may vary from many governments' trends in conceiving of social protection schemes as top-down platforms for individual poverty alleviation or targeted harm reduction. While the profession actively promotes the creation of poverty reduction mechanisms and programmes and alleviates pain, it goes beyond this by focusing on the construction of family, community, societal capital and interdependence as the main first and viable type of social security. This is reflected in the capacity-building notion of society. According to Dreze and Sen (1999), 'the basic idea of social security is to use social means to prevent deprivation and vulnerability to deprivation'.

THE SOCIAL WORKER'S ROLE IN SOCIAL SECURITY

The role of social workers in social security systems is to enable community commonness and meeting within the improvement of structures that may be comprehensive for all individuals and give them self-esteem and respect while confirming human rights and social justice. Social workers can take their abilities understanding and expertise not only from marginalized and excluded people, but also from groups and communities to advocate for positive systems addressing structural, social and cultural obstacles. The function of social workers is to mediate between state services and family and community structures in order to obtain results that strengthen family and community capacity for sustainable self-care and the ability to access social protection systems when needed. In their workplaces and communities, social workers advocate for those integrated services that promote maximum accessibility while avoiding unnecessary duplication.

Social workers are advocates for the communities and within communities of social protection systems that are easily accessible to all members of the community. Advocacy is also a significant factor for the profession, whether or not it operates in highly resourceful social protection schemes, in settings where social protection is based completely on culture and faith or in support-related situations. Social workers support the formation of social protection systems in order to maintain and improve social relations, encourage social integration and create as harmonious interactions between people as possible.

Social security is the structure of programmes, assurance interventions, social support and well-being benefits that are provided by the state, civil society and community actors at local, regional or national level to safeguard the well-being and security of all members of society, particularly socially or economically deprived individuals and groups. The social work profession recognizes the significance of social security and its power to bring about change within a community and between individuals. Social workers drive to promote social harmony as the ultimate goal.

SUMMARY

This chapter deals with the importance of social security and its relevance in the social work profession. Social security is the safety that a society offers to people and families to ensure access to well-being and financial gain, predominantly in certain contingencies of life. Social security is an important safety instrument. It prevents deprivation and vulnerability by ensuring sustainable human development (Dreze & Sen, 1999). Urbanization and modernization have led to essential socio-economic modifications and have provided an increase in new tensions following the erosion of current family and communal security. Social security has a greater influence at all levels of society. Social work in the contemporary context is a professional service based on systematic knowledge and skills. On the other hand, social security means an array of safeguard measures given by society in contradiction of certain contingencies of life. These contingencies include old age, dependency, sickness, unemployment and accidents. In other words, social security can be understood as the safety that society provides to particular organizations in the face of certain hazardous situations. This chapter discusses origin, meaning, types and other various aspects of social security. India has a long history of formulating and implementing social security measures. Since independence, the governments at various levels have implemented a variety of schemes for ensuring the social security of the state's citizens. Social work has always joined hands with the combined efforts of the government as well as other developmental professionals in ensuring the necessary social backing for secure living.

TOP 10 TAKEAWAYS/MAIN POINTS

1. According to Dreze and Sen (1999), 'the basic idea of social security is to use social means to prevent deprivation and vulnerability to deprivation'.
2. Although the wide system of social assurance was shaped by the Government of Germany, the term 'social security' was formally recognized and authoritatively used in the USA in 1935.
3. In his works, Kautilya also referred to a number of pension systems, such as education pensions and public poor relief. He says that 'state itself should provide support to poor, pregnant women, to their new born offspring, to orphans, to the aged, the infirm, the afflicted and the helpless'.
4. The impact of the International Labour Organization also laid the basis for social security actions for labourers to implement the values of safe collective peace based on social justice.
5. According to the Universal Declaration on Human Rights Article 25,

    Everyone has the right to a standard of living adequate for the health and well-being of himself and of his family, including food, clothing, and housing and medical care and necessary social services, and the right to social security in the event of unemployment, sickness, disability, widowhood, old age or other lack of livelihood in circumstances beyond his control. Motherhood and childhood are entitled to special care and assistance. All children, whether born in or out of wedlock, shall enjoy the same social protection.

6. There are two types of social security.
    a. **Social assistance:** It is a method to provide benefits to people, usually for the vulnerable groups in a community (children, mothers, disabled, elderly people and so on) from general revenues of the state. It is non-contributory.
    b. **Social insurance:** A method to provide benefits to individuals through the contributions of beneficiaries, with contributions or subsidies from employer and the state.
7. Modern social work is a professional service based on scientific knowledge and skills.
8. The theoretical and practical understandings of the social work profession are entrenched in the fact that human beings cannot live sustainable, fulfilled lives unless they are interdependently connected in a social context.
9. The role of social workers in social security systems is to enable community commonness and meeting within the improvement of structures that may be comprehensive for all individuals and give them self-esteem and respect while confirming human rights and social justice.
10. Social workers are advocates for the communities and within communities of social protection systems that are easily accessible to all members of the community.

Keywords: Social work profession, human rights, social protection, Indian government

GLOSSARY

Social assistance: It is a method to provide benefits to people, usually for the vulnerable groups in a community (children, mothers, disabled, elderly people and so on) from general revenues of the state. It is non-contributory.

Social insurance: A method to provide benefits to individuals through the contributions of beneficiaries, with contributions or subsidies from employer and the state.

Social security:

Social security envisages that the members of the community shall be protected by collective action against social risks causing undue hardship and privation to individuals whose primary resources can seldom be adequate to meet them. The concept of social security is based on ideals of human dignity and social justice. The under lysing ideal behind social security measure is that a citizen who has contributed or is likely to contribute to his country's welfare should be given protection against certain hazards or as consequence of it. (Government of India, 1969)

Social work profession:

Social work is a practice-based profession and an academic discipline that promotes social change and development, social cohesion, and the empowerment and liberation of people. Principles of social justice, human rights, collective responsibility and respect for diversities are central to social work. Underpinned by theories of social work, social sciences, humanities and indigenous knowledge, social work engages people and structures to address life challenges and enhance well-being. The above definition may be amplified at national and/or regional levels. (Avenir Social, 2014)

ANALYTICAL QUESTIONS

1. Find out about current social security-related acts in India.
2. Write briefly about the relationship between social security and the social work profession.

MULTIPLE CHOICE QUESTIONS

1. Who defined 'social security is to use social means to prevent deprivation and vulnerability to deprivation'?
   a. V. V. Giri
   b. **Jean Dreze and Amartya Sen**
   c. Sir William Beveridge
   d. W. A. Robson

2. Which was the first country to formally recognize social security?
   a. **The USA**
   b. Germany
   c. India
   d. The Vatican City

3. Which aims to create positive collective outcomes by protecting people against financial scarcities?
   a. Social institution
   b. Social work
   c. **Social security**
   d. Social welfare

4. Which was the main guard of social security in ancient India?
   a. Caste
   b. Religion
   c. **Joint family**
   d. Education

5. The term '*zakat*' denotes _____.
   a. Service
   b. Justice
   c. Sharing
   d. **Charity**

6. What are the two types of social security?
   a. Social institutions and social assistance
   b. Social insurance and social work
   c. Social work and social service
   d. **Social insurance and social assistance**

7. Which is the best method to provide benefits to people, usually for the vulnerable groups in the community?
   a. Social institution
   b. Social insurance
   c. **Social assistance**
   d. Social service

8. Social security comes under which list?
   a. Union List
   b. **Concurrent List**
   c. State List
   d. Central List

9. What is the full form of ILO?
   a. International Livelihood Organization
   b. Indian Labour Organization
   c. **International Labour Organization**
   d. Indian Livelihood Organization

10. In which year was the Declaration of Philadelphia passed?
    a. 1934
    b. **1944**
    c. 1966
    d. 1977

REVIEW QUESTIONS

1. Define social security?
2. How is social security important to current human society?
3. Explain the historical development of social security at the international and national level.
4. Write a brief note on social security measures in India.
5. What is the social work profession?
6. Describe the role of social workers in the field of social security.
7. Elaborate the social work profession in social security.

REFERENCES

Avenir Social. (2014). The role of social work in social protection floors. IFSW Delegate Meeting Melbourne. http://www.ifsw.org/wp-content/uploads/ifsw-cdn/assets/ifsw_83600-1.pdf

Beveridge, S. W. (1942). *Social insurance and allied services*. Macmillan, 9, 326.

Beveridge, W. (1942). *Report on social insurance*. p. 6.

Chandra, M. (1976). *Industrial jurisprudence*. N. M. Tripathi.

Dreze, J., & Sen, A. (1999). Public action and social security: Foundations and strategy. In E. Ahmad, J. Dreze, J. Hills, & A. Sen (Eds), *Social security in developing countries* (pp. 3–34). Oxford University Press.

Encyclopædia Britannica. (1963). *Encyclopaedia Britannica* (vol. 20). Encyclopædia Britannica, Inc, p. 891.

Giri, V. V. (1972). *Labour problems in Indian industry*. Asia Publishing House.

Government of India. (1969). *Report of National Commission on labour*. p. 162. https://casi.sas.upenn.edu/sites/default/files/iit/National%20Commission%20on%20Labour%20Report.pdf

Jagdish. (2004). *Social welfare in the 21 century*. Akansha Publishing House.

Robson, W. A. (1945). *Social security*. George Allen and Unwin Limited.

Starr, P. (2017). Social security and the American public household. In T. Marmor & J. Mashaw (Eds), *Social Security: Beyond the Rhetoric of Crisis* (pp. 119-148). Princeton University Press.

United Nations. (1967). International covenant on economic, social and cultural rights. https://treaties.un.org/doc/treaties/1976/01/19760103%2009-57%20pm/ch_iv_03.pdf

United Nations. (1986). *Declaration on the right to development: Resolution/adopted by the General Assembly, 4 December 1986*. A/RES/41/128. https://www.ohchr.org/sites/default/files/rtd.pdf

United Nations. (2015). *Universal declaration of human rights*. United Nations. https://www.un.org/en/udhrbook/pdf/udhr_booklet_en_web.pdf

Universal Declaration of Human Rights. (1948). Articles 22 and 25. http://www.ohchr.org/EN/UDHR/Documents/UDHR_Translations/eng.pdf

Vrooman, J. C. (2009). *Rules of relief: Institutions of social security, and their impact*. Netherlands Institute for Social Research.

RECOMMEND READINGS

Gajendragadkar, P. B., Singh, B., Ram, B., Das, R., Ganguli, B. C., Kothari, D. C., Kotwal, M., Malviye, R. K., Ramakrishnan, P. R., Shashtri, R. R., Ramanujam, G., Tata, N. H., Khandelwal, G. D., Dange, S. A., Ganguly, B. N. (1969). *Report of the National Commission on labour*. Government of India. Ministry of Labour, Employment and Rehabilitation.

Goswami, Y. G. (2019). *Labour and industrial laws*. Central Law Agency.
Khan, A., & Khan, A. (2020). *Commentary on labour and industrial laws*. Asia Law House.
Kumar, A. (2003). *Social security and labour welfare*. Deep & Deep Publications.
Law Commission of India. (1923). *62nd report on Workmen's Compensation Act, 1923*. https://lawcommissionofindia.nic.in/51-100/report62.pdf
Ministry of Labour, Employment and Rehabilitation. (2003). *Report of the second National Commission on labour with emphasis on rationalization of labour laws and unorganized labour*. https://labour.gov.in/sites/default/files/39ilcagenda_1.pdf
Mishra, S. N. (2018). Labour and industrial laws. Central Law Publications.
Rao, Y. J. (2015). Factories laws in A. P. Asia Law House.
Singh, J. K. (2002). *Labour economics*. Deep and Deep Publications.
Spicker, P. (2011). *How social security works: An introduction to benefits in Britain*. Bristol University Press.
Srivastava, K. D. (2012). *Workmen's Compensation Act, 1923*. EBC.
Srivastava, S. C. (2005). *Treaties on social security and labour laws*. Eastern Book Company.

Social Work as a Profession: Principles and Methods, Scope, Theories, Models and Professional Status

- Chapter 12 *Professional Status of Social Work Profession in India*
- Chapter 13 *Professional Social Work Associations in India*
- Chapter 14 *Scope and Fields of Social Work and Emerging Areas*
- Chapter 15 *Principles and Methods of Social Work*
- Chapter 16 *Models of Social Work*
- Chapter 17 *Theories in Social Work*
- Chapter 18 *Skills in Social Work*

12

Professional Status of Social Work Profession in India

Bishnu Mohan Dash, Rajan Prakash and Sheeba Joseph

> **LEARNING OBJECTIVES**
> - To understand the concept of the profession
> - To discuss the status of social work in India
> - To analyse the barriers in the professionalization of social work in India
> - To suggest ways for making the discipline of social work a profession

The science, which teaches arts and handicrafts is merely science for the gaining of a living; but the science which teaches deliverance from worldly existence, is not that the true science?

—Prajñadanda (The Staff of Wisdom), attributed to Nagarjuna

INTRODUCTION

Social work has an undefined area of practice and furthering its scope day by day and venturing into every field. The lack of proper fieldwork manual, proper training in developing skills and competencies as professionals, absence of professional council of social work education, weak professional association, lack of indigenous literature and absence of continuous training for faculty members pose significant hindrances in the professionalization of social work education. The unsystematic fieldwork supervision, lack of seriousness in the evaluation of fieldwork reports and lack of linkages between theory teaching and realities in the fieldwork constitute a significant barrier in the professionalization of social work education in India. Even in some of the universities, social work courses are run by other departments. The academicians without degrees in social work also teach social work in some of the universities. However, the emergence of social work as a profession has Victorian roots, originated in the context of capitalism to mitigate the socio-economic problems caused by it. It had its origin in the 19th century with the emergence of a philosophy of 'scientific charity' which stated that charity should be secular, rational and empirical as opposed to sectarian, sentimental and dogmatic (Huff, 2008). The observations made by Flexner (1915) more than a 100 years ago still characterize the same situation in our country. The social workers still have an identity crisis, and the profession is still struggling for professional status. Many studies report that field education in social work has become a ritual in colleges and universities. There are no objective criteria for fieldwork evaluation. Several factors are responsible for such a pathetic situation of the social work profession in our country.

To make it a profession, academicians have used the same methods and approaches that are prevalent in the West and the USA. Social work philosophy, principles, methods and techniques have been accepted in the same way as they are in the USA. America's socio-economic system is self-centred, whereas Indian social system emphasizes collective welfare. Here, the roots of the majority of the problems are inherent in the social structure. Therefore, they can be resolved only after bringing the required changes in it. Still, schools here have accepted individual approach in social work teaching and training (Singh & Srivastava, 2003). Since ancient times, Indian thinkers have believed that *Seva Parmo* dharma, that is, *Seva* is the ultimate religion.

Nevertheless, some particular service requiring specific knowledge and skill have also been known and practised here. In India, the roots of social work have existed since ancient times in the form of mutual aid, charity and the wish of the welfare of all. Mutual support and mutual assistance to a person in need of help have been a unique feature of Indian society since ancient times. Indian mystics were known as the symbols of renunciation and penance, and they did not wish for profit (Oman, 1903). This chapter, besides highlighting various factors which are hampering the growth of social work education and its professional status in the country, has also suggested various measures for its improvement. It emphasizes the need to reorient social work in India in a new form taking into consideration the unique social structure of the country.

THE CONCEPT OF PROFESSION

Any occupation can be accepted as a profession only if it is based on knowledge, science and skill, that is, all these characteristics of a profession should be present in that work. The same characteristics provide a professional appearance to any occupation. Various scholars have noted the characteristics of the profession. Greenwood (1957) considers the following four qualities to be essential in a profession.

1. *Systematic theory:* It develops general and specific concepts and specialized knowledge.
2. *Authority:* In any profession, some experts have in-depth knowledge about various aspects of the profession and dominate their profession.
3. *Community sanction:* A profession gets the approval of the community and the state, and it exists in line with the interests of the society.
4. *Ethical code:* In any profession, there are some rules and regulations which are mandatory for all the members of the profession.
5. *Culture:* A profession takes into account the cultural context of that particular area in its domain.

> **Box 12.1 University Grants Commission Review Committees on Social Work Education**
>
> Till date, three review committees have been formed by the University Grants Commission, a national level body to advise universities in India on financial and educational matters to review the social work curriculum. The first committee was set up in 1960, the second in 1975 and the third in 2001 for research and practice, training, coordination of social work education and maintenance of standards of education. Given the unique nature and the need for the social work discipline, the first review committee emphasized the autonomy of the social work institutes. This view was also shared by the second review committee, which, besides this, highlighted the need to establish a National Council on Social Work Education for the development and promotion of social work education in India.
>
> The third review committee stressed the need for studying the social realities in social work discipline and recommended that the social work curriculum be divided in three sets, which are as follows:
>
> - The core set includes the theory, concepts, ethics, values, ideology and philosophy.
> - The second, that is, supportive set deals with the skills and knowledge essential to supporting the core set.
> - The third, interdisciplinary, set includes the concepts and theories which are relevant for social work (Thomas, 2010, cited in Botcha, 2012).
>
> However, the implementation of recommendations of these committees have been abysmal, and there is still the lack of coordination in social work education, and the discipline has not been developed on the basis of social realities of India.

MEANING AND DEFINITION OF PROFESSION

The profession is a much common term which people usually use for the sense of belonging to an enterprise, employment or trade. In the modern era, the profession is understood as an organized form of occupation, requiring specific formal knowledge and incorporating the skills of proficient workers. The word 'profession' is derived from the Latin word professiō, which means avowal or public declaration. However, in the 13th and 14th centuries, it began to be used for religious devotion and devotion to the valour of knights. In the 16th and 17th centuries, it gradually began to be used for a form of occupation. Even today, a layman uses it as a synonym for a kind of occupation. Various scholars have tried to define the profession as follows.

- According to Cogan (1953):
  A profession is a vocation whose practice is founded upon an understanding of the theoretical structure of some department of learning or science, and upon the abilities accompanying such understanding. This understanding and these abilities are applied to the vital practical affairs of man. The practices of the profession are modified by knowledge of a generalised nature and by the accumulated wisdom and experience of

mankind, which serve to correct the errors of specialism. The profession, serving the vital needs of man, considers its first ethical imperative to be altruistic service to the client.
- Abraham Flexner (1915) defined it as follows:
  Professions are intellectual and learned; they are in the next place definitely practical. No profession can be merely academic and theoretic; the professional man must have an absolutely definite and practical object. His processes are essentially intellectual; his raw material is derived from the world of learning; thereupon, he must do with it a clean-cut, concrete task. All the activities about the professional quality of which we should at once agree are not only intellectual and learned, but definite in purpose.
- According to Johnson (2016):
  A profession is not an occupation, but a means of controlling an occupation. Likewise, professionalisation is a historically specific process which some occupations have undergone at a particular time, rather than a process which certain occupations may always be expected to undergo because of their essential qualities.
- Freidson (1988) has defined the profession as 'the most strategic distinction lies in legitimate, organised autonomy—that a profession is distinct from other occupations in that it has been given the right to control its own work'.

It is clear from the above definitions that the profession is used in the sense of an organized occupation which requires the particular kind of skill and proficiency. These skills and proficiency are considered to be essential for working in that profession.

CHARACTERISTICS OF THE PROFESSION

Many scholars have written about the characteristics of a profession. Generally, these characteristics are the benchmark for the qualification of a particular occupation for a profession. Some of the characteristics, as identified by Millerson (1964), are as follows:

- Proficiency base on theoretical knowledge
- Provision for training and livelihood
- Evaluation of the abilities of members
- Organization
- Professional code of conduct
- Compassionate service

Abraham Flexner (1915) identified six qualities of the profession and its professionals. These are as follows:

1. Professions involve essentially intellectual operations with enormous individual responsibility.
2. They derive their raw material from science and learning.
3. They work up to a practical and definite end.
4. They possess an educationally communicable technique (their language).
5. They tend to self-organization.
6. They are becoming increasingly altruistic in motivation.

Based on the above characteristics, it can be inferred that systematic and scientific knowledge, specific methods and techniques, education, organizations, community sanction and approval, and a code of ethics are the essential criteria for a profession.

KNOWLEDGE AND TRAINING

All the services provided in any profession should be based on scientific knowledge and specialized art (which is evident from the use of specific methods and skills by the professional practitioners). Social work profession uses a variety of skills, techniques and activities tailored to individuals and their environment. It addresses the barriers in society, inequalities and injustices (Adams et al., 2017). Its mission is to help people develop their full potential, enrich their lives and prevent stagnation. Social work uses many theoretical framework and methods for the study and eradication of various social problems. Rigorous training is required to gain an understanding of the theoretical aspects. There is a misconception in the society that anyone can practise social work which emanates from the ignorance of the various modern and scientifically tested approaches for working with the target group.

SOCIAL WORK AS A PROFESSION IN INDIA

Whether social work is a profession in India or not depends on to what extent it satisfies the criteria of a 'profession'. Also, what are the state of community sanction and approval and the quality of professional education? If it uses the scientific knowledge, skills and theoretical frameworks for practice in India. These are some of the aspects which determine the professional status of the discipline.

PROFESSION OR SEMI-PROFESSION

One often faces the dilemma when asked about the state of social work in India. One of the main reasons for this is that social work in Indian society has not received the kind of social recognition as it has received in America and other Western countries. Social work in India emerged as a discipline in the 20th century but, since its inception, it has faced an identity crisis. As far as India is concerned, social work is not considered anything more than financial aid to the poor (Cnaan et al., 1999). It has ignored the current and contextual realities of India. The education which is imparted in the social work curriculum in India does not conform to the Indian standards. That is one of the main reasons social work could not achieve professional status in the country. It is safe to say that social work is still a semi-profession as far as India is concerned and we have failed to develop the methods and techniques that would take into account the specific problems embedded in Indian society. The education imparted in the social work curriculum has adopted the same content as taught in America. It may be noted that America is a capitalist country, and the socio-economic system is more appropriate for individual-centric approaches.

In contrast, the Indian social system emphasizes collective welfare and the roots of the majority of the problems are because of the dysfunction of the particular aspect of the social system which can be resolved only after bringing the required changes in it. Despite that, the schools of social work in India have failed to incorporate these essential elements in their teaching and do not focus on the real problems (Cox et al., 2006). Indian social workers are proficient at using the American methods, which does not prove to be relevant in the Indian context. The technique of working with the individual, groups and society as well as that of social action needs to be developed techniques and those that have been developed also need to be given Indian form.

Social work is a practice-oriented subject, but many schools have given very little weightage to the fieldwork. The tradition of working with people in the field of social work has been followed since ancient times, which made one aware of the practical problems but, in the modern era, there is much emphasis at the theoretical aspects of social work (Banks, 2012). While this is important, it has also proved to be a hindrance in recognition of the discipline as a profession. There is still a state of confusion about the concept of social work among ordinary people and, even today, it is perceived more as an act of philanthropy, charity or social service. Voluntary workers, social reformers and politicians are all regarded as a social worker, and it has made it very difficult for the discipline to emerge as a profession.

Did You Know?

As per the different sources and experts, there are more than 350 schools of social work in India. Nevertheless, their geographical distribution is not uniform in the country. Karnataka and Maharashtra have the highest number with more than 70 schools in each state, and many South Indian states have a large number of institutions, whereas Bihar, Manipur, Mizoram, Meghalaya, Assam, Himachal Pradesh, Uttarakhand and Jammu and Kashmir have only one department or school, and all five of the north-eastern states have no school at all. Even in those states which have a high number of schools, these are mostly centred in urban areas and rural areas where more than 70 per cent of the population lives have very few schools.

THE GAP IN THEORY AND PRACTICE

There is a lack of Indian literature written for addressing the problem and whatever emerges as a form of knowledge in the West ultimately becomes part of Indian literature. At one hand, it has given rise to an abundance of literature available on every issue it has also added to the stock what is very little relevant. When schools adopt this literature, the new generation of social workers realizes the extent of the gap in theory and actual practice. For example, American books are written on the basis of the fundamental belief that a client comes to the institution themselves and asks for service. However, in India, the situation is different. Here, those who are in need must be encouraged to take the service of the institution or the professionals, and because of these teachings students face disappointment and fail to mature on their own (Bogo & Vayda, 1998). If social work is to achieve professional status in India, then social work principles, methods and techniques will have to be developed and put into practice according to the Indian realities.

LACK OF LEGAL APPROVAL TO PROFESSIONAL ASSOCIATION

There are many professional bodies of social work in India. Notable among these are the Indian Society of Professional Social Work, Professional Social Workers' Association, the Bharatiya Samaj Karya Parishad and the National Association of Professional Social Workers. However, none of these has control over what is being taught in social work curriculum or how it is being practised in India. For example, our social workers talk about the resettlement of unmarried mothers which is the problem of Western countries (Engstrom & Okamura, 2004) and despite the effectiveness of social casework, India has very little utility for it. On the contrary, there is a need in our country to use the method of community organization and social action effectively, but we are not using it to the extent it is required (Specht & Courtney 1995). Even there is no coordination among these bodies and, because of this, schools have failed to adopt a uniform curriculum and are dependent on the content as taught in other countries. Formally, social work education in India started in 1936 AD. Ever since, apart from some fundamental changes, training and practice of social work are still taking place in the same way. Although the number of educational schools and organizations have increased, social work in the country has very little as its achievement. Even today, the schools are dependent on the government for sustenance, and the government has to work more diligently in meeting this need.

Did You Know?

Mahatma Gandhi Chitrakoot Gramodaya Vishwavidyalaya is a rural university at Chitrakoot, India, established by Nanaji Deshmukh, a social activist and reformer, to provide higher education to the people living in rural areas. Apart from social work, it runs many more disciplines and also provides practical training in those disciplines.

NEED TO RESTRUCTURE THE SOCIAL WORK CURRICULUM

There is a need to restructure the social work curriculum in India so that it can be made more fulfilling for the society. Most books of social work have been written by writers and thinkers from American and other Western countries. More literature needs to be written on Indian social work, which describes the social, economic and political life. Even if we adopt the Western literature, the efforts should be made to make it more relevant for Indian society. The curriculum of social work needs to incorporate Indian philosophy, literature and culture, apart from placing more emphasis on fieldwork practice. Also, the lack of books on social work in Indian languages is a significant hindrance in reaching to ordinary people, given the vast linguistic diversity of Indian society.

If social work in India is to achieve professional status, then it must restructure its curriculum based on indigenous knowledge and literature. We have to tailor our curriculum to the Indian scenario and redesign it (Cohen, 2011). This effort requires the inclusion of the traditional knowledge of Indian spirituality, philosophy and culture in line with modern science and technology. Many social reformers and scholars who worked in ancient times may illuminate the path. Today, there is a need to replicate their experiences, knowledge and experimentation in the social work curriculum. Some of the social reformers including Raja Ram Mohan Roy, Swami Vivekananda, Swami Dayananda, Mahatma Gandhi, Dr Bhimrao Ambedkar, Vinoba Bhave and Nanaji Deshmukh and others have a stronghold on Indian society, and inclusion of their ideas and values will give the discipline a firm base and will help the discipline get the community sanction and can be an essential step in the professionalization of the discipline.

DHARMA AS THE GUIDING FORCE OF SOCIAL WORK PRACTICE

Just as all disciplines and practices have their ethics, social work practice also places great importance to ethics. The basic tenets of ethics of social work practice are influenced by the principles of social work, which include helping people according to their needs, raising voice against social injustice, protecting human dignity, promoting mutual interdependence and tolerance in society. For social work practice, all these values are indicative of high human values, and dharma can play an essential role in strengthening it (Williams & Kabat-Zinn, 2011). For Indian society, dharma is not the religion but the duty of one for the others. In the context of social work, it is the duty of social workers towards the service users and vice versa. Dharma refers to living the life decently by holding high values and creates a feeling of working with the person. For those bound by this virtue, their life becomes society-centred rather than self-centred. It implies truth and sacrifice. Inclusion of this value in social work practice, in terms of ethics of social work, will help the development of a person protecting the dignity of all and eliminating the evils such as disharmony and inequality in the society and can also be important in strengthening the hold on Indian society and getting the social approval.

SUMMARY

This chapter deals with the professional status of social work in India. A profession is an organized form of occupation that fulfils a particular function in society and is based on the theoretical knowledge, practical work, a code of conduct, presence of experts and includes the skills and techniques. The rigorous training in any profession is essential as it enables one to gain proficiency and practical knowledge of theoretical understanding. The discipline of social work in India in its modern form came into existence about eight decades ago; despite many achievements in its stock, it is still facing an identity crisis and struggling to get the professional status. As far as the context of India is concerned, it is characterized more by the inheritance of the value of collective welfare and most of its problems are embedded in the sociocultural structure.

Nevertheless, the education and practice of social work in India have ignored the ground realities of Indian context and have imported the contents that are not sufficient for practice in

India. This situation has also been magnified by the lack of original literature on the subject, less weightage to the fieldwork in the curriculum and concentration of the institutes, mainly in urban areas. These factors are responsible for a significant gap in theory and practice, and society has failed to give it a sanction and approval as a profession.

While the role of a professional body in the regulation of curriculum and practice is crucial, the presence of many professional bodies, the lack of coordination among them and no legitimate sanction to any by the government have undermined the autonomy and self-regulation of the schools of social work in India. For a professional status, the discipline needs to restructure its curriculum and must incorporate Indian experience and knowledge. The thinkers and social reformers of India can illuminate the path in this direction and supplementing the code of conduct of practice with the concept of dharma can strengthen the hold of the discipline on Indian society and will reorient it to the needs and aspirations of Indian society.

TOP 10 TAKEAWAYS/MAIN POINTS

1. Indian society is characterized more by the collective welfare than individualistic well-being for most of the problems in India are embedded in the socio-economic-cultural structure.
2. Many scholars have made an active attempt to define the complex concept of profession and notable among these are Cogan, Flexner, Johnson and Friedson.
3. There are many barriers in the professionalization of social work in India; these include a little emphasis on the fieldwork practice in the curriculum, lack of proper training to the social workers and the absence of original literature on the subject.
4. A profession is an organized kind of occupation, including both theoretical knowledge and practical aspects.
5. The essential characteristics of a profession are the existence of an authority, community sanction, ethical code of conduct and a cultural element.
6. There is a significant gap in the theory and practice of social work in India as the content taught in social work curriculum in India is of very little relevance to the actual realities of the field. Nevertheless, no sincere effort has been made for a systematic revision of the curriculum.
7. There are many professional bodies for social work education and practice in India, but none of these has legitimate control over the curriculum, teaching and practice of the discipline.
8. The lack of original literature for social work practice in India has led to the imitation of those methods and techniques of social work which may not be sufficient for the Indian context.
9. Restructuring the social work curriculum in India and including such aspects as Indian culture, philosophy and thinkers may help get social approval.
10. Ethical code of conduct is an integral aspect of social work practice, and the inclusion of the concept of dharma in it may strengthen the discipline in terms of its hold on the society.

Keywords: Profession, professional social work, India, UGC Review Committee

GLOSSARY

Dharma: Dharma is an essential element of Indian philosophy and culture. Indian society believes that it not only shapes social, political and economic aspects of human life but also transcends to the spiritual and psychological aspect of human life.

Individualistic approach: In social work, individualistic approach stresses for adapting the intervention and services to the need of an individual. It is believed that making the intervention more personalized is more effective in alleviating the problem of the individual. This practice is done given the physical, psychological and emotional needs of an individual. While this approach is necessary in social work, reducing the profession only to it can ignore the broader collective approach. There are plenty of instances where a collective focus can work.

Social structure: Herbert Spencer is credited for popularizing the term *social structure* with the publication of his seminal work *Principles of Sociology* in 1885. According to him, as our body is made up of many smaller parts, the same way the society also has its constituent elements. The proper function of each of the constituent part is necessary for the proper functioning of society.

ANALYTICAL QUESTIONS

1. Discuss the professional status of social work in India.
2. How can the inclusion of dharma in social work discipline in India help it gain community sanction?

MULTIPLE CHOICE QUESTIONS

1. Which of the following is not an essential feature of a profession?
   a. Community sanction
   b. Authority
   c. Systematic knowledge
   d. **Voluntary work**

2. Which of the following is the etymological meaning of the word *professiō*?
   a. **Avowal or public declaration**
   b. Trust
   c. A professional body
   d. Authority

3. Who defined a profession as distinct from other occupations in that it has been given the right to control its own work?
   a. Flexner
   b. Johnson
   c. Cogan
   d. **Freidson**

4. How many review committees have been set up to reform social work curriculum in India?
    a. 1
    b. 2
    c. **3**
    d. 4

5. Which of the following is a barrier in the professional development of social work in India?
    a. The importance placed on fieldwork
    b. **Existence of many professional bodies with no legitimate control of any on the teaching and practice of social work in India**
    c. Social approval to the discipline
    d. None of the above

6. Which of the following is responsible for the gap in theory and practice of social work in India?
    a. Lack of professional body
    b. **Teaching those theories and concepts which have very little relevance in Indian society**
    c. Financial dependence of schools of social works on government for sustenance
    d. All of the above

7. According to Abraham Flexner, which of the following is the quality of the profession and its professionals?
    a. Professions involve essentially intellectual operations with enormous individual responsibility
    b. They derive their raw material from science and learning
    c. They work up to a practical and definite end
    d. **All of the above**

8. When did social work education in India start?
    a. **1936**
    b. 1937
    c. 1938
    d. 1939

9. Which of the following characterizes profession?
    a. Evaluation of the abilities of members
    b. Organization
    c. Professional code of conduct
    d. **All of the above**

10. In the context of profession, who has said that 'the most strategic distinction lies in legitimate, organised autonomy—that a profession is distinct from other occupations in that it has been given the right to control its own work'?
    a. Johnson
    b. **Freidson**
    c. Flexner
    d. Cogan

REVIEW QUESTIONS

1. What are the essential elements that make a discipline a profession?
2. How is a profession different from an occupation?

REFERENCES

Adams, R., Dominelli, L., & Payne, M. (Eds.). (2017). *Social work: Themes, issues and critical debates.* Palgrave Macmillan.
Banks, S. (2012). *Ethics and values in social work.* Macmillan International Higher Education.
Bogo, M., & Vayda, E. J. (1998). *The practice of field instruction in social work: Theory and process.* University of Toronto Press.
Botcha, R. (2012). Problems and challenges for social work education in India: Some recommendations. *International Journal of Multidisciplinary Educational Research, 1*(3), 201–212.
Cnaan, R. A., Wineburg, R. J., & Boddie, S. C. (1999). *The newer deal: Social work and religion in partnership.* Columbia University Press.
Cogan, M. L. (1953). Toward a definition of profession. *Harvard Educational Review, 23*(1), 33–50.
Cohen, B. J. (2011). Design-based practice: A new perspective for social work. *Social Work, 56*(4), 337–346.
Cox, D., Pawar, M., & Pawar, M. S. (2006). *International social work: Issues, strategies, and programs.* SAGE.
Engstrom, D. W., & Okamura, A. (2004). A plague of our time: Torture, human rights, and social work. *Families in Society, 85*(3), 291–300.
Flexner, A. (1915). Is social work a profession? *Research on Social Work Practice, 11*(2), 152–165.
Freidson, E. (1988). *Profession of medicine: A study of the sociology of applied knowledge.* University of Chicago Press.
Greenwood, E. (1957). Attributes of a profession. *Social Work,* 45–55.
Huff, D. (2008). *The social work history station.* Boise State University.
Johnson, T. J. (2016). *Professions and power* (Routledge revivals). Routledge.
Millerson, G. (1964). *The qualifying associations: A study in professionalization.* Routledge.
Oman, J. C. (1903). *The mystics, ascetics, and saints of India: A study of Sadhuism, with an account of the yogis, sanyasis, bairagis, and other strange Hindu sectarians.* T. Fisher Unwin.
Singh, S., & Srivastava, S. P. (Eds.). (2003). *Social work education in India: Challenges and opportunities.* New Royal Book Company.
Specht, H., & Courtney, M. E. (1995). *Unfaithful angels: How social work has abandoned its mission.* Simon and Schuster.
Williams, J. M. G., & Kabat-Zinn, J. (2011). Mindfulness: Diverse perspectives on its meaning, origins, and multiple applications at the intersection of science and Dharma. *Contemporary Buddhism, 12*(1), 1–18.

RECOMMENDED READINGS

Alphonse, M., George, P., & Moffatt, K. (2008). Redefining social work standards in the context of globalisation: Lessons from India. *International Social Work, 51*(2), 145–158.
Banerjee, G. R. (1973). *Papers on social work: An Indian perspective* (Vol. 23). Tata Institute of Social Sciences.
Dasgupta, S. (Ed.). (1967). *Towards a philosophy of social work in India.* Popular Book Services.
Dasgupta, S., & Kohák, E. V. (1968). *Social work and social change. A case study in Indian village development* (with Introduction by E. V. Kohák). Porter Sargent Publisher.

Dash, B. M. (2017). Revisiting eight decades of social work education in India. *Asian Social Work and Policy Review, 11*(1), 66–75.
Dash, B. M., & Roy, S. (2019). Eight decades of fieldwork training in India: Identifying the gaps and missing links. In *Fieldwork Training in Social Work* (pp. 151–168). Routledge.
Flexner, A. (2001). Is social work a profession? *Research on Social Work Practice, 11*(2), 152–165.
Gangrade, K. D. (1976). *Dimensions of social work in India: Case studies*. Marwah Publications.
George, P., & Marlowe, S. (2005). Structural social work in action: Experiences from rural India. *Journal of Progressive Human Services, 16*(1), 5–24.
Gray, M. (2005). Dilemmas of international social work: Paradoxical processes in indigenisation, universalism and imperialism. *International Journal of Social Welfare, 14*(3), 231–238.
Gray, M., Coates, J., & Bird, M. Y. (Eds.). (2008). *Indigenous social work around the world: Towards culturally relevant education and practice*. Ashgate.
Healy, L. M., & Thomas, R. L. (2020). *International social work: Professional action in an interdependent world*. Oxford University Press.
Jacob, K. K. (1965). *Methods and fields of social work in India*. Asia Publishing House.
Khinduka, S. K. (Ed.). (1965). *Social work in India*. Kitab Mahal.
Kohli, H. K., & Faul, A. C. (2005). Cross-cultural differences towards diversity issues in attitudes of graduating social work students in India and the United States. *International Social Work, 48*(6), 809–822.
Midgley, J. (1981). *Professional imperialism: Social work in the third world* (Vol. 16). Heinemann Educational Books.
Nagpaul, H. (1972). *The study of Indian society: A sociological analysis of social welfare and social work education*. S. Chand.
Nagpaul, H. (1996). *Social work in urban India*. Rawat Publications.
Palattiyil, G., Blyth, E., Sidhva, D., & Balakrishnan, G. (2010). Globalisation and cross-border reproductive services: Ethical implications of surrogacy in India for social work. *International Social Work, 53*(5), 686–700.
Parmar, P. M. (2002). *Social work and social welfare in India*. Sublime Publications.
Pathak, S. H. (1961). *Medical social work in India*. Delhi School of Social Work.
Shastri, R. R. (1966). *Social work tradition in India*. Welfare Forum & Research Organization.
Sheafor, B. W., Morales, A., & Scott, M. E. (2010). *Social work: A profession of many faces*. Allyn & Bacon.
Wadia, A. R. (1961). *History and philosophy of social work in India*. Allied Publishers.
Williams, E. E., & Ellison, F. (1996). Culturally informed social work practice with American Indian clients: Guidelines for non-Indian social workers. *Social Work, 41*(2), 147–151.

13

Professional Social Work Associations in India

Ram Babu Botcha

LEARNING OBJECTIVES

- To understand the national associations in social work and various categories of associations
- To comprehend the need and functions of national associations in social work and their contributions
- To analyse the role of national associations in improving the standards of social work profession
- To find out the role of national associations of social work towards promoting the core values of the profession

Coming together is a beginning; keeping together is progress; working together is success.

—Henry Ford

INTRODUCTION

Professional social work has completed eight decades in India after its inception in 1936. India is fortunate to have a good beginning of professional social work education and training under the leadership of founding father of social work in India, Dr Clifford Manshardt in Mumbai with the establishment of Sir Dorabji Tata Graduate School of Social Work now popularly known as Tata Institute of Social Sciences (TISS). Many stakeholders including professional associations, institutions of social work, educators, students and practitioners have come up to standardize and streamline the professional training in this country in line with the many developed countries such as the USA, the UK, Germany and Australia.

There are some prominent professional associations in social work in India at state, regional and national levels. The associations are the Bharatiya Samaj Karya Parishad (BSKP; set up in 2018), the National Association of Professional Social Workers in India (NAPSWI; registered in 2005), the Indian Society of Professional Social Work (ISPSW; registered in 1970) and the Association of Schools of Social Work in India (ASSWI; set up in 1959). One of the important associations called the Indian Association of Trained Social Workers (IATSW) was established in 1961 and in between it was made dysfunctional. Every association had put their efforts towards professional advancement in this country.

The author explained the journey of professional associations at national level in India and also to analyse the efforts of various national-level associations on the basis of the available literature. Finally, this chapter gave a set of roles and functions of the national associations of social work in India towards contributing for strengthening of the profession thereby contributing to the society's development.

NATIONAL ASSOCIATION: CONCEPT, SCOPE AND DEFINITION

National associations in any profession in general strive to bring all its students, educators and practitioners work together towards strengthening of their profession. They may concentrate on standardization, public recognition, government's approvals, meeting the demands of professionals and so on. The associations should adopt a common agenda aiming at the prosperity of the professions in their field.

National associations in social work generally work at the national level in bringing students, educators, practitioners and schools/departments together in achieving the goals of the profession. The national associations also organize various events in different parts of the country to provide a common platform to the professionals to share their experiences and learn from each other. The national associations update the current trends and contemporary issues in social work profession and bring all the stakeholders together to meet/solve the needs/problems of the people in the society.

National associations can be defined as 'a group of people organized for a joint purpose at national level working towards attaining their common goals/objectives aiming at well-being of all the professions belongs to that profession'. National associations in social work strive to work for the welfare of the students, educators and practitioners across the country through various activities and engagements for the last five decades.

TYPES/CATEGORIES OF PROFESSIONAL ASSOCIATIONS

In order to fulfil the professional needs of social work profession in India and other parts of the world, there are associations at state, national, regional and international levels. These associations were established based on the circumstances and needs of the profession. Each of those associations are contributing towards strengthening the profession and fulfilling the needs of the social work professionals in their respective states and nations. Various categories of professional associations in social work are provided in Table 13.1.

TABLE 13.1 Categories of Professional Associations in Social Work

S. No.	Level	Names of the Associations	Location
1	State	Kerala Association of Professional Social Workers	Kerala
		Maharashtra Association of Social Work Educators	Maharashtra
2	National	NAPSWI	Delhi, India
		Australian Association of Social Workers	Canberra, Australia
3	Regional	Asian and Pacific Association for Social Work Education	Japan
4	International	International Association of Schools of Social Work (IASSW)	USA
		International Federation of Social Workers (IFSW)	Switzerland

The above associations of professional social work have been rendering their services in bringing social work schools, educators, practitioners and students together in their respective locations in attaining the goals of the profession. These associations are working in their locations in organizing conferences/seminars, sharing the experiences, enriching the existing body of knowledge, involving in productive research and so on. These associations are also fulfilling the needs of the professionals and provide sound solutions to the problems and needs of the people in the society.

VARIOUS NATIONAL-LEVEL ASSOCIATIONS IN INDIA

The idea of establishing professional associations was first mooted by Dr J. M. Kumarappa, the then director of TISS in 1961, at the annual meeting of the Indian Conference of social work (now known as the Indian Council of Social Welfare). With this, the ASSWI was initiated the same year, followed by the establishment of the Indian Association of Alumni of Schools of Social Work later named as the IATSW (Nanavatty, 1997). Later on, the other national-level associations such as ISPSW, NAPSWI and BSKP emerged in India (Table 13.2).

BHARATIYA SAMAJ KARYA PARISHAD

BSKP is a national-level pan-India organization of social work professionals, academicians, researchers and students. In its *Wardha Declaration* on 30 June 2018, the BSKP unanimously adopted a proposal to observe 11 October, the birthday of Nanaji Deshmukh, as Indian Social Work Day or Bharatiya Samaj Karya Diwas. Since then, the Indian Social Work Day is being celebrated in the central as well as provincial social work institutions throughout the country. 'BSKP is happy to associate in the dissemination of the importance of teaching and practice social work from Nanaji Deshmukh's way of serving people in need,' said Professor.

Professional Social Work Associations in India

TABLE 13.2 Prominent Social Work Associations in India

S. No.	Name of the Association	Years of Establishment	Active/Inactive/Defunct
1.	BSKP	2018	Active
2.	NAPSWI	2005	Active
3.	National Coordinating Committee of Professional Social Workers	2003	Inactive
4.	ISPSW	1970	Active
5.	ASSWI	1961	Inactive
6.	IATSW	1961	Defunct

Y. S. Siddegowda (2010), Vice Chancellor, Tumkur University, Karnataka. 'Nanaji Deshmukh is an epitome of India Social Work. With his deep-seated commitment to the sustainable development of villagers and forest dwellers defined by values of self-reliance, compassion and renunciation' (Dash, 2019).

BSKP was established in 2018 under the meticulous stewardship of Dr Bishnu Mohan Dash, faculty of social work from Dr Bhim Rao Ambedkar College, University of Delhi. Its headquarters is located in New Delhi. The prime goal of this Parishad is to Indianize social work profession across the country. The association has been working with various central universities, state universities, both government and private colleges in promoting *Bhartiyakaran of Samaj Karya* in India. It has been working in the direction of the teachings and practices of Bharat Ratna Nanaji Deshmukh who has dedicated his entire life to serve the society with compassion and commitment.

The association has been observing the birthday of Bharat Ratna Nanaji Deshmukh as the Indian Social Work Day on 11 October every year. Many eminent social work educators, practitioners and prominent schools of social work in India are joining this association in bringing recognition to social work profession in this country. In the process of Indianization of social work, the association is striving to incorporate the value system and practices of various religions with an objective to inculcate the strong values among students, practitioners, researchers and educators of social work in India. These efforts will guide them towards building strong society while addressing the problems of the people and fulfilling the needs of various sections of the society in India.

Did You Know?

The emergence of professional associations in social work was the idea of Dr J. M. Kumarappa, the then director of TISS in 1961. He proposed to have a national-level association in one of the annual meetings in Mumbai. After that, all the national associations of social work were established.

NATIONAL ASSOCIATION OF PROFESSIONAL SOCIAL WORKERS IN INDIA

NAPSWI is one of the largest member-based organization of professional social workers in the country. Established in 2005, NAPSWI is a non-profit, non-political, national-level organization dedicated to the promotion of standard and status of social work profession with a vision to create a compassionate fraternity of professional social workers. NAPSWI intends to promote the social work profession across the country with the aim of improving the quality of services in the social welfare and social development sectors on one hand and to protect interests of social work professionals on the other. NAPSWI believes in working with different stakeholders, including social work educational institutions, government, non-government organizations, civil society organizations and others. In order to attain its goals for the social work profession, the following objectives were formulated and being achieved:

1. To promote the profession of social work across the country with the aim of improving the quality of service in the social welfare and social development sectors
2. To act as a national-level organization and to represent social work professionals and profession at national and international levels
3. To improve the quality of social work education training and practice in the country and promote such activities as are conductive to social work profession and social work professionals
4. To undertake, organize and facilitate academic and professional interaction through studies, courses, training courses, conferences, seminars, workshops, lectures and research in matters relating to social work profession and professionals
5. To develop the code of conduct for professional social workers in the field of education, research, action and practice aimed at enhancing the status of social work profession and performance of the professionals
6. To work for better working conditions and conditions for work of social work professionals in general in India and elsewhere
7. To cooperate and collaborate with any such organizations/institutions at regional/state/national or international level having similar objectives and similar international levels
8. To open its branches at state level/regional level/zonal level in order to promote and strengthen the NAPSWI
9. To publish journal research papers, books, encyclopaedia and so on directly or indirectly related to social work profession
10. To work for the protection and promotion of the rights and interests of the members at different levels and initiate measures aimed at providing scholarships, awards, recognitions and improving working conditions and conditions for work professionals
11. To do any activity permissible under the law of land which may be instrumental or incidental in promoting the aims and objectives of the society

NAPSWI has organized 10 annual national seminars on social work response to HIV/AIDS with different themes from 2004 onwards in collaboration with various reputed institutions in India. From 2013 onwards, the association started organizing the Indian Social Congress; till date, seven congresses were organized in various parts of the country. The association also confers Lifetime Achievement Awards every year to the well-known social workers for their incredible contribution to both educators and practitioners in India.

INDIAN SOCIETY OF PROFESSIONAL SOCIAL WORK

ISPSW was formerly known as the Indian Society of Psychiatric Social Work which was established in 1970 by Dr R. K. Upadhyaya and his staff of the Department of Psychiatric Social Work, Central Institute of Psychiatry, Ranchi. It aims at meeting the challenges of present-day social work practice and creating a platform for information exchange among fellow professionals. Later, it has been constantly upgraded to reach this current status of professional identity and recognition by Dr I. A. Sharif and faculty members, Department of Psychiatric Social Work, National Institute of Mental Health and Neuro Sciences, Bangalore.

The nomenclature of the Society was changed in December 1988 at Kolkata, because of an increased representation of educators, practitioners and researchers from all streams of social work in the Society. The Society primarily focuses on uniting the professional social workers to discuss, deliberate and develop conceptual frameworks and feasible indigenous interventions in social work practice. In order to facilitate this cause, the Society has so far conducted 35 annual national conferences along with workshops, seminars and symposia on various issues all over India. The society also confers awards for the best paper presenters in its conferences. It encourages young social workers to contribute more to the Indian social work profession.

NEED OF NATIONAL ASSOCIATIONS IN SOCIAL WORK IN INDIA

The ASSWI disapproved of the practice of appointing persons who are not trained in social work as members of boards of examiners and board of studies in social work and selection committees for appointing social work teachers by the universities in one of its seminar (Nair, 1981). In the same way, only social work professionals can teach, guide and train the students of social work. Likewise, students of medicine can only be trained by medical professors, law students can only be capacitated by law graduates; likewise, same will be applicable for social work profession but, unfortunately, in some universities and colleges other discipline teachers such as anthropology, psychology, sociology and geography teach social work students (Botcha, 2012). Therefore, it is the need of national associations in social work who should seriously strive to work on completely controlling such practices in India.

Social work is a practice-based human service profession across the globe. There are many people engaged in this profession to work at grassroots level in order to enhance the quality of life of marginalized sections and disadvantaged sections in the society. A professional programme has got a set of standards with which it renders services in a systematic way. But in India, there is a need of standardizing the procedures of training and education for providing better services to the people and find robust solutions to the problems being faced by various categories of people in the society.

In order to provide sound solutions and needful interventions for addressing the problems in the society, there is a need to establish and strengthen national-level associations through which standardization, public recognition, reaching the unreached, providing solutions to problems and meeting the needs of professionals and people, and bringing all its stakeholders together can be accomplished. There will be pressing needs in every profession as the world changes. Social work is not exceptional and in India there are very many needs which are unmet and long-pending. There is no National Council for Social Work Education and Training in India which can standardize and streamline the social work profession in India. But the Government of India is not coming forward in establishing the Council. At this juncture, there is a need of proactive involvement of professional associations in putting pressure on the government and meet the needs of the people.

FUNCTIONS OF NATIONAL ASSOCIATIONS IN SOCIAL WORK IN INDIA

Among the national-level associations of the profession, the NAPSWI and the ISPSW are putting reasonable efforts for the professional advancement and for the continuous professional development of educators, practitioners as well as learners of social work across the nation by organizing national-level seminars and conferences. NAPSWI is the only national association in which there are institutional members, life members (faculty, researchers, practitioners and retired professionals) as well as student members associated with it. All these national and state-level associations should be strengthened for the advancement of the profession in future. The efforts put in by these associations are not at all adequate for streamlining this professional programme in India. The social work profession is struggling with various problems for the last several years (Botcha, 2019).

There are very many functions to any association which works at the national level in any profession. National associations in social work have many roles and responsibilities to play. Some of them are listed below:

1. Reaching the unreached
2. Indianization of social work
3. Uniting all the schools of social work
4. Membership in international associations
5. Organizing national and international events
6. Enhancing visibility to social work profession
7. Strengthening social work education and training
8. Bringing all the practitioners and educators together
9. Standardizing social work education, training and practice
10. Expanding services of social work to various corners of the country
11. Achieving professional status and establishment of the National Council for Social Work

The existing national associations such as NAPSWI, ISPSW and BSKP have been functioning aiming at attaining the above-mentioned requirements of social work profession in India. It is clearly evident that there is a need of putting more efforts and collective efforts towards making this profession more visible in Indian society and the world.

CONTRIBUTION OF NATIONAL ASSOCIATIONS IN SOCIAL WORK IN INDIA

The absence of effective functioning of professional association of social work practitioners and educators is the most pronounced handicap in professional development in the country. Unless these are revived and made effective, the future of the profession of social work is likely to remain bleak (Nanavatty, 1997).

Some of the prominent national associations have been contributing to strengthen the social work profession in India. They have been working in bringing all its stakeholders together and discussing the needs of the profession at large. These associations also find suitable interventions to meet the needs of various sections of the people. As mentioned above, NAPSWI has been conducting a series of national events starting from 2004 till date and it has conducted 10 annual national seminars and 7 Indian Social Work Congresses in various parts of the country. Through the above-mentioned programmes, hundreds of students, teachers and practitioners were benefited in terms of building networks, developing knowledge base on social work and understanding best practices.

Similarly, ISPSW has conducted 35 annual national conferences in different parts of the country till date. This is one of the oldest associations in social work. It has contributed a lot in developing the knowledge base for professional social workers in India through its annual meets. It encouraged young social workers in contributing to the conferences and recognized with best paper awards to the contributors.

BSKP is the emerging association in India. It was established in 2018. From its inception, it has been organizing a series of seminars, workshops and meetings with various stakeholders of social work profession in India. It has been propagating to Indianize social work education and training and make social work profession to meet the needs and address indigenous problems of the people. Eminent social work educators and practitioners from across the country have been putting their efforts in strengthening this association at national levels.

All the three associations have been doing commendable job and putting their efforts in the establishment of the National Council for Social Work in India. But it has not been achieved till date. There are many such unmet needs of the professional social workers in India.

NATIONAL ASSOCIATIONS AND PROMOTION OF CORE VALUES OF SOCIAL WORK

Values are the fundamentals of social work profession. A social worker's life and actions are based on and guided by a set of core values. Values are critically important for social workers as they are social doctors working with individuals, families, groups and communities in problem-solving process. Values are priceless but worth to a social worker in their personal and professional life. Professional life is based on values. For a social worker, life is based on and directed by values which set certain standards, principles and believes. Values are like a road map which brings about change in one's attitudes and direction for life. Values help the worker to understand what is 'right' and what is 'wrong' and when to say 'yes' and when to say 'no' with conviction (Thomas, 2016).

There are 12 core values brought out by an eminent social work educator and practitioner, Professor Gracious Thomas. The 12 core values are as follows:

> *Value 1:* Service to humanity
> *Value 2:* Social justice
> *Value 3:* Respect for dignity and worth of the person
> *Value 4:* Importance of human relationships
> *Value 5:* Competence
> *Value 6:* Integrity
> *Value 7:* Hard work
> *Value 8:* Teachership
> *Value 9:* Loyal to profession
> *Value 10:* Cultural sensitivity
> *Value 11:* Responsibility and commitment
> *Value 12:* Patriotism
>
> **Source:** Thomas (2016).

Professional associations at the national level have a significant role in promoting core values of social work among students, teachers and practitioners of social work. As mentioned above, these core values are guiding principles to work with the people who are in need. If the professional social worker understands the above core values in its true manner and practice with passion and compassion, they will be able to provide better services to the society.

Did You Know?

In addition to the six core values of social work disseminated by the National Association of Social Workers (NASW), Professor Gracious Thomas proposed six additional values in social work in 2015 to be followed by all social workers while practising social work.

Similarly, they can contribute to their personal and professional growth and contribute towards strengthening the professional social work. In order to make them understand and imbibe the core values, national-level associations should strive to propagate about the significance and need of practising these core values.

ROLE OF NATIONAL ASSOCIATIONS IN STRENGTHENING SOCIAL WORK PROFESSION IN INDIA

Professional social work organizations, namely the IATSW and the ASSWI, are both dismal and disillusioning. In over 60 years, these professional organizations have witnessed a complete chaos, characterizing ineffectiveness, indifference, inaction, in-fighting and total mismanagement of whatever little resources and goodwill they had in the beginning. As a result, we do not have strong professional organizations to infuse health and vitality to the profession and salvage its sagging morale (Srivastava, 1999).

As mentioned above in the functions, there are very many roles to national association of social work in India. The role of professional associations needs to be understood at three levels: micro, mezzo and macro.

NEEDS OF PEOPLE—MICRO LEVEL

At the micro level, these associations should work in such a direction to meet the emerging needs of the people from time to time (individual and family problems, poverty, unemployment, risk behaviour, health, education and so on). In order to meet the needs of the people, indigenous models and knowledge need to be developed or the existing practices are to be updated. By working with people in the society, the profession can enhance its visibility and get recognition to this professional social work.

REQUIREMENTS OF THE PROFESSION/PROFESSIONALS—MEZZO LEVEL

At the mezzo level, national associations should play a vital role in meeting the requirements and protecting the interests of the profession and professionals. The requirements of the profession can be connecting various institutions of social work in India, putting pressure on the government to establish the National Council for Social Work in India, getting membership in international associations and so on. The requirements of the professionals can be standardization, proper recognition, creating employment opportunities/protecting existing employment opportunities, paying reasonable salaries to the workforce and assuring productive career in professional social work and so on. National associations should work in delivering their role in achieving the above with the support of all their stakeholders.

RESPONDING TO THE NEEDS OF COUNTRY—MACRO LEVEL

At the macro level, there are so many needs to be met with the professional expertise of social work. These needs can be in terms of contribution in policymaking, being part in decision-making bodies, involvement in research and consultancy, responding to natural calamities and emergency situations, working with government departments aiming at providing/designing solutions to the problems of the society and so on. The compassionate response to the above-mentioned needs should be collective and result-oriented. That can be achieved only with the active involvement of national associations.

SUMMARY

It is clearly evident that the presence and proactive involvement of national association/associations in social work in any country are very essential and bring positive result. These associations have specific roles to perform in order to standardize the profession and enable its professionals to respond to the emerging needs of the society from time to time. This chapter provides an outline on various aspects pertaining to national associations of social work in India. The efforts and odyssey of national association in India from its inception, that is, 1961, have been given in the chapter. Mentioning various roles and responsibilities of the association, it highlighted the role of these associations in inculcating the core values of social work among its students, educators, researchers and practitioners in India.

TOP 10 TAKEAWAYS/MAIN POINTS

1. Inception of professional social work in India at Sir Dorabji Tata Graduate School of Social Work which is now popularly known as TISS in Mumbai.
2. Establishment of various national associations of professional social work in India and the long journey which started in 1961.
3. Concept, scope and definition of national associations of professional social work and various types/categories of national associations in the world.
4. Understanding state-, national-, regional- and international-level associations of social work with examples.
5. Need of national associations in social work and their important functions in addressing the problems of the professionals, people and planet.
6. Comprehending the active national associations such as BSKP, NAPSWI and ISPSW, and their efforts in standardizing social work in India.
7. Contribution of various national associations in India from the establishment till date; national seminars/conferences/social work congresses and so on.
8. Role of professional associations in promoting core values of social work which are very essential to any professional.
9. Understanding 12 core values in professional social work given by Professor Gracious Thomas.
10. Roles of national associations at micro, mezzo and macro levels.

Keywords: social work, national associations, core social work values

GLOSSARY

Core values: Core values play a vital role in any profession. These values are the guiding principles to practitioners, educators, researchers and students with which they will systematically practise their profession without any bias. Professional social workers should always remind the six core values given by NASW (USA) and in addition to that six more core values given by Professor Gracious Thomas (IGNOU).

National associations: National associations in social work will work at the national level in bringing students, educators, researchers, practitioners and schools/departments together in achieving the goals of the profession. The national associations also organize various events in different parts of the country to provide a common platform to the professionals to share their experiences and learn from each other. The national associations update the current trends and contemporary issues in social work profession and bring all stakeholders together to meet/solve the needs/problems of the people in the society.

Professional Social Work Associations in India

Professional social work: Professional social work is a professional engagement of attending the needs/problems of the people (individual, groups, communities and organizations) in a systematic way by following the methods, using tools and techniques and applying principles of social work. Professional social worker should not ignore the core values while they engage themselves in practising the profession. Professional social work believes in *teaching a man to fish and feeding him for a lifetime*. Hence, its prime focus is on capacitating the people to solve their own problems and live comfortably.

MULTIPLE CHOICE QUESTIONS

1. In which year was the professional social work started in India?
    a. 1926
    b. **1936**
    c. 1940
    d. 1947

2. BSKP stands for
    a. Bharathiya Samaj Kaushal Parishad
    b. Bharathiya Sanghatith Karya Parishad
    c. **Bharatiya Samaj Karya Parishad**
    d. Bharathiya Samaj Karya Parishodhan

3. ISPSW was established in
    a. **1970**
    b. 1947
    c. 1959
    d. 1961

4. NAPSWI stands for
    a. North-East Association of Psychiatric Social Workers in India
    b. **National Association of Professional Social Workers in India**
    c. National Association of Psychiatric Social Workers in India
    d. Norway Association of Psychiatric Social Workers in India

5. ISPSW stands for
    a. **Indian Society of Professional Social Work**
    b. International Society of Professional Social Work
    c. Indian Society of Personnel Social Work
    d. Indian Society of Professional Social Welfare

6. NAPSWI was established in
    a. 2000
    b. **2005**
    c. 2010
    d. 2015

7. Which one of the following is the International Association?
   a. NAPSWI
   b. ASSWI
   c. **IFSW**
   d. ISPSW
8. How many core values are there in professional social work in India?
   a. **12**
   b. 15
   c. 10
   d. 9
9. Roles of national association are divided into the following sequence:
   a. Macro, micro and mezzo
   b. Mezzo, micro and macro
   c. **Micro, mezzo and macro**
   d. Micro, mezzo and macro
10. IASSW stands for
    a. International Association of Schools of Social Welfare
    b. Indonesian Association of Schools of Social Work
    c. Indian Association of Schools of Social Work
    d. **International Association of Schools of Social Work**

REVIEW QUESTIONS

1. Define association in your words.
2. What are the categories of professionals associations in social work in India?
3. Describe the need of national associations in social work.
4. What is the contribution of professional social work associations in India?
5. Describe the relationship between national associations and core values in social work.
6. What is the role of national associations in strengthening social work profession in India?

REFERENCES

Botcha, R. (2012). Problems and challenges for social work in India: Some recommendations. *International Journal of Multidisciplinary Educational Research, 1*(3), 201–212.

Botcha, R. (2019). *Social work education in India: Retrospect and prospect.* Shipra Publications.

Dash, B. M. (2019). National seminar on Nanaji Deshmukh on Indian Social Work Day. *New Delhi Times.*

Nair, K. (1981). *Social work education and social practice in India.* ASSWI.

Nanavatty, M. (1997). Professional associations of social work: An analysis of literature. *The Indian Journal of Social Work, 58*(2), 287–300.

Siddegowda, Y. S. (2010). Educational and professional concerns of social work education. *The Social Work Journal, 2*(1), 1–8.
Srivastava, S. P. (1999). Addressing the future of professional social work in India. *The Indian Journal of Social Work, 60*(1), 118–139.
Thomas, G. (Ed.). (2016). *Social work: The value based profession.* Rawat Publishers.

RECOMMENDED READINGS

Bharadwaj, T. (2010). Growth of social work education and training. In G. Thomas (Ed.), *Professional social work in Indian perspectives.* Indira Gandhi National Open University.
Desai, A. S. (1994). Five decades of social work in India. In K. K. Jacob (Ed.), *Social work education in India: Retrospect and prospect.* Himamsu Publications.
Devi, R. K. (2009). *Social work education and action.* Omega Publication.
Dupare, S. et al. (2018). *Professional associations in social work in social work profession.* Vikas Publishing House.
IFSW. (2020). *India Network of Professional Social Workers Associations.* https://www.ifsw.org/member-organisation/india/
Indraj, G. (2012). Main ideas of social work. In *Encyclopeadia of Social Work.* Aadi Publications.
NAAC. (2004). *A manual for assessment and accreditation of social work education programme.* New Delhi.
Nanavatty, M. C. (1985). Social work education and professional development. *The Indian Journal of Social Work, 46*(3), 315–325.
Raju, K. (2012). *Strengthening social work education and practice: The imperative for indigenous knowledge base* (a paper presented in the All India Conference held at Jamia Milia Islamia, New Delhi).
Thomas, G., & Joseph, V. (2012). Social work education around the world. In S. Surendra (Ed.), *Encyclopedia of social work in India* (3rd ed., Vol. 4), pp. 1385–1396. New Royal Book Company.
University Grants Commission. (1965). *Social work education in Indian universities.* The author.
University Grants Commission. (2001). *UGC model curriculum.* University Grants Commission.

14

Scope and Fields of Social Work and Emerging Areas

Shashi Rani

LEARNING OBJECTIVES

- To learn the historical evolution of social work practice and expansion
- To understand the concept, nature and meanings of social work practice
- To know contemporary practice areas and settings
- To describe the scope of social work practice in international domain

Cultivation of the mind should be the ultimate aim of human existence.

—B. R. Ambedkar

INTRODUCTION

Social work is a practice-based profession. It is professional in nature and having a professional body of knowledge duly recognized by international standards of practice. Since the beginning of evolution of professional social work services, the emphasis is on education and training. Social workers are trained in identification of social issues and application of social work methods for assisting individuals, groups, communities and society at large. Social work education incorporated all possible social, political, psychological and economic approaches. Edward T. Devine, the pioneer of social work education, at New York in 18th century, very well elaborated on source of knowledge for social workers and stated that, 'Social work appropriates from all sources whatever will be useful in rescue of individuals or the amelioration of adverse working or living' (Devine, 1922, p. 303). The social work professionals assist people on the basis of their felt need and scientific assessment of the

Scope and Fields of Social Work and Emerging Areas

problem. This profession aim is to deal with issues of individuals, groups and communities in their social context. The assistance is majorly provided through government and non-government institutions through policy, planning, programme and services within the larger legal framework of 'human rights and social justice' at local and global levels (IFSW, 1996).

With this background, in order to understand the future scope of the social work practice, it is important to know the social work journey in a continuously changing world. The present chapter is aimed to provide knowledge on the emergence of social work profession, definition and ethical guiding principles, practice areas and scope of social practice at national and international levels.

BACKGROUND OF SOCIAL WORK EDUCATION AND PRACTICE

Social work began its journey with religious and charity-based organizations and philanthropic activities in England in 1860 (Engelbrecht, 1999). Steiner explained the nature of social work and stated that

> the terms used for social work indicates clearly the nature of the field from which modern social work has developed. The social workers of a generation ago were engaged in the work of charity or philanthropy. Their efforts were concentrated upon the disadvantaged and handicapped and represented a growing attempt to understand their problems and solve them through the application of scientific methods. (Steiner, 1921, p. 1).

But gradually with development, the social workers moved from just remedial services to preventive services for various social problems.

> Investigations of the standards of living and housing conditions, social surveys of various kinds, promotion of recreational activities, organization of communities for the purposes of social betterment, arousing public sentiment against the evils of child labor, and organized efforts to give the general public a social point of view—all these and many other activities of a similar nature became a recognized part of the field of social work. (Steiner, 1921, p. 2).

Thus, to study social conditions and provide services, social workers required methods and techniques to be adopted to carry out investigations and organization of services and for this educational training was necessary.

The educational training of social work started at the University of London in 1903 (Engelbrecht, 1999). The social work professionals who had theoretical understanding of human sufferings enriched the educational training on methods to study distressed individuals, families and groups, and techniques for intervention. The academic work of Mary Richmond (1917, 1922) generated important methods and body of knowledge to work with individuals. Jane Addams advocated for social justice and democracy through her practice. Freud's use of psychological and clinical techniques from 1930 onwards created the base for social work education (Engelbrecht, 1999). The psychosocial approaches, scientific methods of need assessment, social and economic issues of the client, identification of need of assistance and aid are considered important from the viewpoint of establishment of social work services. In 1920, Abbott at the Chicago School of Social Work presented the broader framework of social work education; she proposed the study of social treatment, public welfare administration, social research and statistics, law and government, social economics and politics, and social experiments (Augustine & Gentle-Genitty, 2013).

In addition to that, at international institutional level, the establishment of the International Labour Organization (ILO) in 1919, emergence of the United Nations (UN) in 1945, adoption of the Universal Declaration of Human Rights (UDHR) in 1948 and formation of the International Federation of Social Workers (IFSW) in 1956 are some of the landmarks in the expansion of social work activities at national and international levels. The traditional forms of social work practices and working with individuals, families and communities turned in to assisting people within the larger framework of 'Human Rights and Social Justice' (IFSW, 1996).

Indian society was also continuously changing through social and religious movements and reforms. In India, the social issues such as sati *pratha*, compulsory widowhood, child marriage, caste system, untouchability, *devdasi*, restrictions on education for lower caste and women were some of the prominent social issues of 18th and 19th centuries. After political independence, the Constitution of India provided the philosophical base for securing equal rights for all under fundamental rights. The guiding principles for state are laid down to guide the state to perform various governance and administrative duties in the welfare of citizens. Since independence, within this larger framework of social justice and protection of human rights, the special emphasis was always on adopting the right-based approach under the legal framework for protection of marginalized, poor, women, children, differently abled, homeless populations and so on.

In India, the social reformers, various government and non-government organizations are continuously working on social problems of India, but the formal and recognized training of professional social work started with the establishment of the first school of social work in 1936 by Sir Dorabji Tata School of Social Work, Mumbai, in 1936. The Delhi School of Social Work (DSSW) came into existence in 1946. The third important institute of social sciences, Kashi Vidyapith, was established in 1947 and in the same year there was the emergence of Indian Conference of Social Work (Yelaja, 1969).

After India's Independence, many other educational institutes started social work education in a professional manner, such as the University of Baroda in 1950 and the Xavier Labour Relations Institute, Jamshedpur, which started education in social work, the Madras School of Social Work in 1952, the School of Social Sciences in Gujarat University, the Xavier Institute of Social Service Ranchi, Bihar, in 1955, the Department of Sociology and Social Work in Lucknow University and Nirmala Niketan, Bombay, in 1956, the Institute of Social Sciences at Agra University, the Departments of Sociology and Economics, Andhra University and the Indian Institute of Social Welfare and Business Management, Calcutta, in 1957, the PSG School of Social Work, Coimbatore, in 1958, the Udaipur School of Social Work, Rajasthan University, which started social work education in 1959 and the Department of Labour and Social Welfare, Bhagalpur University, which also started a social work course in 1959. After that, in the era of the 1960s, there were many other institutes that started offering social work education in India. These were the National Institute of Social Sciences, Bangalore, the School of Social Work, Roshni Nilaya, Mangalore, the Indore School of Social Work, Indore Christian College (1960), the Department of Social Work, Sacred Heart College, Thevara, Kerala

(1961), the PSG School of Social Work, Coimbatore, the Department of Social Work, Stella Maris College, Madras, the Department of Social Anthropology and Social Welfare, Karnataka University, Dharwad, started in 1962, and the Department of Social Work, Loyola College, Madras, established in 1963 (Yelaja, 1969). Today in India, there are many state and central universities offering social work academic courses/degrees at graduate and postgraduate levels. In an estimate, there are more than 500 educational institutes offering graduate- and postgraduate-level courses in social work subject. Also, at higher studies level, research options are available in social work departments at university level (Thomas, 2018). The educational institutions are providing education and training to students of social work, the curriculum is designed as per international standard and local need of practice/intervention to provide both theoretical and practical knowledge and duly approved by government authorities. The University Grants Commission (2001) provided the framework of the model of social work education curriculum in India. The network of government and non-government organizations, and community practice are being utilized for field work exposure and training.

As far as the model approach to social work education is concerned, there is a debate whether the Eurocentric model can be utilized or appropriate in social work education in India or not. Although there is no straight answer to this debate, Robbins et al.'s (1999) views seem to be relevant that 'Due to the complexity of human behavior and human experience, it is critical that our theory base encompass a broad range of theories and knowledge from the human and social sciences'. In this context, if we have to expand and update ourselves with the growth of global society, the source of knowledge should be broad and blended; the balanced model of international or indigenous social work practice should be adopted and required. Narrowing down the knowledge base in a globalized society would not create a scientific and rational mind for social work practice. The indigenous approach is very well acknowledged by the UN and it gives enough liberty to countries to adopt the policy and practice guidelines as per regional and local needs to protect indigenous communities (see box below).

At a global level, there are also emerging concerns of application of indigenous social work practice keeping in view the interest of indigenous communities. There is no formal and fixed definition of indigenous people. There was demand for giving freedom and flexibility to indigenous communities to define themselves. According to Martinez Cobo:

> Indigenous communities, peoples and nations are those which, having a historical continuity with pre-invasion and pre-colonial societies that developed on their territories, consider themselves distinct from other sectors of the societies now prevailing in those territories, or parts of them. They form at present non-dominant sectors of society and are determined to preserve, develop and transmit to future generations their ancestral territories, and their ethnic identity, as the basis of their continued existence as peoples, in accordance with their own cultural patterns, social institutions and legal systems.

The ILO Convention No. 169 explained that indigenous people are descendants of populations 'which inhabited a country or geographical region during its conquest or colonization or the establishment of present state boundaries' and 'retain some or all of their own social, economic, cultural and political institutions' (UNDP, 2013).

Although in present time the social work practice follows universal principles of social justice and human rights, it is equally important to apply these principles in indigenous context.

SOCIAL WORK PRACTICE—DEFINITION AND ETHICAL GUIDING PRINCIPLES

The core areas of social work practice are mentioned in the internationally adopted definition of social work. The definition which was approved by the IFSW and IASSW in July 2014 defines social work as profession and stated that

> Social work is a practice-based profession and an academic discipline that promotes social change and development, social cohesion, and the empowerment and liberation of people. Principles of social justice, human rights, collective responsibility and respect for diversities are central to social work. Underpinned by theories of social work, social sciences, humanities and indigenous knowledge, social work engages people and structures to address life challenges and enhance wellbeing. The above definition may be amplified at national and/ or regional levels.

IFSW's (2014) definition further provided the road map for social work practice and to adopt general principals with universal applicability. These ethical guiding principles for social work professionals are as follows:

- Recognition of the inherent dignity of humanity
- Promoting human rights
- Promoting social justice
- Promoting the right to self-determination
- Promoting the right to participation
- Respect for confidentiality and privacy
- Treating people as whole persons
- Ethical use of technology and social media
- Professional integrity

The above *Global Social Work Ethical Principles* are referred to as the *Statement of Ethical Principles*. The aim is to provide the framework for social workers to practise with professional integrity by maintaining highest standards of practice. The global acceptance of this policy of ethical statement is also setting expectations from social work practitioners, educators, students and researchers to uphold the core values and principles of the social work profession.

In view of contemporary times, this statement is not only important from an ethical practice point of view but also from the view of expansion of scope of social work practice. The practice is to meet the need of people struggling for their survival and to have a dignified life. Moreover, in contemporary times, the global society in general and nations in particular are facing many pressing social problems. The global goals to deal with various problems are accepted under United Nations Development Programme (UNDP) Sustainable Development Goals (SDGs) and India is also signatory to achieve these SDGs (Figure 14.1).

Scope and Fields of Social Work and Emerging Areas

> **Box 14.1** **UNDP SDGs**
>
>
>
> FIGURE 14.1 17 Goals to Transform Our World
>
> The SDGs, also known as the Global Goals, were adopted by all UN member states in 2015 as a universal call to take action to end poverty, protect the planet and ensure that all people enjoy peace and prosperity by 2030. The 17 SDGs which are integrated to recognize that action in one area will affect outcomes in others, and that development must balance social, economic and environmental sustainability.
>
> **Source:** UNDP (2015).

At international level, there are many professional alliances and networks of social workers. India also marked its representation in Asia and Pacific region of IFSW through working in partnership with India Network of Professional Social Workers' Associations (INPSWA) in 2015. INPSWA is a network of professional social work associations; these associations have their own members (professional social workers) from regional and national levels. At present, in INPSWA, there are six associations which are working in India, these are as follows: the Indian Society of Professional Social Work, Karnataka Association of Professional Social Workers, Professional Social Workers' Association, Bombay Association of Trained Social Workers, National Association of Professional Social Workers in India, New Delhi, and Kerala Association of Professional Social Workers. These associations are working in the area of education, training, practice, knowledge dissemination, advocacy and so on. These associations also take note of local and international concerns and make efforts to build up networks and alliances.

SOCIAL WORK PRACTICE AREAS AND SCOPE

The scope of social work has continuously expanded since its inception. In general, 'the social work profession broadly works for equity, social justice, harmony and peace mainly directing to support the quest of the marginalized groups to meet their needs' (University Grants Commission, 2001). This section highlighted areas of social work practice along with the diverse sections of population for delivering social work services. In social work, diversity is broadly defined and encompasses race, culture, religion, gender, age, sexual orientation and socio-economic status. The social workers work with individuals, groups, families and communities through regional- and global-level government and non-government agencies and organizations (Ritter, 2009). Among other important roles of social workers are to contribute to the expansion and upgradation of the knowledge base for social work practice through research and academia. It includes education, training, research, interdisciplinary studies, writing, publication, policy analysis, social action projects and social change.

At the ground level, social work practice consists of working with a population of all age groups, gender and social background. As social work professionals, social workers according to their interest and expertise can work with government, non-government organizations, community, civil society and so on. At national and international levels, the demand for social workers is increasing in various sectors and areas. In order to provide basic understanding, some of the general practice areas are discussed below.

SOCIAL WORK PRACTICE IN HEALTH

In the health sector, social workers have a huge scope for practice. Ruth and Marshall explored the relationship of social work with public health and explained that

> Although public health predates social work, both fields evolved into their contemporary forms during the early 20th century. Reflecting Progressive Era values, they shared an overlapping commitment to health and social well-being and, by the second decade of the 20th century, collaborated on issues such as maternal and child health, influenza epidemic response, and venereal disease control. (Ruth & Marshall, 2017)

In this context, the areas of social practice are expanded at three levels of health interventions: preventive, curative and rehabilitative. The job of social workers is to assist individuals of all age groups/gender, families, groups and communities with direct services, at clinical/hospital or non-clinical level. The social work professionals work as medical social worker, psychiatric social worker, counsellor, educator or community mobilizer, supervisor, researcher and policy analyst and so on. In the health sector, public–private partnership, alliances and networking with other organizations and agencies is also an emerging field for social work practice. The social workers work closely with patients suffering from different illnesses in need of healthcare and assistance, treatment and counselling, rehabilitation and so on. The maternal and child health, health of elderly population, alcoholism and drug abuse, lifestyle-related illnesses, tuberculosis, HIV/AIDS, viral infections and flu, reproductive and sexual health, disability and so on are some core areas which have a scope of social work practice. Public health issues and requirement of trained frontline workers for creating awareness and education are the need of the hour at national and international levels. Mental health as one of the important sectors required trained professionals to work with people suffering from mental health issues. Social work practice in mental health settings included clinical practice, counselling and psycho-social support units, education, awareness and rehabilitation.

SOCIAL WORK PRACTICE IN WOMEN AND CHILD WELFARE

To provide services for women and children, this area required alliances with other sectors. The national and international agencies are working towards holistic development of women in children by addressing the issues of health, education, gender discrimination, safety and protection, violence and sexual abuse and so on. The SDG no. 5 is for member nations to bring gender equality (UNDP, n.d.). In this context for women, the issue of equality and non-discrimination in matters of health and nutrition, safe spaces at home and public, educational and employment opportunities, empowerment and right to participation in social and political activities and so on are some contemporary areas of social work concerns. The social work professionals in various capacities are playing a very important role in creating awareness and education in all these areas. The ministries at central and state level, government institutions, non-government organizations and civil societies are joining hands together for the cause of women and child development. The legal protection and compensation to women and children are provided through networks of agencies.

Working with children at school and community levels is based on the fundamental right to life and health, right to survival and protection, right to education and psychosocial development and so on. IFSW (2002, p. 13) stated the directions to work for the protection of children's rights.

> The intervention is suggested at three level these are; at the micro level: the rehabilitation of the individual child is the central focus; the meso level: the principal focus is on supporting groups of children to change their value base and build normal patterns of relationships; and the macro level: the focus is on leading and supporting national and international action against the use of child soldiers.

The legal rights of children in need and protection are central to social work practice. 'The Rights of children are interlinked and connected to other socio economic rights such as food, shelter, education, protection from discrimination, abuse, violence, exploitation etc' (Rani, 2015). To ensure these basic rights to children, the social work intervention is required at family, school and community levels. School-based practice is focused on guidance, counselling, personality development, physical and psychological growth, inclusive learning, special education and so on. For child in need and protection, the focus is on child welfare programmes such as child safety and protection, health and education, legal protection and family counselling, adoption, foster care, health and nutrition. The social work interventions in the areas of women and child development are based on scientific knowledge of theoretical aspects of development and growth of women and children. Utilizations of methods and various models of intervention with application of skills is central to social work practice in this area.

SOCIAL WORK PRACTICE FOR CRISIS INTERVENTION AND DISASTER MANAGEMENT

This area of practice required specialized knowledge of providing aid and assistance to the population exposed to crisis and disaster. The natural disasters and conflict in interest of human beings may create life-threatening situations for many vulnerable people. This area of practice demands urgent action and services of social work professionals for the protection of natural and human resources and lives of people irrespective of their class, creed, race, gender, region, religion and so on. The important skills include networking and alliances, fundraising, utilization of internal and external resources and so on. The situations of famine, earthquakes, fire and floods, epidemic and pandemic are some natural disaster situations. Iravani and Parast (2014) highlighted that

> psychological problems, social problems, such as economic destruction, loss of income, occupation, destruction of facilities and resources to communities in crisis, is threatening. Seen this on the social catastrophe, the crisis is a multidimensional phenomenon. Physical, social, economic, psychological, learning, insecurity and an influx of criminals as well as the affected areas all represent different aspects of the crisis, the presence of social workers with specific abilities and capabilities are demanding.

Other than these natural calamities, the human societies are also exposed to political, religious and regional conflicts. Although there are strong international and national political and legal measures to deal with these negative acts of certain forces, in case of any exposure of population of such situations, the requirement of special services is offered immediately through both government and non-government institutions at individual, family, groups and community levels for rescue and relief, shelter and food, transport, emergency services, social and financial support, aid and assistance, counselling, healthcare and so on. The role of social work professionals is to extend humanitarian services and to build up strong networks for advocacy to stop man-made disasters and to prevent loss from natural disasters.

SOCIAL WORK PRACTICE IN CRIMINAL JUSTICE AND CORRECTIONAL SERVICES

The right of equality before law and justice is central to social work practice in criminal justice and correctional services. In order to protect human rights and state of justice, the mandatory provisions of legal aid and counselling are considered as fundamental rights of a person arrested or accused of unlawful activities and wrongdoings. The scope of social work practice in correctional settings is at prison/jail (for adults) and observation homes (for children). In present times, the correctional services are governed by principles of human rights; thus, services and assistance are extended for reformation, restoration and rehabilitation. As very appropriately explained by Ruchi (2019):

> the human rights movement brought forth the rampant abuse of human rights of individuals, especially of individuals in custody. The human rights movement also brought forward the issues of marginalization, vulnerability and abuse within the democratic ideals of equality, freedom, human worth and dignity. The human rights movement transposed the idea of criminality from an individual act to a behaviour that is driven by the process of social exclusion.

With this framework of practice and understanding of structural issues, the social workers may facilitate the process of transformation and reformation through counselling, education and awareness for upgradation of their life skills. The aim is to bring reform in attitude and behaviour through constructive cognitive development.

SOCIAL WORK PRACTICE WITH COMMUNITY

Community practice is a traditional area of practice of social work. The practice area includes working with urban and rural communities. The community practice is aimed to assist individuals, families and groups in the community to enhance their potential and to empower them for assessment and utilization of community resources to solve their issues in an independent manner and organize them for problem-solving. It includes need assessment, resource identification, community mobilization, communication and negotiations, planning, action and advocacy for social change. In this context, Hardcastle et al. (2011) presented Ross' definition of community organization. According to Ross (1967), it is

> a process by which a community identifies its needs or objectives, orders (or ranks) these needs or objectives, develops the confidence and will to work at these needs or objectives, finds the resources (internal and/or external) to deal with these needs or objectives, takes action in respect to them, and in so doing extends and develops cooperative and collaborative attitudes and practices in the community. (Hardcastle et al., 2011, p. 28)

The community practice requires scientific knowledge of ecological perspectives and skills. The community practice requires knowledge of ecological and social structural perspectives. The important skills such as observer, researcher, communicator and facilitator are central to community practice. Creating a nurturing environment through education and awareness is the aim of community organization. Community empowerment should be based on equal rights for all in democratic environment irrespective of social, economic or political background. The scope of social work practice at community level (rural and urban) across all regional boundaries is expanded to social reform, gender development, communal harmony, creation of inclusive communities, removal of caste and racial barriers, infrastructural development, public private partnership, engagement of civil society, creating sustainable livelihood opportunities and linking community members with welfare schemes, benefits and so on.

SOCIAL WORK PRACTICE AT INDUSTRIAL SECTOR

In this area of social work practice, the knowledge of industrial working conditions is required. The ILO is the highest recognized body in the matters of advocacy and administration of industrial standards. Its member countries are expected to adopt international standards of working conditions and employment. Desai (n.d.) explained that 'social work practice in industrial sector has its roots not only in industrialization and urbanization with all consequences, but also in developing social consciousness, expressed through measures of family assistance, labour welfare legislations, regarding safety, hygiene, employment of women, young persons, etc'. Thus, the specific knowledge about the nature of employment, occupational health and safety policy, planning and management of factory systems, social security and welfare programmes, wages and payment, administration and capacity building policy and so on is important from a practice perspective. The scope of social work practice in industrial setting is under labour welfare and human resource development department, the role is expanded to recruitment, wages and leaves, training and skill upgradation, counselling, educational, awareness, health and safety management, welfare of workers, liasioning with management, settlement of disputes, gender equality, prevention of sexual harassment at workplace and so on. The job of social workers includes capacity development programmes, health and safety training, administration of maintenance and cleanliness of working place, use of protective and safety gears to minimize accidents and workplace injuries and so on. The social work professionals deal with problems related to individuals or groups of workers that affect their lives, job and working conditions directly and indirectly. The globalization and adoption of the global approach of right to work and decent conditions of work is in demand of contemporary times. The advocacy for decent work, occupational health, prevention of accident and injury, mental health, rehabilitation and fair compensation to workers, advocacy for social justice in neoliberal era are also some of the important areas of social work practice in industrial sector. With recent advancement of corporate social responsibility, social workers are not just contributing at workplace but also working for larger socio-economic issues in which corporate sector are ready to invest (Rani, 2016, p. 389).

SOCIAL WORK PRACTICE AT INTERNATIONAL LEVEL

Social work practice at the international level is governed by the acceptance of universal human rights principals. The UDHR 1948 opened the door for international community alliances to influence regional policies for the protection of these universal human rights principals. The global definition of social work stated that its aim was generating sense of 'collective responsibility and respect for diversities'. The need of international alliances with acceptance of indigenous model of practice is central for international social work practice. The globalization at one side increasing social mobility, economic opportunities, travel and tourism, political and business alliances and many more but, on the other side, it put forward many challenges for human beings, including problems such as poverty, hunger, inequality, homelessness, immigrant, refugee, unemployment, political conflicts, man-made disaster, financial crisis, overuse of technology, environmental degradation, and gender and racial divide. Various agencies are working in these areas (Box 14.1) and these agencies are working with regional offices in member countries; the services that are being offered are related to relief, assistance, funding, research and action projects in the area of health, education, safety and protection, gender equality, employment generation, infrastructure development, environment protection and so on. Also, the focus is on creating inclusive societies, communal harmony and peace building, advocacy and campaign for social change. Over the decades, the very nature of dealing with the clients also got changed depending upon various forms of human sufferings. Now in the contemporary world, the profession cannot bind itself in geographical boundaries and serve only local clients. When it comes to addressing complex issues at international platforms, there is a need to expand social work practice to international clients. The profession of social work is widely accepted as a helping profession through professional approach (Rani, 2019). There are many international agencies, and its members are from across the global world. Some important agencies are World Health Organization, World Bank (WB), UNDP, United Nations International Children's Emergency Fund, ILO, the United Nations Human Rights Council, United Nations Programme on HIV/AIDS and so on. The *International Social Work* believes in the principle of acceptance of diversity and advocates social justice and human rights. Also, it emphasizes collective responsibilities of the countries at the international level to address the issues of international clients. These issues need to be addressed through different perspectives and should not get influenced by local interest and pressures (Rani, 2019).

SUMMARY

The history of the social work profession presents the scope of social work across the nations. The scope of social work practice is continuously expanding according to the local and international social, economic and political developments. In the 21st century, social work is a well-known professional domain for work with humanitarian and development approach. It is officially recognized almost in all regions of global society. The nature and scope of work is general and specific to meet international and local standards of practice. However, broadly, social work professionals are educated and trained as per global and international standards of education and practice.

The understanding and knowledge of local and regional structural arrangement of society and issues are important for social work practitioners. The education and training of social workers is to create trained professionals with sound knowledge of theories and skills to serve the society. The scope and areas for social work professionals will be largely defined by global and local needs and emerging issues; thus, social work practice must be flexible in its approach to deal and address the issues in an ethical manner. The scope of social work practice is as per the social need that required systematic intervention at international or national level. With professional training and certification, social workers may practice in many areas. Some areas required specific training within social work, but other areas come under scope of general practice.

In present scenario, social work professionals need to generate understanding on international agenda of development, its relevance to local or national needs of the human beings. In present times, the commitment and willingness of young social work professionals to serve the society with rational and scientific temper, knowledge and training is much required to protect human rights and to deliver social justice to all.

TOP 10 TAKEAWAYS/MAIN POINTS

1. Social work is a practice-based profession. It is professional in nature and has a professional body of knowledge duly recognized by international standards of practice.
2. IFSW's (2014) definition provided the road map for social work practice and to adopt general principals with universal applicability.
3. The establishments of the ILO, the UN, the UDHR and the IFSW are some of the landmarks in expansion of social work activities at national and international levels.
4. Social work professionals are required to undergo professional training which is provided through educational institutions at national and international levels as per globally/nationally accepted standards.
5. The area and scope are continuously changing as per the need and expansion of professional education, training and collective consensus of social work professionals to respond positively to the cause of protection of human relationships and the overall well-being of societies.
6. At a micro level, the aim of social work profession is to help the clients to cope up with their individual, family and local issues and to resolve them by utilizing their own potential and strengths. At macro level (national and international), social work professionals contribute back to society through various interventions.
7. In India, the formal and recognized training of professional social work started with the establishment of the first school of social work in 1936 by Sir Dorabji Tata School of Social Work, Mumbai, in 1936. The DSSW came into existence in 1946.
8. Indian society was continuously changing through social and religious movements and reforms. The Constitution of India provided the philosophical base for securing equal rights for all under fundamental rights, assistance and protection to marginalized under special and exclusive arrangements and so on.
9. Although in present time the social work practice follows universal principles of social justice and human rights, it is equally important to apply these principles in indigenous context.
10. The working area of social workers is very vast and thus requires the professional knowledge and understanding of multicultural societies and issues of individuals, families, groups and communities.

Keywords: Social work practice, scope of social work, social justice and human rights, indigenous community

GLOSSARY

Human rights: Human rights are those standards that recognize and protect the dignity of all human beings. These rights are universal and protect all human beings irrespective of their social, economic, political and cultural backgrounds. Human rights are directive principles in nature and define human relationship with each other and with state. Also, they indicate state obligations towards the protection of human beings and society at large.

Indigenous community: The community or group of people identified themselves as indigenous on the basis of identification of descendants of population with historical continuity since pre-colonial or settlers defined territorial linkages having distinct social, economic and political system and maintaining their distinct life and cultural practices.

Scope of social work: The scope of social work practice is huge depending on the nature of social problems and need of individual, group and community. The scope of professional social work includes identification of social problems and with application of social work methods plan for social work intervention. Social work intervention is aimed to restore balanced functioning and promote problem-solving capabilities.

Social justice: Social justice is justice based on the philosophy of social, economic and political justice for people. It includes equal and equitable distribution of resources, opportunities and removal of social imbalances. Social justice also empowers people to protect social, economic, political, cultural rights through social institutions, actions, advocacy, collective and individual pursuance.

Social work practice: Social work practice consists of the professional application of social work values, principles and techniques to work with different client systems. Social work practice is based on principles of social justice and human rights.

MULTIPLE CHOICE QUESTIONS

1. Who introduced social diagnosis approach in social work practice?
    a. **Mary Richmond**
    b. Abbot
    c. James Adams
    d. Freud

2. In India, first social work school started in
    a. **Mumbai**
    b. Calcutta
    c. Uttar Pradesh
    d. Delhi

3. The process of communities to utilize or enhance their capacity and use of internal and external resource is called
    a. Social case work
    b. **Social community work**
    c. Social group work
    d. Social welfare

4. Which of the following Commission deals with the social work curriculum framework in India?
    a. National Commission for Women
    b. **University Grants Commission**
    c. National commission of Minority
    d. Human Rights Commission

5. The global definition of social work advocated for the *principles of*
   a. Social justice and human rights
   b. Collective responsibility
   c. Respect for diversities
   d. **All of the above**

6. Indigenous social work practice is approved by
   a. WB
   b. UNDP
   c. **UN**
   d. None of the above

7. Jyotirao Phule is known for his social reform movement for
   a. Vedic education
   b. Sati *pratha*
   c. Land reforms
   d. **Removal of caste system**

8. Which of the following is not an SDG?
   a. Gender equality
   b. **Capacity building**
   c. Quality education
   d. Zero hunger

9. UDHR stands for
   a. Universal Declaration of Health Rights
   b. Universal Declaration of Housing Rights
   c. Universal Development of Human Race
   d. **Universal Declaration of Human Rights**

10. The ILO was established in
    a. 1914
    b. **1919**
    c. 1923
    d. 1930

REVIEW QUESTIONS

1. What are social reforms of the 18th and 19th centuries in India?
2. Discuss the relation between social work and social welfare.
3. Define indigenous communities in your own words.
4. Write a short note on SDGs.
5. List out international agencies working for human rights and social justice.
6. Enlist some common social work practice areas at national and international levels.

REFERENCES

Augustine, M. G., & Gentle-Genitty, C. (2013). *A perspective on the historical epistemology of social work education.* https://core.ac.uk/download/pdf/81634126.pdf

Desai, M. M. (n.d.). *Industrial social work in retrospect.* http://ijsw.tiss.edu/greenstone/collect/ijsw/index/assoc/HASH01c3/6f125fea.dir/doc.pdf

Devine, E. T. (1922). *Social work.* The Macmillan Company.

Engelbrecht, L. K. (1999). *Introduction to social work.* Lanzo.

Hardcastle, D. A., Powers, P. R., & Wenocur, S. (2011). *Community practice: Theories and skills for social workers* (3rd ed.). Oxford University Press.

IFSW. (n.d.). *Global social work statement of ethical principles.* https://www.ifsw.org/global-social-work-statement-of-ethical-principles/

IFSW. (n.d.). *Global standards for social work education and training.* http://cdn.ifsw.org/assets/ifsw_65044-3.pdf

IFSW. (2002). *Social work and the rights of the child.* http://cdn.ifsw.org/assets/ifsw_124952-4.pdf

IFSW. (2014). *Global definition of social work.* https://www.ifsw.org/what-is-social-work/global-definition-of-social-work/

Iravani, M. R., & Parast, S. M. (2014). Examine the role of social workers in crisis management. *Journal of Sociology and Social Work, 2*(1), 87–97.

Rani, S. (2015). The right based approach towards child development: Issues and challenges. In N. Kumar (Ed.), *Early childhood development, family and community participation in early childhood development* (Knowledge Series 1). Global Books Organization.

Rani, S. (2016). Occupational issues and problems: Scope of social work interventions at work place. In B. Dash & S. Roy (Eds.), *Field work in social work education: Contemporary practices and perspectives*, p. 389. Atlantic Publishers and Distributors.

Rani, S. (2019). International social work practice: Issues, strategies and programmes. In *MSWE International Social Work: Concept, Standard and Regulatory Bodies*, pp. 34–47. IGNOU.

Richmond, M. E. (1917). *Social diagnosis.* Russell Sage Foundation.

Richmond, M. E. (1922). *What is social case work? An introductory description.* Russell Sage Foundation.

Ritter, Jessica A. et al. (2009). *101 Careers in social work.* Springer Publishing Company (ISBN 978-0-8261-5405-7).

Robbins, S. P., Chatterjee, P., & Canda, E. R. (1999). Ideology, scientific theory, and social work practice. *Families in Society: The Journal of Contemporary Human Services, 80*(4).

Ross, M. (with Lappin, B. W.). (1967). Community organization: theory, principles, and practice. Harper & Row.

Ruth, B. J., & Marshall, J. W. (2017). Public health then and now. *American Journal of Public Health, 107*(Supplement 3, S3).

Sriganesh, M. V. (n.d.). *India Network of Professional Social Workers' Associations.* https://www.ifsw.org/member-organisation/india/?dir=regmem&region=asia-pacific

Steiner, J. F. (1921). *Education for social work.* University of Chicago Press.

Thomas, B., & Pradeepkumar, P. C. (2018). Mental health in postgraduate social work curriculum: Review of training contents in Indian schools of social work. *Asian Social Work Policy Review.* https://doi.org/10.1111/aswp.12143

UNDP. (2013). *The United Nations Declaration on the Rights of Indigenous Peoples—A manual for national human rights institutions.* https://www.ohchr.org/documents/issues/ipeoples/undripmanualfornhris.pdf

UNDP. (2015). *The SDGs in action.* https://www.undp.org/content/undp/en/home/sustainable-development-goals.html

University Grants Commission. (2001). Social work education. In *Model curriculum.* The author.

Yelaja, S. A. (1969). Schools of social work in India: Historical development 1936–1966. *The Indian Journal of Social Work, 29*(4).

15
Principles and Methods of Social Work
Nita Kumari

LEARNING OBJECTIVES
- To develop an understanding about the generic principles of social work
- To discuss primary and secondary methods of social work

The moment you give up your principles, and your values, you are dead, your culture is dead, your civilization is dead.

—Oriana Fallaci (Italian journalist)

INTRODUCTION

The profession of social work is primarily concerned with the remedy to psycho-social problems and deficiencies which exist in the relationship between the individual and their social environment. This phenomenon always existed in the society in one form or the other but achieved its scientific basis in the last decades of the 19th century. Friedlander (1955) has defined social work as a professional service, on the basis of scientific knowledge and skill in human relations, which assists individuals, alone or in groups, to obtain social and personal satisfaction and independence. According to Pincus and Minahan, 'Social work is concerned with the interaction between people and their social environment which affects the ability of people to accomplish their life tasks, alleviate distress, and realise their aspirations and values' (Pincus & Minahan, 1978). Social work has been transformed from a simple helping profession into an empowering profession with a right-based approach which is very much evident in the global definition of social work. The International Federation of Social Workers/International Association of Schools of Social Work (2013) in the global definition have defined social work (Box 15.1).

Principles and Methods of Social Work

> **Box 15.1** **Global Definition of Social Work**
>
> Social work is a practice-based profession and an academic discipline that promotes social change and development, social cohesion and the empowerment and liberation of people. The principle of social justice, human rights, collective responsibility and respect for diversities are central to social work. Underpinned by theories of social work, social sciences, humanities and indigenous knowledge, social work engages people and structures to address life challenges and enhance well-being.

The goal of social work is to minimize suffering by solving people's problems. It enhances social functioning of individuals, groups and families by providing much-needed help. It links client system with the available resources and helps the individual in bringing about a change in the environment in favour of their growth and development. Social work always strives and promotes social justice through the development of social policy.

> **Did You Know?**
>
> Professional education for social work in India was started with the founding of Sir Dorabji Tata Graduate School of Social Work in Bombay (now known as Mumbai) in 1936.

In the process of helping clients, a social worker makes use of various skills, techniques, principles and suitable methods to provide help in the correct perspective. A social worker's approach to the problem on the basis of the knowledge of human behaviour and human relationships combined with their ability to use various skills and techniques of social work is very different and result-oriented than that of any other professional. They deal with the client within the framework of a democratic and humanistic way. A social worker helps the client from the moment they approach till the adjustment with the present situation.

The purpose of this chapter is to add to our understanding of the principles of social work as well as look into the application of these principles of social work practice in the field. The chapter further discusses various methods of social work which are systematic and planned ways of helping people.

PRINCIPLES OF SOCIAL WORK

There are some basic principles that all social workers are expected to follow while working in the field. Social work principles are essential to forming effective relationship with people. These facilitate relationship building with people, particularly those in need, crisis or distress. Apart from having good understanding of principles, social workers also require a range of

> **Box 15.2 Skills Required by Professional Social Workers**
>
> 1. Assessment skills
> 2. Communication skills
> 3. Advocacy skills
> 4. Problem-solving skills
> 5. Critical thinking skills
> 6. Respect for diversity
> 7. Intervention skills
> 8. Documentation skills
> 9. Organizational skills
> 10. Understanding of human relationships

skills and competencies while dealing with clients. Some of the prominent skills are observation, analysis, assessment, communication, mobilizing, motivation, advocacy, networking, planning, organizing, implementing, recording, documenting, evaluating, monitoring and so on. Dunlap (2013) has provided 10 core skills that are required by professional social workers (Box 15.2).

Principles are basic rules or guidelines which enable a practitioner to be competent in their profession. In the words of Jagadish, principles are the guideposts for the professional to carry out work in the field. Principles are elaboration of the values in the form of understandable statements to practise a profession. He has explained it by giving an example that the value of worth and dignity of an individual is expressed in the principle of belief in the self-determination of an individual or group or a community (Jagadish, 2007).

There are seven generic principles of social work which are as follows:

1. Principle of acceptance
2. Principle of individualization
3. Principle of communication
4. Principle of confidentiality
5. Principle of self-determination
6. Principle of controlled emotional involvement
7. Principle of non-judgemental attitude

PRINCIPLE OF ACCEPTANCE

The principle of acceptance implies that the social worker must perceive, acknowledge, receive and deal with the client as they really are and not as they wish them to be. A social worker should accept the client with all their limitations, strengths and weaknesses, their constructive and destructive attitudes and behaviour, their positive as well as negative feelings. They should respect the client, maintain a sense of the client's innate dignity and personal worth. The professional relations between the client and social worker should be based on mutual trust and cooperation, and acceptance of each other.

For instance, when a client approaches social worker for help and expresses their negative feelings and attitudes about them or the people in their life during the helping process, the social worker should not be angry, rather they should welcome these feelings or expressions and should be happy that the client was able to express them which would help the social worker in making treatment possible. This is only possible when there is mutual acceptance which is the beginning of the process of establishing a strong professional relationship towards working out a solution to the client's social dysfunctioning.

PRINCIPLE OF INDIVIDUALIZATION

Principle of individualization believes that each client possesses unique qualities. Each person has different life experiences and different external and internal stimuli. Every individual has different emotions and memories that influence their thinking process, feelings, beliefs, perceptions and behaviour in an individual manner. Social worker should deal with the client with their personal differences. Since the client is different from others, the help should be rendered in some way different. Social worker help, therefore, must be differentiated to meet the particular needs of the individual client. The client should be helped by using their own abilities and resources to work out their problem. The social worker should give undivided attention and privacy, and should be encouraged to tell their own story.

PRINCIPLE OF COMMUNICATION

Communication is the core of all social relationships and is a two-way process. In social work, the communication between the social worker and the client is of paramount importance. Most of the problems concerning human relations arise due to faulty communication. When the communication is inadequate or insufficient, the problems appear either automatically or because of misunderstanding. There are mainly three ways in which social worker conceives that clients may have problems of communication of feeling: (a) the client may be confronted with a difficult practical problem which arouses such strong feeling in them that they are unable to cope effectively with the problem (Perlman, 1957); (b) the client may have certain feelings of apprehension or diffidence about asking for help (Moffett, 1968) and (c) the client's feelings may be the main problem about which they are asking for help (Perlman, 1957).

The social worker through their professional skills and techniques should make all the efforts that the communication between them and the client is proper. They can effectively make use of the techniques such as clarification and reclarifications, elaborating, questioning and reframing of what the client has said. The worker must ensure whether the client understands correctly what they are conveying to them. For this, the worker may ask the client to repeat what they have conveyed to them. In this way, miscommunication between the client and worker can be reduced to a great extent.

The principle of communication thereby calls for effective communication between the client and the social worker. The social worker should communicate effectively in a manner that their views are being understood by the client and also whatever the client is communicating is effectively understood by the social worker. Further, the available options available for client should also be communicated effectively by the social worker to the client. Without proper two-way communication, the efficiency of the process will be hampered. There could be several issues arising from miscommunication on any aspect of client's situation or response or understanding; hence, this principle becomes very important. For an effective response thereby, effective communication becomes the key. The client should be made aware of the situation and the responses/options they have in a very comprehensive manner.

In this regard, it becomes important to stress that both verbal and non-verbal communication should be conducted in a professional manner which is neither offensive nor judgemental and respects the client and their situation. Hence, a social worker needs to be aware of the communication through body language and should refrain from responding (both verbally and non-verbally) in a manner which could create miscommunication.

Hence, the importance of the principle of communication.

PRINCIPLE OF CONFIDENTIALITY

Confidentiality is the preservation of secret information concerning the client which is disclosed in a professional relationship. Confidentiality is based upon a basic right of the client. When a client approaches a social agency, he reveals information to the professional social worker. The information may include their innermost feeling or facts about previous behaviour, which they want no one else to know about. He may have a feeling if this information is known to their friends, neighbours or relatives, it would destroy their personal reputation. Therefore, the social worker's preservation of secret information is an essential quality of the relationship. If a client ever becomes aware of the fact that the information shared has been revealed to others, it may destroy professional relationship at any point of time.

However, to follow this principle, the worker faces certain dilemmas. First, should the confidential information be shared with other agency personnel as well as fellow professionals who too can assist in solving the problem. Second, what should they do when there are cases in which the information given may unravel the client's participation in anti-social and anti-legal activities? In the first case, the social worker may share the information in the best interest of the client. But in second case, it becomes really tough for the social worker to withhold information as it has been received under the promise of keeping it confidential. In such circumstances, decision is to be left to the client whether to disclose such information or not to the social worker. If disclosed, social worker should make it clear to the client that the information can be shared with the concerned authorities, if needed. The worker should also exercise their discretion while receiving or sharing confidential information. The social worker should take prior consent of the client before sharing the information with other agencies and individuals.

PRINCIPLE OF SELF-DETERMINATION

The principle of self-determination believes in giving autonomy to individuals to make their own decisions in helping process. Social worker believes that client themselves is the best person to deal with their life situation better and arriving at a decision, they will become a less dependent person. Social worker always motivates the client to think independently about their problem and arrive at a decision for themselves. However, it is the responsibility of social worker to explain the possible consequences of adoption of various alternatives. In case, the client proposes to choose some solutions that are negative and destructive in nature, the social worker either helps the client to change their ideas or simply prohibit that course of action. The goal and responsibility of the social worker is to guide the client towards a right path and suggest availing the facilities and opportunities available to them.

PRINCIPLE OF CONTROLLED EMOTIONAL INVOLVEMENT

This principle of controlled emotional involvement guards social workers from either indulging too personally in the client's predicament or being too objective. Social worker should maintain a reasonable emotional distance during problem-solving process. In case, the social worker starts sympathizing with over-indulging in the client's life, it may adversely affect the worker's ability to work objectively and client's rights to self-determination. Hence, it is highly imperative that a social worker need not get emotionally involved with the client's situation to the extent of getting swayed with emotions arising from the client's situation. If a social worker ends up getting too emotionally involved with the client will affect their ability to look at the situation in an objective manner which will affect an effective response in the situation. In a nutshell, social worker should be sensitive to the client's feelings, should understand their problem situation and should give a purposeful and appropriate response to the client's feelings. Caution needs to be applied that sensitivity to a client's emotions and situation should not result in the social worker getting affected and becoming emotionally involved in the situation. Sensitivity to the feelings of clients comes as a result of many things. It begins with the social worker's real conviction about the importance of feelings in the client's life.

PRINCIPLE OF NON-JUDGEMENTAL ATTITUDE

When a client approaches a social agency for help, they have a feeling of inadequacy, weakness and failure. The intensity of this feeling varies from individual to individual. Approaching a social agency means that the client is incapable of dealing with his problem alone. In the process of helping a client, it is important to understand their failures and weaknesses, but it is not the function of the social worker to judge any individual. The philosophy of social work has grown in love and optimism, and accepts the concept that it is possible to love the sinner without loving their sin. The principle of non-judgemental attitude presumes that the social worker should not have any biases and prejudices of any kind during helping process. They should neither get influenced by the opinions of others about the client or their situation nor should be governed by clients' past experiences. However, it is to be noted that if any professional judgement is needed to be made either about the problem or its various alternatives solutions in order to tackle the problem, the worker should not hesitate in passing the required judgement, keeping in view the best interest of the client.

METHODS OF SOCIAL WORK

There are six methods of social work which are popularly known and being practised across the globe, namely social case work, social group work, community organization, social welfare administration, social action and social work research. These are the methods through which social work is practised. Removing these methods would be like one has removed the soul from the body. In fact, the above said methods are the unique assets to the social work profession. The social work professionals working in different areas can skilfully practise these methods.

SOCIAL CASEWORK

Social casework is a method employed by social workers to help individuals find solution to problems of social adjustment which they are unable to handle in a satisfactory way by their own efforts (Hollis, 1954, p. 474).

The needs of the individuals are not limited to their material wants only as the material benefits alone cannot ensure human happiness. Happiness is achieved when material comforts are accompanied by fulfilment of emotional needs. For example, persons living with HIV and AIDS (PLHA) not only suffer from their physical ailment, but they are also emotionally broken up. In such situations, the role of the family becomes very important. A caseworker makes home visits, conducts sessions with the family members and mobilizes family support for the care of the ill in the hours of need. The caseworker also provides necessary support to the family and helps the family members to understand the needs of the HIV/AIDS patient.

Social caseworker seeks to find a permanent solution to the client's problem by restoring their self-esteem. A caseworker studies the client in totality, that is, in relation to their environment, past experiences, relation with significant others, understanding of the problem and problem-solving capacity and helps to understand themselves. Social caseworker enhances the knowledge and information of the client related to the issue.

The caseworker by careful listening and accepting the client with their feelings facilitates expression of repressed feelings by the client. He respects their worth and dignity as an individual human being. A caseworker helps the client to adjust to the reality and motivates to move ahead. Caseworker also helps an individual to reach a new level of integration by introducing new ideas and new ways of living.

> **Did You Know?**
>
> Mary Richmond's first book, titled *Social Diagnosis* (1917), provided techniques for assessing the situation of the poor.

SOCIAL GROUP WORK

Social group work is a method through which individuals in groups in social agency settings are helped by a worker who guides their interaction in programme activities so that they may relate themselves to others and experience growth opportunities in accordance with their needs and capacities to the end of the individual, group and community development (Trecker, 1955).

Hospitals are important settings for social work practice. Through group work, a client is given holistic care. For example, a social group worker is instrumental in organizing cancer support group and educational groups and guides the group work process. In the educational groups, the information is disseminated about the disease, prevention and treatment. They educate the group members about the pattern of progression and its debilitating effects in near future. They are also taught about the adherence to the treatment process like taking medicines without failure and educate to avoid those behaviour patterns that may worsen the condition.

In the support groups, the group members provide the necessary social and emotional support to the patients. It is an important platform for the cancer patients where they can express themselves freely and share their problems to help each other. Through social group work, the patients are helped to change their attitude for the rest of their life that helps in living a positive life and coping with the situation.

COMMUNITY ORGANIZATION

Community organization is a process by which a community identifies its needs or objectives, orders (or ranks) these needs or objectives, develops the confidence and will to work at those needs or objectives, finds the resources (internal and/or external) to deal with these needs or objectives, takes action in respect of them and in so doing extends and develops cooperative and collaborative attitudes and practices in the community (Ross, 1955).

Community organization is a macro-method in social work. The community organizer possesses required qualities and skills to work with people and conveys information to the community people in an effective way. The community organizer has essential knowledge, skills about the principles, process and steps of community organization and applies same while working in the community.

Through this method, the information is disseminated about various issues to the community people. For example, the community organizer organizes awareness camps related to health and nutrition, governmental programmes and human rights to improve the knowledge and understanding of the people. They conduct street plays, puppet shows, lectures and so on to disseminate the information among the general public. The community organizer also educates the community people about various diseases such as HIV/AIDS, leprosy, keeping in mind their religious beliefs, social taboos and attitude of the community.

SOCIAL WELFARE ADMINISTRATION

According to Walter A. Friedlander (1958), 'administration of social agencies translates the provisions of social legislation of social agencies and the aims of private philanthropy and religious charities into the dynamics of services and benefits for humanity.'

Social welfare agencies play a pivotal role in rendering services to the clients. The social welfare organizations employ professionally trained social workers who work as an administrator and plan, organize, direct and coordinate the delivery of services, prepare budgets for meeting the costs, supervise the staff and finally, reports to the higher authorities about the performance of the organization. The social workers have in-depth knowledge and makes use of available resources together with active community participation in order to achieve the goal of the programme properly.

SOCIAL ACTION

Social action is an individual, group or community effort within the framework of social work philosophy and practice that aims to achieve social progress to modify social policies and to improve social legislation and health and welfare services (Friedlander, 1977). Singh has given a broad definition of social action by stating that social action is a process in which conscious, systematic and organized efforts are made by some elite(s) and/or people themselves to bring about change in the system which is instrumental in solving problems and improving conditions which limit the social functioning of weaker and vulnerable sections (Singh, 1986).

For example, through social action, social worker addresses the issues pertaining to HIV/AIDS. They advocate by raising the voice on behalf of the people living with HIV/AIDS. It is widely accepted that the rights of the PLHAs are being violated in a great way. They are being stigmatized and discriminated in the healthcare setting. Through advocacy social workers influence, motivate and encourage democratic powers to take decisions for the welfare of PLHAs. They fight to bring desired changes in the policies with *the aim to ensure equitable distribution of resources in the social system, protecting their* rights and provide justice. Social action is one of the most effective methods of social work, which social workers can use in fighting for the rights of the PLHAs.

SOCIAL WORK RESEARCH

Social work research is a systematic, critical and careful investigation of a social phenomenon. The findings of social work research may help the social worker, the agency/organization and the policymakers to plan effective programmes based on the needs of a particular community (Thomas, 2010).

The role of social work research is very important for the effective implementation of any programme initiative. Research studies provide useful information about the different dimensions of the issues/problems and facilitate effective planning, policy formulation and implementation of the programme. Hence, research facilitates effective response to a particular issue and is thereby a very important social work method. As the issue of HIV/AIDS is very sensitive, the social workers assess the problem in a broader way with professional competence and suggest appropriate action plans.

SUMMARY

Social work profession has a number of values, principles and methods to guide the professional while practising social work. In this chapter, information has been provided about the generic principles of social work, namely the principle of acceptance, individualization, confidentiality, communication, self-determination, non-judgemental attitude and controlled emotional involvement. It has also looked into the application of these principles of social work practice in the field.

The chapter further discussed various methods of social work (social case work, social group work, community organization, social welfare administration, social action and social work research) which are systematic and planned ways of helping people.

TOP 10 TAKEAWAYS/MAIN POINTS

1. Social work is a welfare activity based on humanitarian philosophy, scientific knowledge and technical skills of helping individuals/groups/communities to live a wealthy and full life.
2. The process of transforming social policy into social services and the use of experience in recommending modifications to policy is called social welfare administration.
3. Confidential information can be defined as a fact or a condition, pertaining to a client's private life which is normally hidden from others.
4. The caseworker must accept the client and everything about the client that is pertinent to the helping process.
5. The function of the social worker is primarily to create an environment in which the client feels comfortable in giving expression to his feelings.
6. The social worker should not have any prejudice or bias while helping the client in solving their problem in a professional relationship.
7. The community as a unit of social work intervention seeks to tackle the needs/problems affecting a large number of people living in a community.
8. At the group-level intervention, the focus may be on a particular member of the group or a specific number of members or the whole group.
9. Social action aims to bring about necessary changes in the social legislations and policy initiatives for mass betterment.
10. The objective of social work research is to produce knowledge that can be helpful in planning and executing social work programmes.

Keywords: Principles, skills, social work, psycho-social problem

GLOSSARY

Confidentiality: To maintain the secrecy of information provided
Individualization: Asserting the uniqueness of a person
Principles: Principles are the basic rules/statements in any profession directing ways to be followed to accomplish a goal.
Social work: Social work is a value based, ethical and spiritual practice-based profession aims at addressing the overall problems of individuals, families, groups and communities to attain a peaceful life (Roy & Dash, 2016).

ANALYTICAL QUESTIONS

1. Critically analyse the principle of acceptance with suitable examples from the field.
2. How social action as a method of social work can be used in changing/modifying social policies of government for mass betterment? Discuss with field experiences.

MULTIPLE CHOICE QUESTIONS

1. Which of the following is the primary method of social work?
    a. Social work research
    b. Social action
    c. **Social case work**
    d. Social welfare administration

2. Principle of non-judgemental attitude presumes that
    a. Social worker should be biased towards the client
    b. **Social worker should begin the professional relationship without any bias**
    c. Social worker should form opinions about clients
    d. Social worker should not respect the client

3. Principle of self-determination emphasizes
    a. **Every individual has the right to assess what is good for them and decide the ways and means to realize it**
    b. Social worker should impose decisions or solutions on the client
    c. Social worker should be authoritative
    d. Client does not have any right to decide what is good for them

4. Principle of acceptance means
    a. **Accepting the client with all their limitations**
    b. Acceptance of the gifts given by client
    c. Deal with the client according to their family background
    d. Imposing ideas on the client

5. A process through which social work services both private and public are organized and administered is called
    a. Social case work
    b. Social group work
    c. Community organization
    d. **Social welfare administration**

6. Social action aims at
    a. Bringing about desirable changes to ensure social progress
    b. Creating awareness about social issues
    c. Encouraging people to raise their voice against undesirable practices
    d. **All of the above**

7. Which of the following cannot be considered as secondary method of social work?
    a. Social work research
    b. Social action
    c. **Social group work**
    d. Social welfare administration

 8. Social work research
    a. Offers an opportunity for social workers to make a difference or modification in their practice
    b. Seeks to accomplish the same humanistic goals as does a social work method
    c. Deals with those methods and issues, which are useful in evaluating social work programmes and practices
    d. **All of the above**

 9. Community organization is a
    a. **Primary method of social work**
    b. Secondary method of social work
    c. Tertiary method of social of social work
    d. None of the above

10. Social group worker should be skilled in
    a. Establishing purposeful relationship
    b. Dealing with group feelings
    c. Using agency and community resources
    d. All of the above

REVIEW QUESTIONS

1. Discuss the principle of client self-determination.
2. Write a short note on the principle of controlled emotional involvement.
3. Discuss social group work as a method of social work.
4. Define social work research.

REFERENCES

Dunlap, A. (2013). *Ten skills every social worker needs.* www.socialworkhelper.com/2013/08/06/10-skills-every-social-worker-needs/

Friedlander, W. A. (1955). *Introduction to social welfare.* Prentice Hall.

Friedlander, W. A. (1958). *Concepts and methods of social work.* Englewood cliffs, NJ: Prentice Hall (p. 208).

Friedlander, W. A. (1977). *Introduction to social welfare.* Prentice Hill.

Hollis, F. (1954). Social case work. *Social work year book.* Open University Press.

International Federation of Social Workers/International Association of Schools of Social Work. (2013). *Global definition of social work.* http://ifsw.org/get-involved/global-definition-of-social-work/

Jagadish, B. V. (2007). Professional social work: Generic principles, values and their application. In G. Thomas (Ed.), *Basics of social work*. IGNOU.
Moffett, J. (1968). *Concepts of case work treatment*. Routledge and Kegan Paul.
Perlman, H. H. (1957). *Social case work*. Chicago University Press.
Pincus, A., & Minahan, A. (1978). A model of social work practice. In H. Specht & A. Vickery (Eds.), *Integrated social work methods*. George Allen and Unwin.
Ross, M. G. (1955). *Community organization: Theory and principles*. Harper and Brothers.
Roy, S., & Dash, B. M. (2016). *Field work practice in social work education: Major components, issues and challenges*. Atlantic Publishers.
Singh, S. (1986). Social action. In S. Surender & K. S. Soodan (Eds.), *Horizons of social work*. Harnam Publications.
Trecker, G. (1955). *Social group work: Principles and practices*. Association Press.

RECOMMENDED READINGS

Batra, S., & Dash, B. M. (2021). *Fundamentals of social work*. Concept Publisher.
Bodhi, S. R. (2019). *Social work: Lectures on curriculum and pedagogy*. The New Vehicle.
Desai, M. (2002). *Ideologies and social work: Historical and contemporary analyses*. Rawat Publications.
Dubois, B., & Karla, M. K. (1992). *Social work—An empowering profession*. Allyn and Bacon.
Lewis, J., & Gibson, F. (1977). The teaching of some social work skills: Towards a skills laboratory. *The British Journal of Social Work, 7*(2), 189–209.
Mathew, G. (1992). *An introduction to social case work*. TISS.
Sheafor, B. W., & Horejsi, C. R. (2003). *Techniques and guidelines for social work practice* (6th ed.). Allyn and Bacon.
Suppes, M. A., & Wells, C. C. (2013). *The social work experience: An introduction to social work and social welfare* (6th ed.). Pearson.
Thomas, G. (2015). *Social work: A value based profession*. Rawat Publications.
Trevithik, P. (2008). Revisiting the knowledge base of social work: A framework for practice. *The British Journal of Social Work, 38*, 1212–1237. doi:10.1093/bjsw/bcm026

16
Models of Social Work
Sayantani Guin

LEARNING OBJECTIVES
- To understand the concept, nature and meanings of social work models
- To examine the historical evolution of charity model, remedial model, developmental model and sustainable model
- To note the current trends of social work models
- To describe the scope of social work models and its relevance in social work teaching and practice

It is not enough to be compassionate. You must act.

—Dalai Lama

INTRODUCTION

The chapter focuses on the development of social work models. Models are the blueprints explaining how and in what way a particular practice may happen. Thus, social work models describe how to apply principles and theories in a wide range of situations in a structured way in order to give the practice consistency. In this chapter, the development of social work models, namely charity model, remedial model, developmental model and sustainable model, will be discussed. The economic crisis of the 1890s triggered the charity model in the 19th century in which friendly visitors, mostly middle-class women, volunteered for charity organizations to offer advice and occasionally some amount of monetary help to the poor and the needy. The remedial model focuses on the welfare aspects wherein social, economic and health benefits are extended to the underprivileged and needy who are unable to access those by themselves. The developmental perspective in social work emerged in the Third-World countries at the end of the Second World War. It emphasized that social programmes contribute positively to economic development and introduced social programmes having developmental goals. The sustainable model of social work introduces the ethical framework based on the values of inclusivity, diversity and integration, and stresses the importance of social justice and human rights.

SOCIAL WORK MODELS: CONCEPT, SCOPE AND DEFINITIONS

Social work models have a wider implication in the practice of social work. Social work models describe how and in what way social work practice evolved in due course of time. Social work, as is widely acknowledged, had its roots in the charity and voluntary aspect inherent in every religion and society across the world. Thus, charity model of social work developed under the aegis of ancient societies and religions. It propagated helping and reaching out to people in need and distress in the form of charity and philanthropy. Gradually, as the number of poor people in need grew manifold and the services of individuals and the philanthropic organizations became insufficient, the government came to the rescue. Thus, the remedial model of social work came into existence where the states enacted several legislations to reach out to individuals, groups and communities. It emphasized on welfare measures covering every citizen. Gradually, social and economic development of the nation gave rise to the developmental model of social work. This aimed in bringing social change within a broad framework of social and economic development. Social programmes that foster social capital, human capital and generate gainful employment are some of the mandates of the developmental model of social work.

CHARITY MODEL OF SOCIAL WORK

The charity model of social work initially emerged out of the necessity of helping people in the form of giving alms to the poor and the needy. This model of social work has essentially developed from the concept of sharing to the needy people which is explained in almost every society, culture and religion in the world. It is well established that all members of the society are not equally privileged with resources and even with basic necessities of survival. Care for the sick, hungry and homeless, helping the poor, disadvantaged, aged, sick, widows and orphans, donation of money and collection of taxes have been encouraged throughout all societies.

An account of several instances of charity work in ancient societies of Asia and Europe are being provided by Robert L. Barker (1995) during a project celebrating the first 100 years of professional social work in the USA. This was a project sponsored by the National Association of Social Workers and the Council on Social Work Education. It goes back to 2500 BC when papyrus scrolls were placed along with the mummies of kings in pyramids which spelt out the duties of the king including the caring for the sick, hungry and homeless. A code of justice was issued by the Babylonian King Hammurabi during 1750 BC requiring the people to help each other during the times of distress. Similar kinds of directives are found in Israel during 1200 BC. During 530 BC, the awakening of Buddha, or Siddhartha Gautama, enlightens people with the concept of love and charity. Gradually, in Greece, the concept of philanthropy, or acts of love for humanity, is introduced during 500 BC, and citizens are encouraged to make donations for public good. Similarly, during 300 BC, the act of helping others in need is expressed by Confucius in China and by Prince Asoka of India. By 100 BC, the provision of free or low-cost grain by the wealthy is well established in the Roman tradition and during 30 CE, the teachings of Christianity propagate donating to those in need. By 400 CE, hospitals and shelter homes for the poor and the disabled are established in India and throughout China, the Middle East and Europe by 542 CE. The five pillars (duties) of Islam propagate Muslims in 650 CE to pay zakat (a 'purification tax') for caring for the poor. Supporting the poor by the rich people is declared to be a moral and legal obligation by the Roman Church in 1100. The Magna Carta in 1215 granted human rights for the privileged class. In 1348, the breakdown of European feudalism is caused partly due to the Bubonic plague, killing many and leaving many more poor and economically vulnerable. Gradually, legislations were enacted, the prominent one in 1531, which provided relief to the poor and license to beg for the elderly and the disabled. The Elizabethan Poor Law of 1601 provided a model for taxing people for the benefit of the poor (Abell, 2010a). Thus, it is evident that the charity model of social work had its roots in the ancient societies, which gradually gave way for professional nature of social work practice.

In North America, before the American Revolution, formal structures of poor relief, child welfare and mental health services were already established. Gradually, the government and eventually the private self-help organizations started to help the poor and the needy. Some untrained social workers, called the friendly visitors, took up the work of helping people. Scientific charity in the form of American Charity Organization Society (COS) emerged after the Civil War and was focused on mutual aid and self-help. The settlement houses gradually broadened the concept of charity to focus on the root causes of poverty and provided working opportunities to the poor by establishing legislations, social insurance and introducing public health reforms. It has been observed that the formal social work in the USA was based on 'the four Ps' (Abell, 2010a), namely patronage, piety, poor laws and philanthropy. Patronage is helping a segment of the society, which is normally the minority group to be self-sufficient so that they become a prominent part of the economy and polity. Piety refers to the moral duty and the religious obligation of a person to help someone in need. The poor laws were meant to help the needy and the poor. Philanthropy was concerned with voluntary financial donations (Abell, 2010a). Thus, it may be said that the charity model of social work has its basis on all these concepts. Charity has also been an integral part of the development of social welfare in Canada in the form of individual charity to the family and private charity. Food poverty, that is, inability to meet basic nutritional needs, has been met by food banks, that is, non-profit organizations which collect, share or distribute surplus food to poor people or to emergency relief programmes (Abell, 2010a).

Did You Know?

Models of Social Work

Charity model of social work
Remedial model of social work
Developmental model of social work
Sustainable model of social work

Charity has also been advocated by the Greek, Roman, Jewish, Christian, Hindu, Islam, Sikh and various other religions. The Greeks considered that the rich and the poor were interrelated in the fact that the rich provided money to the poor and the poor provided the opportunity to the rich to get salvation by receiving alms, that is, good deeds. In the Roman society, the concern for the poor was met by an organized system of collecting and distributing alms and a voluntary social service system also existed along with it. The Jews were required to set aside a part of their harvest for widows, orphans and strangers. The Christian Church had certain specified roles which were directly related to charity, namely deacons, who collected food, clothing and money which were offered during religious services and distributed to the needy. Similarly, the deaconesses helped the deacons, especially on the needs of women and children. Thus, charity in the form of cash and kind existed in the form of providing money, food, clothes directly and also caring for the old, women, elderly and physically sick (Abell, 2010a).

REMEDIAL MODEL OF SOCIAL WORK

The remedial model focuses on the welfare aspects wherein social, economic and health benefits are extended to the underprivileged and needy who are unable to access those by themselves. This model refers to the efforts taken by the state for effective service delivery for the well-being of groups and individuals. The government supports the poor people when other means of support to them are exhausted. It involves both welfare services and social services. Formal organizational structure, institution or agencies are involved to help individuals and groups to develop their full potential. When other institutions of society like the family or market are unable to provide for the basic necessities to an individual or group, the social welfare services come to the rescue. This model of social work involves several programmes and services like access to health and education to women, children, aged and challenged people. Thus, it helps the weaker and the vulnerable sections of the society. It is a specialized form of social work in which direct intervention is made to individuals, groups and communities. The interaction of the individual with their environment is taken into account.

The remedial model of social work evolved after the charity model, the most prominent in the West being the COS movement by Mary Richmond and Settlement House Movement by Jane Adams. The need for scientific techniques encouraged social casework and such professionals joined the social casework agencies. Thus, the voluntary agencies had a steady supply of professionals who would work for the individuals in need (Stoesz, 1989). As a consequence of industrialization, people faced several problems, and the Social Security Act was passed in the USA in 1935. This Act enabled the various states to provide for the aged, poor, physically challenged, public health and maternal and child health, among others. A lot of trained volunteers were engaged to employ case work practice and supervise untrained people. It was realized that money alone could not solve problems of people and that individual problems of people should be addressed to alleviate people from their sufferings.

The need for the involvement of the government to ensure welfare measures for those in need became apparent as charity by individuals and institutions became inadequate. This gave rise to the remedial model of social work. In England, a series of legislations, known as the 'statues of labourers', were passed between 1350 and 1530, culminating in the shifting of the responsibility of relief from the Church to the government. One of the prominent features of the state's involvement in the welfare of people is the passing of the Elizabethan Poor Law in 1601 in the United Kingdom. The Elizabethan Poor Law in 1601 ensured the collection of taxes which were to be used for the benefit of the poor and the needy. According to the Act, the poor were divided into three categories, namely the able-bodied poor, the impotent poor and the dependent children. There were workhouses for the able-bodied poor who had to work in those workhouses. The impotent poor and the dependent children stayed in almshouses where they were given alms. However, as the number of poor increased manifold, merely an Act of the Parliament was unable to solve the problem of poverty and the need for an individualized approach was realized. This was because the problem of every individual was unique and in order to make people self-reliant, it was felt that the cause of individual problem needs to be investigated. Thus, the COSs began to work in this endeavour.

Did You Know?

The Poor Relief Act, 1601 (43 Eliz 1 c 2), was an Act of the Parliament of England.[1] The Act for the Relief of the Poor 1601, popularly known as the *Elizabethan Poor Law*, '43rd Elizabeth' or the Old Poor Law was passed in 1601 and created a poor law[2] system for England and Wales.[3] It formalized earlier practices of poor relief[4] distribution in England and Wales.

During the 18th and the 19th centuries, the social transformations set forth by the Industrial Revolution led to several social problems such as poverty, overcrowding, health issues, addiction issues, prostitution and poor housing. In order to cater to the needs of the people, many social institutions and welfare initiatives were launched. In the 19th century, laws were introduced in the United Kingdom which addressed the working conditions and treatment of children. Programmes on education, policing, public sanitation and juvenile correction were also introduced. The Poor Law Amendment Act was passed in 1834 which ensured the duty of the state to identify the deserving poor from those who were undeserving and thus able-bodied to work. The state also took the responsibility to provide social services such as free education up to the age of 10, public sanitation and laws enabling working conditions in the factory and mines to all citizens (Abell, 2010b). Later in 1942, the Beveridge Report, the report of the Inter-Departmental Committee on Social Insurance and Allied Services, headed by Sir William Beveridge, emphasized the provision of benefits and grants to every citizen in the form of family allowances, national health services and national assistance (Lobo, 2010).

---

[1] https://en.wikipedia.org/wiki/List_of_Acts_of_the_Parliament_of_England,_1485%E2%80%931601
[2] https://en.wikipedia.org/wiki/Poor_law
[3] https://en.wikipedia.org/wiki/England_and_Wales
[4] https://en.wikipedia.org/wiki/Poor_relief

DEVELOPMENTAL MODEL OF SOCIAL WORK

The developmental model of social work emerged after the end of the Second World War particularly in the Third-World countries with an aim of social and economic development of the respective nation. Thus, the developmental model initially was more widespread in the developing nations rather than in the Western industrial nations. Gradually, even industrial nations became interested in developmental perspective with the increasing use of social programmes to promote economic development.

Developmental model of social work aims at the planning and implementation of social policy to bring about positive social change. This affects a large number of people and works within the broad framework of the existing national plans. It helps in the growth and development of the existing social, economic and political institutions and involves systematic analysis of the social policy (Stein, 1976).

Some of the features of the developmental perspective are given below (Midgley & Livermore, 1997).

1. Developmental perspective, also known as social development, promotes economic development of the nations as it encompasses a social policy meant for the whole population to bring about positive social change.
2. Developmental perspective believes that economic progress brings about social progress.
3. Developmental perspective encourages the intervention of the state in the planning of social, economic and developmental programmes.
4. It strives to include all sections of the society including the marginalized and the oppressed.

To understand the contribution of social work in the developmental perspective, it is essential to understand the following three requirements (Midgley, 1995, as cited in Midgley & Livermore, 1997).

1. *The presence of a formal organizational structure:* A structured institution is required at national, regional and local levels to implement the developmental policies. This organization will be able to facilitate the social developmental programmes and encourage coordination and cooperation among the social welfare organizations, thus preventing them from collapsing.
2. *Developmental initiatives should have an impact on the overall well-being of the people:* It had been observed that economic development alone could not facilitate welfare of the masses. So the developmental model of social work advocates for bringing both economic development and social development to a large section of the society. To bring about economic and social development, some of the initiatives that have been proposed include the promotion of the informal sector of the economy, training for jobs, creating job opportunities, job placement, infrastructure development and promoting education.
3. *Developmental policies should contribute to the economy:* In this regard, the developmental model of social work advocates for three types of social development initiatives that

can promote to the nation's economy (Midgley 1995, 1996, cited in Midgley & Livermore, 1997).
  a. *Initiatives that foster human capital:* The developmental model of social work promotes social programmes which works towards providing education, health and nutrition to all in the society, or at least to those who are most deserving. This is because access to education, healthcare and nutrition contributes to healthy individuals who in turn work towards some tangible economic gain.
  b. *Social programmes that promote social capital:* Social capital basically means a network of people who live and work together for the effective functioning of the society. Such social network has close bonding of people with effective coordination and communication resulting in effective contribution to the society. Creation of assets and infrastructure such as roads, schools, drinking water projects and irrigation system which promote social development are also considered social capital. These assets have a positive impact on people's lives who in turn contribute to the growth of the nation's economy.
  c. *Programmes that generate productive employment and self-employment:* The development model of social work promotes social programmes that create jobs and employment opportunities for all citizens, especially the needy and low-income population group. Such kind of employment generation social programmes include self-help groups, vocational education, job placement and micro-enterprises. Such kind of self-employment programmes not only benefit the individual but also contribute to the larger economy.

Thus, the developmental model of social work aims at the strengthening of social organizations by creating social policy which cover all or the majority of the population.

The developmental model of social work involves participating in the process of strengthening of social institutions to enable them to provide better services to the people. It includes social policy and social coverage that have an impact on a larger section of the population (Stein, 1976).

SUSTAINABLE MODEL OF SOCIAL WORK

The sustainable model of social work is based on the understanding of sustainable development and protecting the ecosystem, the balance of which is constantly threatened due to the ever-increasing developmental projects. While the population of the earth is increasing, there is poverty leading to the over-exploitation of natural resources. Sustainability essentially includes protection of the environment and all organisms residing in the ecosystem. Sustainable development involves the growth of the humankind within the framework of inclusivity, diversity and integration. It involves the development of mankind in an eco-friendly way so as to protect the environment and the future generations. Three pillars of sustainable development were initially recognized: the social, the economic and the environmental. The social dimension of sustainable development includes the provisions of basic needs of people and provision of opportunities of a better life. The environmental dimension of sustainable development implies limiting the ill effects of technology on environmental resources. The economic dimension of sustainable development includes the equitable distribution of earth's resources to everyone including the poor for a better standard of life (Mignaqui, 2014). Thus, sustainable development includes a balance between these three dimensions, namely social (people), ecological (environmental) and economic (prosperity). Also, the principle of social justice for an equal society is inherent in sustainable development. The term *sustainable development* became popular in 1987 during the World Commission on Environment and Development (known as the Brundtland Commission) and the Earth Summit in Rio de Janeiro in 1992 (Fergus & Rowney, 2005). The sustainable model of social work focuses on the empowerment of people, socio-economic development, human rights and environment and is also included in the global agenda of Sustainable Development Goals (SDGs). The SDGs were adopted by the United Nations on 25 September 2015 which includes the action plan of 2030 Global Agenda titled 'Transforming Our World: The 2030 Agenda for Sustainable Development'. This agenda focuses on human rights, development, empowerment and environment. There is a great opportunity for social workers to work for human development concerns which include eradication of poverty, providing education and employment opportunities, access to healthcare and so on at the local, national and global levels. Furthermore, the sustainable model of social work also strives to promote social and economic equality, gender equality and empowerment, respect the worth and dignity of the individual and also work towards development which does not harm the environment. This model also supports the protection and promotion of human rights and fundamental rights of individuals irrespective of any discrimination. Thus, the sustainable model of social work strives to promote inclusivity, respects diversity, equality and non-discrimination, and realization of full potential of people. The target group are women, children, migrants and refugees, persons with disabilities, aged and indigenous people (Jayasooria, 2016).

SUMMARY

In this chapter, the concept of the development of social work models were explained. The chapter makes an attempt to trace the development of the models of social work. Four models of social work were explained in this chapter. Social work has its foundation on charity and philanthropy, which are propagated in all religions across the globe. Charity has been practised since the ancient societies of Greek, Roman, Jewish, Christian, Hindu, Islam, Sikh and various other cultures. The charity model of social work highlights the principle of 'giving' or 'donating' to the needy people. While individuals and social organizations make charity, it is also the responsibility of states and governments to make welfare provisions to not only the needy and deserving but also to anyone who qualifies for such provisions. The remedial model of social work strives to promote the several welfare programmes on education, policing, public sanitation, juvenile correction and so on to the deserving and qualified. The development model of social work takes into account the social and economic prosperity of the individual and aims at the planning and implementation of social policy to bring about positive social change. The sustainable model of social work focuses on the empowerment of people, socio-economic development, human rights and environment. Thus, this chapter traced the development of social work models by explaining the charity model of social work, the remedial model of social work, the developmental model of social work and the sustainable model of social work.

TOP 10 TAKEAWAYS/MAIN POINTS

1. Models are the blueprints explaining how and in what way a particular practice may happen.
2. Social work models describe how to apply principles and theories in a wide range of situations in a structured way in order to give the practice consistency.
3. The charity model of social work had its roots in the ancient societies and religion, which gradually gave way for professional nature of social work practice.
4. The remedial model of social work involves the efforts of the states and governments to provide welfare programmes for all sections of the society including the poor and the deserving.
5. In the remedial model of social work, a social worker works for the effective implementation of the welfare programme initiatives of the government for the people.
6. The developmental model of social work aims at the strengthening of social organizations by creating social policy which covers all or the majority of the population.
7. The developmental model of social work aims at the planning and implementation of social policy to bring about positive social change.
8. The sustainable model of social work strives to promote social and economic equality, gender equality and empowerment, respects the worth and dignity of the individual and also work towards development which does not harm the environment.
9. The sustainable model of social work supports the protection and promotion of human rights and fundamental rights of individuals irrespective of any discrimination.
10. The sustainable model of social work strives to promote inclusivity, respects diversity, equality and non-discrimination and realization of full potential of people.

Keywords: Social work models, charity, remedial, developmental, sustainable

GLOSSARY

Charity: Charity is the act of helping others voluntarily, especially those who are the poor and less privileged. Charity may be in the form of money or in the form of some material things. It is different from social work as it provides temporary relief to the recipient and makes the recipient dependent on the donor. However, social work has its roots in charity.

Empowerment: It is the ability to become confident and stronger by being able to control one's own life and being aware of one's own rights. It gives power and status to individuals. It enables people to achieve their goals and enhance the quality of their lives.

Human rights: These are the rights that an individual is born with. These are the inalienable rights of individuals simply because of the fact that they are a human being. Everyone is entitled to human rights without being subjected to any discrimination of race, gender, religion, birthplace and so on.

SDGs: The SDGs were adopted by the United Nations on 25 September 2015. These are also known as 'global goals'. There are 17 SDGs. They include the action plan of 2030 Global Agenda, titled 'Transforming Our World: The 2030 Agenda for Sustainable Development'. This agenda focuses on human rights, development, empowerment and environment.

Social justice: It means protecting and promoting the rights of people. Every society develops certain rules and regulations for the protection and promotion of the rights of its people. Social justice ensures that the rights of all citizens are protected and promoted in an equal manner.

Social welfare: It includes the specialized services for the betterment of the lives of the weaker and most vulnerable sections of the society. It is an organized system of services and institutions. It aims to protect and promote the interest of the most vulnerable section of the society by enabling their potentials, talents and abilities.

Sustainable development: It means economic development which does not have a negative impact on the environment. It is based on the principle that development should meet the needs of the people without compromising the ability of future generations to meet their own needs.

ANALYTICAL QUESTIONS

1. Highlight the concept of the sustainable model of social work.
2. Enlist the global agenda of SDGs.

MULTIPLE CHOICE QUESTIONS

1. Which of the following is the apt meaning of *charity*?
   a. Donating alms
   b. Voluntarily helping others
   c. Helping the poor and the needy
   d. **All of the above**

2. Social programmes that foster social capital, human capital and generate gainful employment are some of the mandates of which model of social work?
   a. Charity model of social work
   b. **Developmental model of social work**
   c. Remedial model of social work
   d. Sustainable model of social work

3. The London COS was founded in which year?
   a. 1820
   b. 1832
   c. **1869**
   d. 1879

4. What was the main recommendation of the Beveridge Report?
   a. Welfare provisions for the poor
   b. Welfare provisions for the sick
   c. **Welfare provision for every citizen**
   d. Welfare provision for women

5. In which year was the Poor Law Amendment Act passed?
   a. **1834**
   b. 1838
   c. 1934
   d. 1860

6. Which of the following is not a part of the types of social development initiatives advocated by the developmental model of social work?
   a. Social programmes that generate productive employment and self-employment
   b. Social programmes that promote social capital
   c. **Social programmes that promote charity**
   d. Social programmes that foster human capital

7. When were the SDGs adopted?
   a. 10 September 2014
   b. **25 September 2015**
   c. 18 September 2016
   d. 20 September 2017

8. SDGs include:
   a. Gender equality
   b. Quality education
   c. **Both a and b**
   d. None of the above

9. Which of the following is not a part of the three pillars of sustainable development?
   a. Social dimension
   b. Economic dimension
   c. Environmental dimension
   d. **Welfare dimension**

10. When was the Magna Carta created?
    a. 1220
    b. **1215**
    c. 1350
    d. 1320

REVIEW QUESTIONS

1. Discuss the main provisions of the Elizabethan Poor Law 1601.
2. Trace the evolution of the remedial model of social work.
3. Define charity in your own words.
4. Write a short note on the concept of charity in different religions.

REFERENCES

Abell, N. (2010a). History of social work in the Americas. In Gracious Thomas (Ed.), *Origin and development of social work*. IGNOU.
Abell, N. (2010b). History of social work in Europe. In Gracious Thomas (Ed.), *Origin and development of social work*. IGNOU.
Fergus, A., & Rowney, J. (2005). Sustainable development: Lost meaning and opportunity? *Journal of Business Ethics*, *60*(1), 17–27. http://www.jstor.org/stable/25075243
Jayasooria, D. (2016). Sustainable Development Goals and social work: Opportunities and challenges for social work practice in Malaysia. *Journal of Human Rights and Social Work*, *1*, 19–29. https://doi.org/10.1007/s41134-016-0007-y
Lobo, J. (2010). Emergence of social work abroad. In Gracious Thomas (Ed.), *Introduction to social work* (Vol. I). IGNOU.
Midgley, J. (1995). *Social development: The developmental perspective in social welfare*. SAGE.
Midgley, J. (1996). Involving social work in economic development. *International Social Work*, *39*, 13–95.
Midgley, J., & Livermore, M. (1997). The developmental perspective in social work: Educational implications for a new century. *Journal of Social Work Education*, *33*(3), 573–585. http://www.jstor.org/stable/23043090
Mignaqui, V. (2014). Sustainable development as a goal: Social, environmental and economic dimensions. *The International Journal of Social Quality*, *4*(1), 57–77. http://www.jstor.org/stable/44174133
Stein, H. (1976). Social work's developmental and change functions: Their roots in practice. *Social Service Review*, *50*(1), 1–10. http://www.jstor.org/stable/30015320
Stoesz, D. (1989). A theory of social welfare. *Social Work*, *34*(2), 101–107. http://www.jstor.org/stable/23715780

RECOMMENDED READING

Batra, S., & Dash, B. M. (2021). *Fundamentals of social work*. Concept Publishers.

17

Theories in Social Work
Sonam Rohta

LEARNING OBJECTIVES

- To provide a detailed understanding of the commonly used social work theories and methods
- To explore the relevance of social work theory and its application in practice
- To understand the role of social workers in utilizing appropriate social work theory in practice
- To encourage the reader to further explore the application of social work theory through case examples

Everything is theoretically impossible, until it is done.

—Robert A. Heinlein

INTRODUCTION

Theory is an important component in social work practice that guides social workers while working with individuals, communities and society as a whole. The theory helps to predict, explain and assess situations and behaviours and provides a rationale for how the social worker should react and intervene with clients who have particular histories, problems or goals (Teater & Kondrat, 2010). Social workers are expected to approach, assess and provide interventions that are based on psychological, sociological and social work theories. Every social worker, whether they recognize it or not, operates within a theoretical framework (Coulshed & Orme, 2006). Some social workers do not try to acknowledge or understand their theoretical framework, instead practising based on assumptions driven from their personal or professional experiences. In that case, social workers could be putting clients at risk of harm by practising from assumptions and the social worker's values versus established theories and the values set by the social work profession (Teater & Kondrat, 2010). Social workers have the ethical and professional responsibility to acknowledge the established and researched theories that are grounded in social work values and make efforts to bring them into practice.

The two concepts, 'theory' and 'method', are both independent and interrelated in social work practice. A theory helps to understand or describe a particular phenomenon, whereas the method specifies the action for the social workers faced with that particular phenomenon. The term 'method' is often used interchangeably with 'approach', 'intervention' or 'practice'. All these terms denote action, which is synonymous with method, in regard to something the social worker does or implements (Teater & Kondrat, 2010).

THE SIGNIFICANCE OF THEORY IN SOCIAL WORK PRACTICE

Theories help social workers to understand or explain different situations or behaviours and provide insight into past experiences and future prospects. For example, the attachment theory of Bowlby explains the disruptive behaviour of children placed in different foster homes. This theory helps the social worker gain an understanding of the behaviour of children raised in foster homes. Theories provide a foundation for understanding the client's situation and problem, and they guide social workers through the possibilities that may happen when certain methods or theories are applied.

Social workers should critically assess, evaluate and reflect on their own practice and implementation of theories and methods in social work situations in order to determine what works, what does not work or what needs to be modified, adjusted or maintained for future situations. This would enable social workers to utilize the most appropriate and effective theories and methods in certain situations. 'Reflecting critically entails reviewing different perspectives and options before deciding on best practice' (Payne et al., 2009, p. 3; Teater & Kondrat, 2010). Critically reflective practice requires social workers to be both reflective and critical about social work practice. Social workers can begin to participate in this process by asking themselves the following questions after a social work encounter (Adams, 2009, p. 234; Teater & Kondrat, 2010):

1. What happened?
2. How did it compare with previous experience?
3. How did I do?
4. How well did I do?
5. What could I have done better?
6. What could I have done differently?

The first three questions above involve the social worker reflecting on the situation and what happened, and the last three questions involve the social worker critically reflecting on the experience, what was learnt and what will be adjusted or modified in future practice.

ECOLOGICAL SYSTEM THEORY

Ecological system theory has had relevance in social work practice since the 1970s when theorists began stressing the importance of the person-in-environment perspective. During this period, the early ecological theorists, notably Germain and Hartman, developed the groundwork for the ecological approach that is currently given emphasis in the field of social work. An ecological model of individual and society and how to practice social work in the current behavioural and ecological sciences refers to a conceptual system about mind-body-environment in transactional relationships. As Germain points out, ecological theory is an appropriate metaphor for social work, which seeks to enhance the quality of transactions between people and their environment (Siporin, 1980). Ecological theory deals with the web of life, at the interfaces between systems and subsystems, so that it relates to 'open, self-organizing, self regulating, and adaptive complexes of interacting and interdependent subsystems'.

THE ECOLOGICAL PERSPECTIVE

From the beginning of the profession of social work, there has been a concern for people and the environment, for their interrelations and for the whole unit that encompasses them. The pioneers of social work, such as Mary Richmond, emphasized the role of the environment in the social functioning of human beings. The ecological approach guides social workers to move from a micro-level to macro-level of interventions. It helps social workers to impact a client system through micro- and macro-level interventions, such as policy and planning activities at macro level and counselling and psychotherapy at the micro-level approaches.

Presently, the ecological framework has developed six distinct professional roles. There are a number of writers who have identified these roles as a complex part of advanced generalist practice (Anderson, 1981; Hernandez et al., 1985). John T. Pardeck (1988) identifies six professional roles that allow the practitioner to work effectively with five basic client systems: the individual, the family, the small group, the organization and the community. The six professional roles are as follows:

1. **Conferee:** Derived from the idea of a conference, this role focuses on actions that are taken when the practitioner serves as the primary source of assistance to the client in problem solving.
2. **Enabler:** The enabler role focuses on actions taken when the practitioner structures, arranges and manipulates events, interactions and environmental variables to facilitate and enhance system functioning.
3. **Broker:** This role is defined as actions taken when the practitioner's object is to link the consumer with goods and services or to control the quality of those goods and services.
4. **Mediator:** This role focuses on actions taken when the practitioner's objective is to reconcile opposing or disparate points of view and to bring the contestants together in united action.

5. **Advocate:** This role is defined as actions taken when the practitioner secures services or resources on behalf of the client in the face of identified resistance or develops resources or services in cases where they are inadequate or non-existent.
6. **Guardian:** The role of guardian is defined as actions taken when the practitioner performs a social control function or takes protective action when the client's competency level is deemed inadequate.

Did You Know?

The science of ecology and professions like social work have a comfortable fit as they share the expressed purpose of fostering healthy and interdependent transactions between individuals and their environment. The earliest ecological model of the social work practice challenged the individualistic casework orientation popular in the early and mid-20th century (Ramsay, 1994; Wakefield, 1996b). As Carol Meyer notes,

> The movement from casework to social work was more than semantic; it meant ultimately that family, group, community, and organisation approaches to intervention were to be included under the heading of social work practice, and that new efforts were to be made to intervene in the client's environment. (Greif and Lynch, 1983, p. 12; Ungar, 2002)

Furthermore, John T. Pardeck (1988) and Max Siporin (1980) summarize the ecological perspective as an appropriate strategy for practice in social work through the following points:

1. Ecological theory is a dynamic holistic approach in social work that stresses emphasizing the person and the sociocultural systems surrounding them.
2. The mutual interdependence among person, behaviour and the environment is emphasized.
3. A social worker is able to move from micro-level to macro-level interventions while working with a client system.
4. It stresses treatment planning and allows the practitioner to work on altering intersystem relationships.
5. It encourages an eclectic approach to practice.
6. Given its multifactorial nature, the practitioner is able to develop and utilize a strong and varied repertoire of assessment and social treatment strategies.

The ecological approach provides a balance between the person and the environment, which is critical to social work practice and treatment. It contributes to facilitating practice effectiveness and accountability. The ecological approach facilitates effective social work treatment by involving the practitioner not only with the client, but also with the social systems and processes of social functioning that involves the client's family, neighbourhood and smaller and larger communities.

THE PSYCHODYNAMIC THEORY

Psychodynamic theory, a theory of personality originated by Sigmund Freud, has a long history in social work practice and social work education, which continues to impact the profession of social work. By the early part of the 20th century, social work practice started showing signs of division between the clinical and macro-level practice traditions. On the one hand, the experience of 'friendly visitors' with the charity organization societies in both England and America in the latter part of the 19th century had gradually evolved into an early, though fundamentally non-dynamic form of social casework, largely owing to the pioneering work of Mary Richmond (Brandell, 2004). The earlier historical emphasis of psychoanalytic ideas in the field of social work seems to have occurred in the 1920s.

During the past century, psychoanalysis has had a revolutionary influence on the field of clinical social work. It can also be argued that psychoanalytic thinking has pervaded a variety of clinical social work approaches. The three classical social casework may illustrate this influence most clearly: the diagnostic or psychosocial school, the functional school and the problem-solving school (Brandell, 2004).

THE DIAGNOSTIC OR PSYCHOSOCIAL SCHOOL

The diagnostic school is basically founded on the Freudian theory of psychoanalysis. Although Mary Richmond is often credited with having originated the diagnostic or psychosocial approach to casework, there were a number of other early contributors. Gordon Hamilton, Bertha Reynolds, Charlotte Towle, Fern Lowry, Marion Kenworthy, Betsey Libbey, Annette Garrett and Florence Hollis are among those whose teaching and scholarship helped to shape this approach to casework (Hollis, 1970; Brandell, 2004).

Since the goal of social casework services is to free individuals from their psychosocial and socio-psychological disabilities, diagnosis is an inseparable part of the helping process. According to Lowry, the process of diagnosis in social casework consists of (a) shifting the relevant from irrelevant data, (b) organizing the facts and getting them into relatedness, (c) grasping the way in which facts fit together and (e) perceiving the configuration of meaning as a whole. The diagnosis done by the caseworker emphasizes an understanding of psychological, social, biological and environmental factors operating on the 'person-in-situation'.

The person-in-situation can be understood and described from three equally perceptible facets. The first is the *dynamic diagnosis*, which is the cross-sectional view of the forces currently operating in the individual's life. It examines an individual's interactions with others in his or her environment. The second is the *etiological diagnosis*, where the focus is on present and historically remote features of the person-environment matrix. The present problem is seen in terms of life situations, past events and experiences. The third is *classificatory diagnosis*, in which an effort is made to classify various aspects of the individual's functioning, typically including a clinical diagnosis (Hollis, 1970, p. 52; Brandell, 2004). Other psychoanalytic ideas, such as resistance, transference and countertransference, have also been integrated into the psychosocial perspective.

THE FUNCTIONAL SCHOOL

Functional social casework was developed by Jessie Taft and Virginia Robinson at the Pennsylvania School of Social Work in the 1930s. Taft and Robinson, both influenced by the teachings and philosophy of Herbert Mead and John Dewey, and later by Freud's disciple Otto Rank, whose theories emphasized human growth, the development of the self, and the will as a controlling and organizing force, became an important force in functional theory as a member of the teaching faculty at the University of Pennsylvania.

As opposed to diagnostics, functionalists believe that human problems are caused by the use of destructive relationships. Therefore, the interaction between the helper and the client is used for positive change through the experience gained in the casework relationship. The functionalists give the utmost importance to the use of agency function in the helping process. It is considered a unifying and direction-giving factor in the helping process.

THE PROBLEM-SOLVING MODEL

The problem-solving model was developed by Helen Harris Perlman in the 1950s at the University of Chicago. Perlman's model of casework is very closely tied to ego psychological theory, and she views the casework process itself as a 'parallel to the normal problem-solving efforts of the ego'. With the use of such concepts as partializing (breaking down large problems into smaller, more manageable tasks), Perlman attempted to translate ego psychology into action principles. The problem-solving model emphasized the significance of the relationship between the caseworker and the client. Casework always aimed to maintain the relationship between client and caseworker to be aware of their separate and realistic identities and their joint goal of achieving a better adaptation between the client and their current problem situation (Brendall, 2004, p. 8).

ANTI-OPPRESSIVE SOCIAL WORK

The primary objective of practising social work is to facilitate change among individuals and within their environments that are oppressing or preventing the individual from positive growth and development. Social workers seek to challenge inequality and injustice and advocate for equal opportunities and resources for individuals, groups and communities. Anti-oppressive practice in social work is a concept that, at its core, is concerned with promoting values of equality and social justice by challenging the power of oppression (Dalrymple & Burke, 1995; Dominelli, 2003).

According to Dominelli (2002, p. 7), conceptualizing oppression simply as cruel or unjust treatment entailing the enforcement of power over others, focuses the exercise of power in social relationships primarily on the interpersonal level. Oppression involves relations of domination that divide people into dominant or superior groups and subordinate or inferior ones. The dynamics of oppression provide the context in which oppressed individuals and groups exercise agency and attempt to shape their world as they envisage it. These dynamics involve processes of oppression that are shared across a range of social divisions, for example 'race', gender, class, age, disability and sexual orientation. Oppressive acts can be implemented in ways that limit or block access to resources or opportunities for particular groups of people, as is often evidenced by advantages for the powerful in systems such as healthcare, education, policy, finance, media and culture (Clifford, 1995; Teater & Kondrat, 2010).

Thus, anti-oppressive practice is empowering in nature as it seeks to provide a working environment that is egalitarian where clients identify their needs and collaborate with social workers to identify clients' strengths and resources to overcome barriers and obstacles within the environment. The end result of this practice will empower the clients and enable them to overcome oppression, access available resources and opportunities and fulfil their needs.

Thompson (2006) developed an approach to analysing anti-discriminatory and anti-oppressive practice by building on the works of Dalrymple and Burke (1995; Teater & Kondrat, 2010).

Thompson's approach, referred to as the PCS model, is often depicted as a set of three circles, each embedded within the other, as illustrated in Figure 17.1. As the figure shows, the personal level (P) involves interpersonal relationships, personal feelings, attitudes, self-conceptions and interactions between individuals, which would often include social work practice relationships (Payne, 2005; Teater & Kondrat, 2010). The personal is embedded within the individual's cultural context (C) that shapes the individual's perspective towards himself and others in society. Culture establishes norms and rules that shape an individual's interaction with other people and the environment. Both the personal and cultural levels are then embedded within the societal framework (S), which sets the structures, norms, rules and order within society. Thompson's PCS model emphasizes to social workers that discrimination or oppression may not take place only at the personal level, where social workers prefer to exercise anti-oppressive practice but may take place on other levels such as cultural and societal, which are embedded within one another. Social workers may intervene on a personal level to change discriminatory and oppressive behaviours, but they might find it difficult to intervene and change such behaviours in larger societies where there is a shared culture as a whole that continues to discriminate and oppress. Thompson's PCS model is helpful for social workers to first begin this process of change by

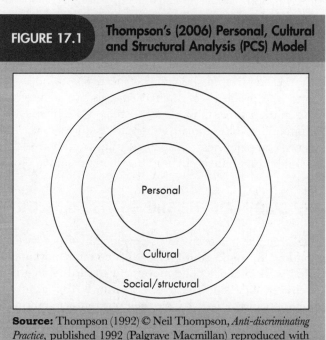

FIGURE 17.1 Thompson's (2006) Personal, Cultural and Structural Analysis (PCS) Model

Source: Thompson (1992) © Neil Thompson, *Anti-discriminating Practice*, published 1992 (Palgrave Macmillan) reproduced with permission of Palgrave Macmillan.

examining themselves and their personal views on culture, societal structures, norms and rules of society. Different aspects of social work practice should be permeated by anti-oppressive practices, which should include the social worker–client relationship, the employer–employee relationship, the ethos of the social service agency and the social context, all with the driving force of challenging inequalities and disadvantage (Burke & Harrison, 2009; Dominelli, 2002; Teater & Kondrat, 2010). In order to accomplish this goal, social workers need to practice self-reflection and become self-aware of inequalities and disadvantages that may have an impact on them. The past experiences and values of social workers shape the way they practice, so it is essential to acknowledge and reflect on what the social worker brings to the working relationship, which can assist in delivering anti-oppressive practice. According to Dominelli (2002, p. 15), social workers are required to consider three key levels when implementing anti-oppressive practice: (a) intellectual—understanding the principles and methods of working in an anti-oppressive way, (b) emotional—ability to deal with oppression and discrimination in a confident way, and the ability to learn from one's mistakes and (c) practical—ability to implement the principles of anti-oppressive practice (Teater & Kondrat, 2010).

STRENGTHS PERSPECTIVE

The strengths perspective in social work was proposed by Saleebey (2006). Since its introduction, it has been widely applied in child welfare, substance abuse, family services and services for elderly people (Guo & Sui, 2010). The strengths perspective is a way of working in which rather than focusing on the problems of clients, social workers try to emphasize interactions and interventions that focus on the client's abilities, resources, accomplishments and strengths. The strengths perspective is based on the fundamental belief that focusing on individual strengths, versus deficits or limitations, is the true avenue for therapeutic progress (Weick et al., 1989).

Practicing from a strengths perspective does not mean that social workers are required to ignore the problems of their clients, as problems such as violence, child sexual abuse and schizophrenia are all real, but it demands a different way of looking at individuals, groups or communities. The strengths approach requires that all be seen in the light of their capacities, talents, competencies, possibilities, values and hopes, no matter how distorted these may have become through their circumstances, oppression and discrimination.

THE ORIGIN OF THE STRENGTHS PERSPECTIVE

The strengths perspective was developed by social work academics, such as Dennis Saleebey, Charles Rapp and Ann Weick, as a counter movement to the problem-focused approach to social work practice. The movement towards strengths-based practice came from two fronts (Weick et al., 1989; Teater & Kondrat, 2010): (a) to respect the dignity and worth of every human being regardless of their current circumstances; focusing only on the problems, limitations or diagnoses reduces a person to a problem-focused label, which is contrary to the values of social work and (b) the diagnostically driven system, which places the social worker in a position of power over the client.

According to Saleebey (2009b), strengths can be framed within a triangle with three points: C, P and R. This triangle is referred to as the CPR of strengths and helps social workers identify clients' strengths under each of these three headings. C represents competence, capacities and courage; P represents promise, possibility, positive expectations and potential, and R represents resilience, reserves, resources and resourcefulness. Therefore, when identifying clients' strengths, social workers must look beyond the obvious personal strengths and delve into clients' possibilities, competencies and resiliencies (Teater & Kondrat, 2010).

ASSUMPTIONS AND PRINCIPLES OF THE STRENGTHS PERSPECTIVE

The strengths perspective consists of the following six guiding assumptions (Saleebey, 2009b, pp. 15–18; Teater & Kondrat, 2010):

1. Every individual, group, family and community has strengths.
2. Trauma, abuse, illness and struggle may be injurious, but they may also be sources of challenge and opportunity.
3. Assume that you do not know the upper limits of the capacity to grow and change, and take individual, group and community aspirations seriously.
4. We best serve clients by collaborating with them.
5. Every environment is full of resources.
6. Caring, caretaking and context—care is essential to human well-being.

The strengths perspective holds that social workers and clients should work collaboratively to assess and identify strengths and resources that can be used and capitalized upon to foster client self-determination and control in order to grow and develop (Greene & Lee, 2002). As an approach, strengths-based practice assumes that all individuals have strengths which can be used to achieve the desired goals. It focuses on clients' strengths and achievements instead of only on their problems and seeks to use those strengths to achieve clients' full potential. Therefore, a strengths-based approach encourages both the social worker and the client; it focuses on clients' strengths to help them counter their problems and move towards self-defined, satisfying goals.

SOCIAL LEARNING THEORY

Understanding human behaviour is an important aspect of social work practice. It is always challenging and difficult for social workers to employ the right theories that come with trying to understand human behaviour and achieve positive results for their clients. From the very beginnings of our profession, our forebears recognized the value of empirical research in social work. To define social learning theory, it is important to understand the term 'behaviour'. The term 'behaviour' refers to what a person does, regardless of the observable nature of the phenomena.

In social learning theory, 'man is neither driven by inner forces nor buffeted helplessly by environmental influences' (Bandura, 1971). Instead, there is a reciprocal relationship between behaviour and the conditions that control it (Weisner & Silver, 1981). The theory integrates prior cues, cognitions, behaviour and reinforcing and punishing consequences. The environment is considered a behavioural creation that acts on the behaviour of the actor who creates it.

To understand behaviour, then, social learning theory looks to (Weisner & Silver, 1981):

1. Environmental cues that precede a particular behaviour
2. Mediational processes (cognitions that mediate stimuli)
3. The behaviour itself
4. Rewarding or punishing (reinforcing) consequences that follow

The most salient contingencies of behaviour, most simply stated, are rewards and punishments.

APPLICATIONS FOR SOCIAL WORK INTERVENTION

The social learning theory foundation of behavioural social work has produced an empirical approach to social work practice that provides a clear understanding of the relationships between human beings and their environments. Over 50 per cent of the controlled studies resulting in positive outcomes that have been published in the social work literature have been based on social learning theory (Reid & Hanrahan, 1982; Rubin, 1985; Sheldon & Gillespie, 1992; Thomlison, 1984; Thyers & Myers, 1998). Thyer and Hudson (1987) offer a definition of behavioural social work:

> Behavioral social work is the informed use, by professional social workers, of interventive techniques based upon empirically-derived learning theories that include but are not limited to, operant conditioning, respondent conditioning, and observational learning. Behavioral social workers may or may not 'subscribe to the philosophy of behaviorism. (p. 1)

Liberman and Bedell (1989) note that practice research has demonstrated that among the psychosocial therapies, behaviour therapy may be considered the initial treatment of choice for a wide variety of disorders, including anxiety disorders, schizophrenia, depression, eating disorders, psychosomatic complaints, sexual dysfunctions, substance abuse, childhood disorders, mental retardation and other developmental disabilities such as autism (Thyers & Myers, 1998). For the treatment of more complex disorders, the application of behavioural principles has expanded consistently over the past few decades. As practice guidelines for various disorders have been developed, the behavioural therapies derived from social learning theory are better represented than any other psychosocial approach to practice (cf. Chambless et al., 1996). The behavioural studies are also considered among the best designed and controlled studies in the social and behavioural sciences (Thyers & Myers, 1998). The behavioural perspectives also have applicability to community practice and the formulation of social welfare schemes. Behavioural principles have been applied in community settings to such topics as reducing unemployment, crime, employee absenteeism, school vandalism and highway speeding as well as promoting public health practices, industrial safety and community-based recycling efforts (Thyers & Myers, 1998). These social problems have always been the concern of social workers and effective interventions are derived from the social learning principles.

> ### Did You Know?
>
> The social learning theory foundation of behavioural social work has produced an empirical approach to social work practice that is committed to understanding the objective relationships between human beings and their psychosocial environments. Over 50 per cent of the controlled studies resulting in positive outcomes that have been published in the social work literature have been based on social learning theory.

TASK-CENTRED APPROACH

The task-centred model is a short-term approach to social work practice that focuses on alleviating specific problems of clients (Reid & Epstein, 1972; Fortune et al., 2009; Teater & Kondrat, 2010). The approach was developed after extensive experimentation with brief interventions and work with clients that focused on identified problems and incremental steps toward reaching a specified goal (Reid and Shyne, 1969; Teater & Kondrat, 2010). The fundamental nature of task-centred social work practice is to help clients clarify the problems, establish goals that are personally meaningful and that alleviate the problems, and implement the task in their life situations to achieve the goal. Task-centred social work holds that clients build confidence and self-esteem by experiencing small successes and completing tasks along their journey towards reaching goals (Doel, 1991). The focus of task-centred social work is initially on problems and goals, but the process of work with the client moves from the identification of problems through a sequence of incremental steps, called tasks, to the desired goal (Doel & Marsh, 1992; Teater & Kondrat, 2010). Task-centred social work is generally a way of working with clients to achieve their goals and alleviate immediate problems.

Reid and Epstein's (1972) book, *Task-centered Casework*, was the first book to illustrate the step-by-step process of implementing the task-centred approach. Reid and Epstein developed an approach that focused on the early establishment of goals, the development of tasks, and a commitment to adhere to time limits. Task-centred social work is a short-term, problem-solving approach and is applicable to work with individuals, families, groups and communities. Reid and Epstein (1972) specified the various problems that the model is suitable to address, which are still applicable today. The problems can include one or more of the following: interpersonal conflict; dissatisfaction in social relations; relations in formal organizations; difficulty in role performance; problems of social transition; reactive emotional distress, and/or inadequate resources. The key to identifying problems is that the client must express a desire to work on the problem either independently or in collaboration with the social worker (Teater & Kondrat, 2010).

The following values are inherent in the task-centred approach and are particularly useful for social work (Doel, 1991; Teater & Kondrat, 2010, p. 180).

1. **Partnership and empowerment:** The relationship between the client and social worker is one of partnership and collaboration. The social worker and the client should have a common purpose in their work, and the client should specify the problem from

their perspective and establish goals that are personally meaningful. In certain situations, the nature of the social work role and the involvement of the client with social services does not lend itself to a truly collaborative or partnership relationship.

2. **Clients are the best authorities on their problems:** Clients are seen as experts on their situation and problem definitions and, therefore, are encouraged to describe their problems from their perspective and establish personally meaningful goals that they perceive will alleviate the problems. Again, in particular situations, the problem may be defined by outside sources (that is, courts, social service agencies) that are not congruent with the client's definition of the problem.
3. **Builds on people's strengths rather than analysing their deficits:** All clients are seen to possess strengths, and the social worker should identify each client's strengths and resources. Acknowledging the strengths and accomplishments of the client enables a greater sense of confidence and self-esteem in the client.
4. **Provide help rather than treatment:** The social worker and client are in a partnership and should work collaboratively through the task-centred process to alleviate problems. The social worker is there to help and guide the client through this process, not to treat the client or alleviate their problems.

Table 17.1 summarizes the five steps with the three main sequences of the task-centred approach. The task-centred approach is well structured and categorizes the steps and sequences into three phases (Fortune et al., 2009). In the initial phase (Session 1–2), client-acknowledged problems and their contexts are identified, explored and assessed. In the middle phase (each subsequent sessions), the social worker and client review the problem and tasks, resolve any

TABLE 17.1 List of the Five Steps with the Three Main Sequences for Task-centred Practice

Steps and Sequences	Purpose
1. Preparation	Establish the justification for social work involvement at this time.
2. Sequence 1: Exploring problems a. Problem scanning b. Problem details c. Problem priorities	Explore and determine the concerns/problems. Develop a list of all identified concerns/problems. Explore each problem in more detail: who, what, when, where, why and how. Rank the problems and identify no more than three to be the focus of work.
3. Sequence 2: Establish goal and time limit	Define a goal in relation to the problem(s) and a time limit to reach the goal.
4. Sequence 3: Develop tasks	Establish the tasks that need to be completed in order to reach the goal.
5. Evaluation	Evaluate the process of work: Has the client achieved what they wanted?

Source: Doel (1991); Doel & Marsh (1992); Reid & Epstein (1972); Teater & Kondrat (2010).

obstacles identified and develop and select new tasks to be accomplished, and in the terminal phase (final session), target problems are reviewed and successful problem-solving strategies are identified, and any further problems remaining are discussed, including any potential future plans to alleviate the problems (Reid, 1997; Teater & Kondrat, 2010).

GANDHIAN APPROACH

Gandhi (1957), one of the most outstanding social activists of recent times, believed that all people are responsible for their immediate environment and for society. This stresses the understanding that knowledge is constantly constructed from community experiences. The Gandhian approach emphasizes that rights and duties are regulated by the principle of interdependence and reciprocity between one's immediate environment and society (George & Krishnakumar, 2014). He emphasized that through continuous social interactions, each layer of social reality is discovered, which gave him a new perception of the community and helped him to understand his own social responsibilities. Social work is an empowering profession with values and principles committed to human rights and social justice (Payne, 2005). The Gandhian approach has a great role to play in social work in India. It strengthens the promotion of human rights and social justice, especially among those who are often neglected. When it is applied to social work, the Gandhian approach is based on a reciprocal, interactive partnership between social workers and the community, particularly community residents. It emphasizes what each has to offer and learns from the other (George & Krishnakumar, 2014).

FOUNDATIONS OF GANDHIAN THOUGHT

Gandhi's ethical system developed out of his lifelong 'experiments with truth' (Gandhi, 1993). These experiments were based on a turn-of-the-century non-Western culture. Gandhian principles stress philosophical beliefs such as cooperation over competition, interdependence over rugged individualism, compassion for others over pursuit of self-interest and social justice over individual achievement. The two main ethics of Gandhian thought are service to others (sarvodaya) and justice for all (Satyagraha). In Gandhian thought, the Sanskrit word 'ahimsa' includes the principles of non-violence, truthfulness and love for all. 'Sarvodaya' includes the principle of self-development through service to others, especially those in need. 'Satyagraha' is a principle of non-violent social change for addressing social injustice, and 'swadeshi' is the principle of human scale and immediacy, as well as material simplicity and the corollary principles of non-attachment, non-stealing and trusteeship (Walz & Ritchie, 2000).

GANDHIAN APPROACH IN SOCIAL WORK

Despite its emergence in 1936, Indian professional social work has failed to gain social recognition because of its lack of clarity in direction and because it has not effectively responded to social issues (Singh, 2005). The significant contributions and developmental models propounded by the great Indian thinkers, particularly Swami Dayanand Saraswati, Swami Vivekananda, Dr Bhim Rao Ambedkar, Mahatma Gandhi, Jyotiba Phule, Nanaji

Deshmukh, Rabindranath Tagore, Narayan Guru, Anna Hazare, Baba Amte and others, should be given sufficient emphasis, which is highly relevant in the reconstruction of Indian society (Dash, 2018). The main objective of integrating the Gandhian Approach is not to create a different knowledge base on social issues but to help social workers develop their own professional identities within their community. The Gandhian approach works as a guide for Indian social workers to obtain community-based knowledge and practice models that could engage them in more productive practices. The Gandhian approach beckons social workers to integrate their education and practice into the local community, which would help the community to realize their own potential and build more responsive social structures.

SUMMARY

This chapter has defined the concepts of commonly used social work theories and methods. A theory helps social workers predict or explain human behaviours and situations, whereas a method provides the techniques or steps that can be adopted to achieve the goals set by social workers. The chapter explores seven social work theories in depth by providing the definition, basic premise or characteristics with a discussion on how social workers can utilize or implement the theory or method in practice. It guides social workers to move from a micro level to macro level of intervention, based on the ecological system theory, which has a long history in social work. The psychodynamic theory has had a revolutionary influence on the field of clinical social work, which pervades a variety of clinical social work approaches like the diagnostic or psychosocial school, the functional school and the problem-solving school. The strengths perspective in social work is based on the fundamental belief that focusing on individual strength, rather than on the limitations of clients, is the true avenue for therapeutic progress. Further, social learning theory fits closely with social work's traditional person-in-environment perspective. Task-centred social work is a short-term, problem-solving approach that can be used to address many different types of problems in various types of settings and in combination with other theories or methods. Finally, Gandhi's approach as a guide for service to others and the pursuit of social justice is complementary to social work practice theory. His method emphasizes both social service and social action, with micro-level and macro-level interventions.

TOP 10 TAKEAWAYS/MAIN POINTS

1. A theory is a hypothesis, an idea or prediction about the possibility of a situation in certain circumstances.
2. The theory helps to predict, explain and assess situations and behaviours and provides a rationale for how the social worker should react and intervene with clients who have particular histories, problems or goals.
3. Aetiology, diagnosis and therapy are inseparably linked theoretically and practically in every approach to any of the disabilities of man.
4. Ecological theory is an appropriate metaphor for social work, which seeks to enhance the quality of transactions between people and their environment.

5. Anti-oppressive practice in social work is a concept that, at its core, is concerned with promoting values of equality and social justice by challenging the power of oppression.
6. The strengths perspective is based on the fundamental belief that focusing on individual strengths, versus deficits or limitations, is the true avenue for therapeutic progress.
7. Task-centred social work is a short-term, problem-solving approach and is applicable to work with individuals, families, groups and communities.
8. The Gandhian approach stipulates that knowledge is constantly constructed from community experiences and that community-based social work learning and practice are necessary to reflect and act on social crisis.
9. Social learning theory offers social workers a comprehensive theory of human personality and a widely applicable approach to clinical practice.
10. Social work is an empowering profession with values and principles committed to human rights and social justice.

Keywords: Social work theory, ecological system theory, psychodynamic theory, anti-oppressive social work, strengths perspective, social learning theory, task-centred approach, gandhian approach

GLOSSARY

Behaviour: Any action or response by an individual, including observable activity, measurable physiological changes, cognitive images, fantasies, and emotions. Some scientists even consider subjective experiences to be behaviour (Barker, 1995, p. 33).
Empowerment: The capacity of individuals, groups and/or communities to take control of their circumstances, exercise power and achieve their own goals, as well as the process by which they are able to help themselves and others to maximize the quality of their lives (Adams, 2008, p. 17).
Perspective: To understand or view certain experiences based on words and principles.
Social work practice: Social work practice consists of the professional application of social work values, principles and techniques to one or more of the following ends: helping people obtain tangible services; counselling and psychotherapy with individuals, families and groups; helping communities or groups provide or improve social and health services, and participating in legislative processes (the National Association of Social Workers).
System: A set of elements that are orderly and interrelated to make a functional whole (Kirst-Ashman & Hull, 2002).

MULTIPLE CHOICE QUESTIONS

1. Who developed the groundwork for ecological theory in the field of social work?
   a. Mary Richmond
   b. Sigmund Freud
   c. **Germain and Hartman**
   d. Garrett and Hollis

2. What does 'sarvodaya' mean?
   a. Non-violence
   b. Trusteeship
   c. Truthfulness
   d. **Progress for all**

3. Which of the following theories emphasizes human behaviour?
   a. Ecological theory
   b. Psychodynamic theory
   c. **Social learning theory**
   d. Gandhian theory

4. Who among the following proposed the strengths perspective?
   a. Thompson
   b. **Saleebey**
   c. Perlman
   d. Jessie Taft

5. Who is the author of the book *My Experiments with Truth*?
   a. A. V. Thakkar
   b. K. D. Gangrade
   c. Dr Ghurye
   d. **Mahatma Gandhi**

6. Who coined the term 'person-in-situation'?
   a. **Florence Hollis**
   b. H. Bartlett
   c. Mary Richmond
   d. Charles Cooley

7. What is the goal of social work?
   a. To reduce social tensions
   b. To provide services to all
   c. **To promote social justice**
   d. To serve the elite

8. Whose work gave rise to the 'problem-solving approach'?
   a. Florence Hollis
   b. Mary Richmond
   c. **H. H. Perlman**
   d. B. Swift

9. Which of the following approaches is empowering in nature?
   a. Task-centred
   b. Psychodynamic
   c. **Anti-oppressive**
   d. Ecological

10. Who is the author of the book *Task-centered Casework*?
    a. Elliot and Merill
    b. **Reid and Epstein**
    c. Fuller and Myres
    d. Louise Weston

REVIEW QUESTIONS

1. Describe how you would prefer to incorporate systems theory or the ecological perspective into your social work practice. Give specific reasons.
2. How does Thompson's PCS model impact the social worker's values in anti-oppressive social work practice?
3. Describe the merits of a strength-based approach. How would you utilize this approach in the community with multiple issues?
4. Describe the significance of the Gandhian approach in modern social work practice. Give reasons.

REFERENCE

Thompson, N. (1992). *Anti-discriminatory practice: Equality, diversity and social justice*. Palgrave Macmillan.

18

Skills in Social Work

Rutwik Gandhe

LEARNING OBJECTIVES

- To discuss the concept and types of skills necessary to become successful a social worker
- To develop an understanding about various skills required to practise professional social work
- To review skills identified required for social workers

The highest skill is the true judgement of values.

—Francois Alexandre Frederic

INTRODUCTION

Human beings require a certain skill set to perform or practise a task or profession. A surgeon requires to have skills of surgery with due dexterity in hands. Authentic knowledge and awareness along with skills only makes a doctor perfect. An engineer would require foresight so that instruments can be used to perform the due activity to create or perform what is desired of. Lawyer may require the skills to win an argument to persuade in the court of law. We see that wherever profession or performance is executed, it requires a skill set that one must possess in order to operate the tools and obtain desired results.

Skills are no tools, neither they are the means to perform one's duty. Skills are abilities to perform a task/behaviour at a given time in a given situation. Before we get into formal definitions of *skills*, let us differentiate between skills, knowledge and tools. Just as skills are different from tools, they are different from knowledge or awareness as well; we shall discuss and understand it by a simple example of a carpenter. The toolbox of a carpenter is where all the necessary equipment is kept. They are known as tools. The knowledge and awareness of different types of woods and other aspects of the work that guide what works and what does not is knowledge or know-how. However, the more subtle and rather invisible characteristic here, which is the ability to apply the tools and knowledge about wooden work in order to create different objects from wood, can be understood as the skills of the carpenter. Every work or profession requires a certain skill set without which that task or professional duties cannot be rendered. So is the case of *social work* as a professional practice. An individual must possess certain skills in order to excel in practising social work. Thus, *knowledge, skills and tools* (KST) can be termed as the trio which makes someone a successful practitioner in any practice. Before we actually look into what are the skills necessary to become a successful social worker in life, let us further decode the word 'skills'. Before the discussion really forwards on skills of social work, it should be noted that it has been conclusively stated that theoretical construct of *skills of social work* is weak (Karpetis, 2017; Trevithick, 2004). Theoretical underpinnings of social work skills are either underdeveloped or missing and, at the same time, there is no evidence from practice world or consensus among scholars on the definitions of core, specific, technical, interpersonal, listening, interviewing, helping, counselling and micro-skills (Diggins, 2004; Travethick, 2013; Trevithick et al., 2004). On the contrary, very soft and humane view of skills for social work has been taken by including only soft skills in it. Communication, observation, listening, assessment, helping, directing, guiding, empowering, negotiating, partnering and virtues such as competence and accountability are the ones described and recognized as skills at many places in the domain of social work.

FORMATIVE COMPONENTS OF SKILLS IN SOCIAL WORK

A social worker regardless of setting or function has to deal with *person and situations* (PAS) and *person in environment* (PIE) in order to render services (Cournoyer, 2008). Here, PAS are keywords requiring due attention. As Cournoyer (2008) suggested, PAS and PIE are important considerations when we determine the skills that are required to be a social worker or skills that a social worker ought to have. This means that the *skills in social work* or any other arena of life is indeed a dynamic concept and depends primarily on two factors: person and situation or environment. This *person* could be the client in social case work setting or otherwise. As situation of the person or the environment of the person who is intended to help professionally changes, the skills required at the end of social worker also change. Thus, we see that range and scope for defining the skills for social workers is quite wide and vivacious. At the same time, Cournoyer (2008) suggests that skills are a derivative of three basic components: (a) *phase of social work practice*, (b) *facilitative qualities consistent with that phase* and (c) *central professional characteristics required at the given situation*.

In this context, the phases or processes of social work practice include *preparing, beginning, exploring, assessing, contracting, working and evaluating,* and *ending* (Cournoyer, 2008). Effective social workers consistently demonstrate the essential facilitative qualities such as *empathy, respect and authenticity* in their work with clients. Finally, competent social workers integrate the characteristics of professionalism such as *integrity, professional knowledge, critical thinking and lifelong learning, ethical decision-making, self-understanding and self-control, cultural competence and acceptance of others,* and *social support and self-efficacy* throughout all aspects of their service. Thus, we can see that there are five components that can potentially define and shape the skills required for practising social work in a professional manner, namely (a) *PAS*, (b) *PIE*, (c) *phase of social work practice*, (d) *facilitative qualities consistent with that phase* and (e) *central professional characteristics required at the given situation*.

Accordingly, many different ways, different skills can be thought for or can be defined for the professional social worker as combination of these five components keeps changing. Looking at the history of literature on skills for social workers, it can be observed that in situations of old-age care, the scholars have first paid heed towards the special set of skills one should have while attending and serving to the aged ones in society. As we are aware, a skill set changes from situation to situation and person to person who needs it, and it has left us with many opportunities to proclaim anything under the sun as 'skills for social work' as long as it serves the purpose of helping people.

Did You Know?

Welford (1958) long ago attempted to compile the skill set that social workers require in the context of helping aged individuals.

DEFINING SKILLS IN SOCIAL WORK

Let us now have a look at various definitions of skills in the context of social work. The term *skill* has assumed significance in popular literature of social work. Several social work texts incorporate skill or skills in their titles. Body of literature generated by Freeman (1998a, 1998b), Henry (1981, 1992), Hepworth et al. (2002), Middleman and Wood (1990), Phillips (1984) and Shulman (1999) is testimony to it. As discussed and hinted earlier, the term 'skill' has been used in different manners according to people and situations or environment in which they are required. It means that skills mean different things to different scholars and there is no single way to reflect the conceptual understanding of the term *skills* in the context of social work.

For example, skill has been described as 'the practice component that brings knowledge and values together and converts them to action as a response to concern and need' (Johnson, 1998, p. 55). Another definition suggests that it is 'a complex organization of behaviour directed toward a particular goal or activity' (Johnson, 1998, p. 451), and a 'social worker's capacity to use a method in order to further a process directed toward the accomplishment of a social work purpose as that purpose finds expression in a specific program or service' (Smalley, 1967, p. 17).

Middleman and Wood (1990, p. 12) define skills as 'the production of specific behaviours under the precise conditions designated for their use'. Henry (1981, p. vii) suggested that skills are 'finite and discrete sets of behaviours or tasks employed by a worker at a given time, for a given purpose, in a given manner'. She (Henry, 1992, p. 20) also cited Phillips (1984), who characterized skill as 'knowledge in action'. Morales and Sheafor (1998, p. 140) described skills as the 'ability to use knowledge and intervention techniques effectively'.

> **Box 18.1** Two Definitions that Are Most Pertinent to Skills in Context of Social Work
>
> Cournoyer (2008) defines the skills as:
>
> A circumscribed set of discrete cognitive and behavioural actions that (1) derive from social work knowledge and from social work values, ethics, and obligations, (2) are consistent with the essential facilitative qualities, (3) reflect the characteristics of professionalism, and (4) comport with a social work purpose within the context of a phase or process of practice.
>
> Barker (1995) defined that
>
> Social worker's skills include being proficient in communication, assessing problems and client workability, matching needs with resources, developing resources, and changing social structures.

SKILLS REQUIRED FOR SOCIAL WORKERS

Different authors and professional bodies mention the skills required depending upon five essential components as discussed previously. Some would suggest 6, some would suggest 10, 12 and so on, more or less, in a similar fashion the various skills that are required by the social workers. Sudbery (2003) has identified 50 skills required for social workers. He provides classification of these skills as well where 15 skills are identified as skills of indirect help (different kinds of interviewing and so on), 20 skills mentioned are related to direct help. In this way, we see that classification and identification of social work skills is possible in many different ways. In a similar but terse attempt, Trevithick (2012) also classified skills in social work; however, the skill set she discussed was just human skills pertaining to indirect help. Here, an attempt has been made to summarize the set of skills commonly understood as necessary skills for professionally practising social work.

Dunlap (2013) has identified 10 core skills that a social worker requires. These are as follows:

1. Assessment skills
2. Communication skills
3. Advocacy skills
4. Problem-solving skills
5. Critical thinking skills
6. Respect for diversity
7. Intervention skills
8. Documentation skills
9. Organizational skills
10. Understanding of human relationships

> **Box 18.2 Twelve Skills Outlined by National Association of Social Workers, USA**
>
> 1. Listen to others with understanding and purpose.
> 2. Elicit information and assemble relevant facts to prepare a social history, assessment and report.
> 3. Create and maintain professional helping relationships.
> 4. Observe and interpret verbal and non-verbal behaviour and use knowledge of personality theory and diagnostic methods.
> 5. Engage clients (including individuals, families, groups and communities) in efforts to resolve their own problems and to gain trust.
> 6. Discuss sensitive emotional subjects supportively and without being threatening.
> 7. Create innovative solutions to clients' needs.
> 8. Determine the need to terminate the therapeutic relationship.
> 9. Conduct research or interpret the findings of research and professional literature.
> 10. Mediate and negotiate between conflicting parties.
> 11. Provide inter-organizational liaison services.
> 12. Interpret and communicate social needs to funding sources, the public or legislators.
>
> **Source:** NASW (1981, pp. 17–18; used with permission).

It is also believed, in general, that there are 11 essential skills in order to successfully render the duties pertaining to social work. We shall look into those very briefly. These skills are enlisted after the discussion with experts from human services consulting firms. Therefore, we can call it the view of the practitioners rather than scholars.

1. *Detailed note-taking ability:* The ability to take excellent notes is extremely important as a social worker listens to their clients and colleagues, and develops interventions and strategies.
2. *Organizational skills:* Being organized is very important as social workers are often asked to multitask and thus the ability to prioritize which work is required to be done in which order is extremely important.
3. *Understanding of human psychology:* Social workers need to understand the way people's mind works.
4. *Knowledge of human developmental stages:* For social workers, it is critical to understand human psychology to know the developmental stages from birth to death.
5. *Knowledge of interventions applicable to one's specialty:* Depending on a social worker's specialty, there might be a variety of different interventions to not only understand in theoretical terms but also in practical application.
6. *A developed sense of empathy:* Empathy is extremely important for without it social workers have an unending series of difficulties working through people's problems

Skills in Social Work

without fully being able to understand their point of view on a given situation. Shulman (2008) has therefore emphatically stated that while working with families and child welfare settings, having empathy is extensively required being the only human skills in this classification.

7. *Exceptional professional boundary setting:* In social work, there are myriad situations in which it is critical sometimes to quickly and effectively establish a boundary in a concise and professional manner. This is important not only for ethical reasons but also due to the fact that social workers as a human being will find themselves burnt out quickly if they do not rigorously apply and stick to professional boundaries.
8. *Ability to facilitate cooperation both among individuals and groups:* One of the main challenges as a social worker is to get reluctant individuals and groups to work with one another. In order to really get the affairs going, one must have the ability to facilitate cooperation.
9. *Active listening skills:* As a social worker, it is important to be able to listen and also ask questions wherever appropriate for clarification otherwise it becomes difficult to read the minds of others.
10. *Critical thinking skills:* Critical thinking is helpful for social workers to make a decision on what a piece of information really means in a given situation.
11. *Verbal and written communication skills:* Social workers time and again need to express themselves cogently to a wide variety of people in a diverse contexts, and having strong written and verbal communications skills is an absolute must.

CORE SKILLS REQUIRED FOR SOCIAL WORKERS: THE SPLENDID SEVEN

It should be noted that numerous scholars and practitioners have identified from their experience and perspectives from time to time the skills for social workers. Therefore, there is so much to write and discuss about it; however, many of these classifications of skills overlap and sometimes find the superficial mention of the skills. Core skills are the ones which find place and evidence in academic literature, whereas numerable skills can be defined and constructed as per the popular belief. We shall discuss here some of the prominent and widely accepted skills recognized for social workers.

1. *Assessment skills*: Like any other professional, social workers too should have skills of being capable of assessing the people and situations. However, the assessment in practice is not much of a kind of mathematical or logical one, but to have the ability to read and understand people for their wants, needs and aspirations. A good social worker must have skills to distinguish and discern between the situations and people for often they are in the middle of a situation when they need to identify the right kind of beneficiaries. Social workers deal with greater accountability and are required to be more transparent while dealing with resources as they are more often available to them in the form of charity or donations from varied sources. In such a situation, people dealing with scant resources demanding high level of accountability and transparency, must know the most

prudent use of such resources. One of the most essential skills to be able to carry forward this dutiful obligation is to make an assessment with great precision so that just and righteous allocation of resources can be done, and it is made sure that no individual group or community worthy of help is denied the opportunity.

2. *Communication skills*: Social workers are some of those fortunate creatures on the soil who deal with people, their emotions and hardships. They are the ones who have best of the chances to interact with and intersperse among a wide range of people, groups and communities that entail them to have the ability to pass on the correct messages through right channels in time and to further take care of the matters on the basis of the feedback of these processes. If these processes are made effective, hearts are touched with humane feelings and joy, satisfaction and other virtues are spread among people; nonetheless, if such process is not paid due heed, it may turn out to be sowing the seeds of animosity and bitterness among people and various stakeholders. Therivel (2017) has brilliantly outlined the need and process for communicating with anxious clients, a skill that is must for social workers. Ayling (2012), through his research, has been a strong propagator of the fact that theatre, drama and acting are important skills for social workers and therefore suggested these skills to be cultivated.

Let us note that good communication results in bridging the gap between different stakeholders, that is, funding agency, which is concerned with proper and intended utilization of resources it offered, implementing agency, which is concerned with greater good to be done to intended beneficiaries and other stakeholders or participants in the loop. Communication skills help social workers build a rapport with all the stakeholders they are likely to deal with in executing their tasks in this empowering profession. Verbal communication being the more informal kind of communication helps in building rapport with beneficiaries, and written communication being more of formal kind helps build rapport with donors and other partners to generate resources and remain relevant. Therefore, a social worker is rightfully suggested to master written and verbal communication skills.

3. *Advocacy skills*: This is one of the typical skills one should have in order to become a successful social worker. As a result of their exposure to people and their problems, mostly social workers are well versed with the ground realities. It naturally puts them into a strong position of knowing problems and situations of people from multifaceted perspectives which is apt for championing the cause of the people and the number of other stakeholders. The ability to forward and champion the cause of the multifaceted stakeholders and beneficiaries in a way that policy-driven changes are possible in a society with respect to the subject championed is known as *advocacy skill.*

4. *Problem-solving skills*: The ability to take the problem(s) head on and duly persuading all possible ways persistently leading to its logical end finally is known as a problem-solving skill. This is a very important skill in any human being whether the person is a social worker or otherwise. For social workers, this particular skill is very important as it is the only way to live with problems. The professional life of a social worker is filled with problems, and many a times social workers find themselves in the middle of a number of problems at once. This is so because social workers deal with no routine, and they are

confronted with new and challenging situations one after another. In such a situation, maintaining the calmness and equanimity of mind becomes extremely crucial. A calm state of mind only is fit to find solutions of the problems that are result of dealing with people, their lives and livelihoods. But for having this skill, the efforts of any individual in any profession not just social work are in vain. Problem-solving skills provide the due impetus to constantly struggle and strive for better in life as well as profession. The life of a social worker is said to be full of struggles; therefore, this skill is said to be a must for social workers.

5. *Critical thinking skills*: The capability to ponder, circumspect and think over a problem or about a situation from multiple angles including those from opposite ones, even to the extent of holding transiently negative opinion, is known as critical thinking skill. This capability is required for a social worker as a society is made up of many contradictions. Groups of people exist in conflict with each other having one view for a group is often tantamount to have opposite view from the point of view of other group. Social workers with critical thinking skills make sound judgements about complicated situations and controversies which are inevitable in social life. Without critical thinking, it is nearly impossible to think from opposite points of views and appreciate contrary opinions which are the heart and soul of balancing peace and harmony in a society. Therefore, having critical thinking is one among absolutely essential skills for those who wish to dedicate their life as social workers.

6. *Appreciating diversity*: The ability to recognize diverse backgrounds, views, opinions and conduct of people around oneself is called the appreciation of diversity. In today's era, the world has become smaller and has practically become a one small place to live in, making true the concept of a global village. People from different cultures, beliefs, values, norms, religions, skin colours, race and appearance come together and work towards common goals. Diversity could be based on age, gender or sexual orientation, race, ethnicity, religion, caste or cultural background, nationality or any other basis. Managing people from different backgrounds requires a great deal of adjustment to be done with people from different backgrounds. A social worker has to be with people of different natures and backgrounds all the time. This skill thus assumes a great significance towards rendering duties in a timely and cohesive manner. A social worker works with people from abroad and hinterlands alike; hence, it is extremely important for them to appreciate the differences among people in order to uphold their dignity. If, therefore, diversity is not recognized and appreciated, perhaps it is impossible to practise social work. Thus, appreciation of diversity is considered here to be among essential skills for social workers.

7. *Intervention skills*: The ability of any individual to mediate between two stationary resource pools or sets of pools, such that the mobility of individual concerned establishes peace, harmony, access to resources leading to greater prosperity for all the resource pool involved, is known as 'intervention skill'. In other words, it is the ability of an individual to intervene between one set of resources (say community or villages) and other set of resources (the group of people who want to bring desired changes in the state of affairs of villagers, say donors or funding agencies) leading to establish peace, harmony and

greater prosperity for resource pools on both sides. Proper intervention is very much required to achieve the end result in any social work process. In case of case work, it is the skill of the case worker how to interfere between agency and the client. In case of group worker as well, the same dictum is true and in case of interventions pertaining to communities or village as a whole, again it is the skill to establish connection between community and agency. In all cases and situations, social workers are always required to play the role of mediators. This mediation is indeed an art and is not something that can be performed by anybody. This requires greater and sophisticated dealing with people, at times artful, some other times the other way things have to be done. A social worker has to display different shades of human behaviour. Social workers have to work out ways in order to deal with different people. A social worker has to be skilful in adapting to display the attribute required, for example, authority or power, prowess, mendicancy, indifference or whichever way it works out the intervention has to be executed taking individual, group or community along.

PROMINENT SUBSIDIARY SKILLS ATTACHED TO THE SPLENDID SEVEN

1. *Organization skills*: A social worker has to organize a number of activities with the client. The client could be individuals, groups or communities. Organization skill is the ability to mobilize the resources and intervene between stakeholders who gather with a common objective. Organization skills could be termed as sub-skill of intervention skills. If one has intervention skills, one could be an effective organizer being a social worker. Thus, we can safely assume organization skill to be one kind of intervention skills only.
2. *Relationship skills*: The ability to manage the relations with other human being or designates is known as relationship skills. In management parlance, experts also refer to this as people skills. This can also be considered as another variant of intervention skills as while intervening between two resource pools, a social worker manages the relationships. Relationship management is a skill bigger than anything else. Martin and Hollows (2016) points out this relationship aspect as significant one for conducting social work with families and children. If we see the management perspective, then we see that management of relations has been considered extremely vital. Point of view differs among academicians and scholars. Since in social work, intervening and helping and execution of the activity takes ascendancy therefore even more than relationships or organizing, the intervention assumes supremacy for social workers.
3. *Documentation skills*: To be able to record well in written form is called documentation skill. This skill requires the command over language and written communication and the art of expressing oneself through pen; therefore, it is considered a subsidiary skill set of communication skills. A social worker, during their professional life, has to demonstrate this skill for every activity requires its authentic documentation.
4. *Interviewing skills:* Many of the domain experts in counselling and clinical social work have emphasized treating interviewing as separate skill; however, all acknowledge it to be part

of communication skill set. Cartney (2006) has also discussed and recognized this as skill for social workers in context of video interviewing.

5. *Human skills*: The set of skills that can be referred to as human skills constitutes a large portion of social work skills. This set of skills first found recognition in the literature of management when Katz (1974) published his path-breaking research in *Harvard Business Review*. Later, this was recognized by the scholars across the domains including social work. Human skills refer to the skill set that exists primarily as a result of humane virtues and most of the time virtues themselves. Rogers (1979) had argued in favour of this category to be deemed as skill set by establishing that people attribute meanings in their lives through feelings. All human virtues can therefore be termed as 'skills of social work'. Tolerance, empathy, compassion, courage, uprightness, honesty and more so, love for mankind are such virtues. In the absence of these humane attributes, one cannot be a social worker. This should also be noted that social work is never done in isolation and is essentially practised among people in various settings. This necessitates the need for people or human skills of which managing relationships, organizing activities and planning interventions are vital manifestations. Ruch (2012) in his seminal study really highlights the necessity of humanly feelings and emotions in practising social work. Empathy has been highlighted by scholars across the social work setting (Cuff et al., 2016).

Did You Know?

Egan's skilled helper model (Egan, 2013) is one such model which highlights the significance of skilled help in counselling work that involves a lot of intervention with individuals, families and groups through interviewing them.

CLASSIFICATION OF SOCIAL WORK SKILLS

There are many ways in which skills pertaining to social work can be classified. Sudbery (2003) classified 50 skills on the basis of roles of helper and nature of help. Katz has already identified effective skills for administrators and further classified them into categories as per the role. Similarly, there can be a number of examples, and there are indeed a number of examples whereby the classification of skills is done either on the basis of nature of skills or their application or role. There can be other classifications as well, for example, based on degree of replication (i.e., popular usage of the application of the skill; most frequently used ones versus rarely used ones and so on) and theoretical underpinning, for example, skills that find sound support and acknowledgement in theory and literature as well. The information given in the box below should further clarify. There can be any number of rows in the table given in the box below based on any criterion taken for classification.

Box 18.3 Classification of Skills Pertaining to Social Work

Criterion	Classification of Skills	Examples
Role of activity	Skills to extend (a) direct help, (b) indirect help and (c) intermediate help	a. Intervention b. Interviewing c. Counselling
Nature of activity	a. Technical skills b. People skills c. Human skills	a. Documentation skills b. Communication skills c. Empathy
Degree of application/replication	a. Highly applied b. Rarely applied	a. Communication b. Critical thinking
Theoretical underpinning	a. Sound b. Weak	a. Counselling b. Advocacy

SUMMARY

Skills are an important aspect of human life. In this chapter, information pertaining to skills in social work has been provided. The chapter first discusses the concept, formative components and definitions of the term 'skills' in the context of social work. Furthermore, various popular skill sets propounded or widely believed have been given. Later, various types of skills that are considered essential or significant from the point of performing duties in line of social work have been discussed. In this context, splendid seven skills and their subsidiary skills have been highlighted. The chapter also reviews the contemporary literature of social work pertaining to skills in social work while discussing these issues. Popular classifications of the skills in social work have also been provided.

TOP 10 TAKEAWAYS/MAIN POINTS

1. Every professional requires a skill set that one must possess in order to operate the tools and obtain the desired results.
2. KST can be termed as the trio which makes someone a successful practitioner in any practice, and they are different from each other.
3. A social worker regardless of setting or function has to deal with PAS and PIE in order to render services.
4. There are five components that can potentially define and shape the skills required for practising social work in a professional manner, namely (a) *PAS*, (b) *PIE*, (c) *phase of social work practice*, (d) *facilitative qualities consistent with that phase* and (e) *central professional characteristics required at the given situation*.
5. Skills have been defined in numerable ways. Every thinker and scholar has an independent perspective on it; however, all indicate certain abilities as skills.

Skills in Social Work

6. Sudbery (2003), Dunlap (2013) and NASW (1981) have identified 50, 10 and 12 skills, respectively, for social workers. Besides, there are 11 essential skills for social workers as per the popular belief.
7. The splendid seven skills are those which have evidence in academic literature in favour of them; at the same time, these are widely accepted and quite popular.
8. Each skill may have a number of sub-skills associated with it.
9. Almost all human virtues are quite significant from the point of view of human skills for social work.
10. A number of classifications may exist for skills pertaining to social work; however, classifications based on 'nature of activities' are still quite logical and applicable.

Keywords: Skills, skill set, social work

GLOSSARY

Intervention: To come in between two different pools of resources in order to achieve common good
KST: The trio that makes a practitioner successful
PAS: Components that help form a skill according to person and situation
PIE: Components that help form a skill according to a person in a given situation
Skill set: The set of abilities in a person that help perform or outperform

ANALYTICAL QUESTIONS

1. Highlight the various types of skills required for a social worker.
2. Discuss the intervention skills in social work.
3. Briefly explain the importance of human skills in social work.

MULTIPLE CHOICE QUESTIONS

1. Skill of a professional is
   a. Toolbox
   b. Information and awareness
   c. **Ability to apply knowledge and tools**
   d. All of the above

2. Who among the following conclusively stated that the theoretical construct of *skills of social work* is weak?
   a. Rogers
   b. Ross
   c. Sudbery
   d. **Karpetis**

3. Cartney (2006) has worked on skills pertaining to
   a. Advocacy
   b. Critical thinking
   c. **Interviewing**
   d. All of the above

4. Egan's skilled helper model is associated with
   a. Counselling
   b. Interviewing
   c. **Both a and b**
   d. None of the above

5. How many components can potentially define and shape the skills required for practising social work?
   a. **Five**
   b. Four
   c. Three
   d. Two

6. Trying to bring about a change for a section of society through persistent persuasion requires the most
   a. Human skills
   b. **Advocacy skills**
   c. Critical thinking skills
   d. Interviewing skills

7. Which one of the following can be termed as a subsidiary skill of communication skills?
   a. Documentation skill
   b. Human skill
   c. Interviewing skills
   d. Both a and c

8. Which one of the following can be termed as subsidiary skill of intervention skill?
   a. Critical thinking
   b. **Organizing**
   c. Listening
   d. Communication

9. PIE as a formative component of skills stands for
   a. Person information equipment
   b. **Person in environment**
   c. Pie
   d. Person innovation environment

10. Formative components of skills such as PIE and PAS were initially propounded by
    a. Egan
    b. Katz
    c. Rawles (2016)
    d. **Cournoyer**

REVIEW QUESTIONS

1. Define skills in context of social work.
2. Discuss the role of PAS and PIE in determining the skills required for social workers.
3. What are the 11 skills deemed essential for social workers?

REFERENCES

Adams, R. (2009). Being a critical practitioner, in R. Adams, L. Dominelli, & M. Payne (eds). *Critical practice in social work* (2nd ed.). Palgrave Macmillan.
Anderson, J. (1981). *Social work methods and processes*. Wadsworth Publishing Company.
Ayling, P. (2012). Learning through playing in higher education: Promoting play as a skill for social work students. *Social Work Education*, 31(6), 764–777.
Bandura A. (Ed.). (1971). *Psychological modeling: Conflicting theories*. Aldine-Atherton.
Barker, R. L. (1995). *The social work dictionary*. National Association of Social Workers, University of Michigan.
Barker, R. L. (Ed.). (1995). *The social work dictionary*. NASW Press.
Brandell, J. R. (2004). *Psychodynamic social work*. Columbia University Press.
Burke, B., & Harrison, P. (2009). Anti-oppressive approaches, in R. Adams, L. Dominelli & M. Payne (eds), *Critical practice in social work* (2nd ed.). Palgrave Macmillan.
Cartney, P. (2006). Using video interviewing in the assessment of social work communication skills. *British Journal of Social Work*, 36(5), 827–844.
Chambless, D. L., Sanderson, W. C., Shoham, V., Johnson, S. B., Pope, K. S., Crits-Christoph, P., Baker, M., Johnson, D., Woody, S. R., Sue, S., Beutler, L., Williams, D. A., & McCuny, S. (1996). An update on empirically validated therapies. *The Clinical Psychologist*, 49(2), 5–18.
Clifford, D. J. (1995). Methods in oral history and social work. *Journal of the Oral History Society*, 23(2), 65–70.
Coulshed, V., & Orme, J. (2006). *Social work practice: An introduction* (4th ed.). Palgrave Macmillan.
Cournoyer, B. R. (2008). *The social work skills workbook* (5th ed.). Cengage Learning.
Cuff, B. M., Brown, S. J., Taylor, L., & Howat, D. J. (2016). Empathy: A review of the concept. *Emotion Review*, 8(2), 144–153.
Dalrymple, J., & Burke, B. (1995). *Anti-oppressive practice: Social care and the law*. Open University Press.
Dash, B. M. (2018). 'Bharatiyakaran of social work': Understanding the meaning and concept. *The New Delhi Times*, 7 December.
Diggins, M. (2004). *Teaching and learning communication skills in social work education*. SCIE.
Doel, M. (1991). Task-centred work, in J. Lishman (ed.), *Handbook of theory for practice: Teachers in social work*. London: Jessica Kingsley.
Doel, M., & Marsh, P. (1992). *Task-centred Social Work*. Ashgate.
Dominelli, L. (2003). Anti-oppressive practice in context, in R. Adams, L. Dominelli and M. Payne (eds), *Social work: Themes, issues and critical debates* (2nd ed.). Palgrave.
Dunlap, A. (2013). 10 skills every social worker needs. https://swhelper.org/2013/08/06/10-skills-every-social-worker-needs/
Egan, G. (2013). *The skilled helper: A problem-management and opportunity development approach to helping* (9th ed.). Brooks/Cole and Cengage Learning.
Fortune, A. E., Reid, W. J., & D. P. Reyome. (2009). Task-centered practice, in A. R. Roberts (ed.), *Social workers' desk reference* (2nd ed.). Oxford University Press.

Freeman, E. M. (1998a). School social work at its crossroad: Multiple challenges and possibilities. *Social Work in Education, 20*(2), 83–89.

Freeman, M. (1998b). The right to be heard. *Adoption & Fostering, 22*(4), 50–59. https://doi.org/10.1177/030857599802200408

Gandhi, M. K. (1993). *An autobiography: The story of my experiments with truth*. Beacon Press.

George, M., & Krishnakumar, J. (2014). *Revisiting the landscape of professional social work in india*.

Greene, G. J., & Lee, M. Y. (2002). The social construction of empowerment, in M. O'Melia & K. K. Miley (eds), *Pathways to power: Readings in contextual social work practice*. Allyn and Bacon.

Greif, G. L., & Lynch, A. A. (1983). The eco-systems perspective, in Carol H. Meyer (ed.), *Clinical social work in the eco-systems perspective* (pp. 35–71). Columbia University Press.

Guo, W., & Tsui, M. (2010). From resilience to resistance: A reconstruction of the strengths perspective in social work practice. *International Social Work, 53*(2), 233-245

Henry, S. (1981). *Group skills in social work*. F. E. Peacock.

Henry, S. (1992). *Group skills in social work: A four-dimensional approach*. Wadsworth Inc.

Hepworth, D. H., Rooney, R. H., & Larsen, J. A. (2002). *Direct social work practice: Theory and skills* (6th ed.). Brooks/Cole-Thomson Learning, the University of Michigan.

Hernandez, S., Jorgensen, J., Judd, P., Gould, M., & Parsons, R. (1985). Integrated practice: Preparing the social problem specialist through an advanced generalist curriculum. *Journal of Social Work Education, 21*, 28–35.

Hollis, F. (1970). *Casework: A psychosocial therapy* (2nd ed.) Random House.

Johnson, L. C. (1998). *Social work practice: A generalist approach* (6th ed.). Allyn & Bacon.

Karpetis G. (2017). Theories on child protection work parents: A narrative review of the literature. *Child Welfare, 95*(2), 33–70.

Katz, R. L. (1974). Skills of an effective administrator. *Harvard Business Review* (September–October), 90–102.

Kirst-Ashman, K. K., & Hull, Jr., G. H. (2002). *Understanding generalist practice* (3rd ed.). Pacific Grove, CA: Cole Thomson Learning.

Kondrat, D. C., & Teater, B. A. (2010). An anti-stigma approach to working with persons with severe mental disability: Seeking real change through narrative change. *Journal of Social Work Practice, 23*(1),35–47.

Liberman, R. P., & Bedell, J. R. (1989). Behavior therapy. In H. Kaplan & B. Sadock (eds), *Comprehensive textbook of psychiatry* (5th ed.). Williams & Wilkins.

Macdonald, G., Sheldon, B., & Gillespie, J. (1992). Contemporary studies of the effectiveness of social work. *The British Journal of Social Work, 22*(6), 615–643.

Martin, R., & Hollows, A. (2016). Practising for social work practice: Integrating knowledge and skills for social work with children and families. *Social Work Education, 35*(5), 576–588.

Middleman, R. R., & Wood, G. G. (1990). *Skills for direct practice in social work*. Columbia University Press.

Morales, A., & Sheafor, B. W. (1998). *Social work: Profession of many faces*. Allyn & Bacon.

Pardeck, J. (1988). The Minuchin Family Stress Model: A guide for assessing and treating the impact of marital disruption on children and families. *Early Child Development and Care, 28*, 387-399.

Payne, M. (2005). *Modern social work theory* (3rd ed.). Palgrave Macmillan.

Payne, M., Adams, R., & Dominelli, L. (2009). On being critical in social work, in R. Adams, L. Dominelli & M. Payne (eds), *Critical practice in social work* (2nd ed.) Palgrave Macmillan.

Phillips, H. U. (1984). *Essentials of social group work skill*. School of Social Work, University of Pennsylvania.

Ramsay, R. (1994). Conceptualizing PIE within a holistic system of social work, in James M. Karls and Karin E. Wandrei (ed.), *Person-in-environment system: The PIE classification system for social functioning problems* (pp. 171–196). NASW.

Rawles, J. (2016). Developing social work professional judgment skills: Enhancing learning in practice by researching learning in practice. *Journal of Teaching in Social Work, 36*(1), 102–122.

Reid, W. J. & Epstein, L. (1972). *Task-centered casework*. Columbia University Press.

Reid, W. J., & Shyne, A. W. (1969). *Brief and extended casework*. Columbia University Press
Rogers, C. R. (1979). The foundations of the person-centered approach. *Education, 100*(2), 98–107.
Rubin, A. (1985). Practice effectiveness: More grounds for optimism. Social Work, 30(6), 469–476.
Ruch, G. (2012). Where have all the feelings gone? Developing reflective and relationship-based management in child-care social work. *British Journal of Social Work, 42*(7), 1315–1332.
Saleebey, D. (2006). Introduction: Power in the People. In D. Saleebey (Ed.), *The Strengths Perspective in Social Work*, (3rd edition) (pp. 1–24). Allyn and Bacon.
Saleebey, D. (2009). Introduction: Power in people. In D. Saleebey (Ed.), *The Strengths Perspective in Social Work Practice*, (5th edition). Allyn and Bacon.
Shulman, L. (1999). The skills of helping individuals, families, groups and communities. F. E. Peacock.
Shulman, L. (Ed.). (2008). The skills of helping individuals, families, groups and communities (6th ed.). Brookes/Cole.
Singh, R. K. (2005). Professional status of social work in India: An overview. In S. Singh & S. P. Srivastava (Eds.), Teaching and practice of social work in India: Realities and responses (pp. 98– 127). New Royal Book.
Siporin, M. (1980). Ecological systems theory in social work. *The Journal of Sociology & Social Welfare, 7* (4), Article 4.
Smalley, R. E. (1967). *Language of social casework*. Routledge and Kegan Paul.
Sudbery, J. (2003). Social work skills: A practice handbook. *Journal of Social Work Practice, 17*(2), 193–194. https://doi.org/10.1080/026505302000145717
Therivel, J. (2017). *Communication: Communicating with clients who are anxious*. EBSCO Information Services. https://www.ebscohost.com/assets-sample content/SWRC_Comm_w_Client_Who_Are_Anxious_SWPS.pdf
Thomlinson, R. J. (1984). Something works: evidence from practice effectiveness studies. *Social Work*, 29, 1–56.
Thompson, N. (2006). Anti-discriminatory Practice (4th edition). Palgrave Macmillan.
Thyer, B. A., & Hudson, W. W. (1987). Progress in behavioral social work: an introduction. *Journal of Social Service Research, 10*(2)/3/4).
Thyer, B. A., & Myers, L. L. (1998). Social learning theory: an empirically-based approach to understanding human behavior in the social environment. *Journal of Human Behavior in the Social Environment, 1*(1), 33–52.
Trevithick, P. (2012). Practice perspectives. *The SAGE handbook of social work*, 113–128.
Travethick, P. (2013). *Social work skills and knowledge: A practice handbook*. Rawat Publications.
Trevithick, P., Richards, S., Ruch, G., & Moss, B. (2004). *Teaching and learning communication skills in social work education*. Social Care Institute for Excellence.
Ungar, Michael. (2002). A Deeper, More Social Ecological Social Work Practice. *Social Service Review, 76*(3), 480–497.
Wakefield, Jerome C. (1996b). Does Social Work Need the Eco-Systems Perspective?. Part 2. Does the Perspective Save Social Work from Incoherence?" Social Service Review *70*(2),183–213.
Weick, A., Rapp, C., Sullivan, W.P. and Kisthardt, W. (1989). A strengths perspective for social work practice. *Social Work, 34*(4). 350–4.
Weisner, S., & Silver, M. (1981). Community Work and Social-Learning Theory. *Social Work*, 26.
Welford, A. T. (1958). *Aging and human skills*. Oxford University Press.

Philosophy, Values and Ethics of Social Work

Chapter 19 *Philosophy of Social Work*

Chapter 20 *Social Work Values: Traditional and Emancipatory*

Chapter 21 *Social Work Ethics*

19

Philosophy of Social Work
Nagalingam

LEARNING OBJECTIVES

* To understand the philosophical foundation of the social work profession
* To describe the philosophical thoughts on humans and society by various Indian scholars
* To comprehend Indian philosophical thought and its relation to social work profession
* To contemplate the solution for contemporary societal problems through the rich philosophical foundation

*India is the cradle of the human race, the birthplace of human speech, the mother of history, the grandmother of legend, and the great grandmother of tradition. Our most valuable and most artistic materials in the history of man are treasured up in **India** only!*

—Mark Twain

INTRODUCTION

Social workers need to have an orientation on their philosophical foundations. The philosophy of social work was first contributed by Eduard C. Lindeman about half a century back. Then Herbert Bisno had expanded it. This chapter will also focus on the philosophical thoughts given by various Indian scholars and their relation to social work. It strived to highlight the contributions of *Panchatantra* and *Arthashastra*. The great message from the Indian treasure tale *Panchatantra* is deliberated. A tiny essence of *Thirukkural* is also added in this chapter. The preaching from Buddha, Mahavira and Shankaracharya, and their relevance to social work philosophy are also given in this chapter. Significantly, how the Bhakti Movement had given the message on equality is portrayed here. The preaching of Sri Ramakrishna Paramahansa and Swami Vivekananda, as well as their notable contributions to mankind, is presented. The successful model of Sree Narayana Guru on the social upliftment of the downtrodden has also been described. The Gandhian philosophical foundation to social work in India is also given.

PHILOSOPHY OF SOCIAL WORK BY EDUARD AND HERBERT

Eduard C. Lindeman, a social worker, was the first to write about the philosophy of social work. According to him, social work represents three distinguished but interrelated parties such as a network of social services, carefully developed methods and processes, and social policy expressed through social institutions/individuals. It is based on the view of human beings, their interrelationships and the ethical demands made on them. Social work has been founded on some assumptions about man and society, and their mutual moral obligations. Social work philosophy is based on humanitarianism, liberty and democracy. A social worker needs to find a method of helping people to gain confidence for rightly adjusting their life themselves. The democracy of philosophy has further emphasized the need to recognize the worth of respect and recognition of every human being.

Herbert Bisno has described the philosophy of social work and he has explained it in four parts: (a) the nature of the individual, (b) the relations between groups, groups and individuals, and between individuals, (c) the functions and methods of social work and (d) social maladjustment and social change. Each individual, by the very fact of their existence, is of worth. The fundamental premise of social work is the belief in the inherent worth of the individual which focuses on equality of opportunity, the rights of minorities and the rights of free expression. Human suffering is undesirable and should be prevented and social work believes that sufferings are the result of the weakness of the social system. Hence, an individual should be helped in alleviating and preventing suffering. In general, human behaviour is the outcome of the interaction between the biological organism and its environment. Social work conceives personality as a unit in which both emotional and physical factors are inseparably involved in some malfunctioning of the organism. Man does not naturally act rationally. There is no innate rationality. Man (includes woman also) is a moral and social being at birth and it means that they are neither moral nor immoral at birth. They are neutral and their behaviour is the outcome of many forces in the environment. There are both individual and common human needs. The individual needs and desires have to be recognized and addressed at the appropriate stage. The failure of handling such needs and desires may be reflected in irrational or antisocial behaviour. Further, family relationships are of primary importance in the early developmental stages of an individual and the type of family atmosphere also plays a vital role in shaping an individual.

Social work rejects the doctrine of survival of the fittest. The rich and powerful are not necessarily fit, and the poor and weak are not necessarily unfit. As the pathological conditions of the community react adversely upon the entire community, the major responsibility for the welfare of its members rests with the community itself.

Interestingly, social work has two opposite approaches, the casework on one side and the social action on the other. Hence, social work supports individuals in adjusting to the institutional framework of the society and also attempts to modify the institutional framework itself for the welfare of the underserved.

There are various types of maladjustment in our culture, namely political, economic and social. The coexistence of serious social–psychological maladjustments urges us to have an urgent need for new ways of social thinking. Evolutionary type of reform is desirable in our society. There is a need for social planning and there should be planning for freedom too.

THE CONTRIBUTIONS OF *PANCHATANTRA*

The *Panchatantra* is an ancient Indian story originally written in Sanskrit verse and prose which is estimated to be written 2,000 years ago by the intellectual scholar Pandit Vishnu Sharma. In the language of Sanskrit, the word *Pancha* means 'five' and 'tantra' means 'parts'. *Panchatantra* is the most frequently translated literary product of India and it is translated in nearly every major Indian language. The stories are based on age-old Indian oral traditions with animal fables that are able to be understood easily. These stories are widely known in the world and available in more than 50 languages around the world. It has reached so many cultures and there are about 200 versions and one version in Europe in the 11th century. Although it is structured as fables and folk tales, the *Panchatantra* has basic morals and ethics to guide through one's life. The book links the most important branch of ancient science of India called *Nitishastra*, meaning 'a book of wise conduct in life'. *Panchatantra* is broadly classified into five parts as given below.

Five parts of classification of *Panchatantra*:
1. Conflict among friends
2. Winning friends
3. Crows and owls (action without due consideration)
4. Separation
5. Union

1. *Conflict among friends:* The loss of true and reliable friends is a great setback to anybody's life and the Pandit explains the ways to handle the problems with patience and care.
2. *Winning friends:* The winning of friends is seen as a profit to a person's life as it is a valuable relationship and trust earned. The book explains the qualities of a good friendship.
3. *Crows and owls (action without due consideration):* It is certainly humane to react out of our impulsions emotionally. This causes us to take unforeseen actions that are done without enough thought process. This results not only in broken relationships but also in regrettable actions and words.
4. *Separation:* How can one handle the difference of opinions or the difference in thoughts and how does one handle a situation of separation in a relationship.
5. *Union:* The power of unity and the power of togetherness are stressed by the Pandit to understand the ease and benefits of being united.

The text of *Panchatantra* is formed in the need of a king who hands over his three sons who are of impressionable ages to the intellectual Pandit Vishnu Sharma. The king expected the Pandit to teach his sons the knack and skill to take over him and the kingdom. Thus forms the story of *Panchatantra* where the Pandit attempts to teach his students the way of life and the quality of conducting ourselves. This is only an overview, and it is given with an aim of introducing such a rich indigenous literature to the social work students. *Panchatantra* sensitizes the readers through its stories about handling human beings and relationships with them and power of unity and the power of togetherness. This kind of knowledge is required for social workers as they have to deal with the micro- and macro-level problems in the professional practice.

ARTHASHASTRA ON WELFARE STATE

Chanakya, who was the minister in charge for the kingdom of Chandra Gupta, was an insightful person with clear ideas about the economic, social and political aspects required for running a kingdom. Chanakya, who was also known as Kautilya, wrote the *Arthashastra* (during 273 BC), the first extensive book on political science and economic conditions, which depicts the basic foundation upon which the kingdom should function.

The *Arthashastra* refers to the constructive work for public good by the joint efforts of the villagers. Through village panchayats, it also refers to such type of social work as care provision for boys, old or diseased men in case they have no sympathetic guardians or protectors. Similar care was also to be taken of widows with or without children. Village elders were also to take after the property of minors without any natural guardians until they attain the age of majority when the property should be returned to them with all the accumulated profits. One of the important forms of social work in ancient India was free education (*Vidyadana*) to people by learned Brahmins. The learned teachers used to give day-to-day commons (dining room, cafeteria) of food to poor lads and taught them for free. *Vidyadana* was considered to be the best of all gifts. Even the poorest man gave something to eat to the hungry students begging at their door. Rich persons sometimes built free educational institutions as a matter of charity or in commemoration of a departed soul. The responsibility for the care of the poor, the aged, the infirm, the destitute and so on was that of the king. Also, there is a mention of the workshops having been set up for economically disadvantaged people. The division of labour was practised and various departments were established such as military, foreign affairs, laws, agriculture and social work. He encouraged the participation of villagers in many social works which included provisional care for old, young and diseased who are orphaned. They are also required to take care of properties belonging to stray minorities and return these lands with added benefits once they attain the mature age. Free food and education were provided to everyone in need of them. The affluent built educational institutions for the welfare of the people. The state was responsible for providing irrigation facilities, assistance, sanitation and food crisis relief to its masses. The root of wealth is economic activity and lack of it brings material distress. In the absence of fruitful economic activity, both current prosperity and future growth are in danger of destruction. As *Arthashastra* shows us the road map for the welfare state, the knowledge of *Arthashastra* is essential for social workers.

THIRUKKURAL AND ITS RELEVANCE TO SOCIAL WORK

Being one of the oldest literatures in Tamil language from India, *Thirukkural* comprehends knowledge in a pod for all stages and events of life. It is denoted as the short poetic form with only seven words in each couplet. This was written by Thiruvalluvar between 2nd and 8th centuries BC. He divided 1,330 couplets under 133 chapters into 3 broad areas such as dharma (path of rightness), *artha* (wealth) and *kama* (pleasure/desire). This book mainly denotes the ways to lead a happy life with a good code of conduct. This literature was widely adapted all over the world. Thiruvalluvar, who was a weaver, was also a renowned philosopher who distinguished the spirituality and the social needs of an individual. He shared his thoughts between the relationships among different individuals, among an individual and society and symbiotic relationship of individual and society over spiritual, material and intellectual development. *Thirukkural* is compact and universal in nature. A couple of couplets are explained here to experience the richness of *Thirukkural* (ValaiTamil, n.d.). According to Chapter 39 titled 'Qualities of a Ruler', some light is shed here. A ruler has to understand how a person can lead a nation and what basic qualities they should have and also their requirements as a leader and their knowledge on laws and reforms. A ruler is considered to be majestic and successful when they own military, citizenry, adequate resources, knowledgeable advisors, honest friends and fortresses. But having qualities such as generosity, courage, insight and vivacity are appreciated. A ruler should always be bold, follow culture and be aware of things around them. An ideal ruler would neither deviate from justice nor encourage violations. They should be capable of managing resources by carefully strategizing and allocating resources. Rulers should be available to the public at all times and refrain from rude admonitions. People would appreciate a ruler who always follows justice and shows kind gestures to the people. Protecting the people by leading the nation in a just, honest and strategic way brings the people closer to the ruler, thereby enriching their bond. The ruler is loved by the people by the charity they do, their justice and also in protecting people when they are in danger. Chapter 52 titled 'Assessing and Assigning Task' emphasizes exploring good and evil tasks before starting and the ability to endure the obstacles in the tasks. Further, it explains the need to examine the nature of the doer, the nature of the action and realize the relevance of the appropriate time. Then, the task should be handed over to a person after examining whether the person can do this work. After

> Three broad areas:
> 1. Dharma (path of rightness)
> 2. *Artha* (wealth)
> 3. *Kama* (pleasure/desire)

> Out of 133 chapters, a few chapters are given below:
> 'The Power of Righteousness, Family Life, Hospitality, Speaking Pleasantly, Neutrality, Charity, Being Compassionate, Truthfulness, Avoiding Anger, Qualities of a Ruler, Learning, Not Learning, Listening, Assessing before Executing, Knowing the Strengths, Assessing and Assigning Tasks, Being a Minister, Country, Friendship, Assessment before Entering a Friendship, Rapport, Adverse Friendship, Undesirable Friendship, and so on.'

examining whether a person is qualified to do a profession, the person should be made to belong to that profession. The chapters given in the box are very relevant to social workers and their knowledge is very much helpful to train the social workers (Thirukkural in English, n.d.).

THE RELEVANCE OF PREACHING OF BUDDHA AND MAHAVIRA TOWARDS SOCIAL WORK

Prince Siddhartha Gautama was born to the rulers of Sakyas kingdom in Nepal during 623 BC who then became Buddha, an inspiring teacher of the world. Buddha always acknowledged himself as a human rather than God. He accredited his realizations to hard work and intelligence. He also encouraged people to follow their will with hard work so that they can achieve whatever they believe in. He was called a superhuman owing to his humanity. Buddhism is considered superior over other religions because it does not idolize a supernatural system. This religion inculcates in humans that one can attain salvation by *self-exertion*. This religion also teaches their disciples to lead a life full of pure thoughts to acquire wisdom and away from all befoulment. This religion believes that there is no supernatural power or supreme being who needs to be obeyed or dreaded. Generally, people follow two extremes to attain happiness, one is through the pleasure of their *senses* and the other one is through *self-mortification*, both these ways are unprofitable. He follows *four noble truths* upon which his foundation is built on.

Four noble truths:
1. The truth of suffering
2. The truth of the cause of suffering
3. The truth of the end of suffering
4. The truth of the path that leads to the end of suffering

1. *Life means suffering*, as soon as we enter the world, we are subjected to physical and mental suffering, it all depends on how we cope from it and start a journey towards *truth and inner peace*. Suffering is also associated with our activities towards each other and to the environment.
2. *Suffering* is originated *through attachments to temporary earthly things*. We always wanted to achieve our goals of having possessions of impermanent things and also having ardent desires and passion towards money, drive towards popularity. But these qualities will further bring suffering to us because only when our thoughts are right and pure that we would understand that desire on attachments is ignorance.
3. *Once* when we stop our association with attachments associated with senses or physical pleasure, *our mind becomes clear as our thought process gets cleared*. This clarity is essential to remove bad thoughts and speech. One can reach this level through meditation.
4. *Finally,* the path where suffering dissolves. This happens only when an effort is made towards *self-actualization and realization* that occurs nearly at the end of the rebirth cycle. One realizes who they are, with the help of meditation, they achieve peace and happiness. In Buddhism, he has created a middle path which is composed of eight categories and will help an individual to attain their inner peace and also purify their mind. *These eight notions* are the modes through which peace and happiness are attained by the individual. They are *right understanding, right thoughts, right speech, right actions, right livelihood, right effort, right vigilance* and *right concentration*.

A proper understanding of a situation would make a person have good thoughts such that their speech and actions are towards the well-being of them, which would reflect in their livelihood, and through their continued effort and concentration on the work and suitable awareness, they attain self-mortification (Dormgrandpop, 2007).

Fivefold path given by Mahavira:
1. Non-violence
2. Truthfulness
3. Abstaining from sexual pleasures
4. No possession of property
5. Non-purloin

Mahavira is one of the 24 Jain prophets, born to Siddhartha and Priyakarani 2,500 years ago, rulers of Kaundinyapura, Patna. He got this name because of his *bravery*. He excelled in his academics with his sharpness and deep insight about everything and also exhibited physical skill and was blessed with good health. Hailing from a prosperous background did not push him into the pleasures of enjoying the richness but he underwent *atonement for more than 12 years*. He dealt with his ill-behaved and roguish countrymen with utmost calmness and also bore with the rigours of nature. He finally understood what self-realization was and continued with his life helping people to redeem themselves. Mahavira proved to be a great tool in making people understand what actually the Vedas or religions teach us through various spiritual practices. He found that people blindly followed certain traditions which in no way was beneficial to them or to their environment such as animal sacrifice and they did a lot of rituals on the basis of superstitions just to earn *punya* (a Sanskrit word that means merit or virtue) in the process of forgetting what was actually being implied—dharma (a code of conduct of one's duty). He played a huge role in trying to simplify and break down a lot of superstitious beliefs and rituals such that the people could understand the true spiritual significance and practise them with good conduct. His way of appealing to the supreme power soon made everyone turn their heads towards him, and he soon gained a lot of followers. He would deliver a message implying that non-violence should be practised at all times and he would substantiate his words through some questions he would ask the people, *can they hold a red-hot iron rod in their hand just because someone wishes to*, which would be answered negatively by everyone. He would then ask the listeners to not to inflict pain to others because they wish to, because they will experience the same pain on their body or mind as them. He would conclude by saying, 'Do unto others as you would like to be done by.' He did not support violence and always encouraged his disciples to not harm any person or animal as they would feel the same pain as them. *Unity of life*, given by Mahavira, is a great ideology to be followed by humans. The era we are in always focuses on selfish needs and endless thirsts of man to exploit everything around them till they reach a level of fullness. This inordinate hunger would land the human race in crisis and jeopardy. *Mahavira created a simple fivefold path to all people, which is very easy to follow.*

THE RELEVANCE OF PREACHING FROM SHRI SHANKARACHARYA

Shri Adi Shankaracharya is an Indian philosopher who consolidated the doctrine of Advaita Vedanta. He was born in a village named Kalady in Kerala, a southern Indian state and lived 32 years during 700 AD. Shri Shankaracharya has said, 'The cause itself is the effect. Everything we do has bliss in it; let this bliss be enjoyed in our experiences.' At the age of eight, he desired for liberation and left home in search of his guru, a spiritual leader. He travelled more than 2,000 km in search of his teacher which he eventually found in the banks of Narmada, Ashram of Govinda Bhagavatpada. Under his teacher's guidance, he developed the philosophies of Vedas, Upanishads, Brahma Sutras and Bhagavad Gita. As per the directions of his guru, Shri Shankaracharya composed 72 devotional and meditative hymns, wrote 18 commentaries on the major scriptural texts including the Brahma Sutras (a fundamental text of the Vedanta school of Hinduism), the Bhagavad Gita and 12 major Upanishads and authored 23 books on the fundamentals of the Advaita Vedanta philosophy. At the age of 16, he completed all his major writings. On those days, the essence of Sanatana Dharma, with its all-embracing message of love, compassion and the universality of humankind was completely lost in the blind performance of degraded ritualism, superstitions and scriptural misinterpretations. Shankaracharya travelled all over India along with his disciples and challenged various eminent scholars and leaders of various religious sects through philosophical discourses and debates. He established four maths in Sringeri, Puri, Dwarka and Badrinath. It is concluded that debates helped in establishing a new philosopher and also helped to acquire disciples from the person who loses in the debate. By using the tools of discourses and debates to persuade them, he has shown the way to social workers how to handle leaders and followers of various religious sects.

BHAKTI MOVEMENT AND ITS CONTRIBUTION

'Bhakti' means *devotion or unconditional love* towards God. This movement has its deep roots in South India and then spread to other parts of India. The expression of love towards God required a form which was Shiva, Vishnu, Murugan and many others. Saints and poets from all over the country paid their respects towards God through various poems which inscribed traditional values and beliefs as mentioned in Vedas. Irrespective of the caste and livelihood, everyone had their love delivered to God through various means. There were two communities of people within this Bhakti Movement, they were (a) Alwars, who were 12 in number and worshipped lord *Vishnu* and there were (b) Nayanmars, who were 63 in number who worshipped Shiva. These Alwars and Nayanmars showed their devotion to God through their hymns, which were later compiled into books. In Nayanmars, the following saints were distinguished: Sundarar, Appar, Sambandar and Manikkavasagar, whereas the hymns of Alwars who were *12* in number were called *Nalayira divya prabandham* and these verses were recited in temple rituals as a form of devotion. This Bhakti Movement took its course towards North India during the 14th–17th centuries, where preliminary importance was given to Lord Rama and Krishna (Jayaram, V., n.d.). To mention some of the great poets of those times, Kabir, Ravidas, Meerabai, Surdas and Tulsidas were pioneers of Hindi literature towards God. Their hymns are widely used for daily rituals. Narsinh Mehta's work in Gujarati, Samarth Ramdas and Eknath's work in Marathi, Purandara Dasa and Kanaka Dasa in

Saints of the Bhakti Movement have the following aspects in common

- Surrendering oneself to the omnipotent
- Unconditional irrevocable love towards the deity
- Bhakti in the form of poem or songs in their regional dialect
- Breaking the restrictions built by the society based on their caste or creed or sex
- The contributions of the composers in each language enriched in the literature

Kannada, Chaitanya Mahaprabhu in Bengali, Tyagaraja and Bhadrachala Ramadasu in Telugu and Vallathol in Malayalam were some of the great minds during the period of time. It can be learnt from the Bhakti Movement how the restrictions based on caste, creed and sex were overcame in the society and how a unity was arrived. This kind of philosophy from the past will show the way in the present and also in the future (Wikipedia, n.d.).

THE PREACHING OF SRI RAMAKRISHNA PARAMAHANSA AND SWAMI VIVEKANANDA AND THEIR NOTABLE CONTRIBUTION TO MANKIND

Sri Ramakrishna, known as *the prophet of human religion*, is the primary originator of the concept of *pluralism*, which is to say that all religions are different in their own way, despite their differences; all religions have the same ultimate goal: self-realization. His doctrine of harmony of religions has high importance in the modern world. According to him, the goal of human life should be towards the realization of *ultimate reality* through a purity of mind free from greed or lust through spiritual practices. He believes that God dwells in all people, but the complete manifestation of God is possible only when one prays sincerely, practises discrimination between external and internal matter and remains unattached. Their life history has encouraged thousands of people to have faith and re-establish the ideal of God realization in the modern world irrespective of materialism and atheism. They give emphasis on being truthful and devoid of lust and greed and lead a moral and ethical life. Sri Ramakrishna's ideology of *God is love* elevated love from the level of emotions to a state of unity and realization. As stated in Upanishads, the principle of oneness of supreme self-acts as a central dogma and rarely applied in regular practical life. He made it possible that divinization of love and human relationships would take us towards our realization and can be easily done in our regular life. Life is an expression of the creativity of the lord; one must handle pleasure, pain, success, failure with patience and submit oneself to God's will. He encouraged people to be sincere in their prayers and determined in their work, not let worldly thoughts disturb the mind, if so, one can attain God through pure love by constantly repeating the name of God (Radhakrishnan, 1962).

Swami Vivekananda is a world-famous spiritual leader and reformer from India. Being *the first cultural ambassador to the West*, he played a major role in building a bridge between Indian and Western culture by interpreting Hindu scriptures and philosophies of Western people. He made everyone realize the value of Indian culture and how great a contribution it is to the world. He also adapted concepts from Western world symbolizing ideas of individual freedom, social equality, justice and respect for people. He harmonized the East and the West, religion and science, past and present, and made countrymen gain unprecedented self-respect, self-reliance and self-assertion. According to him, religion is the manifestation of divinity already in man. It is a universal experience of transcendent reality which is common to all humanity. He said that religion is a science of consciousness; as such, religion and science are complementary and not contradictory. His understanding of religion is the pursuit of freedom, knowledge and happiness rather than superstitious beliefs, witchcrafts and intolerance. His concept *of potential divinity of the soul* prevents the deterioration of the humankind, divinizes human relationships by making the life lead as meaningful and happy through spiritual humanism which manifests throughout the world through neo-humanistic movements and meditation. His theory of ethics and principle of mortality are entirely based on the inner pure mind and the feeling of oneness of the self. He depicts that the soul always changes to what a person believes. Purity, patience and perseverance are three fundamental prerequisites to success. So when one believes in themselves and has all these qualities, they manifest every movement of their life. *Education* helps in building character, increasing the strength of mind, expansion of the intellect and helps a person to stand on their own feet in the society, and also enables them to help others in need and to serve humanity. Both Ramakrishna Paramahansa and Swami Vivekananda gave a foundation to understand the human sufferings of ordinary people and confidence to handle the situation (Vivekananda, 1989).

SREE NARAYANA GURU'S MODEL ON SOCIAL UPLIFTMENT OF THE DOWNTRODDEN

Sree Narayana Guru was a Hindu saint and a social reformer. Being born to a backward community, he always faced social injustice and he fought against the caste system in Kerala by leading a reform movement and also propagated new values of freedom and social equality. At the age of 21, he underwent educational training under Kummampilli Raman Pillai Asan and excelled in Sanskrit, literature criticism and logic rhetoric values and also had his training in Vedas and Upanishads. His proficiency, Vedic philosophy, unrelenting resolve to solve people's problems made him a great leader and a reformer. He followed non-violence and inculcated the need of spiritual growth and upliftment of the backward castes through educational reforms and institutions. His thirst for knowledge made him meet Chattampi Swamikal, who appreciated his philosophies and introduced him to Hatha yoga. He continued his journey towards truth after mastering various yogic practices. He came across a lovely place in the forest surrounded by hills and rivers, called Aruvippuram. At this place, he built a temple for Lord Shiva which was accessible to everyone irrespective of their caste. In 1913, he established an ashram in Aluva for the sole purpose of studying various religious beliefs and everyone was treated equally in the fraternity. Later, a gurukul was acclaimed by the name of Narayana Gurukulam in the Nilgiri hills. His literary contributions like *Atmopadesa Satakam* are a masterpiece which revolves around the concept of self-instruction. He was a democratic person with moralist thoughts and heightened perspective towards social equality. He built a lot of schools, institutions and ashrams to accommodate people irrespective of their caste, educated them and improved their quality of life. He was presented with the most prestigious title, 'guru'. He had influenced a lot of reformers in his period and was respected by everyone. On raising a number of caste-based discriminations and hatred among different caste groups, the philosophy and model of Sree Narayana Guru is the need of the hour. Not only the social workers but also the community and political leaders can follow his path and replicate his model for uplifting the downtrodden people (Prasad, 2003).

THE GANDHIAN PHILOSOPHICAL FOUNDATION TO SOCIAL WORK IN INDIA

Mahatma Gandhi is the embodiment of truth, loyalty and ahimsa. His understanding of truth is fascinating. He devised a society and called it *Ramrajya* where he wanted to practise social and gender equality, where there would not be a difference in the treatment for rich and poor people, everybody would be respected, and he also considered villages as the backbone of the country. He believed that villages are the strongest society which was self-sufficient and republic. Village structure implied that all homes were properly ventilated with sufficient light and people raise their own food and do their own clothing. The government would appoint five panchayat members on the basis of the voting who would be the legislature, executive and judiciary. Gandhi believed in individual freedom, and he wanted every individual to acquire the skill required to protect him and his society. Mahatma Gandhi also instilled in the minds of people a sense of unity, where people of various religions, irrespective of their differences in their beliefs, come together and build on their friendship, which makes them realize their individual identity as an Indian. His philosophies include self-sufficiency and sustainability. His vision of making one's own clothes from khadi was revolutionary. He recommended that if every village is involved in the production of khadi, surplus to their own needs, they could export all over India and to other countries as well. In this way, unemployment and poverty would never occur in the first place. Primary education has been useful in preparing the mind and body of young children in facing the difficulties in the society in the future and makes them equipped, develops their skill and talent and helps children in realizing their dreams and aspirations. When the children are well educated, their home and their village would simultaneously be developed.

SUMMARY

This is a kind of a drop from an ocean when compared to the vastness of the Indian philosophy. This is a small effort to give an overview and it needs to be elaborated further. Ongoing through this chapter, it is sure that the budding social workers can get a bird's eye view on the philosophical fundamentals of India which are relevant to social work.

TOP 10 TAKEAWAYS/MAIN POINTS

1. The story of *Panchatantra* taught the sons of king the knack and skill, and it continues to teach the way of life. These stories explain handling human beings and relationships with them and the power of unity and the power of togetherness.
2. *Arthashastra* is the first extensive book on political science and economic conditions and it explains how a ruler should function. It also shows a road map for the welfare state.
3. *Thirukkural* had 1,330 couplets and it is divided into 133 chapters into 3 broad areas such as dharma (path of rightness), *artha* (wealth) and *kama* (pleasure/desire). It is one of the oldest works of literature in Tamil, comprehends knowledge in a pod for all stages and events of life. It is denoted as the short poetic form with only seven words in each couplet.
4. According to Buddha, people attain happiness through the pleasure of their senses and self-mortification and both these ways are unprofitable. He follows *four noble truths* upon which his foundation is built: (a) *life means suffering*, (b) *suffering* is originated *through*

attachments to temporary earthly things, (c) *once* when we stop our association with attachments, *our mind becomes clear as our thought process gets cleared* and (d) *finally*, the path where suffering dissolves and this happens only when an effort is made towards *self-actualization and realization*.
5. Mahavira created a simple fivefold path to all people, which is very easy to follow: *non-violence, truthfulness, abstaining from sexual pleasures, no possession of the property* and *non-purloin*.
6. Shri Shankaracharya fought against the blind performance of degraded ritualism, superstitions and scriptural misinterpretations and protected the real Sanatana Dharma which conveys the all-embracing message of love, and shows compassion and the universality of humankind. He has shown the practical model of discourses and debates with scholars and leaders of various religious sects for bringing unity.
7. Saints and poets of the Bhakti Movement were from all over the country, and they were irrespective of caste and livelihood. Saints have the following things in common: (a) surrendering oneself to the omnipotent, (b) unconditional irrevocable love towards the deity, (c) bhakti in the form of poems or songs in their regional dialect, (d) breaking the restrictions built by the society based on their caste or creed or sex and (e) the contributions of the composers in each language enriched the literature.
8. Ramakrishna Paramahansa and Swami Vivekananda have given a foundation to understand the human sufferings of ordinary people and confidence to handle the situation.
9. The philosophy and model of Sree Narayana Guru are successful for uplifting the downtrodden people without creating any hatred with other caste groups. Replicating his model is the need of the hour and the social workers, community and political leaders can follow his path.
10. Mahatma Gandhi devised a society and called it *Ramrajya* where he wanted to practise social and gender equality, where there would not be a difference in the treatment for rich and poor people, everybody would be respected, and he also considered villages as the backbone of the country.

Keywords: Philosophical foundation, philosophical thoughts on humans and society, Indian philosophical thought

GLOSSARY

***Arthashastra*:** The first extensive book (during 273 BC) written by Chanakya on political science and economic conditions, which depicts the basic foundation upon which the kingdom should function.
***Panchatantra*:** An ancient Indian story originally written in Sanskrit verse and prose which is estimated to be written 2,000 years ago by the scholar Pandit Vishnu Sharma.
Philosophy: The study of the fundamental nature of knowledge, reality and existence.
***Thirukkural*:** One of the oldest literatures in Tamil language from India written by Thiruvalluvar which comprehends knowledge in a pod for all stages and events of life. This was written between 2nd and 8th centuries BC.

ANALYTICAL QUESTIONS

1. What are the common aspects of various saints and poets of the Bhakti Movement?
2. Discuss the Gandhian philosophical foundations to social work.

MULTIPLE CHOICE QUESTIONS

1. The *Panchatantra* stories are
   a. **Animal fables**
   b. Plant fables
   c. Human fables
   d. Both animal and plant

2. Chanakya wrote the *Arthashastra* during
   a. 372 BC
   b. **273 BC**
   c. 237 BC
   d. 723 BC

3. The book *Arthashastra* is about
   a. Economic
   b. Political science
   c. **Political science and economic conditions**
   d. History

4. How many couplets and chapters are there in *Thirukkural*?
   a. 1,220 couplets under 122 chapters
   b. 1,320 couplets under 132 chapters
   c. **1,330 couplets under 133 chapters**
   d. 1,230 couplets under 123 chapters

5. The *Thirukkural* is divided into how many numbers of broad areas?
   a. Two
   b. Four
   c. Five
   d. **Three**

6. Each couplet in *Thirukkural* is with how many words in each couplet?
   a. **Seven**
   b. Eight
   c. Five
   d. Three

7. Prince Siddhartha Gautama was born to the rulers of Sakyas kingdom in Nepal during
   a. 633 BC
   b. **623 BC**
   c. 622 BC
   d. 632 BC

8. Indian philosopher Shri Adi Shankaracharya had said that
   a. Everything we do has bliss in it
   b. **The cause itself is the effect**
   c. Both of the above
   d. None of the above

9. The philosophy of Sree Narayana Guru for uplifting the downtrodden people is
   a. Creating conflict among the downtrodden community and others
   b. **Uplifting the downtrodden without creating hatred with other caste groups**
   c. Both
   d. None of the above

10. Mahatma Gandhi devised a society and called it *Ramrajya*. *Ramrajya* aimed for
    a. Practising social and gender equality
    b. No difference in the treatment for rich and poor people
    c. Villages are considered as the backbone of the country
    d. **All of the above**

REVIEW QUESTIONS

1. What are the five classifications of *Panchatantra*?
2. Write down the names of any five chapters of *Thirukkural*.
3. What are the four noble truths of Buddha?
4. What is the fivefold path given by Mahavira?

REFERENCES

Belurmath. (n.d.). *The story of Vivekananda*. https://belurmath.org/kids_section/category/the-story-of-vivekananda/
Dormgrandpop. (2007). *This year's Christmas newsletter*. https://dormgrandpop.blogspot.com/2007/12/
Jayaram, V. (n.d.). *Bhakti marg, the path of devotion*. https://www.hinduwebsite.com/hinduism/concepts/bhaktimarg.asp
Radhakrishnan, S. (1962). *The cultural heritage of India, itihas puranas, dharma and other sastras* (Vol. II). https://estudantedavedanta.net
Swami Muni Narayana Prasad. (2003). *The philosophy of Narayana Guru*. D. K. Printworld (P) Ltd.
Thirukkural in English. (n.d.). *Chapter 114: Shedding shyness*. https://thirukkural133.wordpress.com

Valai Tamil. (n.d.). *List of 1330 Thirukkural with Mu VA Urai and Parimelazhagar Urai in English and Tamil.* http://www.valaitamil.com/thirukkural.php

Vivekananda, S. (1989). The Complete Works of Swami Vivekananda. Advaita Ashrama.

Wikipedia. (n.d.). *Bhakti movement.* https://en.wikipedia.org/wiki/Bhakti_movement

RECOMMENDED READINGS

Agarwal, S. P. (1997). *The social role of the Gita: How and why.* Motilal Banarsidass Publications.

Swami Ranganathanada. (2003). *Sri Narayana Guru—An appreciation.* Bharatiya Vidya Bhavan.

Viswanathan. (2011). *Thirukkural: Universal Tamil scripture.* Bharatiya Vidya Bhavan.

20

Social Work Values
Traditional and Emancipatory
Poonam Gulalia

LEARNING OBJECTIVES
- To help students understand the core values of social work profession
- To enable students to operationalize the values in the practice situation
- To enable students to understand the challenges which they may have faced in the field
- To reflect upon and critically examine ethical dilemmas, conflicts and power relations in social work

There will always be people in your life who treat you wrong. Be sure to thank them for making you strong.
—Zig Zaglar

INTRODUCTION

Practice wisdom is the foundation for effective practice which is taught and measured by supporting the development of critical thinking and reflection skills of student learners in social work. As an experienced practitioner and administrator, one has come to understand that one of the most essential requirements for effective social work practice at all levels is that of the relationship. It is the skills in developing these relationships which build and strengthen over time with the purpose of enhancing one's overall sense of practice wisdom.

This being clubbed with the skill component includes the practice component which brings knowledge and values together and converts them into action as a response to concern and need. Through the use of skills, a social worker displays their capacity to use interventions towards a goal-directed purpose. Since skills get developed and refined through exposure and experience, it becomes essential to acknowledge that this involves conscious use of one's own self and one's abilities. It is the skill laboratory which serves as a platform on which the principles get translated into practice skills, that is, 'learning by doing'. It enables students to learn through simulated situations and reflections carried out in a relatively safe environment. This, clubbed with group learning and peer support, enables students in such a way that it facilitates the process of introspection.

SOCIAL WORK VALUES: CONCEPT, SCOPE AND DEFINITION

Essentially, values are belief narratives which sharpen one's approach and help steer the teaching–learning trajectory. In an era of connectivity through social media and rapid change in technology, the ability of the student learner to anchor themselves in universal values-based strategic action is extremely vital. When people embody and act from the universal values of dignity, fairness and compassion, they engage in what they care about deeply, self-organize, self-correct and operate as independent and interdependent entities. It also needs to be appreciated that values influence one's decision-making process and it is extremely difficult to objectively determine the 'best' value. Even when values differ from person to person, society to society and community to community, the fact is that often one is hardly aware of a value one holds unless of course that value is violated by others. Also, even when one believes in certain values, not at all times is one able to 'live' by one's values due to various social norms or group customs.

The primary mission of the social work profession is to enhance human well-being and help meet the basic human needs of all people, with particular attention to the needs and empowerment of people who are vulnerable, oppressed and living in poverty.

The six core values of the social work profession are as follows:

- Service
- Social justice
- Dignity and worth of the individual
- Importance and centrality of human relationships
- Integrity
- Competence

Did You Know?

Indic Values of Social Work
Dharma
Ahimsha
Nishtha
Upeksha
Satya

Source: Dash (2019).

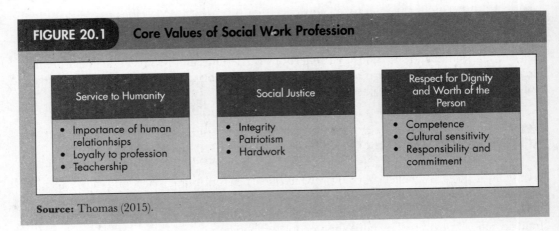

Source: Thomas (2015).

While enhancing students' knowledge and enabling them to tap resources, it also becomes essential that they tap their inner potential with the purpose of sharing universal space of values such as dignity, equity, compassion beyond class, caste, gender, social identity and skill set. Dash (2018) has clarified that '....In Indian context, social work profession being a spiritual profession, Indic values are extremely relevant for Indian social workers.... *Upeksha* is a Sanskrit term which means self-control, tolerance and also non-attachment....' Thomas (2018), in his edited book on social work values, agreed that 12 core values are integral to the profession. Those values are as follows (Figure 20.1).

In further discussing the Indianization of social work, Dash (2018) elaborated on the need for incorporating Indian concepts of social welfare such as dharma, *danam*, *yagna*, *punya*, *purushartha* and bhakti in the social work curriculum. Dash (2019) also elaborated that the Indic values which were the lifeline of Indian society have been neglected. In this critical situation of the country as well as turbulent situation of the social work profession, there is a need to revive the Indic social, moral and spiritual values and integrate them into the fold of social work profession. The Indic values are eternal and universal values which can be applied not only in the Indian context but also at the global level. This has been reinforced by Sharma, Monica (2019) in transforming leadership through universal values. She writes about the need for sourcing inner power and universal values for transforming cultures and systems.

SKILL BUILDING IN THE CONTEXT OF A VALUE FRAMEWORK

Additionally, in an attempt to socialize students to the profession, the effort is to help students increase their ability and comfort in working with and interacting with people, issues and sectors. By attaining practice skills appropriate to working with people and communities and by developing the ability to critically reflect on self and systems, the students are encouraged to achieve the objectives laid out as first-year field placement objectives. It provides a space for students to begin to understand the socio-economic and cultural realities and to acquire the self-awareness necessary to assess one's own values, attitudes, strengths and limitations.

In attempting to create the 'means by which we create meaningful representations of reality' (Gray, 2002), social work becomes an art of connecting with people where values play an extremely prominent role. It includes creativity, intuition and inductive reasoning in combination with values, morals and beliefs. It also embraces the importance of human relationships with community in congruence with the self in practice (East & Chambers, 2007). While valuing the importance of *learning-in-action* and *reflecting-in-action*, the researcher began to value the likes of Cooper and Lousada (2005) who highlighted the value of learning from the lived experience. It also stays in consonance with treating student learners and mentors as co-learners and co-constructors of knowledge as suggested by Lay and McGuire (2010). Additionally, it resonates with Thompson and West (2013) in that practice wisdom is a process which captures values and motivation in supporting the development of practice skills for student learners. Dash (2018) too highlighted the need to revisit values such as service to humanity, social justice, respect for dignity and worth of the person, importance of human relationships and hard work, responsibility and commitment besides competence, integrity and loyalty to the profession. This movement of understanding from the traditional to the emancipatory and vice versa is the beauty of the inherent quality of the values of the profession.

HOW DO WE UNDERSTAND VALUES?

Additionally, in enabling students to practice empathy, it becomes essential for the supervisor-cum-mentor to enact that empathy is the ability to project oneself into the personality of another in order to better understand that person's emotions and/or feelings. Empathetic listening is a core skill that strengthens the interpersonal effectiveness of individuals in many aspects of their personal and professional lives. It is through the use of skilled listening that the 'mediational negotiations' can be managed by giving importance to the use of open-ended questions, sensitivity to the emotions being expressed and ability to reflect and use critical thinking spaces. According to Burley-Allen (1982), a skilled listener 'takes information from others while remaining non-judgmental and empathetic, acknowledges the speaker in a way that invites the communication to continue and provides a limited but encouraging response, carrying the speaker's idea one step forward'.

Drawing from student A's (master's student in social work) recordings:

> My learnings from the home visits were basically to have patience and to develop the skill of listening. The tools I learnt for application in the field came in handy which included active listening. I listened all day to what people were saying, to what they were sharing about their families, issues, background, how they were feeling while narrating the same. ...I listened carefully without giving advice. ...The second thing I learnt was observation. ...I felt it was my duty to observe what was happening, what people were saying, how they were interacting and behaving when some stranger was there, how they responded, how open they were about their problems, how they felt while narrating it or what their concerns were related to the issues which were being discussed...

HOW DO VALUES IMPACT US WHILE WORKING WITH PEOPLE?

From the excerpt of the recording, it is possible to understand how to engage with people in varied settings. It also provides an opportunity to enter various worlds and to appreciate and understand them through various engagements by making meaning of narratives of these people who have had their share of suffering, including students. As a learner, mentor and professional, the effort is to know, understand and appreciate empathy, equanimity and *upeksha*. The discussion notes cannot be conclusive or exhaustive enough. They can be ongoing and a lifetime project accepting that we have a long way to go.

Excerpts from student B's recordings (of field placement):

> Today was hectic but worth interacting day. What I feel about the organization is that they trust us. The student found that the mentee selection was very intense and a difficult task, but the organization gave the students the said task reposing faith in them.... I began my first learning today of linking theory with practice when I was non-judgemental and maintained confidentiality as well as retained the dignity of the person whom I interacted with...

These excerpts ably highlight the learnings of the student at field practicum and have been utilized as evidence to discuss further during individual engagements with the students at the organization and back on campus. They also enabled the researcher to draw from the students learnings and take it further to enable the said student to connect it with their own lived realities and see and understand suffering as a given.

SUFFERING AND APPROACHING IT WITHIN A VALUE FRAMEWORK

Suffering is proposed to be defined as an unpleasant or even anguishing experience, severely affecting a person at a psychophysical and existential level. Pain and suffering are considered unpleasant. However, the provided definitions neither include the idea that pain and suffering can attack and even destroy the self nor the idea that they can constructively expand the self; both perspectives can be equally useful for managing pain and suffering, but they are not defining features of the same.

Suffering is a subjective experience which is conceptualized in diverse ways by researchers. When students encounter suffering, theirs or others, they perceive it as a state of hopelessness, helplessness, lowered self-esteem and isolation in which the person concerned is preoccupied with merely trying to survive. Suffering has been constructed as an expression of alienation from the self and an alienation from the social order (Cassell, 1991). Given this premise, how are we as professionals addressing suffering. This 'existential vacuum' (Lantz, 1995) is also the lived reality of many of the students who are part of the classroom and who hail from various marginalized and varied identities. Suffering also exists for them because it is connected with the notion of freedom and suffering tends to result due to abuse of this freedom. We are familiar with conscious suffering and find ways and means of dealing with it. Unconscious suffering, according to Krishnamurti (2004[1982]), is what which has been inherited through the centuries. *The Mother* (Sri Aurobindo, 2004, p. 21) explains the meaning and redeeming feature of suffering by stating,

'Suffering is not something inevitable or even desirable but when it comes to us, how helpful it can be...brings once more anew and intense life to the organism on the brink of destruction.'

It is this view of suffering which requires an integrated non-disciplinary approach to understand it as a holistic experience. When working with students in the field practicum, the attempt of the supervisor is to undertake an examination of the complex web of physical and social worlds of the people while simultaneously having access to the personal–spiritual domain. In understanding the field, the Buddhist way of dealing with pain and suffering is by altering conditions internal to the person and not by controlling external factors.

The quest for peace and well-being is as inherent in humankind as the cycle of inhaling and exhaling. In psychological literature, the terms closer to suffering and healing are stress and coping. These terms are basically rooted in Western scientific culture which is taught as part of social work curriculum. In Eastern cultures, however, field practicum has taught the researcher that there is no distinct boundary between self and environment, and the goal of a person is to live in harmony with nature. Neimark (2000) says that 'healing is that which makes us whole, that which helps us to reach our fullness of expression and purpose in life'. As Siegel (1991) had said, 'In our acceptance of our vulnerability is our healing.' Many students who hail from various rural and tribal belts are first-time learners, have families who believe in the Buddhist ideology, easily come to terms with this framework and find it 'normal' to accept the lived realities of the people they engage with in the field.

SITUATIONAL LEARNING AND DAILY COPING IN FIELDWORK

Students are faced with circumstances wherein they begin to believe that to know oneself is the journey and to master oneself is the destination. The question which students constantly grapple with is 'how do we come to know ourselves?' It needs to be understood that as a supervisor and field practitioner, the researcher attempts to teach students to get to know ourselves largely by doing and not by thinking. Fieldwork has traditionally taught the need to focus on 'situational learning' and 'daily coping' rather than developing a sense of belonging. The other aspect which has emerged, and which requires some reflection, is how classroom learning can be applied or questioned in the field.

While attempting to reiterate the need for compassion towards the student, self and the situation, it can be understood that what one tends to perceive as a quest for truth is sometimes communicated through non-violent communication. This cognitive craving for words and explanations is in contrast to experiential learning: the non-thinking mind. When inequalities are not desirable in a democratic society, students need to be encouraged to take positions such that the value of equality, justice and non-exploitation are internalized. The pressing question which needs to be addressed is how do we develop compassion and continue to deal with ambiguity? Additionally, how do we look at the tools by which to understand social realities and the need for working on the most important instrument, that is, the mind? When studying the Indian texts, one finds that it is the attitude of unconditional love and compassion which forms the basis of the Mahayana. In the Tibetan tradition, the inner journey is mapped with precision. For each stage of the practice, there are oral explanations and explanatory texts. Moreover, the underlying principles of wisdom, meditation and ethical awareness are collectively known as 'the three trainings' and are also suitable for adoption by Western psychology as part of a unified operational approach.

Buddhist meditation involves a process of training and developing the mind and insight (Dalai Lama, 2001). Additionally, analytical meditation (or *vipassana*) is the process of uprooting the afflictions (Rabjam, 2002). The Buddhist notion of wisdom differs from the Western depiction in which wisdom is measured against parameters of knowledge and socio-environmental mastery (Baltes & Staudinger, 2000). Additionally, the term 'deluded' (or delusional) is used within Buddhism, but it has a different meaning when compared to its use in psychology. Mindlessness (as different from mindfulness) refers to a lack of present moment awareness when the mind is preoccupied with future or past occurrences. Mindlessness could be a form of inverted hallucination. It was with this approach that student C wrote in her recordings:

> ....With only two full-time paid employees and the amount of workload, it is unsure how they are managing... Once again, I felt that the work at the NGO is so well organized and well planned and that there is pretty good communication between the two professionals, that there is something to learn from.... They appreciate the work done by student learners, but I was wondering in due course if it is ok to tell the other person about work which has not been completed? If there is division of responsibility, where does the space for 'blame game' arise? If co-workers are not conscious of their duties, whose responsibility is it to get the work completed or to see where to set the work boundaries?

HOW IS THE SELF UNDERSTOOD AND INTERPRETED IN THE CONTEXT OF FIELDWORK?

When relating to self and self-awareness, there is persisting controversy over understanding the self and the 'other'. In Western literature of human personality, social relationships and cognitive processes, the self exists as an inherently existing 'I' (Chan, 2008). Within Buddhism, the term *non-self* or *I* is absent (Dalai Lama, 2005). As regards the term non-attachment, the concept of 'non-self' is innately woven with the concept of non-attachment. And can be defined as the over-allocation of cognitive and emotional resources towards an object, construct or idea. Within the Buddhist framework, impermanence occurs as all phenomena are perceived to be transient and are subject to decay and dissolution (Rinpoche, 1998). This universal law of impermanence applies to thoughts, feelings and perceptions and to material phenomenon. In addition, the term 'emptiness' is closely related to the principle of non-self. According to Prajnaparamita-Hrdaya sutra (Heart Sutra—a key Buddhist teaching), 'form does not differ from emptiness, emptiness does not differ from form' (Soeng, 1995, p. 1). *Impermanence* refers to the moment-by-moment transitory nature of existence (Dalai Lama, 2005) which has been substantiated by the phrase 'nature of mind' which is used to express the view that all phenomena are 'mind born' (Norbu & Clemente, 1999). Buddhism expounds that the mode of abiding of everyday reality exists in the same manner (Dalai Lama, 2004[1995]; Urgyen, 2000). 'Wake-up' is therefore a term used by Buddhist teachers (e.g., Norbu & Clemente, 1999) to refer to the process of recovering from ontological addiction (Shonin et al., 2013). Buddhist teachings are evidence-based and correspond with Chan's (2008) understanding of non-self-stating that therapeutic techniques work at the surface level of behaviour and cognition.

According to Branden (1995), the six pillars of self-esteem are living consciously, self-acceptance, self-responsibility, self-assertiveness, living purposefully and personal integrity. How much are these in consonance with the Buddhist framework propagated and practised by Asians and Indians in different contexts needs to be understood. The learnings for the researcher again from student D's recordings are as follows:

> Today was a very challenging day for me emotionally. I was confused what was bothering me and the fact that I was not able to talk in front of my organization's contact person or the fact that I need to work on myself. I realized that I am not too concerned about changing myself but transforming my image from the perspective of others. This realization made me question my own values and it took me tremendous courage to accept this reality. …I need to reflect further and talk about this to myself and my supervisor.[1]

One cannot undermine the value of relationships in social work practice more so because both formal and informal support networks for students and new practitioners are essential for growth of practice wisdom. It is in the fieldwork experiences which are learning spaces where students get an opportunity to learn from field contacts, peers, para-professionals, community workers and outreach workers in a multidisciplinary way. Subsequently, they return to campus and meet up with other student learners, attend review meetings, interact in formal and informal networks and exchange views with faculty, supervisors and advisors. These processes foster the development and enhancement of their practice wisdom and that of the mentors. In fact, Carson et al. (2011) have identified social work supervision as a key component in the skill building of students which facilitates experiential learning and supports the growth of practice wisdom (Thompson & West, 2013). It is pertinent to add here that the constructivist approach to practice too is based on 'experienced relationships and interaction' which in turn enables 'humanization' (Cooper, 2001) valuing the fact that people and students think at multiple levels and understand the world through their own personal constructs.

HOW DOES 'TRADITIONAL' PRACTICE FARE IN TERMS OF NEWER APPROACHES?

If one is to truly meet the challenges of shifting 'traditional' practice towards newer approaches, one needs to accept that together they constitute 'developmental social sciences'. Acknowledging that many of the students themselves hail from various marginalities, it is uncalled for that they be assessed and evaluated on the same or similar parameters as those hailing from other backgrounds with varied profiles. In the formative period of professional work, a formal facilitator in the form of a mentor provides valuable support to students who may challenge

---

[1] *Beliefs* are the ideas and concepts that we hold to be true, even without complete knowledge or evidence. Beliefs are generally not provable, but they are important nonetheless because they form the basis for our values systems. Values, then, are ideas that we hold to be important. They tend to form directives for us to follow. As we weave together values we choose to live by, we create a values system, a coherent and internally consistent set of related values.

prevalent assumptions. Despite the need to maintain standards, the facilitation of learning and supervision is sometimes at conflicting purposes (Hughes, 2004). Once the power or lack of trust enters a relationship—a learning relationship—the openness otherwise essential for questioning may tend to dissipate. Wadsworth (2001, p. 420) described different ways of providing guidance based not on supervision but also on 'stewardship without control'.

It needs to be reiterated that the formative professional education and experience places certain parameters around what we know, how we know and what we are competent to do (Flyvberg, 2001; Hall, 2005). Has the secular mindfulness movement lost its way by negating ethics for the purpose of material gain? Dawson and Turbull (2006) had argued that a secular meditation practice is disconnected from the traditional framework of Buddhist ethics. For Buddhists, right mindfulness (*samma sati*) is a core aspect of following the eightfold path and is the equivalent of right mindfulness (Bodhi, 1999, p. 279). In the *Abhidhamma*, mindfulness is classified as one of the 19 universal factors. It arises simultaneous with other mind states including faith (*sadds*), non-greed (*alobha*), non-hatred (*adosa*), neutrality of mind (*tatramajhatta*) and tranquillity (*Passaddhi*). As a part of the Buddhist practice, mindfulness is practised with the 'sila' aspects of right speech (*samma vaca*), action (*samma kamnaste*) and livelihood (*samma ajiva*) of the path while adopting attitudes of Brahmavihara of compassion (*karuna*), loving kindness (*metta*), sympathetic joy (*mudita*) and equanimity (*upeksha*) for eradication of delusion (Bodhi, 1999, pp. 85–90).

While social work profession speaks of critical reflection, it fails to take into account the Buddhist context wherein mindfulness involves the concept of discrimination and use of critical judgement with the purpose of developing wholesome states. In the Buddhist context, mindfulness involves the concept of discrimination and use of critical judgement. It includes application of right view (*samma ditthi*) and right effort (*sammavayama*) *of the eightfold path* (Bodhi, 2011). Thus, it is this mindfulness which becomes a gradual transformation in the process of thoughts, feelings and behaviour (Olendzki, 2011, p. 64). Additionally, when Biestek (1957, p. 93) propagated 'non-judgemental' attitude, it did not mean indifference or rejection of a value system. Further, the caseworker's 'function is to help the individual within the law and within the basic values of a society which is based upon the belief in God' (Biestek, 1957, p. 94). However, the question arises as to whose value system shall inform and constitute the reality? There cannot be any qualm that the universal human values emanating out of the human rights and social justice concern should inform the non-judgemental attitude instead of the prevalent dominant world view of a constricted elite minority.

In fact, the contemporary psychological definition used terms such as 'non-judgemental' differ vastly from the traditional Buddhist understanding of mindfulness (Dreyfus, 2011). In fact, the more contemporary meditation teachers introduced the notion of non-judgemental awareness and paid attention to paying attention as the observation of an object without any value judgement of what is being observed. This involves observation without any value/judgement of internal states of the mind such as anger, which allows the observer to develop a deeper understanding of the nature of the mind (Dhammasami, 2000, pp. 4–5). There are many multifaceted perspectives surrounding the alternate views of traditional Buddhist thought and the introduction of secular mindfulness. Why it is important to flag the Buddhist teachings here is because all along we have considered 'the relationship' as the soul of social casework or working with individuals. It is based on the philosophy of life which is both realistic and idealistic, which includes reason, faith, time and eternity (Biestek, 1957).

What one is questioning here is as to why Biestek ignored the idea that in any relationship gain is possible at both ends and that the casework relationship experiences can have different scripts. In our everyday lived realities, the power dynamics of dominant castes and other castes, between the majority and minority, are unmet challenges.

ON CREATING A SOCIAL WORK IDENTITY

What has been attempted is to base the understanding of the field on a reasoned normative foundation wherein one not only describes changes in discourses and in institutional ways of thinking but is also able to critique the changes and provide reasons for the same. This is the precondition for human beings' ability to follow their version of the good life and participate as a morally sane individual in social and democratic processes of decision-making.

Also, it raises certain pertinent questions, namely how do social work students create a professional identity while focusing on socio-economic justice in a world/space where there is expansion of bureaucratization of institutions and organizations and where social welfare benefits are otherwise getting reduced? What and how do budding social work learners exercise the plurality of social work functions and roles withing communities and across organizations? The discretion they use can range from significant decisions or suggestions which have meaningful consequences for individuals and others involved including 'numerous micro-decisions' (Munro, 2002, p. 110). If appropriate tools and frameworks are used and systematic processes are used, effective discretion and judgement of social work professionals can be enhanced. As supervisor and mentors, we need to question whether we are focusing on outcomes which are informed by evidence or supporting creativity and compassion in a troubled world. Herein lies the secret of values being traditional yet transformative and emancipatory.

SUMMARY

In this chapter, the concept and definitions of social work values are provided. It has been explained that values influence one's decision-making process and it is extremely difficult to objectively determine the 'best' value. Even when values differ from person to person, society to society and community to community, the fact is that often one is hardly aware of a value one holds unless of course that value is violated by others.

The primary purpose of the social work profession is to enhance human well-being and help meet the basic human needs of all people, with particular attention to the needs and empowerment of people who are vulnerable, oppressed and living in poverty. At this juncture, it is meaningful to explain the concepts of pain and suffering as understood in the Asian and Indian context and culture by citing Buddhist philosophies, Krishnamurti, Sri Aurobindo and Nhat Hanh, among others. Explaining the concept of mindfulness and the self, the author charts the journey from the traditional to the emancipatory, attempting to highlight how both aspects merge and draw from each other. By explaining the need for situational learning and daily coping in fieldwork, the author concludes the said chapter by focusing on the aspect of identity in the social work profession and leaves the reader with points to ponder.

TOP 10 TAKEAWAYS/MAIN POINTS

1. Practice wisdom is based on sustaining and maintaining meaningful relationships.
2. The primary objective of first-year fieldwork is to enable students to learn basic principles, values, ethics and skills, and gain a perspective of social work practice.
3. It is essential that students anchor themselves in universal values of dignity, compassion and fairness.
4. Social work becomes an art of connecting with people where values play an extremely prominent role. It includes creativity, intuition and inductive reasoning in combination with 'values, morals and beliefs'.
5. Student learners and mentors are essentially co-learners and co-constructors of knowledge.
6. The constructivist approach to practice is based on 'experienced relationships and interaction' which in turn enables 'humanization'.
7. The process of learning is critical for students to help them acquire, practice and improve the values, skills and knowledge needed for the profession.
8. Mindlessness (as different from mindfulness) refers to a lack of present moment awareness when the mind is preoccupied with future or past occurrences.
9. Mindfulness involves the concept of discrimination and use of critical judgement with the purpose of developing wholesome states.
10. Self-exploration is the process of finding out what is valuable to oneself by investigating within oneself.

Keywords: Practice wisdom, values, skill building, suffering, empathy

GLOSSARY

Empathy: Empathy is the ability to imagine oneself in someone else's situation and to feel some of what that person may be experiencing.

Practice wisdom: Practice wisdom is the foundation for effective practice and encompasses both the *art* and *science* of social work. Practice wisdom is the foundation for effective practice and encompasses both the *art* and *science* of social work. Practice wisdom is acquired through the application of social work values in practice.

Skill building: It comprises five domains, namely concept driven, an understanding and knowledge of varied theoretical approaches to practice, the identification and refining of core practice skills, capacity for knowledge production skills and direct field-based intervention skills.

Social work values: Values are belief-narratives which sharpen one's approach and help steer the teaching–learning trajectory.

ANALYTICAL QUESTIONS

1. Analyse how empathic ability and critical reflection impact us from a traditional and emancipatory point of view?
2. Reflect upon and critically examine ethical dilemmas, conflicts and power relations in social work.

MULTIPLE CHOICE QUESTIONS

1. _____ tend to guide one's actions and judgements across a variety of situations.
   a. Reasoned action
   b. **Values**
   c. Social influence
   d. Dispositional approach

2. Attitudes equal
   a. Values and perception
   b. **values and beliefs**
   c. Values and personality
   d. Values and motivation

3. Mindfulness is exhibited when
   a. We are open to new information that focuses on the communication process
   b. We strive to avoid stereotyping
   c. We pick up signals that alert us to potential misunderstandings
   d. **All of the above**

4. What do we mean by ethics?
   a. Moral judgements
   b. Determinants of what is right or wrong
   c. Rules or standards governing a profession
   d. **All of the above**

5. An individual's moral judgements about what is right or wrong are called
   a. Belief systems
   b. **Ethical values**
   c. Cultural assumptions
   d. Social responsibility
   e. Values posture

6. An act which ends in itself with no benefit to the individual would be
   a. Pro-social
   b. **Sadistic**
   c. Hedonistic
   d. Altruistic
   e. None of these
   f. All of these

7. The values and culture that affect the way people feel about the organization they are in and about work itself is
   a. **Sociological factor**
   b. Political factors
   c. Economic factors
   d. Psychological factors

8. The challenge of creating teams is less demanding for management when teams are introduced where employees have strong _____ values
   a. Collectivist
   b. Competitive
   c. Pluralistic
   d. **Cooperative**

9. A set of principles and expectations that are considered binding on any person who is member of a particular group is known as
   a. Code of ethics
   b. **Values**
   c. Ethics
   d. None of the above

10. According to Branen, the pillars of self-esteem are
    a. Living consciously, self-acceptance and responsibly
    b. Self-assertiveness, living purposefully and personal integrity
    c. None of the above
    d. **All of the above**

REVIEW QUESTIONS

1. What are the core values of social work?
2. Describe briefly the importance of Indic values in social work.
3. Define social work values in your own words.
4. Write a short note on 'how do our values impact us while working with people'?
5. Analyse and critically examine how relationship and one's own values and attitudes influence the relations with various stakeholders in the field.
6. Identify and evaluate one's own ability to relate theoretical knowledge and skills to practical action.

REFERENCES

Baltes, P. B., & Staudinger, U. M. (2000). A meta heuristic (pragmatic) to orchestrate mind and virtue toward excellence. *American Psychologist, 2*(1), 122–136.

Biestek, F. P. (1957). *The casework relationship.* Loyola University Press.

Bodhi, B. (1999). *The Buddha and His Dhamma.* Retrieved from https://www.accesstoinsight.org/lib/authors/bodhi/wheel433.html

Bodhi, S. R. (2011). Professional social work education in india: A critical view from the periphery. *The Indian journal of Social work, 72*(1), 289–300.

Branden, N. (1995). *The six pillars of self-esteem.* Bantam Doubleday Dell Publishing Group Incorporated.

Burley-Allen, M. (1982). *Listening: The forgotten skill.* Wiley.

Carson, E., King, S., & Papatraianou, L. H. (2011). Resilience among social workers: The role of informal learning in the workplace. *Practice*, *23*(5), 267–278.

Cassell, E. J. (1991). Recognizing suffering. *Hastings Center Report*, *21*(3), 24–24.

Chan, W. S. (2008). Psychological attachment, no-self and Chan Buddhist mind therapy. *Contemporary Buddhism*, *9*(2), 253–264.

Cooper, A., & Lousada, J. (2005). Theory and practice: Psychoanalytic Sociology as psychosocial studies. *Sociology*, *40*(6), 1153–1169.

Cooper, B. (2001). Constructivism in social work: Towards a participative practice viability. *British Journal of Social Work*, *31*(5), 721–738.

Dalai Lama. (2004[1995]). *Essential teachings*. Souvenir Press.

Dash, B. M. (2018). Bharatiyakaran of social work: Understanding the meaning & concept. *New Delhi Times*.

Dash, B. M. (2019). Indic social work values. *New Delhi Times*. https://www.newdelhitimes.com/indic-social-work-values/

Dawson, G., & Turnbull, J. (2006). Is mindfulness the new opiate of the masses? Critical reflections from a Buddhist perspective. *Psychotherapy*, *12*(4), 60–64.

Dhammasami. (2000). *Different aspects of mindfulness, the aim and technique of Vipassana meditation*. Wisdom Library.

Dreyfus, G. (2011). Is mindfulness present-centered and non-judgmental? A discussion of the cognitive dimensions of mindfulness. *Contemporary Buddhism- an Interdisciplinary Journal*, 41–54.

East, J., & Chambers, R. (2007). Courage to teach for social work educators. *Social Work Education*, *26*(8), 810–826.

Gray, M. (2002). Art, irony and ambiguity: howard goldstein and his contribution to social work. *Qualitative Social Work*, *1*(4), 413–433.

Hughes, M. (2004). How schools of social work perceive and are responding to juvenile violence: a national survey. *Social work education*, *23*(1), 63–75.

Krishnamurti, J. (2004). *On living and dying* [originally published 1982]. Krishnamurti Foundation Trust Ltd.

Lama, D. (2005). *Many ways to Nirvana: reflections and advice on right living*. Penguin Books.

Lama, D. (2011). *Stages of meditation: training the mind for wisdom*. Random House.

Lantz, J. (1995). Frankl's concept of time: Existential psychotherapy with couples and families. *Journal of Contemporary Psychotherapy*, *25*(2), 135–144.

Lay, K., & McGuire, L. (2010). Building a lens for critical reflection and reflexivity in social work education. *Social Work Education*, *29*(5), 539–550.

Munro, E. (2002). *Effective child protection*. SAGE.

Neimark, N. F. (2000). *The handbook of journaling: Tools for the healing of mind, body & spirit*. R.E.P. Technologies.

Norbu, C., & Clemente, A. (1999). *The supreme source: the fundamental tantra of the Dzogchen Semde*. Snow Lion.

Olednzki, A. (2011). The construction of mindfulness. *Contemporary Buddhism*. https://www.tandfonline.com/toc/rcbh20/current.

Rinpoche, P. (1998). *The words of my perfect teacher*. HarperCollins.

Rabjam, L. (2002). *The practice of Dzogchen*. (H. Talbot, Ed., & Tulku Thondup, Trans.) Snow Lion.

Sharma, M. (2019). *Radical transformational leadership: strategic action for change agents*. North Atlantic Books.

Shonin, E., Van Gordon, W., & Griffiths, M. D. (2013). Buddhist philosophy for the treatment of problem gambling. *Journal of Behavioral Addictions*, 2.

Siegel, H. (1991). The generalizability of critical thinking. *Educational philosophy and Theory*, *23*(1), 18–30.

Soeng, M. (1995). *The heart of the universe: exploring the heart sutra*. Wisdom Publications.

Sri Aurobindo. (2004). *The mother*. Sri Aurobindo Ashram.

Thomas, G. (2015). Social work education through distance learning in india: Areality. In *Bhatt, S. & Pathare, S. (Eds.), Social Work Education and Practice Engagement*. Shipra Publication.

Thomas, G. (2018). *Social work: The value-based profession*. Rawat Publications.

Thompson, L. J., & West, D. (2013). Professional development in the contemporary educational context: encouraging practice wisdom. *Social Work Education, 32*(1), 118–133.

Wadsworth, Y. (2001). The mirror, the magnifying glass, the compass and the map: facilitating participatory action research. In P. Reason & H. Bradbury (Eds.), *Handbook of action research: Participative inquiry and practice* (pp. 420–432). SAGE Publications.

RECOMMENDED READING

Dash, B. M. (2019). Importance of Indic Values for Bharatiyakaran/Indianisation of social work education. In B. M. Dash, B. Ramesh, K. G. Parshumara, & M. Kumar (Eds.), *New frontiers in social work practice Bharatiya contexts, perspectives and experiences*. Tumkur University.

21

Social Work Ethics

K. Rajeshwari and Vijay Kumar Sharma

LEARNING OBJECTIVES

- To understand the social work Code of Ethics
- To identify the roles and responsibilities of social workers in different sectors
- To know the principles and values of social work profession
- To understand the problems related to social work profession

A socially embodied medium of understanding and adjustment in which people account to each other for the identities, relationships, and values that define their responsibilities.

—Walker (2007, pp. 67–68)

INTRODUCTION

Social work is a field that studies and improves the lives of individuals, groups and societies through the use of social theory and research methodologies. Other social sciences are incorporated and used as a means of improving the human condition and changing society's reaction to chronic problems. It is a profession dedicated to the pursuit of social justice, the improvement of quality of life and the full development of each individual, group and community in society. As a result of the post-Second World War growth of social work education at the Tata Institute of Social Sciences in 1936 and later the employment of medical social workers in J. J. Hospital, India has accepted social work as a profession. It was designed to generate professionals who may be appropriately referred to as social doctors or social engineers, with its knowledge base embracing subjects such as psychology, sociology, medicine, psychiatry, development theories, management and welfare administration. However, more than seven decades after its inception, the profession of social work in India is still fumbling for professional space.

According to Jamal and Bowie (1995), codes of ethics are designed to address three major issues. First, codes address problems of moral hazard, or instances when a profession's self-interest may conflict with the public's interest (e.g., whether accountants should be obligated to disclose confidential information concerning serious financial crimes that their clients have committed, or whether dentists should be permitted to refuse to treat people who have a serious immune disease, such as HIV-AIDS). Second, codes address issues of professional courtesy, that is, rules that govern how professionals should behave to enhance and maintain a profession's integrity (e.g., whether lawyers should be permitted to advertise and solicit clients, whether physicians should accept gifts and free trips from pharmaceutical company representatives or whether psychotherapists should be permitted to engage in sexual relationships with former patients). Finally, codes address issues that concern professionals' duty to serve the public interest (e.g., the extent of nurses' or social workers' obligation to assist when faced with a public emergency or to provide low-income people with pro bono services).

Like other professions such as medicine, nursing, law, psychology, counselling and engineering, social work has developed a comprehensive set of ethical standards. These standards have evolved over time, reflecting significant changes in the broader culture and in social work's mission, methods and priorities. They address a wide range of issues, including, for example, social workers' handling of confidential information and electronic communications, dual relationships and boundary issues, conflicts of interest, informed consent, termination of services, administration, supervision, education and training, research and political action.

The major goal of social work is to improve people's well-being and assist them in meeting their basic human needs, with a focus on the needs and empowerment of those who are vulnerable, oppressed or living in poverty. The primary mission of the social work profession is to enhance human well-being and help to meet basic human needs of all people, with particular attention to the needs and empowerment of people who are vulnerable, oppressed and living in poverty. A historic and defining feature of social work is the profession's focus on individual well-being in a social context and the well-being of society (National Association of Social Workers [NASW]). The profession's dual focus on individual well-being in a social environment and the well-being of society is a historic and defining element of social work. Environmental forces that produce, contribute to and address issues in living are at the heart of social work. With and on behalf of clients, social workers seek to promote social justice and change. Individuals, families, groups, organizations and communities are all referred to as 'clients'. Social workers are culturally and ethnically aware and try to eliminate prejudice, oppression, poverty and other types of social injustice. Direct practice, community organizing, supervision, consultation, administration, advocacy, social and political action, policy development and implementation, teaching, and research and evaluation are examples of these activities.

Professional ethics are the base of social work. The profession has its own obligations to come up with its basic values, ethical principles and ethical standards. NASW Code of Ethics (National Association of Social Workers, 2008) focused on values, principles and standards to guide social worker's conduct. The code explains to all social workers and social work trainees, regardless of their professional functions, the settings in which they are working, or the populations in which they exist.

The International Association of Schools of Social Work and the International Federation of Social Workers adopted the following international definition of social work in July 2001:

Social Work Ethics

'The social work profession promotes social change, problem solving in human relationships, and people's empowerment and liberation to improve well-being.' Social work intervenes at the places where people interact with their environments, on the basis of ideas of human behaviour and social systems. Human rights and social justice principles are crucial to social work (NAAC, 2005).

All social workers are beholden to the Social Work Code of Ethics—otherwise known as the NASW Code of Ethics—during their studies and vow to abide by its standards and principles throughout their careers. The following is an outline of the aetiology of its creation and major points.

The NASW Delegate Assembly created the first version of the Code of Ethics in October 1960. It has since been revised several times, but it maintains many of the original principles.

Unless someone like you cares a whole awful lot, nothing is going to get better. It's not.

—The Lorax

SIX PURPOSES OF THE CODE

The core of social work ethics is professionalism. The profession owes it to its members to express its core values, ethical principles and ethical standards. These ideals, concepts and standards are outlined in the NASW Code of Ethics, which serves as a guide for social workers. Regardless of their professional functions, the settings in which they work, or the people they serve, all social workers and social work students are subject to the Code.

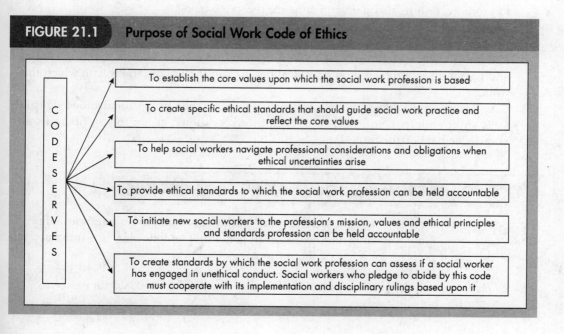

FIGURE 21.1 Purpose of Social Work Code of Ethics

The code is also based on the six core values of the social work profession.

1. *Service:* Social workers put others' needs ahead of their own. To assist individuals in need and to address social issues, social workers draw on their knowledge, values and abilities. Social workers are urged to provide some of their professional expertise without expecting a large monetary reward (pro bono service).
2. *Social justice:* Social workers work to bring about social change, notably on behalf of and alongside vulnerable and oppressed individuals and communities. Poverty, unemployment, discrimination and other types of social injustice are the primary targets of social workers' social change initiatives. These activities aim to raise awareness and understanding of discrimination, as well as cultural and ethnic diversity. Social workers seek to ensure that all people have equal access to required information, services and resources, as well as meaningful participation in decision-making.
3. *Dignity and worth of the individual:* Social workers treat each person in a caring and respectful fashion, mindful of individual differences and cultural and ethnic diversity. Social workers promote clients' socially responsible self-determination. Social workers seek to enhance clients' capacity and opportunity to change and to address their own needs. Social workers are cognizant of their dual responsibility to clients and to the broader society. They seek to resolve conflicts between clients' interests and the broader society's interests in a socially responsible manner consistent with the values, ethical principles and ethical standards of the profession.
4. *Importance and centrality of human relationships:* Relationships between and among people are a key vehicle for transformation according to social professionals. People are engaged as partners in the assisting process by social workers. Individuals, families, social groups, organizations and communities attempt to develop relationships among people in order to promote, restore, maintain and enhance their well-being.
5. *Integrity:* Social workers are always conscious of the profession's goal, beliefs, ethical principles and ethical standards, and they practise in accordance with them. Professionally and individually, social workers should take care of themselves. Social workers are honest and responsible, and they support ethical practises in the organizations with which they work.
6. *Competence:* Social workers continually strive to increase their professional knowledge and skills and to apply them in practice. Social workers should aspire to contribute to the knowledge base of the profession.

MAJOR POINTS FROM THE SOCIAL WORK CODE OF ETHICS

The code is composed of thematic sections that outline a social worker's responsibility to clients, colleagues, employers and the profession in general. The following is a summary of some of the major points from a few of the sections.

Ethical challenges in social work, discussion with practitioners and students suggests at least four main themes.

—Banks (2012, p. 21)

CONDUCT

Social workers must:

- Maintain high standards of personal conduct
- Aim to maintain a high degree of professionalism throughout their careers
- Hold service to be the most important element of social work
- Maintain a high level of professional integrity
- Engage in lifelong learning to maintain competence
- Guide practice according to scholarly enquiry and use evidence to inform best practices

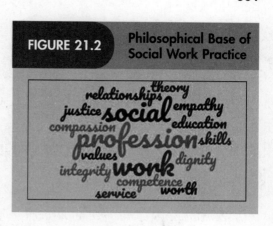

FIGURE 21.2 Philosophical Base of Social Work Practice

RESPONSIBILITY TO CLIENTS

Social workers must do the following.

- *Make clients their primary responsibility:* The major job of social workers is to enhance the well-being of their clients. In general, clients' needs come first. Clients should be informed that social workers' responsibilities to the greater society or specific legal commitments may, on rare circumstances, override the allegiance owed to them (e.g., a social worker may be compelled by law to report a client who has abused a child or threatened to hurt themselves or others).
- *Foster maximum self-determination in clients:* Clients' right to self-determination is respected and promoted by social workers who support clients in identifying and clarifying their goals. Clients' right to self-determination may be limited by social workers when their acts or projected actions, in the social workers' professional judgement, represent a severe, foreseeable and urgent risk to themselves or others.
- *Respect the privacy of clients and keep information that has been shared during the course of their duties confidential:* Except for compelling professional reasons, social workers should maintain the confidentiality of any information received during professional service. When disclosure is required to avert substantial, foreseeable and urgent harm to a client or others, the usual assumption that social workers will keep material confidential does not apply. In all cases, social workers should only divulge the minimum amount of personal information required to achieve the targeted goal; only information directly related to the reason for the disclosure should be shared.
- *Charge fees for services that are fair and considerate to clients:* Clients' goods or services should not be accepted as payment for professional services by social workers. In social workers' relationships with clients, bartering arrangements, particularly those involving services, can lead to conflicts of interest, exploitation and improper limits. Bartering should be considered and used by social workers only in very limited circumstances, such as when

it can be demonstrated that it is a common practice among professionals in the community, that it is considered necessary for the provision of services, that it is negotiated without coercion and that it is done at the client's request and with the client's informed consent. Social workers who receive products or services from clients in exchange for professional services bear the complete responsibility for establishing that the agreement will not harm the client or the professional relationship.

RESPONSIBILITY TO COLLEAGUES AND EMPLOYERS

Social workers should do the following.

- *Treat colleagues with respect, fairness and courtesy:* Social worker should treat colleagues with respect, fairness, courtesy and good faith.
- *Adhere to professional obligations as determined by their employers:* The social workers' responsibility is to relate to the clients colleagues with full professional consideration. If the colleagues are not available, the social worker should take up as they deal with their own.
- *Ensuring cooperation with colleagues:* Social workers should cooperate with colleagues and with colleagues of other professions when such cooperation services the well-being of clients.
- *Abstain from criticizing colleagues in front of clients:* Social workers should avoid unwanted negative criticism of colleagues in communications with clients or with other professionals. Unwanted negative criticism may include demeaning comments that refer to colleague's level of competence or to individuals attributes such as race, ethnicity, national origin, colour, sex, sexual orientation, age marital status, political belief, religion and mental or physical disability.

RESPONSIBILITY TO THE SOCIAL WORK PROFESSION

Social workers should do the following.

- *Uphold, represent and advance the values of the social work profession:* The social workers should uphold and advance the values, ethics, knowledge and mission of the profession. Social workers need to remember that they are a part of a large community of professionals and their actions will positively or negatively affect the profession and its professionals.
- *Help the profession make social services available to the general public:* Social workers should not misrepresent their professional qualifications and abilities.
- *Educate themselves to become culturally competent and understanding of diversity:* Social workers should not misunderstand the facts related to the clients even when it seems to benefit them. Social workers should be more responsive to their behaviour.
- *Engaging effectively for the advancement of social work profession:* Social workers should contribute time and professional expertise to activities that promote respect for the value, integrity and competence of the social work profession. These activities may include teaching, research, consultation, service, legislative testimony, presentations in the community and participation in the professional organization.

Social Work Ethics

At its most basic level, social work is about promoting the general welfare of society by representing those who are most vulnerable. Providing social services can sometimes be a difficult task, wrought with ethical uncertainties and challenges.

The Social Work Code of Ethics helps social workers navigate these challenges throughout their careers and provides a framework for the principles and standards that they must uphold.

One of the hallmarks of a profession is its willingness to establish ethical standards to guide practitioners' conduct (Greenwood, 1957; Hall, 1968; Lindeman, 1947). Ethical standards are created to address ethical issues in practice and to provide guidelines for determining what ethically acceptable or unacceptable behaviour is.

Professions typically publicize their ethical standards in the forms of codes of ethics (Bayles, 1986; Banks & Gallagher, 2009; Kultgen, 1982; Reamer, 2006). According to Jamal and Bowie (1995), codes of ethics are designed to address three major issues.

Every day, social workers stand up for human rights and justice and give voice to unheard and marginalized populations. They contribute to bettering individuals' lives and, by doing so, they improve society as a whole. Social workers are employed by non-profits, the government and private practices. Each of those social workers, regardless of the setting in which one chooses to provide services, must adhere to the professional Code of Ethics established in 1996 by the NASW Delegate Assembly and revised in 2017.

VALUES OF SOCIAL WORK PROFESSION

According to the NASW website, the NASW Code of Ethics 'is intended to serve as a guide to the everyday professional conduct of social workers'. It outlines six ethical principles that 'set forth ideals to which all social workers should aspire'. When ethical dilemmas emerge, the Code provides a set of values, principles and standards to govern decision-making and behaviour. It does not lay out a set of guidelines for how social workers should behave in all circumstances. The context in which the Code is being applied, as well as the possibility of conflicts among the Code's ideals, principles and standards, must be considered.

All human connections, from personal and family to societal and professional, have ethical duties. See NASW Procedures for Professional Review for more information on the NASW Professional Review Process. In addition, the NASW Code of Ethics makes no distinction between which values, principles or standards are most important and should take precedence over others when they contradict. When it comes to how values, ethical principles and ethical standards should be ranked when they contradict, reasonable differences of opinion can and do exist among social workers. Informed judgements of the individual social worker must be applied to ethical decision-making in a given scenario, as well as consideration of how the concerns would be appraised in a peer review process using the profession's ethical standards. Making ethical decisions is a process. When conflicting commitments develop, social workers may be confronted with difficult ethical challenges for which there are no clear solutions.

All of the values, ideas and standards in this Code should be considered by social workers in every scenario when ethical judgement is required. The spirit as well as the letter of this

Code should guide social workers' judgements and activities. This chapter will explore those six social work core values, which comprise service, social justice, dignity and worth of the person, importance of human relationships, integrity and competence.

SERVICE

Social services are a range of public services intended to provide support and assistance towards particular groups, which commonly include the disadvantaged. They may be provided by individuals, private and independent organizations, or administered by a government agency. Social services are connected with the concept of welfare and the welfare state, as countries with large welfare programmes often provide a wide range of social services. Social services are employed to address the wide range of needs of a society. Prior to industrialization, the provision of social services was largely confined to private organizations and charities, with the extent of its coverage also limited. Social services are now generally regarded globally as a 'necessary function' of society and a mechanism through which governments may address societal issues.

Addressing social ills and helping others is a primary goal of all social workers. Service is the value from which all other social work values stem. Social workers regularly elevate the needs of others above their own personal interests and use their skills and knowledge (from education and experience) to help people. Social workers often volunteer their time—in addition to their paid services—with no expectation for financial reward.

SOCIAL JUSTICE

Social justice is a political and philosophical theory which asserts that there are dimensions to the concept of justice beyond those embodied in the principles of civil or criminal law, economic supply and demand, or traditional moral frameworks. Social justice tends to focus more on just relations between groups within society as opposed to the justice of individual conduct or justice for individuals.

Historically and in theory, the idea of social justice is that all people should have equal access to wealth, health, well-being, justice, privileges and opportunity regardless of their legal, political, economic or other circumstances. In modern practice, social justice revolves around favouring or punishing different groups of the population, regardless of any given individual's choices or actions, based on value judgements regarding historical events, current conditions and group relations. In economic terms, this often means redistribution of wealth, income and economic opportunities from groups whom social justice advocates consider to be oppressors to those whom they consider to be the oppressed. Social justice is often associated with identity politics, socialism and revolutionary communism.

Social workers advocate on behalf of the oppressed, the voiceless and others who are unable to advocate for themselves. They often focus on issues such as poverty, homelessness, discrimination, harassment and other forms of injustice.

Social workers provide information, help and other resources to people seeking equality, and they educate people who may not directly experience discrimination about the struggles of the less fortunate.

DIGNITY AND WORTH OF THE PERSON

Every person is different, with different cultural and social values. Social workers are mindful of those differences, treating each person with dignity and respect and promoting their clients' capacity and opportunity to address their own needs and improve their personal situations.

Social workers must be cognizant of their duties to both individual clients and to society as a whole and seek solutions for their clients that also support society's broader interests.

IMPORTANCE OF HUMAN RELATIONSHIPS

Social workers connect people who need assistance with organizations and individuals who can provide the appropriate help. Social workers recognize that facilitating human relationships can be a useful vehicle for creating change, and they excel at engaging potential partners who can create, maintain and enhance the well-being of families, neighbourhoods and whole communities.

INTEGRITY

In order to facilitate these relationships and improve others' lives, social workers must exhibit trustworthiness at all times. Each social worker must be continually aware of the profession's mission, values and ethical principles and standards, and set a good example of these components for their clients.

By behaving honestly and responsibly, social workers can promote the organizations with which they are affiliated while also creating the most value for the populations they serve.

COMPETENCE

Professional social workers often hold undergraduate or master's degree in social work, but a fair amount of their knowledge comes from gaining on-the-job experience. As part of the social work values outlined in the NASW Code of Ethics, each social worker must practise within their scope of competence and avoid misrepresenting their skills or experience to potential clients. Social workers must continually strive to expand their knowledge base and competence in order to make meaningful contributions to the profession.

The importance of ethics and values in social work is more than just compliance with regulations and requirements. In a profession in which the clients are often vulnerable and unable to advocate for themselves, it is necessary that those advocating for them be passionate about empowering those who are vulnerable, oppressed or poverty stricken.

PROBLEMS FACED BY SOCIAL WORKERS IN INDIA WITH REGARD TO SOCIAL WORK ETHICS

Ethical decision-making is difficult in any society as it can result in adverse consequences for the social worker. They may have to suffer losses because their decisions more often than not harm the interests of some individuals or groups that intend to benefit from the situation.

CRISIS OF VALUES IN INDIAN SOCIETY

Many social scientists have commented on the crises of values in Indian society. Values of honesty, propriety, concern for others, accountability among government officials and corporates, are seen as lacking in Indian society. According to some, the crises are caused because we have forgotten our ancient values. On the basis of personal and professional values, a social worker may have apprehension working with a particular client or population.

For others, crises of value have been caused because Indian society is still undergoing the modernization process. Social workers have to live and work in such situations and are naturally affected.

VOLUNTARY ASSOCIATIONS AS A MONEY-MAKING VENTURE

The availability of large funds from international and national donors as well as local and government sources have led to the setting up of numerous voluntary agencies. Many of these agencies claim to work for the people but the real purpose seems to be to make money. Corruption, misappropriation of funds, lack of accountability and improper accounting procedures are some of the allegations that are made against these agencies. In the process, the very purpose and ideals of setting up voluntary organization (VOs) and NGOs get defeated.

LACK OF COMMON PERSPECTIVES IN SOCIAL WORK-RELATED ISSUES

Women, Dalits, tribals/indigenous peoples, nomadic communities, landless and small farmers, the labour class, children, youth, persons with disabilities, mental or terminal illnesses, or varying sexual orientations, and others have all been marginalized as a result of systemic discrimination based on sex, ethnicity, age, health, economic background and sexual orientation, among others. Designed to preserve and improve human security, family, community and state socio-economic–political institutions/systems have taken on a life of their own.

In many ways, Indian society is in a state of transition. Certain issues related to individual autonomy, collective orientation, individual rights and responsibilities are difficult to resolve in any society. Indian society, caught between traditional and modern forces, faces a number of problems related to such issues. Also, different groups are influenced by Westernization to varying degrees. All these cause problems for social workers in interpersonal relationships. Instances may arise when social workers' ethical obligations conflict with agency policies or relevant laws or regulations. When such conflicts occur, social workers must make a responsible effort to resolve the conflict in a manner that is consistent with thee values, principles and standards expressed in this code.

POWERLESSNESS OF THE SOCIAL WORKER

The social worker, in many cases, intends to do the work with propriety but lacks the power to do so. There are other institutions and authorities on which the social worker has to depend on while facing difficult situations. Their methods of functioning are very often found to be different from that of the social worker. Sometimes, there are problems of lack of accountability, the negligence of staff, vested interests and even the presence of criminals in welfare institutions. The social worker has no choice but to go along with these as they have no power to change the situation. At best, they can achieve minimal changes. Anything beyond this involves risk and not everyone can afford to go to that extent.

LACK OF SUPPORT FROM THE CIVIL SOCIETY

In India, the social work profession has not gained much recognition from the government and the society at large. The misdeeds of a few social workers, many of them not even professionals (sadly, Indian society does not distinguish between professional and voluntary social workers) have contributed to the loss of image and the moral authority of social workers. People suspect social workers of having ulterior motives when they take up social issues. All these have resulted in lack of public support for the social worker and weakened their power to achieve social change.

LACK OF PROFESSIONAL BODIES AND PROFESSIONAL SUPPORT

The existence of a professional body can give the much-needed training and support for social work professionals. Second, if any social worker is being harassed for legitimately raising relevant issues the professional body can give them support. This will enable social workers to take up public causes without fear.

LACK OF IMPORTANCE GIVEN TO STUDYING AND DISCUSSING PROFESSIONAL ETHICS

While all social work educators consider social work ethics to be important, it is given secondary importance in the curriculum. Students frequently consider it to be idealistic, rather than something, which should be practised in the field. In fact, social work syllabuses of many universities in India do not have ethics as a component for classroom teaching.

SUMMARY

The Code identifies core values on which social work's mission is based summarizes ethical principles that reflect the profession's core values, establishes a set of specific ethical standards that guide social work practice and provides the basis on which the public can hold a practitioner accountable. Social workers face situations that may challenge their personal beliefs and values. However, they have responsibility to uphold the values and ethics of social work. Effective social work practice is guided by knowledge, skills and values. The values of the profession reflect the historical foundation of the field and the ideological underpinnings of contemporary practice. Ethical standards can also be used to hold social workers accountable for poor decisions, through malpractice suits, regulatory board's sanctions and other adjudication mechanisms. Values are core beliefs about what is right, good or preferable.

TOP 10 TAKEAWAYS/MAIN POINTS

1. Social work is a field that studies and improves the lives of individuals, groups and societies through the use of social theory and research methodologies.
2. The major goal of social work is to improve people's well-being and assist them in meeting their basic human needs, with a focus on the needs and empowerment of those who are vulnerable, oppressed or living in poverty.
3. The International Association of Schools of Social Work and the International Federation of Social Workers adopted the following international definition of social work in July 2001.
4. The core of social work ethics is professionalism. The profession owes it to its members to express its core values, ethical principles and ethical standards.
5. Relationships between and among people are a key vehicle for transformation according to social professionals.
6. Clients' right to self-determination is respected and promoted by social workers, who support clients in identifying and clarifying their goals.
7. Except for compelling professional reasons, social workers should maintain the confidentiality of any information received during professional service.
8. Social services are a range of public services intended to provide support and assistance towards particular groups, which commonly include the disadvantaged. They may be provided by individuals, private and independent organizations or administered by a government agency.
9. Social justice is a political and philosophical theory which asserts that there are dimensions to the concept of justice beyond those embodied in the principles of civil or criminal law, economic supply and demand or traditional moral frameworks.
10. Every person is different, with different cultural and social values. Social workers are mindful of those differences, treating each person with dignity and respect and promoting their clients' capacity and opportunity to address their own needs and improve their personal situations.

Keywords: Values, ethics, social work, NASW

GLOSSARY

Competence: The ability to do something successfully or efficiently
Ethics: Moral principles that govern a person's behaviour or the conducting of an activity.
Integrity: The quality of being honest and having strong moral principles
Service: The action of helping or doing work for someone
Social justice: Justice in terms of the distribution of wealth, opportunities and privileges within a society
Social work: Work carried out by trained personnel with the aim of alleviating the conditions of those people in a community suffering from social deprivation.
Values: The regard that something is held to deserve the importance, worth or usefulness of something.

MULTIPLE CHOICE QUESTIONS

1. The NASW Delegate Assembly created the first version of the Code of Ethics in
   a. **October 1960**
   b. January 1952
   c. August 1947
   d. None of these

2. Social workers stand up for human rights and justice and give voice to unheard _____ populations.
   a. Privileged
   b. **Marginalized**
   c. Both
   d. None of these

3. In India, the _____ has not gained much recognition from the government and the society at large.
   a. Service
   b. **Social work profession**
   c. Both
   d. None of these

4. Ethics are the particular statements about _____ for a profession
   a. Manage
   b. Conduct
   c. **Both**
   d. None of these

5. The primary mission of the social work profession is to enhance human well-being and help to meet basic human needs of _____
   a. **Whoever is in need**
   b. Particular group
   c. Individual only
   d. None of these

6. Tata Institute of Social Sciences started in _____.
   a. **1936**
   b. 1948
   c. 1956
   d. None of these

7. When social workers are urged to provide some of their professional expertise without expecting a large monetary reward, it is referred to as _____
   a. **Service**
   b. Conduct
   c. Both
   d. None of these

8. When social workers treat each person in a caring and respectful fashion, being mindful of individual differences and cultural and ethnic diversity, it is referred to as _____
   a. **Dignity of the client**
   b. Service
   c. Conduct
   d. None of these

9. Code is based on _____ core values
   a. 8
   b. **6**
   c. 5
   d. None of these

10. The International Association of Schools of Social Work and the International Federation of Social Workers adopted the international definition of social work in
   a. **July 2001**
   b. October 1936
   c. Both
   d. None of these

REVIEW QUESTIONS

1. What are the six core values of social work profession?
2. Identify the purpose of social work ethics.
3. Elucidate the roles and responsibilities of social work profession.
4. Describe the conduct of social work.
5. Elaborate the role of social work in understanding human rights and justice.
6. What are the six codes of social work profession according to the NASW?
7. Describe the values of social work profession.
8. How do you describe the problems related to social work profession?

REFERENCES

Banks, S. (2012). *Ethics and values in social work*. Palgrave Macmillan.
Banks, S., & Gallagher, A. (2009). *Ethics in professional life*. Palgrave Macmillan.
Bayles, M. (1986). Professional power and self-regulation. *Business and Professional Ethics Journal*, 5(2), 26–46.
Greenwood, E. (1957). Attributes of a profession. *Social Work*, 2(3), 44–55.
Hall, R. H. (1968). Professionalization and bureaucratization. American *Sociological Review*, 33(1), 92–104.
Jamal, K., & Bowie, N. (1995). Theoretical considerations for a meaningful code of ethics. *Journal of Business Ethics*, 14(9), 703–714.
Kultgen, J. (1982). The ideological use of professional codes. *Business and Professional Ethics Journal*, 1(3), 53–69.
Lindeman, E. (1947). *Social work matures in a confused world*. State Conference on Social Workers.
NAAC. (2005). A manual for self-study of social work institutions. The National Assessment and Accreditation Council.
National Association of Social Workers (NASW). (2008). *NASW code of ethics*. The Author.

RECOMMENDED READINGS

IGNOU. (2020). *Code of ethics for social workers*. https://egyankosh.ac.in/bitstream/123456789/59008/1/BLOCK%201.pdf

INPSWA. (n.d.). *Welcome to India Network of Professional Social Workers' Associations*. http://inpswa.org/

Thomas, G. (2016). *Social work—The value based profession*. Rawat Publications.

Tulane University. (2021). *6 core social work values and ethics*. https://socialwork.tulane.edu/blog/social-work-values

University of Buffalo. (n.d.). *Social work core values and code of ethics*. http://socialwork.buffalo.edu/admissions/is-social-work-right-career-for-me/values-ethics.html

Wikipedia. (n.d.). *Professional Social Workers' Association*. https://en.wikipedia.org/wiki/Professional_Social_Workers%27_Association

SECTION D

Approaches to Social Work

Chapter 22 *Ideologies Background of Social Work*

Chapter 23 *Modern Indian Thinkers and Their Relevance in Social Work*

Chapter 24 *Radical Social Work*

Chapter 25 *Gandhian Social Work*

Chapter 26 *African Social Work*

22

Ideologies Background of Social Work

Saumya and Tushar Singh

LEARNING OBJECTIVES

- To understand the concept and meaning of an ideology
- To examine the historical origin and development of ideologies of humanism, socialism, liberalism, utilitarianism and feminism
- To describe the role of ideologies in informing social work practice

I suppose it is tempting, if the only tool you have is a hammer, to treat everything as if it were a nail.
—Abraham Maslow, in *The Psychology of Science: A Reconnaissance*

INTRODUCTION

Social work has traversed a long distance from its inception as mutual aid and charity to philanthropic actions of groups and individuals to an activity of liberating and empowering people. Today, it is internationally recognized in as many as 141 countries across the world as a discipline and a profession (International Federation of Social Workers [IFSW], n.d.). It is supported by an amalgam of various theories, values and perspectives inherent in a wide array of ideologies that also inform and influence social work practice approaches.

Social workers plan informed interventions supported by thoughts, beliefs, explanations and justifications rooted in ideologies. They apply a broad base of theoretical knowledge to explain human behaviour and the impact of the environment and the social structure on human beings. This chapter, on the ideological background of social work, thus explores the meaning, origin and development of different ideologies, and the key ideas contained in each ideology for social work practice.

IDEOLOGY: CONCEPT AND DEFINITIONS

Ideology is often remarked as a concept that eludes definition (McLellan, 1995). An ideology, at best, provides a 'lens' to see and explain the world. The term 'ideology' (Greek for 'science of ideas') was coined in the late 1790s during the French Revolution by French ideologue Claude Antoine Destutt de Tracy for what he called the 'science of ideas'. Destutt de Tracy, rejecting the use of the words 'metaphysics' and 'psychology', used 'ideology' because it was 'very sensible since it supposes nothing doubtful or unknown....' (Memoire sur la faculte de penser [Memory on the Faculty of Thinking], p. 323, as cited in Kennedy, 1979).[1]

The meaning that ideology as a term embodied, however, changed traits in no less than 50 years since its coining in 1796. Now, a variety of meanings exist; and though de Tracy meant ideology to be an unprejudiced, methodical term (Cranston, n.d.), it has had several connotations: emotive and extremist (Michael Oakeshott, Edward Shils, Albert Camus, Karl Popper and so on), positive (György Lukács and so on) and even critical (Karl Marx, Max Weber, Karl Mannheim, Antonio Gramsci and so on) ascribed to it.

A definition marking ideology as 'manifested' in the practices (Althusser, 2014[1995]) of its subjects (individuals or groups) paint a picture of the promiscuities that the term holds:

> Ideology does not exist in the 'world of ideas' conceived as a 'spiritual world'. Ideology exists in institutions and the practices specific to them. We are even tempted to say, more precisely: ideology exists in apparatuses and the practices specific to them.
>
> —Louis Althusser (2014[1995], p. 156)

Another definition by Patricia Marchak (1975), for social work educators and practitioners, helps in understanding the term 'ideology':

> Ideologies are screens through which we perceive the social world. Their elements are assumptions, beliefs, explanations, values and orientations. They are seldom taught explicitly and systematically. They are rather transmitted through example, conversation and casual observation.
>
> —Patricia Marchak (1975, p. 1 as cited in Carniol, 1984)

Thus, an ideology can be described as a broad set of notions that underlies humanitarian actions by an individual or a group of individuals, involved in social work practice.

HUMANISM

Humanism, variously described as a system of education, a mode of enquiry, a Western belief (Grudin, n.d.), a mode of thinking, a philosophy, a school of thought and an ideology is a perspective from which the world is viewed. It 'assigns to human beings a special position in the scheme of things' (Kolenda, 1999). All humanists present an idea of the 'ideal man' before humanity.

---

[1] For more info, see Destutt de Tracy (1796, pp. 283–328).

The American Humanist Association (n.d.) defines humanism as follows:

> Humanism is a progressive philosophy of life that, without theism or other supernatural beliefs, affirms our ability and responsibility to lead ethical lives of personal fulfilment that aspire to the greater good.

Humanism is usually variously understood under three frameworks: (a) as classicism: the scholastic re-examination of classical literature of the earlier times, irrespective of the when or where it happens; (b) as the body of subjects: the *humanities* and (c) as a rationalist, human-centred view of the world that 'does not affirm traditional views of theism or the supernatural' (Blankholm, 2017, p. 4).

HISTORICAL ORIGINS AND DEVELOPMENT

Renaissance humanism, or humanism, was used to depict (and study) intellectual scholarship and education in the early eras. However, it came to describe values, qualities, talents and limitations that made one human (in stark contrast to the omnipotent divine) in the early 19th century. The term has been derived from the word *humanist*, coined in the late 15th century 'to designate a teacher and student of the "humanities" or *Studia humanitatis*' (Kristeller, 1979, as cited in Kristeller, 2008, p. 113) to describe a group of unscientific subjects that included grammar, rhetoric, literature, history and moral philosophy (Kolenda, 1999). It omitted subjects from the liberal arts (namely, mathematics, astronomy, and so on), the fine arts, the performing arts, divinity and legal philosophy, among others (Kristeller, 1980, as cited in Kristeller, 2008).

The term *studia humanitatis* was based on Roman statesman and philosopher Marcus Cicero's (circa 106 BC–43 BC) idea of *humanitas* contained 'the ideals of both humanism and humanitarianism and ennobled the *Lebensanschauung* [literally, *view of life*] of those...who understood its principles and acted according to them' (Nybakken, 1939, p. 396).

Renaissance humanism, with its humanists—philosophers, educationists, architects and so on—reformed education via poetry, rhetoric and so on first in Italy and then in the rest of Europe (Kristeller, 2008). Humanism found a cause in philology (the study of literature and pertinent disciplines, especially the works of Aristotle and several others), to perceive reality.

Did You Know?

The following definition of secular humanism appeared as a footnote on page 29 in Leon Pfeffer's 1958 book *Creeds and Competition*: 'The term "secular humanism" is used in this book not to mean a consciously nontheistic movement, but merely the influence of those unaffiliated with organized religion and concerned with human values' (Pfeffer, 1987, p. 495).

Secular humanism is a philosophy that attempts to equalize humans and exclude the existence of any concept of God or Gods. As such, primacy is given to the individual, who is a secular member of an enlightened society. The belief of secular humanism is rooted in the process of education, which is used to impart atheism or agnosticism and to believe in science above all. Its belief is displayed in Charles Darwin's theory of evolution.

HUMANISM AND SOCIAL WORK PRACTICE

Humanism 'believes in the capacity of conscious human beings to reason, make choices and act freely, uninfluenced by higher beings such as gods and religion or superstition' (Payne, 2014, p. 275). Social work is implicitly assumed as being humanistically oriented. There are two reasons behind this: first, a shift in the provision of welfare of individuals from the church to the secular state; second, the practice of social work affords an assumption of high estimate to research and rationality of individuals, a central idea of humanism (Payne, 2014).

Rejecting the idea of micromanaging social work interventions, the humanistic technique believes in the capacity of human beings to transcend the given and look beyond the influences to create their destinies. It 'seek[s] to re-establish the focus of social work as empowering and liberating rather than problem-solving in character' (Payne, 2014, p. 273).

SOCIALISM

Socialism is an ideology and a social and economic system that, as an alternative to capitalism, calls for the collective ownership of the means of production and the natural resources. It opposes the free market economy of capitalism and believes that co-ownership of the resources and means of production will lead to a just society with economic equality.

HISTORICAL ORIGIN AND DEVELOPMENT

The term 'socialist' derives from Latin *sociare* and means to combine or to share. Its earliest usage was in an 1827 issue of the *Cooperative Magazine* in the United Kingdom (Heywood, 2017). The origins of socialism date back to the times of ancient Greek, when Plato depicted an ideal society in his dialogue, *Republic*, circa 360 BC (History, 2019). Men and women in this utopian society collectively used goods and also shared partners and offspring (Ball & Dagger, n.d.). More recent background of the ideology relates to Thomas More (1478–1535), Robert Owen (1771–1858) and Claude Henri de Saint-Simon (1760–1825).

The emergence of the socialist ideology was the result of the onslaughts of capitalism brought by the Industrial Revolution, which increased the inequality among the bourgeois and the proletariats. According to socialism, individuals did not live in isolation but as members of cooperative bodies. Further, because people controlled their labour and were the ones manufacturing the products, they were eligible to at least a share of the means of production used to manufacture those products.

Early socialism was a witness of the severe and inhuman conditions and thus often resorted to *utopianism*. For example, early socialists such as Robert Owen and Henri de Saint-Simon offered their models of collective societies, which worked on cooperation rather than competition (Ball & Dagger, n.d.). The early socialists, having witnessed the inhuman onslaughts of the Industrial Revolution on the working class, often resorted to a radical and sweeping stance to bring change to the capitalist society. The modern socialists, however, witnessed improved conditions of the working class as well as their participation in politics. This divide between the early and modern socialists grew wide open after the First World War. The former group of socialists adopted the term 'communism' for their revolutionary ideas for the reform of society. The latter group, with their reformist (rather than revolutionary) ideas, adopted either 'socialism' or 'social democracy' to describe their concepts (Heywood, 2017).

SOCIALISM AND SOCIAL WORK PRACTICE

Ideas informing social work practice under socialism form an eclectic mix and can be covered under critical and radical social work practice with Marxism as their base. Critical and radical perspectives to social work practice emphasize *social change* rather than problem-solving. Critical and radical social work look critically at the present social structure and the way it functions. Radical social work takes a progressive view of the Marxist view of social work (Rojek, 1986, as cited in Payne, 1991), asserting that social work, acting as a change agent, connects the exploiting bourgeois society to the exploited proletariats, encourages praxis and dialectics and conscientizes the proletariats to achieve a revolution leading to social change, while simultaneously recognizing that the status quo cannot be taken for granted (Payne, 1991).

Critical practice also stresses the concept of *cultural hegemony*, popularized by radical Marxist scholar Antonio Gramsci (1891–1937). According to Gramsci, the ideology of any society can be described by an analysis of the ideology of those who control it. It is those in power who exert indirect influence and uphold dominance over others by gaining social consent of individuals for their (the elites') ideas of society. Critical social work practitioners argue that authority is maintained by applying social control *indirectly* through the social institutions that leverage ideas, beliefs, practices and so on in favour of the ruling elite. As such, it casts a shadow of doubt over social work, asserting that it furthers social control and is a vital tool for its exertion; ergo, critical social workers should challenge social control by social workers, especially those working for the government and its agencies (Payne, 2014).

Critical and radical social work practice agrees to the fact that the root cause of all troubles is the society and, thus, they strive to gain autonomy for the individuals, assuming they gain an insight into what it is that leads to their sustained oppression. Such practice is constantly transformed with the transformation of the societal structure.

LIBERALISM

Liberalism is one of the major sociopolitical ideologies, pioneered by celebrated authors such as John Locke (1632–1704), John Stuart Mill (1808–1873) and John Rawls (1921–2002). The central theme of the liberal ideology is a commitment to the people as individual units and the conception of an egalitarian society where people, as individual units, gratify their wants and desires (Heywood, 2017). The principles usually associated with liberalism are those manifested in an egalitarian society, usually, personal autonomy, equality of individuals and their rights and opportunities, freedom of conscience and religion, democracy, human reason, initiative and rationality, capitalistic economics, separation between the state and religion, and tolerance.

HISTORICAL ORIGINS AND DEVELOPMENT

The roots of the liberal doctrine (classical liberalism) date to the 13th, 14th and 15th centuries, the latter being the Renaissance era, when it grew noticeably in scope, but under the moniker of an earlier cultural movement, namely humanism (Borghini, 2018). Two significant years for the liberal doctrine were 1688 and 1689, when the people of the middle class overthrew aristocracy and the Catholic Monarch James II in the *Glorious Revolution* of 1688, making way for constitutional and, subsequently, representative governance. And it was in 1689 when John Locke published *An Essay Concerning Human Understanding*, in which he talked of philosophy, education and the theory of knowledge and defended individual autonomy and liberty. Locke reasoned that ideas were not innate but born out of experiences attained only through sensation and perception (Borghini, 2018; Dagger et al., n.d.).

In the 19th century, the liberals refined their ideology to focus more intensely on the novel social and economic conditions brought by the Industrial Revolution. Liberalism advocated an industrialized *laissez-faire* economy, free from government interventions and in which businesses were to pursue profits and states were to be encouraged to trade freely among themselves (Heywood, 2017). The forces of supply and demand would keep the economy in check. It developed in the United Kingdom in the 18th century and spread throughout Europe and into the North American continent.

Liberalism as an ideological force changed stance with passing time and went from a radical to a conservative nature. Where classical liberalism stood for free markets, minimal government interference (i.e., only in matters of security), individual autonomy and initiative, modern liberalism supported a more welfarist approach to society. It backed the intervention of the state in the areas of education, healthcare, the welfare of the poor and in other matters of public and private life (Ball et al., n.d.).

LIBERALISM AND SOCIAL WORK PRACTICE

Social work practice informed by liberal ideas relates primarily to the achievement of human rights through challenging injustices, oppression and empowerment practice for the reason that while 'rights' (such as civil rights of citizens) are possessed under a status, human rights are *absolute* and *universal*, possessed by virtue of being born a human.

Along with the fundamental freedoms (provided by Articles 19, 25 and 26–28 of the Constitution of India), human rights allow individuals to develop qualities and intelligence, nurture talents and exercise liberty not just by removing external restrictions (*negative* liberty) but also by allowing individuals to act in a manner of their choosing (*positive* liberty).

The human rights have their roots in the pursuit for economic, political and social rights (Desai, 2002[2015]) and gained ascendancy after the Second World War, when human rights as a term was first used (Morsink, 1999, as cited in Reichert, 2003) and the Universal Declaration of Human Rights (United Nations, n.d.) was adopted by the UN General Assembly in December 1948.

To gain an understanding of how human rights translate into social work practice, practitioners need to acquire an 'understanding of government agencies, clients, and social

> **Box 22.1** **A Summarized Structure of The Universal Declaration of Human Rights**

	Articles 1–15 are *negative* rights. Articles 16–30 are *positive* rights.
Articles 1–3	Establish basic concepts of life, liberty, dignity, security and non-discrimination
Articles 4–5	Establish rights against servitude and torture
Articles 6–12	Establish legal recourse in case of breach of a fundamental right(s)
Articles 13–17	Establish individual rights towards the state
Articles 18–21	Establish fundamental freedoms/liberties such as those of religion, thought and expression
Articles 22–27	Establish the economic, social and cultural rights such as those of just and fair wages and free and compulsory education
Articles 28–30	Establish the practice and manner in which the rights are to be realized

work concepts' (Reichert, 2003, p. 224), besides the scope of the concept itself, that is, not just the Universal Declaration but also the International Covenant on civil, political, economic, social and cultural rights.

It is worth mentioning that both Mahatma Gandhi and Paulo Freire fought against the injustices meted out through 'paralysis of despair' and 'culture of silence' over the years, respectively (Narayan, 2000, p. 194). Broadly understood, the paralysis of despair refers to a system of education that focuses on rote learning, leaving little by means of critical thinking and curiosity and thereby rendering those useless receiving the education (Dehury, 2008), while a culture of silence can be understood as the 'indoctrination' of oppression through education, making one unable to think for themselves and thereby perpetuating oppression (Phnuyal, 1998).

In the same vein, empowerment through practice is gained through examining the treatment of individuals in society and their ability to access resources. The opportunity to participate in decision-making to voice opinions and the entitlement to rights are tools to ensure empowerment.

UTILITARIANISM

English philosopher and social reformer Jeremy Bentham (1748–1832) in *An Introduction to the Principles of Morals and Legislation* (1789) put forward the idea of utilitarianism. It is an abstract ideology advocating the maxim of the greatest good of most people which also establishes the basis for correct action in a situation (Driver, 2014).

HISTORICAL ORIGINS AND DEVELOPMENT

Although Bentham was the first to give a systematic account of the idea of hedonistic utility (balancing the intrinsic values of pleasure and pain), he was by no means the first. Bentham attributed his theory to a number of individuals including Joseph Priestley (1733–1804), Claude-Adrien Helvétius (1715–1771), Cesare Beccaria (1738–1794) and David Hume (1711–1776). The core ingredient of utilitarianism, the hedonistic theory of the value of life, appeared first in the school of stoicism (circa 3rd century BC).

More recently, Richard Cumberland (1631–1718) and John Gay (1699–1745) believed in promoting human happiness as a task assigned by God (Driver, 2014). Francis Hutcheson (1694–1746) proposed an arithmetical account for calculating the consequences of best possible action in any given situation. David Hume studied epistemology to conclude that there could be no knowledge beyond human perception. John Stuart Mill (1806–1873) was a follower of Jeremy Bentham. His work, *Utilitarianism* (1861), was an elegant defence of utilitarianism, though he differed with Bentham and argued that pleasure differed not only in quantity but also in quality, pleasures derived from complex and intellectual activities were greater than simple-minded, basal pleasures.

UTILITARIANISM AND SOCIAL WORK PRACTICE

Utilitarianism being a *consequentialist* theory informs social work ethics and the ideas of social justice. It means the resulting (relevant) consequences of an act determine whether an action is good or bad. The utilitarian conception of the theory of social justice holds actions accountable based on whether they can provide the greatest good of the greatest number of individuals, that is, the maximum possible well-being. It holds that, in some cases, the equity or individual well-being can be sacrificed in the interest of the common good (Van Soest, 1994). A society, under classical utilitarianism, can be called fair and non-partisan when, after compensating for everything, it achieves the greatest net remainder of welfare.

Different countries follow a different code of ethics for social workers working within their boundaries. Accordingly, the National Association of Professional Social Workers in India [NAPSWI] has provided a list of principles from which emanate all the ethics for social work professionals in India. Covered under NAPSWI's Code of Ethics for Professional Social Workers in India, they are 'human rights and human dignity; social justice; integrity and belongingness; sustainability; services; and human relations' (National Association for Professional Social Workers in India, 2015, pp. 12–15).

However, this often leads to questions about the objectivity of said ethical principles for social workers are often involved in situations where ethical decisions are difficult to make and where one is marked either an *absolutist* or a *relativist* (Reamer, 2019). In such situations, premeditated ideas cannot decide what is only 'assumed' to be right. It can be resolved only through 'a process of moral reasoning, where existing knowledge, theory, skills, values, and ethical guidelines are brought together to inform the decision-making process' (Gray & Gibbons, 2007, p. 224).

FEMINISM

Feminism has variously been described as an elaborate set of theories, moral philosophies, agendas, movements and actions to achieve personal, social, economic and political equity and equality for women (Dominelli, 2002; Heywood, 2017) while largely advocating the equality of sexes and the end of sexism (Burkett & Brunell, n.d.; McAfee, 2018). Feminism seeks to neutralize the society of patriarchal ascendency and the practices that put women at a disadvantage to men, and thus ameliorate the status of women through organized efforts.

HISTORICAL ORIGINS AND DEVELOPMENT

The terms 'feminist' and 'feminism' are used contemporarily to promote individuals and ideologies championing the liberty and autonomy of women. The usage of the term is primarily attributed to Charles Fourier (1772–1837), sometime during the 1830s. The term was popularized by suffragist Hubertine Auclert (1848–1914), who formally established the world's first *Société le suffrage des femmes* [Women's Suffrage Society] in 1882 (Ménard, 2010). The term *féministe* [feminist], though, appeared first in Alexandre Dumas' play from 1872 *L'homme-femme* [The man-woman] (Offen, 1988, p. 47).

> **Did You Know?**
>
> Mary Wollstonecraft (1759–1797), an English author, social theorist, philosopher and advocate of women's rights, holds an important place in the feminist ideology. Drawn into politics by the French Revolution, her treatise, *A Vindication of the Rights of Woman: With Strictures on Political and Moral Subjects* (1792), was a seminal work in feminist history. It blamed the lack of education for the pitiful condition of adult women and called for men and women to be educated to be provided with work and for their participation in politics on an equal footing. In the same work, she also opposed the notions of subjectivity and trivialization of women (that women exist only to quell men's desire; and that they are best fit for household jobs).

First-wave feminism was characterized by the demands for abolitionism, education, suffrage, equality, property, equal pay and other political and legal rights for women. Contrary to popular belief, the first wave was not made up of the first feminists but the women-led political movements demanding economic and political rights for women (Ménard, 2010). Suffrage was believed to lead the way to the departure of sexual discrimination against women. The first wave of feminism slowed down during the period of the Great Depression in the 1930s.

Simone de Beauvoir's (1908–1986) *Le deuxième sexe* [The Second Sex] (1949) and Betty Friedan's (1921–2006) *The Feminine Mystique* (1963) made way for the appearance of a *second wave* of feminism (term devised by Martha Lear) in the mid-1950s–early-1960s USA. The second wave tried to bring women into the centre from the margins of life with their reproductive rights and employment being the key concerns. It tried to depict women's social inequality, frustrations, sexual exploitation and patriarchal oppression (Turner & Maschi, 2014). The second wave led women to win key political and legal rights for themselves, such as the right to equality in pay, no discrimination in employment opportunities and the right to equality in education, among others.

The *third wave* of feminism began in the early 1990s. Rebecca Walker is credited with coining the term in a 1992 essay. This wave was everything the second wave was not and stressed on 'socially structured forms of bias on women's lives' (Kinser, 2004, as cited in Ménard, 2010, p. 121). It involved fighting against harassment at the workplace, discrimination based on race, colour, origin, sexuality and sexual preferences and so on and fighting for positions of power in the government.

FEMINISM AND SOCIAL WORK PRACTICE

Dominelli (1998, p. 918) states that feminist social work practice 'takes women as its starting point for intervention and advocates social changes linked to advancing women's welfare'. It is, therefore, the practice of social work intervention and education requiring acquaintance with the personal, social, economic and political aspects of women's thoughts, theories, and social and political movements. It is practised on both the micro- and macro-levels of society, and requires, among other things, the recognition of women's needs, meeting said needs through qualified services, and, lastly, contesting social assumptions about women's inequality (Dominelli, 1998).

In many societies where women make the majority of social work service providers as well as service users (Hyde, 2013; Payne, 2014), feminist social work practice provides the necessary *gendered viewpoint* to view the society from the women's perspective: to understand how relationships, roles and responsibilities are shaped by the gender dynamics. It also leads to the realization of how differences arise based on women's location in the social hierarchy.

Another important idea of practice in feminist social work is that of *consciousness-raising*, which began during the 1960s as a chief organizing tool of groups championing women's rights. *Reflexivity* is a related theme, which has resulted in a consistent analysis of changing realities of women's needs and situations and also changes how workers practice interventions (White, 2006). *Ending patriarchal dominance* is another idea central to feminist social work practice. Patriarchal domination of women exists beyond power and entitlement of privilege and extends to sexual and reproductive rights (O'Rand, 1992, as cited in Desai, 2015[2002]; Napikoski, 2020).

Feminist social work also works through *democratic* ideals, which involves a *collective style of work* such as collective decision-making and problem-solving. Collective action also works as a source of authority and autonomy (Dominelli, 2002) devoted to achieving an egalitarian society.

SUMMARY

This chapter deals with the ideological background of social work. An ideology can be understood through various explanations ascribed to it, which vary from 'a meaning-making process' to 'illusion' and 'identity thinking'. But it is best understood as a set of beliefs that call for a variety of actions.

Details on five ideologies, namely humanism, socialism, liberalism, utilitarianism and feminism, and how they inform several elements of various social work practice methods—humanistic and existentialist; radical and critical; anti-oppressive; empowerment and human rights; ethics and social justice and feminist—have been provided in a lucid and precise manner.

TOP 10 TAKEAWAYS/MAIN POINTS

1. The term 'ideology' is Greek for 'science of ideas' and was coined in the late 1790s by French ideologue Claude Antoine Destutt de Tracy.
2. An ideology is an object-oriented view of the world held by an individual or a group of individuals.
3. An ideology can either be positive, negative or neutral in its outlook.
4. Humanism and other related ideas centred around it focus on developing the personality of individuals, both in its totality and relative to those of the others.
5. Ideas informing social work practice under socialism form an eclectic mix and can be covered under critical and radical social work practice with Marxism as their base.
6. Social work practice informed by ideals of liberalism relates primarily to the achievement of human rights through challenging oppression and empowerment practice.
7. Utilitarianism as theory informs social work ethics and the idea of social justice.
8. Concerning the espousal of social justice, social work practitioners are expected to stand against the prejudicial practice, subjugation, to respect cultural diversity and to provide access to equitable resources, while building camaraderie.
9. Feminist practice in social work is the practice of social work intervention and education well-versed in the personal, social, economic and political aspects of the range of women's thoughts, theories, and social and political movements.
10. Feminist social work is practised on both micro- and macro-levels of society and provides a gendered viewpoint of the society: to understand how relationships, roles and responsibilities are shaped by gender dynamics rather than rational, logical provisions.

Keywords: Ideology, social work, humanism, socialism, liberalism, utilitarianism

GLOSSARY

Belief: A psychological predisposition because of which a person acts in a certain specified manner. It points to how a person conducts oneself because of the held view.

Discourse: A conversation or methodical arrangement of sentences forming part of a dialogue. It might assume various genres ranging from academic to journalistic.

Social work:

Social work is a practice-based profession and an academic discipline that promotes social change and development, social cohesion, and the empowerment and liberation of people. Principles of social justice, human rights, collective responsibility and respect for diversities are central to social work. Underpinned by theories of social work, social sciences, humanities and indigenous knowledge, social work engages people and structures to address life challenges and enhance wellbeing. The above definition may be amplified at national and/or regional levels. (International Federation of Social Workers, n.d.).

Weltanschauung: It is German for *world view* and represents 'a perspective and interpretation of the universe and its events held in a sustained way by an individual or by a group' (Ashmore, 1966, p. 215).

MULTIPLE CHOICE QUESTIONS

1. The term 'ideology' was coined by
   a. György Lukács
   b. Karl Mannheim
   c. Étienne Bonnot de Condillac
   d. **Claude Antoine Destutt de Tracy**

2. What best represents an ideology?
   a. **A set of beliefs**
   b. A system of false ideas
   c. An illusion
   d. Identity thinking

3. *Weltanschauung* refers to
   a. A part of a larger whole
   b. A set of beliefs
   c. Cognition
   d. **A view of the world**

4. Which among the following options would not be included in *studia humanitatis*?
   a. **Mathematics and astronomy**
   b. Rhetoric
   c. Literature
   d. Moral philosophy

5. Important ideas in feminist social work do not include
   a. Consciousness-raising
   b. **Emotionality**
   c. Reflexivity
   d. Democracy

6. Who among the following is not a popular utilitarian philosopher?
   a. Jeremy Bentham
   b. **Giovanni Pico della Mirandola**
   c. David Hume
   d. Francis Hutcheson

7. Which book among the following has been written by Simone de Beauvoir?
   a. *The Feminine Mystique*
   b. ***The Second Sex***
   c. *A Vindication of the Rights of Woman*
   d. *The Color Purple*

8. Who among the following is not counted as a socialist?
   a. Robert Owen
   b. Claude Henri de Saint-Simon
   c. Thomas More
   d. **John Rawls**

9. Critical and radical social work practices would relate to which of the following the ideologies?
   a. Humanism
   b. **Socialism**
   c. Liberalism
   d. Feminism

10. The maxim 'greatest good of the greatest number' is associated with which of the following ideologies?
    a. Humanism
    b. Socialism
    c. **Utilitarianism**
    d. Feminism

REVIEW QUESTIONS

1. Define ideology.
2. Why is critical social work practice linked to socialism?
3. How does cultural hegemony work in maintaining social control under socialism?
4. Describe the role of feminism in achieving a distinction between the concepts of sex and gender.

REFERENCES

Althusser, L. (2014[1995]). *On the reproduction of capitalism: Ideology and ideological state apparatuses* (translated by G. M. Goshgarian). Verso.
American Humanist Association. (n.d.). *Definition of humanism.* https://americanhumanist.org/what-is-humanism/definition-of-humanism/
Ashmore, J. (1966). Three aspects of weltanschauung. *The Sociological Quarterly, 7*(2), 215–228.
Ball, T., & Dagger, R. (n.d.). *Socialism.* Encyclopaedia Britannica. https://www.britannica.com/topic/socialism
Ball, T., Dagger, R., Girvetz, H. K., & Minogue, K. (n.d.). *Liberalism.* Encyclopaedia Britannica. https://www.britannica.com/topic/liberalism
Blankholm, J. (2017). Secularism, humanism, and secular humanism: Terms and institutions. In P. Zuckerman & J. R. Shook (Eds.), *The Oxford handbook of secularism.* Oxford University Press. http://dx.doi.org/10.1093/oxfordhb/9780199988457.013.42
Borghini, A. (2018). *What is liberalism in politics?* ThoughtCo. https://www.thoughtco.com/liberalism-2670740
Burkett, E., & Brunell, L. (n.d.). *Feminism.* Encyclopaedia Britannica. https://www.britannica.com/topic/feminism
Carniol, B. (1984). Clash of ideologies in social work education. *Canadian Social Work Review, 2,* 184–199.
Cranston, M. (n.d.). *Ideology.* Encyclopaedia Britannica. https://www.britannica.com/topic/ideology-society
Dehury, D. (2008). Mahatma Gandhi's contribution to education. *Orissa Review,* 1–5.
Desai, M. (2015[2002]). *Ideologies and social work: Historical and contemporary analyses.* Rawat Publications.
Destutt de Tracy, A. (1796). Memoire sur la faculte de penser [Memory on the Faculty of Thinking]. *Mémoires of the National Institute of Sciences and Arts, 1.*
Dominelli, L. (1998). Feminist social work: An expression of universal human rights. *Indian Journal of Social Work, 59*(4), 917–929.

Dominelli, L. (2002). *Feminist social work theory and practice*. Palgrave Macmillan.
Driver, J. (2014). The history of utilitarianism. In Edward N. Zalta (Ed.), *The Stanford encyclopedia of philosophy* (Winter 2014 ed.). Stanford University. https://plato.stanford.edu/archives/win2014/entries/utilitarianism-history/
Gray, M., & Gibbons, J. (2007). There are no answers, only choices: Teaching ethical decision making in social work. *Australian Social Work, 60*(2), 222–238. http://dx.doi.org/10.1080/03124070701323840
Grudin, R. (n.d.). *Humanism*. Encyclopaedia Britannica. https://www.britannica.com/topic/humanism
Heywood, A. (2017). *Political ideologies: An introduction* (6th ed.). Palgrave Macmillan.
History. (2019). *Socialism*. https://www.history.com/topics/industrial-revolution/socialism
Hyde, C. (2013). Feminist social work practice. *Encyclopaedia of Social Work*. https://doi.org/10.1093/acrefore/9780199975839.013.151
International Federation of Social Workers. (n.d.). *What we do*. https://www.ifsw.org/about-ifsw/what-we-do/
Kennedy, E. (1979). 'Ideology' from Destutt de Tracy to Marx. *Journal of the History of Ideas, 40*(3), 353–368. https://doi.org/10.2307/2709242
Kolenda, K. (1999). Humanism. In R. Audi (Ed.), *The Cambridge dictionary of philosophy* (2nd ed., pp. 396–397). Cambridge University Press.
Kristeller, P. O. (2008). Humanism. In C. B. Schmitt (Ed.), *The Cambridge history of Renaissance philosophy* (pp. 111–137). Cambridge University Press.
McAfee, N. (2018). Feminist philosophy. In E. N. Zalta (Ed.), *The Stanford encyclopedia of philosophy* (Fall 2018 ed.). Stanford University. https://plato.stanford.edu/archives/fall2018/entries/feminist-philosophy/
McLellan, D. (1995). *Ideology* (2nd ed.). Open University Press.
Ménard, K. S. (2010). Feminism. In W. A. Darity Jr. (Ed.), *International encyclopedia of the social sciences* (2nd ed., Vol. 3, pp. 119–122). Macmillan.
Napikoski, L. (2020). *Patriarchal society according to feminism*. ThoughtCo. https://www.thoughtco.com/patriarchal-society-feminism-definition-3528978
Narayan, L. (2000). Freire and Gandhi: Their relevance for social work education. *International Social Work, 43*(2), 193–204. https://doi.org/10.1177/002087280004300205
National Association for Professional Social Workers in India. (2015). *NAPSWI's code of ethics for professional social workers in India*. https://www.napswi.org/pdf/NAPSWI_Code_of_Ethics).pdf
Nybakken, O. E. (1939). Humanitas romana. *Transactions and Proceedings of the American Philological Association, 70*, 396–413. https://doi.org/10.2307/283098
Offen, K. (1988). On the French origin of the words feminism and feminist. *Feminist Issues, 8*(2), 45–51. https://doi.org/10.1007/BF02685596
Payne, M. (1991). Radical and Marxist approaches. In *Modern social work theory* (pp. 201–223). Palgrave Macmillan. https://doi.org/10.1007/978-1-349-21161-6_10
Payne, M. (2014). *Modern social work theory* (4th ed.). Palgrave Macmillan.
Pfeffer, L. (1987). The 'religion' of secular humanism. *Journal of Church and State, 29*(3), 495–507. https://doi.org/10.1093/jcs/29.3.495
Phnuyal, B. (1998). Commemoration of Paulo Freire. *Participatory Learning and Action Notes, 32*, 120–123.
Reamer, F. G. (2019). Ethical theories and social work practice. In S. M. Marson & R. E. McKinney (Eds.), *The Routledge handbook of social work ethics and values*. Routledge. https://www.routledgehandbooks.com/doi/10.4324/9780429438813-3
Reichert, E. (2003). Applying human rights to the social work profession. In *Social work and human rights: A foundation for policy and practice* (2nd ed., pp. 224–248). Columbia University Press. https://www.jstor.org/stable/10.7312/reic14992

Turner, S. G., & Maschi, T. M. (2014). Feminist and empowerment theory and social work practice. *Journal of Social Work Practice*, *29*(2), 151–162. https://doi.org/10.1080/02650533.2014.941282

United Nations. (n.d.). *The Universal Declaration of Human Rights*. https://www.un.org/en/universal-declaration-human-rights/

Van Soest, D. (1994). Strange bedfellows: A call for reordering national priorities from three social justice perspectives. *Social Work*, *39*(6), 710–717.

White, V. (2006). *The state of feminist social work*. Routledge.

RECOMMENDED READING

Adams, R., Dominelli, L., & Payne, M. (Eds.). (2009). *Social work: Themes, issues and critical debates* (3rd ed.). Red Globe Press.

23

Modern Indian Thinkers and Their Relevance in Social Work

Chittaranjan Subudhi and J. Raja Meenakshi

> **LEARNING OBJECTIVES**
> - To acquire knowledge about the social transformation made by modern Indian thinkers
> - To understand the ideas of modern Indian thinkers
> - To understand the relevance between the modern thinkers and the social work profession

A person's true beauty is honor and knowledge.

—Periyar E. V. Ramasamy

INTRODUCTION

India has a long history of intellectual discourse and has a distinct identity due to its social, cultural and historical variation in the globe. Despite its culture, the country is struggling with caste hierarchy, inequality and poverty, which are major hindrances in the process of development of the nation. Many eminent personalities have made an enormous contribution from time to time for social development. The chapter is an attempt to comprehend the four modern Indian thinkers, specifically Babasaheb Ambedkar, Jyotirao Phule, Rabindranath Tagore and Periyar E. V. Ramasamy, and their contribution to the eradication of the social evil practices and constructive upliftment of the society. It describes their contribution to different areas for the sociocultural development of the country. B. R. Ambedkar is the father of the Indian Constitution and fought for the Dalit upliftment in the country. Jyotirao Phule was a social reformer in Maharashtra who emphasized status and rights of women in society and fought against unfair discrimination due to the caste system in the Hindu religion. Tagore was a great thinker, philosopher and educationist who believes in every individual's freedom. Periyar was the founder of the Dravidian movement and associated with several social reforms like eradication of the caste system, supported widow remarriage and women's rights which still have their echoes in the political economy of Tamil Nadu.

BHIMRAO RAMJI AMBEDKAR (14 APRIL 1891–6 DECEMBER 1956)

Dr Bhimrao Ramji Ambedkar (popularly known as Babasaheb Ambedkar) had given a strong effort to the removal of caste alienation and untouchability in the country and he is the architect of the Indian Constitution. He fought for the upliftment of the untouchables until his very last breath. He had a strong belief that the progress of the nation depends upon the progress of the depressed class. He stood as a pillar for the untouchables to provide them justice, liberty and equality. He was the first law minister of independent India and was the chairman of the Drafting Committee of the Indian Constitution.

PERSONAL HISTORY

Dr Bhimrao was born on 14 April 1891 in Mhow Cantt in Madhya Pradesh. He was the 14th child to his parents (Ramji Maloji Sakpal and Bhimabai). From birth, he was a victim of caste discrimination as they belonged to the Hindu Mahar caste. But this caste barrier could not stop him to achieve his dream. He studied higher education in various countries such as Britain, Germany and the USA and made his career in legal practice and teaching.

STEPS TOWARDS THE REMOVAL OF THE UNTOUCHABILITY

The origin of the fourfold caste system in India has a long history that is practised even today. Ambedkar faced the evil practices of untouchability throughout his life right from his schooling days and it continued when he worked as a professor in Sydenham College of Commerce and Economics in Bombay. In 1923, he started Bahishkrit Hitakarini Sabha (Outcaste Welfare Association) and, through this association, he took many steps to uplift the social and economic condition of untouchables. In 1927, through *Mahad Satyagraha*, he fetched water from the public tank with all his supporters. As a mark of opposing untouchability, he burnt the copies of *Manusmriti* publicly as it did not support social equality. After that, he started a movement to enter the Hindu temples that were a revolutionary movement for providing human rights and social justice to the oppressed section of the society. He advised five principles (Pancha Sutras) to all Dalits for their upliftment in the society, that is, self-improvement, self-progress, self-dependence, self-respect and self-confidence. He strongly believed that education could bring positive changes in the life of lower caste people.

SEPARATE ELECTORATE FOR UNTOUCHABLES

Dr Ambedkar realized that to get elementary human rights and status in the existing society, oppressed class people should come forward and participate in the electoral process. So he thought for a separate electorate and reservation in political elections. When he had been invited to testify before the Southborough Committee (which prepared the Government of India Act, 1919), he argued for creating separate electorates and reservations for the depressed class and other religious communities. In 1928, when the Simon Commission visited India, he raised the same issue of separate electorate for lower caste people. The long demanding issue was resolved on 24 September 1932 in *Poona Pact*. Special concession like reservation in the legislative assembly and government jobs was approved. Dr Ambedkar formed a separate political party in 1936 named 'Independent Labour Party'.

INDIAN CONSTITUTION AND AMBEDKAR

Ambedkar was the Chairman of the Constitution Drafting Committee, and his constitutional draft is referred to as the first and foremost social document since most of its portion is aimed at social revolution and established path to achieve constructive social change. The Constitution gave protection for every individual citizen of India, and it has included the abolition of untouchability, all forms of discrimination and freedom of religion. Ambedkar introduced the reservation system in government jobs and education for the Schedule Caste, Schedule Tribes and Other Backward Class people. Article 32 framed by Ambedkar is called the heart and soul of the Indian Constitution as it provides the right to constitutional remedies. With Article 32, any individual can approach the Supreme Court on violation of their fundamental rights.

After going through the meticulous life history of Dr Ambedkar, the author can say that Ambedkar was the living God for all the depressed class and untouchable people in India. He tried and applied all kinds of strategies to provide justice to the untouchables and struggled for the eradication of the caste system. Dr Ambedkar spent his whole life for the upliftment of untouchable people. He can be called the 'saviour of the untouchables' in India. Nehru described Ambedkar as a 'symbol of the great revolt against all the oppressive features of Hindu society'. On 14 October, he adopted Buddhism with many of his followers, and on 6 December 1956, he took his last breath. Later in 1990, he was honoured with *Bharat Ratna*, India's highest civilian award for his remarkable contribution towards the development of the Indian society.

Did You Know?

Important publications by Dr Ambedkar

- *Annihilation of Caste* (1936)
- *Riddles in Hinduism* (2008)
- *The Buddha and His Dhamma* (1957)
- *Castes in India: Their Mechanism, Genesis, and Development* (1916)
- *Who Were the Shudras?* (1948)

JYOTIRAO PHULE (11 APRIL 1827–28 NOVEMBER 1890)

Jyotirao Phule also is known as Mahatma Phule or Jyotiba Phule. He was a unique social reformer in the state of Maharashtra in the 19th century. During that period, many reformers focused to bring reformation in social institutions such as family and marriage, whereas Phule emphasized status and rights of women in the society and worked against the unfair discrimination in the caste system in the Hindu religion. He was a pioneer and the first person in modern India who talked about women's education and caste discrimination (Begari, 2010). He believed that the emancipation of women and lower caste people was the only solution to bring social development and to eliminate the existing social evil practices. He was greatly influenced by the book *The Rights of Man* by Thomas Paine and also philosophically inspired by Lord Buddha and Kabir.

PERSONAL HISTORY

He was born on 11 April 1827 at the Satara district of Maharashtra. He belonged to the agricultural (Mali) caste, traditionally occupied as gardeners, and considered to be one of the Shudra varnas in the caste system of Hinduism.

FEMINISM AND WOMEN EMPOWERMENT

His first and foremost work focused on women's education. He strongly believed that education is the foremost weapon that sensitizes the people about their rights and creates self-empowerment among them. To achieve this idea, he opened a school for girls in 1848. His wife Savitribai Phule supported him to run this school as a teacher. Later in 1851, he opened a bigger school for the girls, and everyone was allowed to pursue their education without any discrimination. He always opposed child marriage and was a supporter of widow remarriage. He opened a home for the distressed poor and exploited women, and enhanced their well-being.

EFFORTS TOWARDS THE ELIMINATION OF CASTE DISCRIMINATION

He was strong combat against the hierarchical caste system and the practice of untouchability. He was the person who referred to the untouchables as Dalits. Jyotiba strongly opposed the Brahmins and other upper caste calling them hypocrites. He was a firm believer in gender equality. For the upliftment of the lower caste people, he established Satyashodhak Samaj (Society of Truth Seekers) on 24 September 1873. The main objectives of the Samaj were to fight for the rights of depressed groups such as women, the Shudras and the Dalits. The Samaj campaigned for the spread of rational thinking and rejected the need for priests. Phule's ideas were human well-being, happiness, unity, equality and easy religious principles and rituals. The *Satyashodhaks* believed that all humans were the children of one God and that, to connect with God, humans do not need intermediaries such as priests.

Jyotiba Phule devoted his entire life as a social activist and a social reformer to fight against the practice of untouchability and other social evil practices towards women. He was the pioneer of women's education in India. He was the founder of many movements: (a) movement against discrimination, (b) movement of Dalits, (c) movement of women's education, (d) peasant's movement and (e) movement against blind faith. Jyotiba suffered a stroke in 1888 and was rendered paralyzed. On 28 November 1890, the great social reformer, Mahatma Jyotiba Phule, passed away.

RABINDRANATH TAGORE (7 MAY 1861–7 AUGUST 1941)

Rabindranath Tagore was a Nobel laureate poet, writer and is the greatest versatile genius of Bengali literature. Besides, he was known as a great thinker, philosopher and educationist and, at the same time, an outstanding social reformer. He was the original composer of the Indian National anthem 'Jana Gana Mana'. He won the Nobel Prize in 1913 for his work in literature. He was against the conventional classroom teaching and believed that interaction with nature is essential for learning. He believed in the principle of self-sufficiency and cooperation which are highly required among the rural population for agricultural reconstruction, education and social development (Roy, 2008).

RURAL RECONSTRUCTION PROGRAMME

Tagore felt that rural areas lagged behind urban areas in terms of development and access to services. Rural development is possible through bringing constructive development in the field of healthcare, education, empowerment (both male and female), handicrafts and empowering the backward class (Sinha, 2011). He had developed 15 points of rural reconstruction programme (Roy, 2008).

> **Did You Know?**
>
> **Fifteen points of rural reconstruction programme by Rabindranath Tagore**
>
> 1. To create unity and fraternity among various communities and by finding out harmful social ills to redress them
> 2. To bring compromises to all the conflicts through arbitration *Salishi*, that is, through hearing and settling of differences between parties by a person or persons chosen or agreed to by the villagers
> 3. Making use of homemade industry products, taking arrangements to make the products cheaper and also for advancement of the local industries.
> 4. To make arrangements of quality education for boys and girls by selection of competent teachers and by establishment of schools, where necessary night schools under village development society.

5. To develop unity and moral values spiritually through narration or discussion about great scientists, historians and other noble persons to the rural people
6. Setting up dispensary and medical facilities in every village; making available medicines, medical care and also helping the poor to make funeral arrangements for their dead
7. To improve the quality of health of the rural people by making necessary arrangements for safe drinking water, cleaning rivers and canals, making roads, grounds for gymnasium or sports and cremation grounds
8. To establish ideal farming fields and farmhouses for young men and other village people so that they can get agricultural education and earn their livings through agricultural work and cattle farming
9. To form cooperative grain stores in order to cope with famine
10. To make arrangements of raw materials and provide training in arts and crafts to the village women so that they can contribute to their family income as and when required
11. To restrain people from consuming alcohol and drugs
12. To develop meeting places such as clubs so that the rural people can assemble and discuss issues related to the upliftment of rural areas
13. To collect information through frequent surveys regarding population, houses, condition of various crops, agricultural demands of crops, number of high schools and basic schools and its students, birth and death condition, number of patients with contagious or epidemic diseases such as malaria, smallpox and cholera
14. To cultivate fraternal feelings and sense of unity among each and every village and district
15. To assist districts, provinces and country-based societies to fulfil their aims regarding human development or village upliftment

These 15 points of the rural reconstruction programme are still useful for the development of the rural areas in the country.

REFORM IN THE EDUCATION SYSTEM

In his views, education is not only sharing the knowledge or information but also the holistic development of the student. Teachers should be more like mentors and guide the students towards emotional, intellectual and spiritual upliftment. He started an experimental school at Santiniketan (a place in Bolpur, West Bengal) in 1922 where he tried his Upanishadic ideals of education. It was one of the major contributions of Rabindranath Tagore to society. The Santiniketan experiment had four general programme areas, namely agriculture, crafts and industries, village welfare and education. Different activities were designed under each programme with the help of modern technologies and scientific temper.

EMPLOYMENT GENERATION AND REVIVAL OF COTTAGE INDUSTRIES

Handloom training centres were set up to restore local industries and to make the trainees self-independent. A separate entity called 'Shilpa Bhaban' was established in 1922 to provide vocational training to rural craftsmen and training to the students of academic departments of schools. The cottage industries for both boys and girls were set up in different villages for spinning, weaving, dyeing and printing, needlework and basket-making (Roy, 2008; Sinha, 2011).

SET-UP RURAL BANK

To save the poor farmers from the clutches of the moneylenders, he took initiative to establish a 'Krishi Bank' at Shelaidah in 1894 (Hussain, 2018). Later on, he established the same in Patisar in 1905 to provide easy loans to the farmers. In 1927, Visva Bharati Central Co-operative Bank was established. It had 236 Agricultural Credit Unions attached to it along with 69 irrigation societies and 12 health societies (Hussain, 2018).

HEALTH SERVICES

A medical section was also part of Tagore's scheme of rural and community development. This section tried to improve rural sanitation and health conditions by organizing local health societies. Initially, maternal and child health was an important component of healthcare services. Rural women were trained to provide such services to the mother and children. Another important innovation was tried by organizing cooperative health societies in which villagers could become members that entitled them to free treatment for some ailments. In 1924, an OPD was opened at Sriniketan followed by a health cooperative centre, that is, Swasthya Samanvay Kendra in Bengali in 1932. There were only two hospitals in 1930 (Sinha, 2011).

YOUTH EMPOWERMENT

Tagore believed in youth empowerment and he formed different youth organizations such as Brati-Balaka (for male) and Brati-Balika (for female). He used them as a weapon for the rural development programme.

Women's Association or Mahila Samitis were established to play facilitating roles in the economic and social welfare of the community, thereby ensuring women empowerment. For the development of youth, 'youth groups' were organized in villages to promote volunteerism and it was recorded that, by 1928, there were 800 members organized in 30 centres that were established. The village societies were also established to settle disputes by arbitration. For knowledge dissemination, a rural circulating library, the first of its kind, was set up in this part of the subcontinent.

SOCIAL INCLUSION

Tagore believed in the inclusion of all in the development process even in those days. He formed Dom Samiti (low-caste association) representing Doms in more than 30 different villages for the improvement of the condition of the excluded classes (Hussain, 2018).

Rabindranath Tagore was a versatile leader. His contribution towards the rural community development was the founding stone for the community development programme in India. His contribution towards different areas of community development such as auricular development, credit bank for the farmers, women empowerment and social inclusion has greater prominence. On 7 August 1941, he passed away.

PERIYAR E. V. RAMASAMY (17 SEPTEMBER 1879–24 DECEMBER 1973)

Erode Venkatappa Ramasamy is popularly known as Periyar or Thanthai Periyar (respected father). He was a politician and social activist and mostly social reformer. He was the founder of the Self-Respect Movement and Dravidar Kazhagam. His work was against the dominance of Brahmanism and inequality in the caste system. He had started his political career with the Indian National Congress in 1919.

PERSONAL HISTORY

He was born on 17 September 1879 at Erode, Tamil Nadu, in a wealthy business family. He had little formal education and gained knowledge through critical discussions with scholars whom his father used to patronize. At a young age, he ran away from his home and spent time in Varanasi and other religious centres. He became disillusioned with religion as a result of his experiences in the orthodox Hindu religion. He was a popular personality in Erode due to his public service and forthrightness and he was the chairman of the Erode Municipal Council. He is known for his work on women empowerment, social equality, anti-Hindi, alcoholism and anti-Brahmin stance. He died at the age of 94 on 24 December 1973.

POLITICAL JOURNEY

Periyar made his political entry as a member of the Congress party and worked intensively. He resigned from all his government positions to support the Non-Cooperation Movement. He promoted khadi, boycotted foreign products, worked against toddy shops and worked to abolish the caste system and untouchability. He became the president of the Tamil Nadu Congress Committee. His wife and sister also joined him, leading to women's participation in public work in Tamil Nadu. He strongly advocated the reservation system in education and government jobs. As Congress did not address these issues, he quit Congress in 1917 and started the Self-Respect Movement. In 1944, the Justice Party merged with the Self-Respect Movement and was renamed Dravidar Kazhagam.

DRAVIDAR KAZHAGAM

Dravidar Kazhagam was a social movement which started with the objectives to eliminate caste evils, untouchability and to get the separate Dravidian Republic. It mainly worked to eradicate inequality and superstitious beliefs based on religion. It vehemently opposed Brahmanism and it had a strong anti-Hindi stand. It did social reform work and paid attention to women's education, widow remarriage and liberation of women. He promoted rationalism and motivated the exploited people to think and act to get their rights. His famous quote is, 'any opposition not based on rationalism, science, or experience will one day or another, reveal the fraud, selfishness, lies and conspiracies'. Periyar had spread rationalist thought through newspapers and journals. *Kudi Arasu* was the official newspaper of the Self-Respect Movement, and he expressed his opinion on social issues in his writings.

ERADICATION OF CASTE

Periyar had played a predominant role against the caste system, and he proposed a resolution regarding the rights of untouchables to entry in temples. In Kerala, in the name of caste dharma, the lower caste people were not allowed to enter temples and also to the surrounding streets of temples. In Vaikom town of Kerala, Periyar led a movement against caste dharma and got imprisoned. People hailed him as the hero of Vaikom for his vigorous work against inequality in the name of caste and religion. He was once refused a meal because of his caste in Kasi temple, which drove him to atheism. He met with many prominent social activists all over India and he strongly supported Ambedkar's demand for separate electorates for the Scheduled Castes. Periyar vehemently opposed the caste-based education scheme introduced by Rajagopalachari when he was the chief minister of Madras state.

WOMEN RIGHTS AND WIDOW REMARRIAGE

Periyar was highly critical of patriarchy and emphasized women's right to property and divorce. He condemned child marriage and the devadasi system. He insisted on equal rights for males and females in property, guardianship and adoption. He also supported birth control and contraception. He insisted women to pursue education and thereby attain women empowerment. His important work on women's subject is why the women are enslaved. Widow remarriage was accepted in Tamil Nadu due to Periyar's writings. He stated that women have the right to remarry and he advocates that only education, self-respect and rational qualities will make women empowered. He was not in favour of tying *mangal sutra* around the neck of women at the time of marriage as no such activity was being done for males. The admirers of Periyar, which was a part of the government of Tamil Nadu in 1989, introduced equal rights to the ancestral property for women in inheritance. As a token of respect to his contribution for women development, he was conferred with the title 'Periyar' in the Tamil Nadu Women's Congress in 1938. Periyar strongly opposed women being treated as secondary citizens and advised women to come out of the kitchen to understand the world in a better way.

RELEVANCE IN SOCIAL WORK

Social work is a profession that attempts to help individuals, groups and communities to face the actual situations and taking actions to improve the condition (Kher, 1947). The aim of social work, as generally understood, is to remove social injustice, to relieve distress, to prevent suffering and to assist the weaker members of the society to rehabilitate themselves and their families and, in short, fight the five giant evils of physical want, disease, ignorance, squalor and idleness. The work of Babasaheb Ambedkar, Mahatma Phule, Rabindranath Tagore and Periyar E. V. Ramasamy is highly relevant to the social work profession as they were social workers too. The objectives of social work are to fulfil humanitarian needs, create self-sufficiency, strengthen and make harmonious social relations, develop democratic values, provide opportunities for development and social progress, bring change in the social system for social development and also provide socio-legal aid. The modern thinkers of India either directly or indirectly contributed to the growth of social work profession in India by bringing social reform in the nation. They had resolved both individual and social problems by applying social methods and techniques. All these modern Indian thinkers have applied the methods of community organization and social action predominantly to make social changes in the society. Community organization is a process by which a social worker uses their insight and skill to help communities geographically and functionally to identify and to work towards a solution of the problems. Social action is a group effort to solve mass social problems or to further socially desirable objectives by attempting to influence basic social and economic conditions or practices. It is concerned with system change and seeks to alter the structure of roles and distribution of power, prevent problems, expand opportunity and enhance the quality of life. Social work improves the standard of living and social relations in a society and this work was systematically performed by modern social thinkers of India by the application of all social work methods.

SUMMARY

This chapter has given an overview of the role of social reformers in the social development of India. India, though rich in culture and tradition, the people suffered from social evils such as untouchability, caste system, religious discrimination and women ill-treatment. Many social reformists took action to eliminate social evils and the most prominent reformers in India are Babasaheb Ambedkar, Mahatma Phule, Rabindranath Tagore and Periyar E. V. Ramasamy. Ambedkar was the father of the Indian Constitution and uplifted the life of lower caste people. Jyotirao Phule focused on women's education, rights of women and struggled against the caste system. Rabindranath Tagore was firm in individual freedom and emphasized education and equality. Periyar was associated with many reforms such as widow remarriage, women education and equal rights. Social work is undertaken to raise the socio-economic standard of living by removing social injustice to relieve distress, prevent suffering and assist the weaker members of the society to rehabilitate themselves and their families.

TOP 10 TAKEAWAYS/MAIN POINTS

1. Dr Ambedkar is honoured as the 'architect of the Indian Constitution'.
2. Dr Ambedkar's five principles (Pancha Sutras) to all Dalits for their upliftment in the society, that is, self-improvement, self-progress, self-dependence, self-respect and self-confidence.

3. Jyotirao Phule believed that education is a strong weapon to sensitize the people to realize the rights and it promotes self-empowerment.
4. Jyotirao Phule started the Society of Truth Seekers with the purpose to work for the rights of women and Dalits.
5. Tagore insisted to improve the fields of healthcare, education, empowerment of all genders and backward class people.
6. Tagore founded an experimental school, namely Santiniketan, that promoted agriculture, crafts and industries, village welfare and education.
7. E. V. Ramasamy was named as Periyar who founded Dravidar Kazhagam and worked to eradicate the inequality and superstitious beliefs based on religion.
8. Periyar was highly critical of patriarchy and emphasized women's right to property and divorce. He condemned child marriage and the devadasi system.
9. Social work is a profession that attempts to help individuals, groups and communities to face actual situations and taking actions to improve the condition.
10. Social work makes a fight against the five giant evils of physical want, disease, ignorance, squalor and idleness in a society.

Keywords: Social action, social reforms, community organization, social development

GLOSSARY

Community organization: Community organization is a process in which efforts are directed towards meeting the community needs and developing integration within the community.

Social action: Social action may be defined as an organized effort with the aim of securing social progress and of solving mass social problems by influencing social legislation or the administration of social services.

Social development: Social development is enhancing the well-being of every individual in a society to develop the entire society. It is an all-inclusive concept connoting the well-being of the people, the community and society.

Social reform: Social reform refers to any attempt made to correct the injustice in society. It is a movement that works to bring gradual changes in certain aspects of society rather than fundamental changes.

Social work: Social work is the art of bringing various resources to bear on individual, group and community needs by the application of a scientific method of helping people to help themselves (Stroupe, 1960).

ANALYTICAL QUESTIONS

1. Discuss the contributions of modern Indian thinkers towards social work education and practice.
2. Discuss Dravidar Kazhagam movement.

Modern Indian Thinkers and Their Relevance in Social Work

 MULTIPLE CHOICE QUESTIONS

1. Jyotirao Phule was the founder of
   a. Arya Samaj
   b. Brahma Samaj
   c. **Satyashodhak Samaj**
   d. Ramakrishna Mission

2. Jyotirao Phule was influenced by the book
   a. ***The Rights of Man***
   b. *Progress and Poverty*
   c. *The Poor and Their Money*
   d. *My Experiments with Truth*

3. Tagore founded the experimental school called
   a. Sriniketan
   b. **Santiniketan**
   c. The New School
   d. Sabarmati Ashram

4. The bank established by Tagore for the development of agriculture was
   a. **Krishi Bank**
   b. Bank of Hindustan
   c. Bank of Calcutta
   d. General Bank of India

5. E. V. Ramasamy's work against the caste system in Kerala gave him a name
   a. Guardian of human rights
   b. **Hero of Vaikom**
   c. Dalit leader
   d. Thanthai Periyar

6. E. V. Ramasamy was the founder of
   a. **Self-respect Movement**
   b. Pure Tamil Movement
   c. Adi Dravida Mahajana Sabha
   d. Madras Labour Union

7. Social work profession attempts to help
   a. Individuals
   b. Groups
   c. Communities
   d. **Individuals, groups and communities**

8. Which one of the following is the basis of membership of caste?
   a. By religion
   b. By name
   c. By economic status
   d. **By birth**

9. Who was the chairman of the Drafting Committee of the Indian Constitution?
   a. **B. R. Ambedkar**
   b. Jyotirao Phule
   c. E. V. Ramasamy
   d. Rabindranath Tagore

10. Who was the first law minister in independent India?
    a. Sardar Vallabhbhai Patel
    b. Ravi Shankar Prasad
    c. Subramanian Swamy
    d. **B. R. Ambedkar**

REVIEW QUESTIONS

1. Write the contribution of Dr Ambedkar to the Indian Constitution.
2. Discuss Ambedkar's contribution towards the upliftment of the untouchables.
3. Discuss Mahatma Phule's contribution towards women empowerment.
4. Discuss the 15 points of Rural Reconstruction Programme of Rabindranath Tagore.

REFERENCES

Begari, J. (2010). Jyotirao Phule: A revolutionary social reformer. *The Indian Journal of Political Science*, 399–412.
Hussain, A. (2018). Capitalism, consciousness and development. In *Economic Theory and Policy amidst Global Discontent* (pp.41-60). Routledge India.
Hussain, K. (2018). A new variety of anti-secularism. *Postsecular Feminisms: Religion and Gender in Transnational Context*, p.75.
Kher, B. G. (1947). *Training for social workers: An International survey*. Department of Social Affairs.
Roy, B. K. (2008). *Rabindranath Tagore: The Man and His Poetry*. Read Books.
Sinha, S. (2011). Ghostly Predicament: Narrative, Spectrality and Historicality. In Rabindranath Tagore's 'The Hungry Stones'. *Interventions*, *17*(5), 728–743.
Stroup, H. H. (1960). *Social work- An introduction to the field* (2nd edition). American Book Company.

RECOMMENDED READINGS

Bakane, C., Ali, S. Z., Murlidhara, M., & Buwa, S. P. (2012). Equality: Contribution of Jyotiba Phule (1827–1890). In S. Ghose (Ed.), *Modern Indian political thought* (Political Science Paper II, MA PART I), pp. 30–31. University of Mumbai.
Queen, C. S. (2008). Dr Ambedkar and untouchability: Fighting the Indian caste system (Book review). *Buddhist-Christian Studies*, 2, pp.30–31.
Sirswal, D. R. (2013). Mahatma Jyotiba Phule: A modern Indianphilosopher. *Darshan: International Refereed Quarterly Research Journal for Philosophy an Yog*tem.168–172
Venkatachalapathy, A. R. (2020). Periyar E. Vamasamy. In *Oxford Research Encyclopedia of Asian History*. https://oxfordre.com/asianhistory/view/10.1093/acrefore/9780190277727.001.0001/acrefore-9780190277727-e-340?rskey=NrmMdA&result=3

24

Radical Social Work

Binod Kumar

LEARNING OBJECTIVES

- To understand the concept and meaning of radical social work
- To examine the relevance of radical social work in current scenario
- To enable students to use radical social work perspective in designing social work intervention
- To help learners understand about the limitations of radical social work practice

Be the change you wish to see in the world.

—Mahatma Gandhi

INTRODUCTION

Human beings are continuously influenced by their social surroundings. A professional approach to emancipate the people, who are incapable due to personal weakness and social barriers, may be examined in context of social work. The emancipatory approach is a departure from the traditional methods of social work practice. As a practice-based academic discipline, radical social work tries to alleviate people and social problems through enabling them. Social work as a profession envisages controlling and minimizing sympathetic relation between the client and social worker. However, an empathetic feeling is expected from a social worker so that a genuine understanding and a respect for the plight of the client is realized.

In response to the traditional social work practice, radical social emerged with a promise to provide appropriate and suitable intervention. Radical social work is a most viable and comprehensive approach to understand and solve the problem of society at large. However, the concept of radical social work is embedded in the fundamental principles and methods of social work. The philosophical basis of the discipline of social work is based on the idea of principle of social justice which aims to enable the client to access services and help themselves. The role of a social worker as an enabler in practice-based settings may be fully exercised once client's status is radically transformed. The transformation of status may be achieved through structural changes in the society in a rights-based approach. Social action as a method of social work revolves around structural changes which results into a long-lasting solution to a problem. Radical social work as a concept might look like a revolutionary idea, though it is already embedded in the fundamentals of social work practice. The usual interpretation of radical social work emanates from the political theory and practice focused on the understanding of the change in the political system. However, radical social work differentiates from the mainstream approaches due to its emphasis on social change, thereby meaning that entrenched poverty and widespread inequality have a devastating impact on clients in social work settings and a social worker may ignore it at their own peril. Therefore, service to the client without addressing a fundamental issue may work just like pain killer which reduces pain but keep the root cause intact (Ioakimidis, 2016).

Radical social work creates a scope within the methodological practice of social work to engage with the broader structural and fundamental issues that social worker engages with on a daily basis while dealing with the client's problem. Radical social work also equips professional social workers to meaningfully incorporate social and political action to solve larger issue in the community.

A term denoting attempts in the 1970s to achieve a fundamental reorientation of social work practice ('radical' denotes a concerted attempt to change the *status quo*). The 1970s saw a loose movement known as radical social work, with its roots in an undifferentiated political left. Its main contention was that social problems, including thosehabitually addressed by social workers, had their roots in structural inequality, principally social class, and not in personal inadequacy as earlier theory seemed to imply.

Key ingredients to radical social work as a method were *conscientizatian* (in Paolo Freire's sense), the *empowerment* of clients, the opening up of social work processes to public and indeed client participation, and attempts to make broad political alliances of 'progressive' forces (community groups, client groups, trade unions and political parties). In general, radical social workers perceived ambiguity in the stat e apparatus to the point that real gains were held to be achievable for the working classes.

Currently, a radical right has emerged in social work, stressing individual, family, and to a lesser extent community responsibility for social problems. This has been associated with policy shifts in government, leading to the closing of large institutions for the mentally ill and handicapped, the growth of a private welfare sector, and the recent emphasis on community care in welfare provision. Faced with these changes the tendency has been for the radical left in social work to fragment, focusing on narrower, albeit significant, issues, such as racism, sexism and other aspects of equality. (The Free Dictionary by Farlex, n.d.)

The radical social work as a practice raises many inconvenient questions for government and dominant communities. It tries to dodge the traditional approach of blaming the victim for their plights and raises macro-issues which may be interconnected to each other. As a professional worker, an individual cannot ignore widespread reality which is directly connected to the problem which they are trying to solve on a daily basis. If a social worker ignores the widespread reality, then intervention would be reduced to a futile exercise. Therefore, comprehensive understanding of the issues enhances the knowledge base of radical social work practice. The radical social work approach empowers a client to shape policy which directly impacts them, as opposed to the traditional approach where the social worker assumes the role of a policy guardian.

TRACING RADICAL SOCIAL WORK

The radical social work is embedded in the profession from the beginning. The social work practices and movements such as the Anti-race Movement in the USA, the Gender Rights Movement across the globe, the Labour Right Movement and the Settlement Movement in the West have been part and parcel of the conception of radical social work. The movements related to land rights, anti-caste movements and development-led resettlement movement like *Narmada Bachao Andolan* falls in the framework of radical social work in Indian perspective. The radical social work practice has generated a body of knowledge which intersects various methods and practices of social work. It has altered the curriculum of social work in India and around the globe. It also helped in developing an inclusive character of social work discipline, practice and curriculum in India by integrating question of exclusion and discrimination based on the social structures. The radical social work practice has been able to generate such a body of knowledge that it has also been able to transform the global definition of social work.

Social work is a practice-based profession and an academic discipline that promotes *social change* and development, social cohesion, and the *empowerment and liberation of people*. Principles of social justice, human rights, collective responsibility and respect for diversities are central to social work. Underpinned by theories of social work, social sciences, humanities and indigenous knowledges, social work engages people and *structures to address life challenges* and enhance wellbeing.[1]

The global definition of social work aims to promote social change, empowerment and liberation of people and it engages with structures to address life challenges which means that the global definition of social work already has a very strong component of radical social work. It is manifested in the terminologies such as social change, empowerment and liberation of people and engages with structures to address life challenges.

Did You Know?

Global Definition of Social Work

The following definition was approved by the IFSW General Meeting and the IASSW General Assembly in July 2014:

> Social work is a practice-based profession and an academic discipline that promotes social change and development, social cohesion, and the empowerment and liberation of people. Principles of social justice, human rights, collective responsibility and respect for diversities are central to social work. Underpinned by theories of social work, social sciences, humanities and indigenous knowledges, social work engages people and structures to address life challenges and enhance wellbeing. The above definition may be amplified at national and/or regional levels.

---

[1] https://www.iassw-aiets.org/global-definition-of-social-work-review-of-the-global-definition/

What connects all the various forms of radical social work is addressing issues with the help of structural changes in the community. It is important to note that the purpose of radical social work practice is to empower the community rather than facilitating the structural changes.

THEORETICAL FOUNDATIONS OF RADICAL SOCIAL WORK

The term *radical social work* denotes fundamental reorientation of social work practice in the 1970s to alter the status quo through structural changes. The root of radical social work may be traced in the political Left influenced by Marxism. The radical social work practice assumes that problems addressed by the social workers had their roots in the existing structural inequality rather than personal inadequacy. It was believed that without removing the causes of structural inequality, the problems could not be addressed holistically. The key ingredients of radical social work methods are *conscientization, the empowerment of clients, the opening up of social work processes to the public, client participation* and *attempts to make broad political alliances of progressive forces* (The Free Dictionary by Farlex, n.d.).

> **Did You Know?**
>
> The key ingredients of radical social work methods are *conscientization, the empowerment of clients, the opening up of social work processes to the public, client participation* and *attempts to make broad political alliances of progressive forces.*

The emergence of radical right in the social work stresses on the responsibility of individual, family and community for social problems. The sudden policy shift by the government led to the closure of various social welfare measures like closure of shelter homes for especially able people, children and estranged women. Faced with these challenges, radical left in the social work is narrower though significant issues like racism, sexism and equality. (The Free Dictionary by Farlex, n.d.)

Regardless of political affiliation, social workers across the globe feel that social welfare sector is not able to cater to the need of the poor and marginalized. Those unfamiliar with the nature and scope of radical social work practice often mistake to identify radical social work in traditional Marxism and Leninism, though radical social work goes beyond it. The analysis of social problems under radical social work is based on the fundamental organizing principle of society rather than dealing with its manifestations. Therefore, society needs to be principally reorganized in order to solve the social problem than just a reformation. Often, people tend to reject the radical paradigm because it differs from the analysis they are accustomed with (Galper, 1976).

Theoretically, radical social work practice developed in response to the traditional casework practice. It was a departure from the reformist approach which was incremental in nature. The radical social work approach tried to reconceptualize the traditional approach and shifted focus towards the marginalized section of the society. It was developed in the 1960s and the 1980s in

Britain by Bailey and Brake (1975), in the USA by Galper (1980), in Australia by Throssell (1975) and in Canada by Moreau (1979). Moreover, Peter Leonard (1978) proposed Paulo Freire's concept of conscientization as a radical praxis for social work (Desai, n.d.).

The radical social work approach provides a wider perspective to deal with social problem. Where traditional approach focuses on individual problems, radical approach tries to find and remove the root cause of the problem. Therefore, critical theory provides theoretical foundations to the radical approach in social work practice. The approach also raised questions on professional social work in dealing with fundamental social problems and dubbed it as a cosmetic effort to temporarily resolve the issue and getting away from the larger issues in the interests of the state. The approach is primarily rooted in the idea how professional social workers are trying to change individuals to alleviate the problem rather than changing systems and structures which are at the core of the problems.

SALIENT FEATURES OF RADICAL SOCIAL WORK PRACTICE

- *Thrust in structural and systemic change:* The radical social work aims at a structural or systemic advancement to solve the social problem. Traditionally, there has been a thrust on the immediate problem-solving in social work rather than addressing the larger issue.
- *Individual problems are rooted in the socio-economic and political structures:* The approach to solve the social problem in radical social work is not individual one, rather it engages with the contemporary social, political or economic structures in order to address the problem. It goes beyond the immediate solution and tries to provide a long-lasting solution to the social problem.
- *Systemic and structural change may solve the individual problems which traditional social work practice is trying to address:* Essentially, radical social work is taking a different route to address a social problem. Where traditional social work engages individuals and alleviates life conditions, traditional social work engages with social structures to address individual problems.
- *A commitment to emancipatory and revolutionary change is opposed to incremental and reformist approach:* The radical social work believes in the emancipatory framework. It also alters the relationship between the social worker and the client by enabling and empowering the client. It seeks to facilitate radical change by empowering clients.

CONTEXTUALIZING RADICAL SOCIAL WORK PRACTICE

Radical social work practice uses various methods such as case work, group work, community organization and social action. The adoption of diverse methods depends upon the context and situations, and methods are means to an end rather than end itself. The underlying objective of adopting any method in radical social work is to liberate, enable and empower the client in the persuasion of a just and equitable society.

Often, radical social work has been seen as romantic idea limited to the classrooms and there is no relevance of it in practice. However, trade union movements in the USA and the UK in the late 1970s refute this claim as they were largely led by radical social work practitioners. In practice, the term *radical social work* has often been misinterpreted. Etymologically speaking, radical social work manifests a serious commitment to structural change and altering the status quo. However, the concept becomes irrelevant when diverse persuasions of social worker themselves describe as 'radical' or not identify them as 'radical' (Desai, n.d.). Moreover, there are some terms such as *Marxist*, *socialist*, *black panther* and *Dalit panther* which have been used interchangeably for radical social work from time to time. The land right movement, forest right movement, anti-caste movement, gender rights movement and queer movements in India constituted a robust component of radical social work practice. These movements have been perceived as a watershed development and have been able to make structural changes in the life of the community at large.

RADICAL SOCIAL WORK: AN INDIAN PERSPECTIVE

India is a diverse country having varied culture, ethnicity and language. The diversity of social systems in India makes it more complex in terms of employing a social work intervention. Radical social work practice helps in realigning the existing social structure to alleviate people out of the problems. The anti-oppressive movement, anti-caste movement and Dalit panther movement in some parts of the country are testimony to the indigenous examples of radical social work practice.

The early support to NGOs in post-Independence India came in the form of social work which was entirely funded either by the government or overseas funders. The support was in the form of supporting government's development work in the post-Independence period. In the 1970s, NGOs started taking radical positions to alleviate people's sufferings and wanted some structural changes in order to fulfil the aspirations of the people envisioned in the pre-Independence period. The radical standpoint and questions by the NGOs made government uncomfortable. The radical standpoint by various Gandhian NGOs had far-reaching consequences. Later, the government considered NGOs as a potential threat to the national security and started scrutiny of their intervention on the ground.

LIMITS TO RADICAL SOCIAL WORK

The radical social work practice did not get prominence despite its ability to address the problem holistically. There are multiple factors behind this problem: it includes both internal and external factors. Internal factor directly relates to the profession of social work. For example, social work education in India is designed in such a way that fieldwork education properly regimented. There is hardly any scope left when a student during their fieldwork education will get exposure and tool to deal with radical approach in social work. The trainees during their fieldwork education are expected to do routine work and produce the fieldwork report. They are not equipped with tools to pursue radical social work as it is strenuous task for both host institute and trainee to develop rapport, build community solidarity and facilitate the change. Due to a lack of exposure, a trainee is disinclined to address structural issues and goes for a quick-fix approach which is suitable for both organization and professional social worker. The external factor which restricts the radical social work practice is the dependency of organizations on external fund either from overseas donors or the government. Therefore, organizations' work and approach are donor-driven and there is a rare opportunity for organizations to go for a radical social work approach.

SUMMARY

Human beings are continuously influenced by various activities in their surroundings. Therefore, there are varied forms to deal with individual and social problems. Social work as an academic discipline gives a professional approach to deal with the social problem in a sustained manner. Radical social work might be a long-term process; however, it has the capacity to resolve the issues for a longer period. It approaches problem from the root and therefore intervention transcends beyond merely solving the immediate problem. Employing and practising radical social work in India is not an easy task. It takes a lot of time and resources to actualize radical social work to address the social problem.

The scope and scale of radical social work practice is complex and dynamic. Therefore, it is almost impossible to give a universally accepted meaning of it. It has been defined and understood by different individuals in various ways on the basis of understanding and requirement of society. Some problems may appear impossible to bridge and resolve today and method may also appear illegal and unethical. However, after a certain period of time, dynamic nature of radical social work practice finds its ways to resolve the problem ethically and legally.

TOP 10 TAKEAWAYS/MAIN POINTS

1. Radical social work approach is already embedded in the traditional social work.
2. It is never easy to be radical in social work as it directly challenges the institutional and systemic perspective.
3. Radical social work denotes concerted attempts to alter the status quo.
4. Radical social work practice is based on the foundations of social justice and has emancipatory potential.
5. Radical social work practice is an attempt to eliminate the root cause rather than addressing the manifestation of root cause.
6. Key ingredients of radical social work practice includes *conscientization, enabling client, client participation* and *making a broad political alliance*.
7. Radical social work aims to improve the life of individuals through reducing poverty and inequality.
8. Radical social work transcends beyond the individual-centric intervention and strive for a holistic and structural change.
9. It challenges the culture of managerialism and helps in developing a radical perspective to deal with social problems.
10. Radical social work practice is both within and against the state.

Keywords: Critical theory, social work, traditional approach, radical approach

GLOSSARY

Critical theory: Social work practice grounded in critical social theory begins with a commitment to recognize how personal and political are interconnected. The critical theory finds its origin in the Frankfurt school of thought and developed in response to the reactionary and totalitarian thought. Critical theory is an ideological framework that can bring stronger cohesion to the profession. A discussion of critical theory and how it can be effectively applied to our profession is valuable as we progress into the 2nd century of the social work profession. To engage critical practice in social work, professionals must consider factors such as (a) historical and cultural context, (b) power distribution, (c) self-reflection, (d) non-judgemental enquiry, (e) values and (f) action (Salas et al., 2010).

Structural social work:

Structural social work (Corrigan & Leonard, 1978; Lundy, 2004; Moreau, 1989; Mullaly, 1997, 2007; Payne, 2005; Wood & Tully, 2006) is part of a critical, progressive tradition that has been concerned with the broad socio-economic and political dimensions of society, especially the effects of capitalism, and the impact of these influences in creating unequal relations amongst individuals. Its primary goals have been to reduce social inequality through the transformation. The lens of this theoretical approach has been focused on the interplay between the agency of individuals and structures, particularly the broad structural barriers which influence and limit the material circumstances of service users. (Weinberg, 2013)

ANALYTICAL QUESTIONS

1. Discuss limits to the radical social work practice in India.
2. Examine the relevance of global definition of social work vis-à-vis radical social work practice.

MULTIPLE CHOICE QUESTIONS

1. Which of the following is the foundational principle of radical social work practice?
   a. **Social justice**
   b. Social problem
   c. Ethics
   d. Self-determination

2. Radical social work practice is influenced by
   a. Socialism
   b. **Marxism**
   c. Welfarism
   d. Positivism

3. The radical social work employs methods of social work
   a. Case work
   b. Group work
   c. Social Action
   d. **All of the above**

4. Radical social work attempts to
   a. Maintain the status quo
   b. **Make structural change**
   c. Address the individual problem
   d. Address the root cause

5. Which of the following is not an ingredient of radical social work?
   a. Conscientisation
   b. Empowerment
   c. Client participation
   d. **Non-judgemental**

6. Radical social work came in response to the
   a. **Traditional social work practice**
   b. Group work
   c. Social action
   d. Community work

7. Match the following in context of radical social work in different countries.

Bailey and Brake	Britain
Galper	USA
Throssell	Australia
Moreau	Canada

8. Who proposed Paulo Freire's concept of conscientization as a radical praxis for social work?
   a. Moreau
   b. Galper
   c. **Peter Leonard**
   d. Bailey and Brake

9. Which of the following is not an example of radical social work?
   a. Anti-caste Movement
   b. Black Rights Movement
   c. Transgender Right Movement
   d. **Right to livelihood**

10. Which of the following components of global definition of social work represents radical social work perspective?
    a. Social change
    b. Empowerment and liberation of people
    c. Engages people and structures to address life challenges
    d. **All of the above**

REVIEW QUESTIONS

1. Define radical social work in your own words.
2. Write a short note on the theoretical base of radical social work.
3. Provide some indigenous examples in the context of radical social work practice.
4. Examine Marxian approach as a foundation of radical social work practice.

REFERENCES

Bailey, R., & Brake, M. (1975). *Radical social work*. Hodder & Stoughton Educational.
Desai, D. K. (n.d.). History and philosophy of social work. In *Critical theory*. EPG Pathshal.
Galper, J. H. (1976). Introduction of Radical Theory and Practice in Social Work Education: Social Policy. *Journal of Education for Social Work*, 3–9.
Galper, J. H. (1980). *Social Work Practice: A Radical Perspective*. Prentice Hall.

Ioakimidis, V. (2016). *A guide to radical social work*. https://www.theguardian.com/social-care-network/2016/may/24/radical-social-work-quick-guide-change-poverty-inequality

Salas, L. M., Sen, S., & Segal, E. A. (2010). Critical theory: Pathway from dichotomous to integrated social work practice. *Practice Issues and Social Change*.

Moreau, M. (1979). A Structural Approach to Social Work Practice. *Canadian Journal of Social Work Education*, 78–94.

The Free Dictionary by Farlex. (n.d.). *Radical social work*. https://encyclopedia2.thefreedictionary.com/radical+social+work

Throssell, H. (1976). *Social Work: Radical Essays*. University of Queensland Press.

Weinberg, M. (2013). *Structural social work: A moral compass for ethics in practice*. http://ethicsinthehelpingprofessions.socialwork.dal.ca/wp-content/uploads/2013/10/Weinberg-2008-Structural-Social-Work-CSW.pdf

RECOMMENDED READING

Brake, M., & Roy, B. (1981). *Radical social work and practice*. SAGE.

25

Gandhian Social Work
Mithilesh Kumar and Rajan Prakash

LEARNING OBJECTIVES

- To understand the fundamental elements of Gandhian thought
- To describe the various dimensions of Gandhian social work
- To explain *Satyagraha* as a method of conflict resolution
- To discuss the ethics of Gandhian social work

Generations to come, it may well be, will scarce believe that such a man as this one ever in flesh and blood walked upon this Earth.

—Albert Einstein, in *Out of My Later Years*

INTRODUCTION

Social work is a recognized profession in many countries, and more and more universities are establishing the department for teaching and research in the subject. The traditionally held notion about social work, that the work done from time immemorial, is changing now. In its mission of making the society self-reliant, it uses many methods, techniques, principles and philosophy. In the West, social work traces its initial history to the Church and religious organizations of Europe and America but, in the process of evolution, many alternative perspectives and associated models have emerged from the Third-World countries. The conviction in the academic community of social work has now become firm that the Western models of social work are insufficient to address the needs and aspirations of a different society, for every society has its cultural values and embedded problems in its sociocultural structure. This realization has also paved way for the inclusion of Gandhi's way of work into social work discipline.

This chapter sheds light on one such perspective, that is, Gandhian social work. For doing so, it looks into the fundamental elements of Gandhian thought, dimensions of Gandhian social work and the values and principles of Gandhian social work.

FOUNDATION OF GANDHIAN THOUGHT

Mahatma Gandhi (1869–1948) was a thinker, freedom fighter and spiritual yogi and now academicians in social work recognize him as a social worker, for he experimented and tested his principles and found its utility in solving day-to-day practical problems of human life. We can pinpoint the two dimensions of Gandhi's thought: idealistic and pragmatic. Gandhi wanted to maintain the synergy between idealism and pragmatism. He believed that every person has a soul, and the ultimate goal of a person was to realize that soul (Dāsa, 2005, p. 216). Gandhi's ideas were based on the purity of means in life. Only through pure means persons can bring happiness in their life. Gandhi did not distinguish between means and end. He believed that the end would be attained according to the nature of means, and the means is the manifest or latent form of the end (Cortright, 2020).

Gandhi's pragmatic aspect of thought centred on spiritualizing society. On the one hand, Gandhi believed in the divinity of a person and, on the other hand, prepared the ground to actualize that divinity. In his view, religion or spirituality should not be limited to a temple or church or a mosque (Richards, 2005). The whole society is dependent on spiritual values and can contribute to achieve the ultimate goal of human life.

INFLUENCE ON GANDHI

During his lifetime, Mahatma Gandhi had met many scholars from Europe, Asia and South Africa and had studied their books. These included Leo Tolstoy, Victor Cousin, Henry David Thoreau, John Ruskin and Max Muller. He was also influenced by scriptures such as Gita, Bible, Quran and religious teachings of Buddhism. During his stay in England, Gandhi had met two theosophist unmarried siblings who were the devoted readers of the Bhagavad Gita. They invited Gandhi to read the original Gita in Sanskrit. Despite insufficient knowledge in Sanskrit, he first read the Gita with the two brothers in England in 1888–1889. He considered the Gita to be the best treatise of philosophy and decided to memorize one or two verses daily from it and, in his way, he memorized the entire Gita.

Gandhi accepted at one place that

> When doubts haunt me, when disappointments stare me in the face, and I see not one ray of hope on the horizon, I turn to *Bhagavad-Gita* and find a verse to comfort me; and I immediately begin to smile in the midst of overwhelming sorrow. Those who meditate on the Gita will derive fresh joy and new meanings from it every day. (Perumpallikunnel, 2013)

He considered the teachings of the Gita as an accurate reflection of non-violence and believed that the characters of Pandavas and Kauravas were the symbols of auspicious and inauspicious (Desai, 1946). It was the impression of Gita on his mind that he wrote a book *Gita, My Mother*.

Gandhi said that he did not believe in the things inconsistent with the logic, and his mind does not consider it as scripture (Lal, 2013), that is, he did not believe in the scriptural credibility of anything inconsistent with the universal principles of virtue. For him, Gita gave exact reasons for sticking to it. Gandhi took pride in calling himself a Hindu which, according to him, is so vast that it not only has tolerance towards other religions but also assimilates them. He was flexible enough to suggest that those who do not have faith in the Gita should follow other scripture.

Gandhi's life was equally influenced by various aspects of Christianity. He believed that Christianity was the source of motivation for love, truth, sacrifice and compassion (Gandhi & Desai, 1966, p. 157). Gandhi accepted these in his autobiography *My Experiments with Truth*. He had infinite respect for the *Sermon on the Mount* and its lines, which suggest that 'whosoever shall smite thee on thy right cheek, turn to him the other also' (Gandhi & Desai, 1966). Gandhi considered Jesus Christ the greatest *Satyagrahi* of the world who used the *Satyagraha* against the evils. However, he condemned the way Christian theologians interpreted the doctrines of Bible. He was against the view that Christ was the only Prophet of God and believed that he was one like Rama, Krishna, Buddha, Mahavir and Prophet Muhammad.

Gandhi believed in pluralism. He had studied Buddhism and considered it as a part of Hinduism. Gandhi considered Mahatma Buddha to be an illustrator of the new vision rather than a founder of a new religion. The Buddha revived the philosophy of Vasudhaiva Kutumbakam, that is, the whole world is a family. Gandhi said that he had immense respect for Buddha, and he was the greatest preachers of peace, and the mantra of Buddha is the mantra of peace (Gandhi, 1924, p. 86). Gandhi was of the view that Buddha understood the soul, its purity and immortality in a different way. Islam also had a profound impact on Mahatma Gandhi. Gandhi acknowledged that he read the biography of the Prophet Mohammed and the translated text of the Quran.

INDIVIDUAL AND SOCIETY

Gandhi tried to maintain a harmonious relationship between the individual and society. In Gandhi's view, a person is born good. He possesses virtues such as truth, non-violence and love. He believed that a person is born social and as such is a social organism (Mandelbaum, 1973). He considered the individual as a unit of society. The character and attitude of an individual are shaped by society. However, he viewed that society has the responsibility to socialize a person through values such as truth, non-violence, sacrifice, compassion and love.

Gandhi spent his entire life in building an egalitarian society free from exploitation. For this, he tried to use truth, non-violence, *Satyagraha* and constructive programmes as the methods. His overall goal was to establish Sarvodaya, where the focus was on the development of the last one in the social ladder. To realize this, he worked in the area of poverty eradication, drug de-addiction, women empowerment and making society self-reliant. He continuously strived for environmental protection and adoption of Swadeshi. Gandhi advocated for following an utterly nature-based way of life. He said:

> when I say that there was a time when society was based not on exploitation but justice, I mean to suggest that truth and ahimsa were not virtues confined to individuals but were

practised by communities. To me, virtue ceases to have any value if it is cloistered or possible only for an individual. (Gandhi, 1959, p. 15)

He believed that a society built on the foundation of these values would be egalitarian and free from any problem.

> **Did You Know?**
>
> **Seven Social Sins**
>
> In March 1925, an Anglican priest Frederick Lewis Donaldson delivered a sermon and referred it to the seven deadly social evils. Gandhi published a similar list in his weekly *Young India* on 22 October 1922 and wrote in the commentary that a 'fair friend' had sent him the list and he wanted the readers of *Young India* to know these social sins. Gandhi wanted the individuals to learn the list and abide by heart. During his last years, he used to keep his grandson, Arun Gandhi, close to him and days before his assassination he gave the list to his grandson. Below is the list that was believed by Gandhi to cause social harm and weaken the society:
>
> - Politics without principles
> - Wealth without work
> - Pleasure without conscience
> - Knowledge without character
> - Commerce without morality
> - Science without humanity
> - Worship without sacrifice

DIMENSIONS OF GANDHIAN SOCIAL WORK

As it has been written, Gandhi wanted to build an egalitarian society. He coined the term 'Sarvodaya' for such society in 1908 as he translated the book of John Ruskin on political economy, *Unto This Last*, and lived by this philosophy for the rest of his life. Sarvodaya means the upliftment of all, and its three principles are as follows:

- The good of an individual is contained in the good of all.
- A lawyer's work has the same value as the barber's in as much as all have the same right of earning their livelihood from their work.
- A life of labour, that is, the life of tiller of the soil and the handicraftsman is the life worth living.

Gandhi was of the view that earth has enough to feed people but cannot satisfy their greed. In the Sarvodaya society, as conceived by him, everyone will be free from limitless greed and will simply live their life. For realizing the dream of Sarvodaya or the upliftment of all, he proposed a constructive programme which is discussed in the next section.

CONSTRUCTIVE PROGRAMME FOR THE RECONSTRUCTION OF SOCIETY

Gandhi envisaged constructive programmes as a way to make a self-reliant society. By self-reliant, he meant the independence of every unit. Through his programme, he wanted to develop the Indian society with a regional balance. According to him, if the plan of this programme is worked out, the 'end of it would be the independence we want' (Gandhi, 1945, p. 1).

The constructive programmes are 18 in number and include communal unity, removal of untouchability, promotion of khadi and other village industries, village sanitation, new or basic education, adult education, women, education in health and hygiene, provincial languages, national languages, economic equality, kisans, labours, adivasis, lepers and students. This programme is a balanced vision for the development of society. Main aspects of the constructive programme, such as Gram Swaraj, development, social empowerment, linguistic development, drug addiction and education are particularly relevant for social workers.

GRAM SWARAJ

Even today, a large number of people dwell in villages. Gandhi was particularly interested in Indian society and believed that the roots of Indian culture lie in these villages (Jodhka, 2002). He was in favour of the preservation of these villages and wanted to make it a politically independent entity for the sake of development, which, according to him, was the prerequisite for the attainment of self-reliance of the village of Gram Swaraj. Further, he advocated for the establishment of khadi and other small-scale industries in these villages. In his words, 'when we have become village-minded, we will not want imitations of the West or machine-made products, but we will develop a true national taste in keeping with the vision of a new India in which pauperism, starvation and idleness will be unknown' (Gandhi, 1959, p. 18). The issues like village production and consumption can be decided collectively in a participatory manner. Gandhi conceived of such a society in which the produce would be divided equally among all, no one will have personal property, and all will be equal. From this perspective, the attainment of Gram Swaraj was the goal of Gandhi, whereas the constructive programme as a means to attain this goal.

DEVELOPMENT

The concept of development is very complicated. Different scholars described it differently. Gandhi did not consider it appropriate to achieve material development through modern technology. He thought that the machine helps to climb on the backs of millions of people (Radhakrishnan, 2019). Gandhi believed that growth does not mean growth of material goods; instead, it meant the development of values. He viewed competition as unfair for the sake of development and believed that competition should be in life values rather than material development. Gandhi was in favour of the creation of such a society in which there would be no uncontrolled production and consumption of very physical goods and exploitation of the natural environment but an attempt to move towards an equitable life by establishing a balance between man and nature. Today, we talk about sustainable development. Gandhi's development vision is in line with the Sustainable Development Goals, as preserving nature while maintaining the pace of development is the basis of sustainable development. Gandhi's vision can help to achieve sustainable development goals.

SOCIAL EMPOWERMENT

Social empowerment means the welfare, development and empowerment of all sections of the society. Gandhi envisioned building a society free from poverty, illiteracy, untouchability and communalism through constructive programmes.

LINGUISTIC DEVELOPMENT

Gandhi considered language an essential medium for the development of society. That is why he gave equal importance to the national as well as the provincial language in the development of a nation. He believed that education imparted in mother tongue is effective, and there should be a national language which could connect the whole country.

DE-ADDICTION

Gandhi worked for the eradication of the prevalence of intoxication in society. Drug addiction makes society hollow, and the creation of a self-reliant society is possible only through drug de-addiction. So there is a need for self-control in order to make the society free from this evil.

EDUCATION

Gandhi considered education to be a significant agent for the development of society. His vision of education was not only theoretical but also practical, which is known as 'basic education' or 'new education'. He considered education as a medium of physical, mental and spiritual development rather than as a medium for physical development. That is why Gandhi's conceptualization of this education is known as '3H', that is, balanced development of heart, head and hand is the primary goal of education. He was in favour of such teachers in basic education, whose ideas are original, who have true enthusiasm and who can think every day what to teach students today (Gandhi, 1951). For this, there should be a revolution in the education system; there should be a revolution in the eyes of the teacher.

He believed that 'basic education' could connect all the children in India, whether they are residents of villages or cities, with its eternal and permanent elements. He advocated for such an education which could develop both the mind and body of the children, connect them to the earth and country, show them a glorious picture of themselves and the future of the country. According to Gandhi, poverty and injustice were the outcomes of illiteracy (Box 25.1).

> **Box 25.1 Gandhi's Work in Timeline**
>
> | | |
> |---|---|
> | 1899 | Indian Ambulance Corp established during the Boer war |
> | 1904 | Phoenix Settlement established |
> | 1906 | The advent of *Satyagraha* against the Black Act in South Africa |
> | 1910 | Tolstoy Farm established |
> | 1915 | *Satyagraha* Ashram in Kochrab established |
> | 1917 | Established Sabarmati Ashram |
> | 1918 | Addressed about 5,000 peasants in Nadiad against pay and land revenue |
> | 1920 | Established Gujrat Vidyapith |
> | 1925 | Established All-India Spinners' Association |
> | 1932 | Established Harijan Sevak Sangh |
> | 1933 | Satyagraha Ashram, Sabarmati, was given to Harijan Sevak Sangh |
> | 1934 | Established All-India Village Industries |
> | 1947 | Tour to communal violence-affected areas of Noakhali and Bihar |

SATYAGRAHA AS A METHOD OF CONFLICT RESOLUTION

Conflict is a process in which two or more persons, groups or organizations struggle and one person, group or organization tries to achieve the target by defeating the other by competition or other means. The target for the struggle can be anything such as money, land or a vital position. Gandhi considered the process of struggle as a situation between justice and injustice in which the unjust persons or groups arbitrarily exploit the rights or resources of other persons or groups for their benefit. A person seeking justice in such a situation can demand their rights using the Gandhian method of *Satyagraha*. According to Gandhi, a *Satyagrahi*, who is a justice seeker, will believe in the divinity and humanity of the unjust person (Prabhu & Rao, 1967). Gandhi believed that the goodness in unjust person is buried somewhere in the heart. So the main goal of *Satyagrahi* is to promote goodness in the unjust person. In this way, Gandhi's *Satyagraha* is the method to change the heart of the unjust person and thereby to resolve the conflict. There are three steps in the method of *Satyagraha* method of conflict resolution. These include understanding the nature, dynamics and feasibility of conflict resolution. Once the nature of the conflict, its goal and the reason for its persistence is understood, one can think of the shared goal that is beneficial for both the parties. Besides, the Gandhian method of conflict resolution stresses the need to bring a positive transformation in the lives of the conflicting parties as well as in society.

In the process of resolution of conflict, Gandhi argued for following specific life values, for instance, he talked of faith in God and not to use the path of non-violence psychologically, physically or verbally under any circumstances (Rosenberg & Chopra, 2015). Gandhi was against the idea of causing harm to public property to get the voice heard and believed that non-cooperation could be more effective if the cause is just.

Gandhi considered negotiation, compromise and acknowledgement of mistakes as the essential tools for maintenance of peace in society. With these tools, two or more parties can understand each other's interests and needs, and can succeed in making decisions at a mutually agreeable condition. Gandhi expected the *Satyagrahis* to accept their shortcomings and be ready for a compromise (Hardiman, 2005). This method requires a commitment for a time as the relevance of any conflict and its resolution is for a particular time. Therefore, a *Satyagrahi* must keep his time in focus and try to achieve his primary goal peacefully. It is necessary for a *Satyagrahi*, in Gandhi's view, that they always communicate with the opposition peacefully.

> **Did You Know?**
>
> **SEWA**
>
> Self Employed Women's Association (SEWA), is an organization for poor working women headquartered in Ahmedabad, Gujarat. It traces its evolution from the Textile Labour Association (TLA) whose one of the founding members was Mahatma Gandhi. Earlier, the women's wing of TLA used to work for working women, working outside textile mill for higher wages from employer and protection of labour rights. In 1972, Ela Bhatt, a leader of women's wing of TLA and Arvind Buch came out as a trade union registered under the Trade Union Act of 1926. As of 2016, its membership across India was 1,339,621 and it is one of the leading trade unions of India.

ETHICS OF GANDHIAN SOCIAL WORK

Social workers work with a diverse range of target groups. These can be individuals, groups, family, community or society. As a humanitarian profession, the role of ethics is significant in social work as it guides the social workers and the target groups as well in such questions as what is acceptable and what is not, or what is right and what is wrong. Gandhi was very firm in his belief and practised what he believed to be right. His fundamental values were truth and non-violence for all his thoughts and actions. He wrote, 'We have to make truth and nonviolence, not matters for mere individual practise but practise by groups and communities and nations. That, at any rate, is my dream. I shall live and die in trying to realise it' (Gangrade & Misra, 1990, p. 41). Gandhi believed truth to be God, and non-violence was the means to reach that God. Gandhi's truth was ideal as well as practical. He always tried to hold his truth to the test of non-violence and, to check his credentials, applied its principles on him before applying it to the society. In this way, Gandhi's idea of truth and non-violence came out after rigorous practice. Gandhi also applied this principle of truth and non-violence during his stay at Sabarmati and Sevagram ashrams; he made it almost mandatory for the residents of the ashram to chant 11 vows or *Ekadash Vrat*. These vows are useful for social workers as moral principles and can play a vital role in bringing about a comprehensive and spiritual transformation in the lives of both social workers and target groups. The first two of these 11 vows, that is, truth and non-violence, have already been dealt with in the section foundation of Gandhian thought. Rest nine vows proposed by Gandhi are explained below.

TRUTH

The first in the principle of *Ekadash Vrat* is *Satya* or truth. Truth means the prohibition of lies from mind and word. Gandhi believed that if the individual follows the principles of truth, the others will follow them in word and action (Bilgrami, 2003). Only then society can be changed. This principle is vital for a social worker as well as the client in the sense that no one should mislead the other and must follow the principle of truth at their level of behaviour. In Gandhi's view, the person who follows the truth does not make any distinction between personal and public life and their personal and public life is utterly transparent. This virtue makes them more receptive to society, and society will believe in their words and deeds.

NON-VIOLENCE

Ahimsa or non-violence is the second in the list of Gandhi's *Ekadash Vrat*. It means not to hurt any person or organism with mind, speech or deed. Gandhi's non-violence applies not only to the action but also to the cognitive level of mind for the fact that Gandhi knew that violence originates in the mind and comes out in the form of word and action. When a person commits violence at the level of the mind and tries to prevent it at the level of word or deed, then they hurt themselves emotionally. Gandhi believed that violence arises out of a person's ego; therefore, one should be egoless (Borman, 1986). He believed that where there is ego, there is arrogance and where there is no ego, there are civilization and pride (Borman, 1986). Those who take pride will behave with everyone in a friendly manner, and that will be their dharma. They see themselves in others and others in themselves, whereas an arrogant will see themselves above all.

BRAHMACHARYA (CELIBACY)

Brahmacharya is the third principle of Gandhi's 11 vows. *Brahmacharya* refers to staying away from indulgences from every kind of things. Gandhi believed that the attainment of God is possible only when celibacy is followed. Gandhi considered the prohibition of indulgence in sex while observing the celibacy. He instructs the people working in public life not to get married and follow celibacy in their life. According to him, adherence to *Brahmacharya* makes a person physically, mentally and characteristically healthy (Lal, 2000). While social workers may not follow celibacy in a strict sense, it is essential as a guiding principle for directing them to stay away from over-indulgence into anything.

ASTEYA (NON-STEALING)

Asteya, the fourth principle, implies no stealing. Gandhi considered any form of stealing unethical and believed that it arises out of a person's greed. When we take away the belongings of a person, they feel sad; therefore, this act is uncivilized. This act is the hindrance to the development of sound thought of humanity. So this principle is essential for a social worker for remaining faithful to the society.

APARIGRAHA (NON-POSSESSION)

Aparigraha means the prohibition of over-collection of anything or any resource. Gandhi believed that non-possession is the highest kind of justice with nature and society (Pantham, 1983). At the same time, over-possession is a crime against nature and society. An act of non-possession creates a balance among individuals, society and nature. The same grace creates an imbalance between person, society and nature. A social worker must not possess what is not needed.

BREAD LABOUR

Physical labour is essential for a person doing social work in Gandhi's views. A person should earn their livelihood by doing manual labour themselves. Gandhi believed that living on the labour of others is a form of theft (Gandhi, 1960). A social worker is accepted by society if they earn their livelihood by their labour. It is an essential fact that Gandhi continued to do manual labour during his whole life. This practice made his personality attractive to society.

ASWAD—CONTROL OF PALATE

Aswad is the sixth of the 11 vows of Gandhi. Gandhi was against the idea of the intake of food for taste. He considered flavoured food as the root of uncontrolled behaviour as it creates insensitivity in humans (Iyengar, 2006). Gandhi used to eat neem chutney regularly to control his taste. However, Gandhi was very supportive of nutritional food. In Gandhi's view, a social worker must observe fast along with control of taste which, according to him, purifies one's mind. Fasting is one such method by which the person or society moves from material things to develop their consciousness towards non-material things.

FEARLESSNESS

In Gandhi's view, it is impossible to realize God without the virtue of fearlessness. However, Gandhi's God was not the religious God; it was the virtue of truthfulness (Richards, 2005). He devoted his life in the service of humanity and argued for believing in human service rather than in some imaginary God. When individuals live a selfless life, fearlessness manifests itself in their life. In Gandhi's view, there is no need to be afraid of any kind of threat because the consciousness of the individual is eternal and immortal. There is a need to use this consciousness in the duty of society. For a social worker, this principle is essential, as there arise many problems in society, a social worker instead of fearing from these problems should confront and look into the solution.

EQUAL RESPECT FOR ALL RELIGION

Gandhi considered religion to be an integral part of human life. He believed that every religion follows the same absolute God (Rao, 1990). So he had a clear vision that all religions are equal and should be treated equally. Discriminating in the name of religion is not righteousness. Religion always helps human beings to advance their consciousness towards one supreme God. Therefore, all human beings, irrespective of their religion or belief, must have a sense of respect for all religions and faiths. A social worker should keep the same attitude towards all religions.

SWADESHI (INDIGENOUSNESS)

Indigenousness or Swadeshi refers to the use of locally available resources for the fulfilment of one's need. Gandhi saw Swadeshi as a service to society and called it the law of laws. A person can support their neighbour in the right way by adopting Swadeshi. Adoption of Swadeshi makes a person and their neighbour self-reliant. Gandhi's vision behind Swadeshi was related to ecological balance. He supported the development of India based on the lines of Indian models. Gandhi cautioned India against the blind imitation of the Western civilization. While commenting about Europe, Gandhi wrote:

> European civilisation is no doubt suited for the Europeans, but it will mean ruin for India if we endeavour to copy it. This is not to say that we may not adopt and assimilate whatever may be good and capable of assimilation by us, as it does not also mean that even the Europeans will not have to part with whatever evil might have crept into it. The incessant search for material comforts and their multiplication is such evil, and I make bold to say that the Europeans themselves will have to remodel their outlook if they are not to perish under the weight of the comforts to which they are becoming slaves. It may be that my reading is wrong, but I know that for India to run after the Golden Fleece is to court certain death. (Rao, 2017)

Gandhi was not against the Western civilization and was of the view that each place has its potential, and people living in that place can attain development using those possibilities. He believed that if people imitate the pattern of development outside their region, it will be incompatible and lead to the disturbance of balance. A social worker working in the spirit of Swadeshi will be more devoted to their environment and society.

REMOVAL OF UNTOUCHABILITY

Gandhi was aware of the discriminatory behaviour of untouchability, particularly prevalent in the Indian society, and considered it as a curse. He believed that there is the same soul created by one God in all human beings, and no one is superior or inferior by birth, and instructed the people living in his ashram to work against untouchability (Gandhi, 1955). He thought that untouchability makes individuals so arrogant that they even consider the loving touch of their cohabitant as impure. The way fire burns all things put in it, a social worker is also expected to create the same human spirit by eliminating the evils of society at their level.

Gandhi's 11 vows can prove to be a milestone in the development of social work. These 11 vows must be appropriately used as the ethics of social work while diagnosing problems and working with the target groups.

SUMMARY

This chapter deals with Gandhi's approach to social work and shows how his philosophy and principles provide a vision to build a balanced, prosperous and self-reliant society. Based on the foundation of truth and non-violence, Gandhi's ideas are practical for social work practice. *Satyagraha* is a method of conflict resolution. Gandhian social work is not only for India but for the whole world and humanity. Gandhi worked for the creation of egalitarian society through constructive programmes which transcend across economic, political and social spheres. Ethics is particularly crucial for Gandhian social worker, and it is proposed as 11 vows. Gandhi's 11 vows illuminate social work practice.

TOP 10 TAKEAWAYS/MAIN POINTS

1. Gandhi considered a person divine and advocated to realize that divinity.
2. Gandhi was influenced by thinkers such as Leo Tolstoy, Victor Cousin, Thoreau, Ruskin and Max Muller.
3. Gandhi considered Gita as his mother and followed its teaching in his life.
4. The essential elements of Gandhian social work are truth and non-violence.
5. Gandhi stressed the need for the creation of national and provincial language.
6. *Satyagraha* is a method of conflict resolution.
7. *Aparigraha* is the fifth principle of 11 vows which means that over-possession of material things is not right.
8. A social worker must respect all religion equally.
9. Gandhi stressed the purity of means for the achievement of a means.
10. Gandhi viewed untouchability as a curse.

Keywords: Gandhi, Gandhian social work, truth, non-violence

GLOSSARY

***Aparigraha*:** It literally means free from control on anything. In practice, it means not to over-possess material things. It is one of the principles of Jainism which influenced Gandhi.

***Brahmacharya*:** It is the first ashram in Vedic religion in which a person of age 1–24 years is suggested to get education and live a life free from other worldly things. Gandhi adopted it from Jainism, which places equal importance to it.

Gandhian Social Work

 MULTIPLE CHOICE QUESTIONS

1. Which of the following thinkers did not influence Gandhi?
   a. Leo Tolstoy
   b. Victor Cousin
   c. Thoreau
   d. **All of the above**

2. Which of the following is not included in the constructive programme?
   a. Communal unity
   b. Khadi
   c. Kisan
   d. **Transgender**

3. Which one is not an element of '3H' proposed by Gandhi?
   a. Heart
   b. **Heel**
   c. Head
   d. Hand

4. What is bread labour?
   a. **Livelihood by doing manual labour**
   b. Livelihood by charity
   c. Livelihood by beggary
   d. Livelihood by loan

5. Which of the following is not an element in Gandhi's 11 vows?
   a. **Education**
   b. Truth
   c. *Brahmacharya*
   d. Non-violence

6. Which of the following is an element in Gandhi's 11 vows?
   a. Development
   b. **Bread labour**
   c. Social empowerment
   d. De-addiction

7. When did Gandhi first used *Satyagraha*?
   a. **1906**
   b. 1907
   c. 1908
   d. 1909

8. Who wrote the book *Unto This Last*?
   a. Thoreau
   b. Victor Cousin
   c. Max Muller
   d. **John Ruskin**

9. When was Tolstoy farm established?
   a. 1931
   b. **1932**
   c. 1933
   d. 1934

10. The number of constructive programmes as proposed by Gandhi are
    a. 17
    b. **18**
    c. 19
    d. 20

REVIEW QUESTIONS

1. What are the religious scriptures that influenced Gandhi?
2. What kind of relationship did Gandhi envisage between individual and society?
3. What are the three principles of Sarvodaya?
4. What do you understand by Gram Swaraj?
5. What does truth mean?
6. What do you mean by Swadeshi?

REFERENCES

Bilgrami, A. (2003). Gandhi, the philosopher. *Economic & Political Weekly*, 4159–4165.
Borman, W. (1986). *Gandhi and non-violence*. SUNY Press.
Cortright, D. (2020). *Gandhi and beyond: Nonviolence for an age of terrorism*. Routledge.
Dāsa, R. (2005). *The global vision of Mahatma Gandhi*. Sarup & Sons.
Desai, M. H. (1946). *The gospel of selfless action: Or, the Gita, according to Gandhi*. Navajivan Publishing House.
Gandhi, M. K. (1924). *Collected works* (Vol. 40, p. 160; speech at a Buddha Jayanti meeting in Bombay on 18 May 1924, in *The Collected Works* (Vol. 24).
Gandhi, M. K. (1945). *Constructive programme—Its meaning and place*. Prabhat Prakashan.
Gandhi, M. K. (1951). *Basic education*. Navajivan Publishing House.
Gandhi, M. K. (1955). *Ashram observances in action*. Prabhat Prakashan.
Gandhi, M. K. (1959). *Panchayat raj*. Prabhat Prakashan.
Gandhi, M. K. (1960). *Bread labour: The gospel of work*. Navajivan Publishing House.
Gandhi, M. K., & Desai, M. (1966). *An autobiography or the story of my experiments with truth*. Navajivan Publishing House.
Gangrade, K. D., & Misra, R. P. (Eds.). (1990). *Conflict resolution through nonviolence: Science and ethics* (Vol. 1). Concept Publishing Company.
Hardiman, D. (2005). *Gandhi: In his time and ours*. Orient Blackswan.
Iyengar, S. (2006). *Liberty and individualism in Gandhian perspective*. Gujarat Vidyapith.
Jodhka, S. S. (2002). Nation and village: Images of rural India in Gandhi, Nehru and Ambedkar. *Economic & Political Weekly*, 3343–3353.
Lal, V. (2000). Nakedness, nonviolence, and Brahmacharya: Gandhi's experiments in celibate sexuality. *Journal of the History of Sexuality*, 9(1/2), 105–136. www.jstor.org/stable/3704634
Lal, V. (2013). Gandhi's religion: Politics, faith, and hermeneutics. *Journal of Sociology and Social Anthropology*, 4(1–2), 31–40.
Mandelbaum, D. (1973). The study of life history: Gandhi. *Current Anthropology*, 14(3), 177–206. www.jstor.org/stable/2740760
Pantham, T. (1983). Thinking with Mahatma Gandhi: Beyond liberal democracy. *Political Theory*, 11(2), 165–188.
Perumpallikunnel, K. (2013). Discernment: The message of the Bhagavad-Gita. *Acta Theologica*, 32(2S), 271–290.
Prabhu, R. K., & Rao, U. R. (Eds.). (1967). *The mind of Mahatma Gandhi*. Navajivan Publishing House.
Radhakrishnan, S. (Ed.). (2019). *Mahatma Gandhi: Essays and reflections on his life and work*. Routledge.
Rao, K. S. (1990). *Mahatma Gandhi and comparative religion*. Motilal Banarsidass Publications.

Rao, U. M. (2017). *The message of Mahatma Gandhi*. Publications Division Ministry of Information & Broadcasting.
Richards, G. (2005). *The philosophy of Gandhi: A study of his basic ideas*. Routledge.
Rosenberg, M. B., & Chopra, D. (2015). *Nonviolent communication: A language of life: Life-changing tools for healthy relationships*. Puddle Dancer Press.

RECOMMENDED READINGS

Bakker, H. (1993). *Toward a just civilisation: A Gandhian perspective on human rights and development*. Canadian Scholars' Press.
Bondurant, J. V. (1965). *Conquest of violence: The Gandhian philosophy of conflict* (Vol. 243). University of California Press.
Bose, A. (1981). A Gandhian perspective on peace. *Journal of Peace Research, 18*(2), 159–164.
Burrowes, R. J. (1996). *The strategy of nonviolent defense: A Gandhian approach*. SUNY Press.
Chabot, S. (2012). *Transnational roots of the civil rights movement: African American explorations of the Gandhian repertoire*. Lexington Books.
Dayal, P. (1986). *Gandhian approach to social work* (Vol. 27). Gujarat Vidyapith.
Diwan, R. K., & Lutz, M. A. (1985). *Essays in Gandhian economics*. Gandhi Peace Foundation.
Fox, R. G. (1990). *Gandhian utopia: Experiments with culture*. Beacon Press.
Gandhi, S. (2007). *Gandhian way: Peace, nonviolence, and empowerment*. Academic Foundation.
Ghosh, B. N. (2007). *Gandhian political economy: Principles, practice and policy*. Ashgate Publishing, Ltd.
Gupta, V. K. (1992). *Ahimsa in India's destiny: A study of the ethico-spiritual ahimsa, its roots in ancient Indian history, and its role as a political weapon during the Gandhian era*. South Asia Books.
Hardiman, D. (2001). *Champaran and Gandhi: Planters, peasants and Gandhian politics* by Jacques Pouchepadass, pp. xxii; 277 (Book review). *Journal of the Royal Asiatic Society, 11*(1), 99–101.
Jesudasan, I. (1987). *A Gandhian theology of liberation* (Vol. 3). Gujarat Sahitya Prakash.
Jha, S. N. (1961). *A critical study of Gandhian economic thought*. Lakshmi Narain Agarwal.
Kripalani, J. B. (1961). *Gandhian thought*. Gandhi Smarak Nidhi.
Kumar, R. (1971). *Essays on Gandhian politics: The Rowlatt Satyagraha of 1919*. Clarendon Press.
Kumarappa, J. C. (1951). *Gandhian economic thought*. AB Sarva Seva Sangh Prakashan.
Mantena, K. (2012). Another realism: The politics of Gandhian nonviolence. *American Political Science Review, 106*(2), 455–470.
Mazzarella, W. (2010). Branding the Mahatma: The untimely provocation of Gandhian publicity. *Cultural Anthropology, 25*(1), 1–39.
Mishra, A. D., & Dadage, M. S. (Eds.). (2002). *Panchayati Raj: Gandhian perspective*. Mittal Publications.
Misra, R. P. (1989). *Gandhian model of development and world peace* (Vol. 1). Concept Publishing Company.
Mukherjee, S. (1991). *Gandhian thought, Marxist interpretation*. South Asia Books.
Pani, N. (2001). *Inclusive economics: Gandhian method and contemporary policy*. SAGE.
Rani, A. (1981). *Gandhian non-violence and India's free struggle*. Shree Publishing House.
Ray, R. (1982). *My reminiscences: Social development during the Gandhian era and after*. South Asia Books.
Rigby, A. (1985). Practical utopianism: A Gandhian approach to rural community development in India. *Community Development Journal, 20*(1), 2–9.
Rosen, G. (1982). Gandhian economics: A Schumpeterian perspective. *Journal of Economic Issues, 16*(2), 435–438.
Roy, R. (1984). *Self and society: A study in Gandhian thought*. SAGE.

Sethi, J. D. (1990). *International economic disorder (a theory of economic Darwinism) & a Gandhian solution* (Vol. 68). Indian Institute of Advanced Study.

Singh, R. (1983). *The relevance of Gandhian thought.* Classical Pub. Co.

Sørensen, G. (1992). Utopianism in peace research: The Gandhian heritage. *Journal of Peace Research, 29*(2), 135–144.

Spodek, H. (1994). The Self Employed Women's Association (SEWA) in India: Feminist, Gandhian power in development. *Economic Development and Cultural Change, 43*(1), 193–202.

Walz, T., & Ritchie, H. (2000). Gandhian principles in social work practice: Ethics revisited. *Social Work, 45*(3), 213–222.

Weber, T. (2001). Gandhian philosophy, conflict resolution theory and practical approaches to negotiation. *Journal of Peace Research, 38*(4), 493–513.

Weber, T. (2006). *Gandhi, Gandhism and the Gandhians.* Lotus Collection, Roli Books.

26

African Social Work

Safia Winifred Ahmadu

LEARNING OBJECTIVES

- To understand and articulate the generics of African social work practice involving traditional methods of social services revolving around various traditional cultures and values of African societies
- To address the strategies involving traditional practices that reduce problems and issues in human relationship that improve human interaction through kinship and clan relationship, thereby enriching individual's life maximally

I could go into their reality any time I chose to, but they could never come into mine. This is what I called 'helping' them.

—Agnostic Zetetic

INTRODUCTION

Social work is becoming increasingly popular in Africa. It is one of the helping professions in the world today, concerned with helping individuals, social groups and communities that are socially and economically disadvantaged in mobilizing or transforming appropriate resources within and outside the individual's environment, problem-solving and enhancing the quality of individual's life.

Social work is also an enabling life task that tends to meet an individual's daily living that is as old as the family system. The life tasks and challenges come from family, marriage, work and business. Traditionally, in most African countries, social services were provided within the family, clan and communities to individuals in need whose members are living within the communities. Such services were in terms of helps at home, on the farms, contributions and provisions of basic amenities. However, the colonialization of some of the African countries changed these communal lifestyles of most African countries, which is highly attributed to labour mobility and migration from rural areas to urban areas for white-collar jobs and menial work by indigenous Africans on farms and manufacturing outfits for the colonialists.

The structures of traditional social services, however, embrace more than all of these, including the essential services which are required to ensure that the purpose behind the framework of traditionalism is accomplished.

AFRICAN TRADITIONAL STRUCTURES FOR SOCIAL SERVICES

The African traditional structures for social services provide useful background for understanding the successes and failures of African social services and how some of the non-indigenous structures have managed to change the structures to social work to meet the changing needs of the evolving traditions of the African societies.

African traditional structures consist of the following:

1. Council of elders
2. Institution of traditional historians
3. Age grade
4. Oracles
5. Nuclear and the extended family
6. Town criers
7. Custodians of traditional professions
8. Local training institutions for personal development, especially for women before marriage (Chukuma, 2013)

a. In all traditional African society, the Council of elders is the highest decision-making body concerned in the running of the society. Their decisions were final concerning marriage, work, death, burial and even work.
b. The institution of traditional historians are the traditional priests (i.e., in Nigeria, they are called *Boka* and in the southern Africa they are called *sangoma*). They consulted for the good of the land. They consulted the oracles to interpret the decisions of the Gods of the land. They also perform sacrifices on behalf of the people for healing, land production, rain and appease the Gods against vengeance for the land. They are mandated to defend the tradition of the people.
c. People in African traditional societies are divided into age grade with peculiar responsibilities. For example, there is a particular age grade responsible for waging war and defending the integrity of the land. There is also another age grade responsible for the development of communities and also for the arrangement of various traditional ceremonies.
d. Oracles are the Gods and deity worshiped in most African traditional societies. These control the day-to-day actions of the people in the societies and give directions for the rulership of the various societies.
e. The nuclear family is the basic family unit responsible for raising children and bringing them up. It consists of the father, mother and children. One thing we must take note of

is that most African traditional families are polygamous in nature, where a man can have many wives and concubines. This forms part of the extended family system that exists to protect members of the family from family troubles and ancestors, thereby ensuring that everyone is his brother's keeper.

f. Town criers are the society's disseminators of information from one corner of the community to another. People within the community depend on town criers for any information they might need for their well-being within the community on decisions taken by the Council of elders (Chukuma, 2013).

After the Second World War, so many of the African countries suffered some setbacks for lack of what to do for sustenance, there were so many orphaned children who needed help in terms of food and medical care. This culminated to the introduction of social welfare services by the British within their colonies. However, these services were not viable enough because they were exposed to the winds and risks of change which led to the introduction of social work. Africa is characterized by a number of factors that play a substantial influential role in facilitating the emergence of social work. The missionaries, other African mutual aid organizations, in partnership with Europe and other parts of the world came up with various activities that led to the colonization of the continent by external powers there by contributing to social work development on the continent (Umoren, 2016). This chapter seeks to discuss African social work, its generics as social work practice in most African countries, involving traditional methods of social work, which focuses on reducing problems in human relationships and on enriching individual's life maximally and way of living through improved human interaction. The traditional structures for social work practice were mainly centred around provision and counselling which were already in place traditionally, but now modelled after the structure in Britain. These are as follows:

1. Care for families, especially children
2. Care for members of the community, deterrence from social problems
3. Providing assistance to the needy
4. Training in agricultural production and handcrafts
5. Counselling

AFRICAN SOCIAL VALUES

Social values and beliefs in most African societies and cultures seem to have been well established since pre-colonial times (Bernstein & Gray, 1996). Most of these values are activities which were so important that they form part of their belief systems in solving their social, economic, political and infrastructural challenges. MacPherson and Midgley (1987) noted that some of these

> Most societies continued to hold firm to the framework in which they lived most of their lives; the social organization of production and consumption, marriage and inheritance, communal and religious relationships were guarded and regulated by traditional institutions.

important values are a result of the extended family systems, where individual needs were seen as part of the needs of the wider society; the household was the centre for economic production, distribution and consumption; all individual needs were collectively met through joint effort and cooperative work within extended families, clans, villages and similar communities with similar types of work and skills. As a result, members within these groups were assured of some type of basic material and social services.

Culturally, clan and kinship family relationships are broadly defined and carry lots of weight with extensive obligations and duties from members of the family in most African societies. The extended family strategy has been used to confront social realities and problems of the individual member of the group. This is a kind of strategy which allows people with blood relationship and common ancestral relationship confront their social problems and enjoy other benefits from the extended family in many ways:

1. They share the same family name.
2. For economic reasons, that is, family farmlands and ascriptive roles.
3. For protection, where there is a problem with a member of the family, other members of the extended group are always there for rescue.
4. In social engagements such as marriage, birth and even in death, the head of the family is always there to prevail over the various ceremonies.

Other values which form part of African societies are their belief systems, the role of exhibiting their faith is always conspicuous and this tightens their relationships with one another. The two types of family relations are so organized to deal with social situations and other circumstances that could arise within the family structure. In Africa, the extended family system is seen as a great strategy in dealing with social problems. It is actually believed that blood and ancestry relationships were strategies for helping individuals adjust to the acceptable ways of life within the community in which they live in. Traditionally, the management and administration of social work and the provision of social services in most African pre-literate societies rely on the elders within the clan and kinship family. The elders interpreted every social, economic, political and all spiritual action according to the revelation of the Gods; decisions' concerning the running of most African societies make it impossible for members of the family and community to challenge or question their decisions.

Traditional strategies of social services extend to all strata of the society, these strategies have been put in place to help the children, women, the elderly, widow, people living with disabilities and for community development. The extended family system is always there to protect its members from the ancestral threats and also from the clan, kinship and other members of the community.

Social change in Africa as everywhere else is ubiquitous. Such influences as end of intra- and inter-tribal warfare with the coming of European colonialism, the Western money economy, industrialization, migration and urbanization have certainly transformed the traditional African family from what it was 50–100 years ago (Tembo, 1988). Midgley (1981) describes the colonial rule as the major social change that has ever taken place over time in Africa. It disorganized tribes, families and individuals from the support of the household extended family and kinship relationship. Although most societies continued to hold firm to the framework in which they lived most of their lives, the social organization of production and consumption, marriage and inheritance, communal and religious relationships were guarded and regulated by traditional institutions. However, some tribes and families were disbanded and some of the members were forced to leave their ascriptive ways of life for cheap labour in the developing cities. This movement disrupted most of the African traditional lifestyles and systems of social services.

POLITICAL SYSTEMS AND STRUCTURES IN AFRICA

In Africa, political systems and structures are divided among thousands of separate tribes, each with its own language, organization, custom and beliefs which represent their economic, political and social way of life as primitive, feudal or capitalist society (Radcliffe-Brown, 1931).

In West Africa, Turaki (1993) describes the political systems and structures in line with the Islamic belief in conjunction with the economic, social and political systems of what is called *Barantaka* (the local name for service in a capitalist and imperialistic environment in Hausa land in Northern Nigeria). This clearly shows that within this social system, the political and economic institutions, the kinship organization and religion are intimately related and interdependent, and cannot be separated. Everything that has to do with the individual social services is linked to the religious organization that is predominant within the specific communal or societal social setting. This shows that in pre-colonial Africa, most societies were organized on kinship occupational systems and within the territorial framework. The local police, *yandoka*, were the instruments by which coercion is exercised and crime deterred. Offenders were usually extricated, expelled and banned from societies for offences committed. With the introduction of colonialism, offenders were punished by actually jailing them for a number of days or months. These were done as directed by the men in authority within the society.

AFRICAN TRADITIONAL HISTORY

The importance of African history is embedded in the continuity in tradition and culture; therefore, in almost all African societies, there are traditional historians who are vast in the history and tradition of the people. They are always called upon to give an account of what happened in the past as it concerns the truth and justice. Examples of these are on land issues, crowning a king or ruler, marriage and death rites and so on; stories to uphold cultures and tradition have to be repeated on and on so that no one is short-changed or cheated. By this, the society remains peaceful with advancement socially, politically and economically.

Traditionally, African ways of meeting the social needs of the individuals were enhanced in the social functioning of individuals within the family clan or kinship group. During the pre-colonial era, in many of the African societies, social activities focused on the social relationships which constitute the interaction between man and his environment, and on their ascriptive occupational capacity (Federico, 1976). Festivals are organized for different reasons and were highly scheduled. Festivals are strategies used to promote social development, recreation and socialization among the youth; the youth meet their marriage partners during such festivals. There is also traditional thrift and cooperative groups that help the families financially. This method of saving money has been of immense benefit to most people living in African societies to have capital to run their small-scale businesses. The profits from such businesses have enabled people to marry off their children, engage in communal social functions and improve their welfare. There are also traditional courts established within societies that settle family dispute, land dispute and other forms of conflict that may arise from time to time. The traditional courts were some sort of deterrence.

Bernstein and Gray (1996), in the traditional social work theory, examine the psychological explanations of social problems, taking for granted the existing social order; this approach resulted in a number of issues. First, the explanations of traditional social work in meeting the social needs of the people are seen to reduce complex social problems to individual psychological problems and potentially blaming the victim. Second, approach used by traditional social work such as ecology theory encourages adaption to the present social order rather than questioning and fighting the undesired aspects of society. Third, traditional theory isolates people with social problems by seeing their problems as confidential and thus not allowing contact between the client and others. Finally, traditional theory strengthens and follows the oppressive social order of capitalist societies. So for the African people to cope with the modern challenges in traditional social work, it is important to have a look at the foundations of the indigenous cultures, norms and values of the societies (Mungai, 2015).

HISTORICAL EVOLUTION OF SOCIAL WORK IN AFRICA AND AFROCENTRIC SOCIAL WORK

Administratively, social services in African countries which were formerly colonies under Britain were changed from the traditional models and modelled after services already provided in Britain. The British policy of meeting the social needs of the people resulted in localizing welfare benefits only in areas where colonial interests were best served rather than spreading the services to where they are needed. Besides, the social services provided to the people were financed from the revenue collected from the colonies. However, as a result of the reports contained in the 'Ashridge Report' sponsored by the colonial office in 1954, greater concern for social services started to be given to almost all the British colonies, which led to the gradual expansion of social and welfare services (Haruna, 1986).

> So for the African people to cope with the modern challenges in traditional social work, it is important to have a look at the foundations of the indigenous cultures, norms and values of the societies (Mungai, 2015).

The organizational structure of social work has gone through lots of changes in Africa; this was due to the fact that overriding the traditional methods of social services and introducing social work services created a vacuum which would later on become less beneficial to the people. This vacuum could be termed as the loss of values and norms which hold the society together and gave the people a sense of belonging.

Social work emerged in most African countries in the 1980s and was mostly categorized into three parts:

1. Provision of services which was the responsibility of the administrative officers
2. Services were made the responsibility of departments of governments
3. Integration of services within various ministries

The development of social work was viewed as an agent for social change, which was intended to meet the challenges of our contemporary societies. Theoretically, this phenomenon was actually the product of social, economic, political and technological innovation in most developing countries in Africa (Haruna, 1986).

Social work has its roots in the Western theories and discourses which may not be compatible with the cultural values of non-Western people, especially those who have in the past been victims of Western imperialism. Afrocentric social work has its origin in the academic work of African–American academics in response to the needs and issues of African people and people of African descent around the world (Graham, 2002).

Bernstein and Gray (1996) see social work as focusing on the interaction between people and the institutions of society by identifying four purposes of social work; that the central approach is how to empower the client/people so that they can achieve their goals, work towards changing themselves and their environment. In relation to Vass (1996), Bernstein and Gray (1996) also state the importance of the development of the abilities of the people which would allow them to integrate knowledge, values and skills in order to produce competent practice.

Mungai (2015) examines the role of social workers as helping families within the communities and sometimes work with the individuals directly or indirectly, making referrals to resources in the community. One type of community social work he identified is community organization, of which most communities already have their own organized way of life. But he points out that social workers could help organize communities in ways which transcend service provision when traditional support structures fail in times of war or natural disasters. Afrocentric social work means social workers not only help people with their immediate needs but also set up systems that will endure after they leave.

Social work may be defined as an '....Art, science, and a profession that helps people solve personal, group (especially family) and community problems and attain satisfying personal relationships through social work practice. It addresses the multiple complex transactions between people and their environments' (Hussayn & Adah, 2012).

'Social work is a profession that promotes social change, problem solving in human relationships and the empowerment and liberation of people to enhance well-being' (Umoren, 2016).

Schiele (1997, p. 805) defines Afrocentric social work as 'a method of social work practice based on traditional African philosophical assumptions that are used to explain to solve human and social problems'.

Theories of human behaviour and social systems have been utilized to intervene at various points of peoples' interaction with their environments, indicating human rights and social justice principles as fundamental to social work. Seeking to discuss Afrocentric social work practice in Africa, the basic argument advanced in this chapter centres on the curative or remedial approach, which is currently used in many African countries, though it does not adequately address the needs of the numerous populations residing largely in rural areas of the continent. But it advocates for the adoption of the 'Afrocentric social work paradigm'.

The mission of Afrocentric social work is to enable all people to develop their full potential, enrich their lives and prevent dysfunction. Professional social work is focused on problem-solving and change. As such, social workers try to become change agents in society and in the lives of the individuals, families and communities they serve. Social work should be looked at as interrelated systems of values, theory and practice. These interrelated systems of values could be looked at from three different angles:

1. That the person is important,
2. That the person has personal, family and community problems resulting from interacting with others,
3. That something can be done to alleviate these problems by solving the challenges of the contemporary societies, which could be social, economic, political and technological innovations taking place in most developing countries (Schiele, 2000).

Mungai (2015) explains that Afrocentric social work has a wider application. The paradigm has identical principles with most African tribes, like in Nigeria and the Ubuntu, where African values and ethics are highly appreciated in the service of humanity. The paradigm is based on African philosophies, history, culture, values and ethics. Mungai (2015) further explains that African people can only cope with modern challenges when they seek strength in the foundations of their indigenous cultures because of the value of collectivity, reciprocity, spirituality and their interconnectedness.

Graham (2002) also pointed out the many interpretations of African values, which underpin the paradigm of the Africa-centred world view, which are the interconnectedness of all things and beings, collective/individual identity and the collective/inclusive nature of the family structure, oneness of mind, body and spirit and the value of interpersonal relationship. These African values were further explained by Peil (1977) as she defines society '….as a group of people with shared values, beliefs, symbols, patterns of behavior and territory'. She further explains that society can be broken down into components such as social structures/institutions, social values/beliefs/cultures and persons/people. It is the interactive relationships of these social variables that generate social change or social processes that affect the state of social structures or institutions, social values or culture or beliefs or meanings and persons in the society or a people.

The second African value is culture. Geertz (1973) defines culture '….as the fabric of meaning in terms of which human beings interpret their experience and guide their actions…'. He explains the two concepts of culture and social structure that could bring about social problems in the form of integrator. He focuses on integrating social structure alongside cultures so that the values that are not appreciated could be done away with and replaced by acceptable ones.

In the third value, Bidney (1970) sees 'man as the measure of culture and society'. He explains the role of man as a modernizing agent which could be of a limited value or subject to conditioning by his environment. He reiterates that

> ….people's ethos is the tone, character, quality of their life, its moral and aesthetic style and mood; it is the underlying attitude towards themselves and the world that life reflect, [while] their worldview is their picture of the way things in sheer actuality are, their concept of nature, of self, of society. It contains their most comprehensive ideas of order.

These two human values could be very important in understanding how people see and view themselves as humans, how they interact with one another and bring about solutions to their problems under their own proscribed order.

Afrocentric social work also draws on sociology to explain the context of need and provision. So wherever we are trying to improve people's well-being, it is helpful to understand something about the way they are, and how policies such as social work and welfare relate to their situation. The International Council on Social Welfare (2002) has argued that policies are dominated in practice by the dominant values of the society, which are issues of family, work and the nation; therefore, financing for development whether human or social structure has to correspond with the dominant values of the societies concerned.

Afrocentric social work is enhanced by the African world view so as to be relevant to the needs of the African people and the emerging developing worlds. Graham (2002) draws a distinguishing feature in Afrocentric social work that in Africa, the person is the centre of promoting empowerment, growth, transformation and development. In a Northern Nigerian village, the whole community could contribute to send one person to school, of which after he graduates, he could empower others Turaki (1993).

Schiele (1997) identified goals of Afrocentric social work as optimal thinking, the fight against political, economic and cultural oppression; building on community strength, engendering affective professional relationship and mutuality within relationships. One of the disappointing facts that Schiele (1997) sees is marginalization, which has become a reality in most African countries (like Nigeria) because of the long history of colonization, racial discrimination and capitalism. He points out the argument of Afrocentric social work that all cultural groups need to be treated equally in all aspects. Afrocentric social work promotes social relationships that break the boundaries of the helper and the helped in which social work would be regarded as professionalism. Schiele (1997) argues that emotional connection (as in kinship and clan relationship) leads to a more trusting and authentic helping relationship and transformation of the person.

Afrocentric social work sees the aspect of mutuality from both the social worker and the client learning from each other of which the end result would be the transformation of the society (Mungai, 2015). Schiele (1997) suggests sometimes that the social worker creates problems that could affect the client despite the benefits of being a professional. He explains that the social worker is not part of the client's problem, but they are just there to help in organizing the client directly or indirectly.

SUMMARY

African tradition, values, culture and aspirations did not vanish with the long years of colonization; instead, new cultures emerged from the existing cultures and were only reformed to attract integration between cultures in the form of marriages and businesses. In Africa, norms and values are still very strong and woven around our aged cultures. The family is responsible for their offspring and all strata of age have a mandate. The aged among the family are being cared for by members of the family till they die. No one thinks of taking their aged parents to the old people's home or the hospice. Everything that pertains to the need of the family is being taken care of by the family. Mungai (2015) explains that Afrocentric social work is the only answer to the quest for indigenized social work in Africa that can only work with the people of Africa (African descent and other similar cultures). His reasons were because there has already been a strong network of history and culture in Africa with strong foundations for indigenized social work. He identifies India and China too as having rich and unperturbed cultural traditions with indigenized social work, of which he suggests that social work theories and frameworks could be centred and drawn on these cultures, which historically have been there for the people and their authentic experiences.

TOP 10 TAKEAWAYS/MAIN POINTS

1. Cultures and values of African societies have been well established over time.
2. Kinship and clan relationship are well defined and carry weight with extensive obligations and duties.
3. The belief systems of most African societies are conspicuous, and this tightens their relationship with one another.
4. The social organization of production, consumption, marriage and inheritance, communal and religious relationships are guided by traditional institutions.
5. Most African institutions have their own instruments of deterring crime.
6. Social activities are focused on social relationships between man and his environment.
7. African social work allows African people to cope with modern challenges.
8. Afrocentric social work generics can help people develop their full potentials.
9. Afrocentric social work allows people to value themselves as human and this brings about solutions to their challenges under their own proscribed order.
10. The family is the central focal point of the African society.

Keywords: African social work, kinship, clan, *Barantaka*, *yandoka*, mutuality, ubuntu, culture, tradition, colonization, social work, social services

GLOSSARY

Afrocentric social work: Afrocentric social work can be defined as 'a method of social work practice based on traditional African philosophical assumptions that are used to explain and to solve human and social problems' (Schiele, 1997, p. 805).
***Barantaka*:** The local name for service in a capitalist and imperialistic environment in Hausa land in Northern Nigeria.
Ubuntu: Ubuntu is a Nguni Bantu term meaning 'humanity'. It is sometimes translated as 'I am because we are' (also 'I am because you are') or 'humanity towards others'.
***Yandoka*:** The local police, *yandoka*, were the instruments by which coercion is exercised and crime deterred.

MULTIPLE CHOICE QUESTIONS

1. Which of the following consists of African Traditional structures?
   a. Council of elders
   b. Institution of traditional historians
   c. Nuclear and the extended family
   d. **All of the above**

2. Which of the following statement is not true?
   a. Social work is becoming increasingly popular in Africa and is one of the helping professions in the world today, concerned with helping individuals, social groups and communities that are socially and economically disadvantaged.
   b. Traditionally, in most African countries, social services were provided within the family, clan and communities.
   c. Colonialization of some of the African countries is attributed to low level of labour mobility and migration from rural to urban areas.
   d. **The African traditional structures for social services do not provide useful background for understanding the successes and failures of African social services.**

3. Which of the following does not characterize African traditional structures?
   a. Presence of local training institutions for personal development especially for women before marriage
   b. Oracles
   c. **Highly self-centric society**
   d. Age grade

4. The institution of traditional historians in Nigeria are called
   a. **Boka**
   b. *Sangoma*
   c. Oracles
   d. None of the above

5. Who are town criers?
   a. Traditional priests
   b. Responsible for waging war and defending the integrity of the land
   c. Gods and deity worshiped in most African traditional societies
   d. **Society's disseminators of information from one corner of the community to another**

6. The structures for social work practice in Africa include
   a. Care for families
   b. Care for members of the community, deterrence from social problems
   c. Providing assistance to the needy
   d. **All of the above**

7. Which of the following statement does not characterize the African social values?
   a. Social values and beliefs in most African societies and cultures seem to have been well established since pre-colonial times.
   b. Social values and beliefs in most African societies are so important that they form part of their belief systems in solving their social, economic, political and infrastructural challenges.
   c. Some of the important values are a result of the extended family systems.
   d. **It stresses that individual needs are completely independent of the needs of the wider society.**

8. Which of the following characterizes clan and kinship relationship in Africa?
   a. They share the same family name.
   b. For protection, where there is a problem with a member of the family, other members of the extended group are always there for rescue.
   c. In social engagements such as marriage, birth and even in death, the head of the family is always there to prevail over the various ceremonies.
   d. **All of the above**
9. According to Bernstein and Gray (1996), which of the following is the purposes of social work?
   a. To empower the client/people
   b. To make clients achieve their goals
   c. To change themselves and their environment
   d. **All of the above**
10. Which of the following is the value of Afrocentric social work?
    a. The person is important.
    b. The person has personal, family and community problems resulting from interacting with others.
    c. Something can be done to alleviate these problems by solving the challenges of the contemporary societies, which could be social, economy in political and technological innovations taking place in most developing countries.
    d. **All of the above**

REVIEW QUESTIONS

1. Identify and explain four African traditional structures of social work.
2. Explain the functions of the African traditional religious structure in upholding the African societies.
3. Explain the significance of the extended family system in the provision of welfare services in the African traditional system.
4. Explain how you would introduce Afrocentric social work framework and theories to social work practice.
5. Describe the social structures in Africa.
6. Identify ways in which Afrocentric social work can help Africans to further cope with modern challenges in social work.
7. What are the benefits of integrating formal social work strategies with the African traditional social work strategies?
8. Why is it difficult to integrate the African traditional social welfare strategies with the formal social work strategies?
9. Explain the success of African traditional social work strategies in confronting social problems.
10. Can be it be argued that the African traditional social work strategies offered better services than the formal social work strategies introduced by the British?
11. Explain how the belief systems of most African traditional societies tighten kinship and clan relationship.

REFERENCES

Bernstein, A., & Gray, M. (1996). *Social work: A beginners text.* Juta Academic.
Bidney, D. (1970). *Theoretical anthropology.* Schocken Books.
Chukuma, G. (2013). *Perspective of social development.* Ahmadu Bello University Press Ltd.
Federico, C. R. (1976). *The social welfare institution, an introduction.* D.C.
Geertz, C. (1973). The interpretation of cultures: selected essays. Basic Books.
Graham, M. J. (2002). *Social work and African centred world views.* Venture Press. https://www.goodreads.com/quotes/tag/social-work
Haruna, A. H. (1986). *Issues in social work: Policy, research and action.* Tofa Commercial Press.
Hussayn, U. I., & Adah, A (2012). *Implementation and management of social policy in Nigeria.* Oriel Publishers.
MacPherson, S., & Midgley, J. (1987). Comparative social policy and the Third World. In *Studies in International Social Policy and Welfare* (Vol. 1). Wheatsheaf Books.
Midgley, J. (1981). Professional imperialism: Social work in the Third World. *Journal of Social Policy, 11*(3), 404–405.
Mungai, N. (2015). *Afrocentric social work: Implications for practice issues.* Allied Publishers Private Limited.
Peil, M. (1977). Consensus and conflict in african societies. Longman Publishing Group.
Radcliffe-Brown, A. R. (1931). *The social organization of Australian tribes.* Melbourne Macmillan & Co. Ltd.
Schiele, J. H. (1997). The contour and meaning of Afrocentric social work. *Journal of Black Studies, 27*(6), 800–819.doi:10.2307/278407.
Schiele, J. H. (2000). *Human services and the Afrocentric paradigm.* Haworth Press.
Tembo, M. S. (1988). *The traditional African family.* Wp.bridgewater.edu/mtembo/articles
Turaki, Y. (1993). *The British colonial legacy in Northern Nigeria: A social ethical analysis of the colonial and post-colonial society and politics in Nigeria.* Challenge Press.
Umoren, N. (2016). Social work development in Africa: Encouraging best practice. *International Journal of Scientific and Engineering Research, 7*(1).
Vass, A. (Ed.). (1996). Social work competences: Core knowledge, values, and skills. SAGE.

RECOMMENDED READINGS

Idyorough, A. E. (2002). *Sociological analysis of social change in contemporary Africa.* Deka Publications.
Idyorough, A. E. (2008). *History and philosophy of social welfare services in Nigeria 1900–1960.* Aboki Publishers.

Index

advocacy skills, 254
advocate, 234
Africa
  historical evolution of social work, 374–77
  political systems and structures, 373
  social change, 372
  social values, 371–73
  traditional history, 373–74
African social work, 369
  traditional structures, 370–71
Afrocentric social work, 376–77
  defined by Schiele, 375
  mission, 375
Annie Besant
  Theosophical Society, 35
anti-oppressive social work, 236–38
aparigraha, 362
Arthashastra, 270
Arya Samaj, 39
assessment skills, 253
Association of Schools of Social Work in India (ASSWI), 181
Aswad, 362

Babasaheb Ambedkar, 331
  Indian Constitution, 332
  personal history, 331
  publications, 332
  separate electorate for untouchables, 332
Bala-diksha Pratibandha Andolana, 93
Baroda School of Social Work, 54
Beveridge Report, 18
Bhagavad Gita
  Yogah Karmasu Kausalam, 22
Bharatiya Samaj Karya Parishad (BSKP), 178–79
Bombay Association of Trained Social Workers, 195
Bombay Social Service League, 83

book
  Task-centered Casework, 241
bread labour, 362
broker, 233

Central Social Welfare Board (CSWB), 67
charity, 221
charity model, 220
Charity Organization Society (COS), 20, 221
  movement, 18
Children in Conflict with Law, 127
codes of ethics
  Jamal and Bowie's view, 298
colonialism
  aftermaths, 137
communication skills, 254
community organization, 213
community practice, 199
conferee, 233
conflict, 359
continuous professional development, 182
Council on Social Work Education, 220
Criminal Law (Amendment) Act, 2013), 126–27
critical thinking skills, 255
culture, 376

de-addiction, 358
Debendranath Tagore, 40
Delhi School of Social Work (DSSW), 54, 192
Deoband movement, 40
Dependency theory, 138
development, 357
developmental model, 224–25
  aims, 224
  features, 224
diagnostic school, 235
documentation skills, 256

Downward filtration theory, 19
Dowry Prohibition Act, 1961, 123
Dravidar Kazhagam, 337
  eradication of caste, 338
  women rights and widow remarriage, 338

early reformer in India
  Annie Besant, 92
  Atmaram Pandurang, 92
  Bankim Chandra Chatterjee, 93
  Dhondo Keshav Karve, 92
  discussion, 94–95
  Ishwar Chandra Bandyopadhyay, 92
  Jyotirao Phule, 92
  King Shahu Chhatrapati, 93
  Mahadev Govind Ranade, 92
  Rabindranath Tagore, 93
  Raja Ram Mohan Roy, 91
  social problems addressed, 96
  Sri Ramakrishna Paramahamsa, 93
  Swami Dayanand Saraswati, 92
  Swami Vivekananda, 93
ecological systems theory, 233
education, 358
  social work, 190
Elizabethan Poor Law, 16, 28, 82, 223
  changes through amendments, 17
  four principles, 17
empathetic listening, 285
Employees' Provident Funds Act, 1952, 153
Employees' State Insurance Act, 1948, 152
enabler, 233
Equal Opportunities, Protection of Rights and Full Participation Act, 1995, 128

Erode Venkatappa Ramasamy, 337
  personal history, 337
  political journey, 337

Federal Emergency Relief
  Administration, 50
feminism, 323
  historical origins and
    development, 323–24
  social work practice, 324
formative professional education,
  290
French Revolution, 104
functional school, 236

Gandhian approach, 243
  foundations, 243
  social work, 243–44
Gandhian social work
  aparigraha, 362
  Asteya, 361
  Aswad—control of palate, 362
  Brahmacharya, 361
  bread labour, 362
  constructive programme for
    society, 357
  de-addiction, 358
  development, 357
  dimensions, 356–360
  education, 358
  equal respect for all religion, 363
  ethics, 360–64
  fearlessness, 362
  foundation, 354
  Gram Swaraj, 357
  linguistic development, 358
  non-violence, 361
  removal of untouchability, 363
  Satyagraha, 359
  social empowerment, 358
  Swadeshi, 363
  truth, 361
government welfare programmes,
  50
Gram Swaraj, 357
Great Depression, 48, 49
  social work education in India,
    52, 53, 54, 55
guardian, 234

Henry Louis Vivian Derozio
  Young Bengal movement, 38

Hull-house Model, 20
humanism, 316
  defined by American
    Humanist Association, 317
  frameworks, 317
  historical origins and
    development, 317
  social work practice, 318
human skills, 257

ideology
  concept, 316
  definitions, 316
  meaning, 316
impermanence, 288
India, history of social work, 21
  ancient time, 21–24
  Medieval period, 24–25
  reform during colonial period,
    25–28
Indian Constitution
  Ambedkar, 332
  Article 42, 152
  Article 43, 152
  Article 43A, 152
India Network of Professional
  Social Workers Associations
  (INPSWA), 195
Indian social system, 168
Indian Society of Professional
  Social Work, 195
Indian Society of Professional
  Social Work (ISPSW), 181–82
International Federation of
  Social Workers (IFSW), 192,
  195
International Labour
  Organization (ILO), 192, 200
intervention skills, 255
interviewing skills, 256
Ishwar Chandra Vidyasagar, 41

justice, 105
Juvenile Justice Act, 2000, 127
Juvenile Justice (Care and
  Protection of Children) Act,
  2015, 127
Jyotirao Phule, 333
  elimination of caste
    discrimination, 333
  personal history, 333
  Satyashodhak Samaj, 333

Kautilya's Arthashastra, 23
Kerala Association of Professional
  Social Workers, 195
Keshab Chandra Sen, 40
knowledge, skills and tools (KST),
  249
Krishi Bank, 336

liberalism, 319
  historical origins and
    development, 320
  social work practice, 320–21
linguistic development, 358
London Charity Organization
  Society, 18

Madras School of Social Work, 54
Mahatma Gandhi, 354
  individual and society, 355
  influence, 354–55
  seven social sins, 356
Mahatma Jyotirao Govindrao
  Phule, 36
  Satyashodhak Samaj, 36
Mahavira, 273
Maternity Amendment Act 2017,
  125
Maternity Benefit Act, 1961, 153
Mediatom, 233
Mental Health Act, 1987, 128
mental health legislation, 128
Mirza Ghulam Ahmad, 42
modernization theory, 137
Muhammad Iqbal, 42

Narmada Bachao Andolan, 345
NASW Code of Ethics, 299
  centrality of human
    relationships, 300
  civil society, lack of support, 307
  colleagues and employers,
    responsibility, 302
  competence, 300, 305
  conduct, 301
  dignity and worth of
    individual, 300
  dignity and worth of person, 305
  importance of human
    relationships, 305
  integrity, 300, 305
  lack of common perspectives,
    306

Index

money-making venture, 306
powerlessness of social worker, 307
professional bodies and professional support issue, 307
purposes, 300
responsibility to clients, 301
service, 300
social justice, 300, 304
social services, 304
social work profession, 302
studying and discussing professional ethics importance issue, 307
values crisis in Indian Society, 306
values of social work profession, 303–04
National Association of Professional Social Workers in India (NAPSWI), 180–82
National Association of Social Workers (NASW), 184
national associations
   concept, 177
   contribution in social work in India, 183
   definition, 177
   functions in social work in India, 182
   role in strengthening social work profession in India, 185
   scope, 177
New Deal, 51
   social work, 51
New York Charity Organization Society, 49
Nishkama karma, 22
Nitishastra, 269
non-judgemental awareness, 290

Panchatantra, 269
   conflict among friends, 269
   crows and owls, 269
   separation in relationship, 269
   Union, 269
   winning of friends, 269
Paramatman, 23
Payment of Gratuity Act, 1972, 153
person and situations (PAS), 249

person in environment (PIE), 249
philosophy
   Eduard and Herbert's theory, 268–69
pluralism, 275
Poor Relief Act, 1601, 223
Prarthana Samaj, 37, 92
problem-solving model, 236
problem-solving skills, 254
profession
   characteristics, 166
   concept, 164
   gap in theory and practice, 168
   meaning and definition, 165
professional associations
   national level, 184
   national level in India, 178
   types, 177
professional ethics, 298
professional social work, 176
Professional Social Workers' Association, 195
Prohibition of Child Marriage Act, 2006, 128
Protection of Women from Domestic Violence Act, 2005, 124
psychodynamic theory, 235
purification tax, 221

Rabindranath Tagore, 334
   employment generation and cottage industries revival, 335
   reform in education system, 335
   rural reconstruction programme, 334
   youth empowerment, 336
radical social work, 344
   contextualizing, 347
   Indian perspective, 348
   limits, 349
   salient features, 347
   theoretical foundations, 346–47
   tracing, 345–46
Raja Ram Mohan Roy
   Brahmo Sabha, 35
   education, 34
   ideology for social transformation, 34
reformers
   Ishwar Chandra Vidyasagar, 25
   Raja Ram Mohan Roy, 25

remedial model, 222–23
Renuka Ray Committee, 67

Sadharana dharma
   concept, 23
Sakama karma, 22
Sanatana Dharma, 27
Satyagraha, 359
Satyashodhak Samaj, 37, 333
Scheduled Castes and Tribes (Prevention of Atrocities) Act, 1989, 128
secular humanism, 317
   definition, 317
Self Employed Women's Association (SEWA), 360
self esteem, six pillars, 289
service
   delivery, 78
   ethical principles, 80
Settlement house movement, 20
Sexual Harassment of Women at Workplace (Prevention, Prohibition and Redressal) Act, 2013, 126
Shatra-mudrana Virodhi Andolan, 93
Sir Syed Ahmed Khan
   Aligarh movement, 39
situational learning, 287–88
skilled helper model, 257
skills, 248
   advocacy, 254
   appreciating diversity, 255
   assessment, 253
   communication, 254
   critical thinking, 255
   defining, 250
   definition in context of social work, 250
   problem-solving, 254
   required for social workers, 251
social action, 214
social casework, 212
   functional, 236
   services, 235
social development, 142
   definitions, 139
   genesis, 135–36
   nature, 139
   relevance of social work practice, 141–42

unified approach to development, 140–41
social developments, 135
social empowerment, 358
social group work, 212
socialism, 318
  historical origin and development, 318–19
  social work practice, 319
social justice, 304
  aim, 105
  barriers to access, 108
  concept and definition, 105–06
  concept of access, 107
  constitutional perspective, 110
  Constitution of India, 107
  Directive Principles of State Policy, 111
  historical background in India, 108
  judiciary role, 113
  theories, 106
  vulnerable groups, 109
  welfare legislations, 112
social learning theory, 239
  applications to social work intervention, 240
social legislation
  awareness generation, 121
  defined, 119
  role of social worker, 120–21
  social change, 122
  social justice, 122
  social work, 120
  specific in country, 123
social legislative
  addressing social problems, 123
social reform
  defined by Rajeswar, 90
  definition, 90
  Heimsath's view, 90
  Islam, 93
  Jains, 93
social reform movements in India
  19th century, 33
  Arya Samaj, 39
  Brahmo Samaj, 35
  Deoband movement, 40
  Muslims, 41, 42
  Pandita Ramabai, 43
  Parsis, 42

Ramakrishna Mission, 36
Sarojini Naidu, 43
Sikhs, 43
Theosophical Society, 35
Widow Remarriage Association, 40
women reformers, 43–44
social sector development, 70
social sector expenditure, 70
social security, 147
  aim, 147
  defined, 148
  defined by International Labour Organization, 65
  definitions, 148
  historical development, 150–51
  meaning, 65
  measures in India, 151–53
  need, 149
  Sir William Beveridge's statement, 65
  social work, 153, 154
  types, 66, 149
Social Security Act of 1935, 50
social services, 75, 304
  characteristic, 80
  concept, 76
  correlation with social work, 80
  defined by Collins Dictionary of Sociology, 77
  definitions, 76
  examples, 83
  historical background, 81–83
  meaning, 76
  Middle Ages, 81
  modern era, 81
  premodern era, 81
  types, 84
  values, 80
  worthiness, 77
social values, 371
social welfare
  concept, 60
  philosophical base, 63–64
  scope, 62–63
  scope and practice, 68–70
  trends, 68
  Wilensky and Lebeaux's definition, 61
social welfare administration, 213

social work, 3, 10, 99, 163, 297, 353
  acceptance, 208
  anti-oppressive practice, 236, 245
  Ashokan Empire, 23
  Bhakti Movement and contribution, 275
  by-product of the changes, 89
  communication, 209
  concept and scope, 6, 7, 8
  confidentiality, 210
  controlled emotional involvement, 211
  creating identity, 291
  definitions, 4, 5
  developmental model, 224–25
  ecological perspective, 233–34
  education, 190
  education post-Great Depression, 52–53
  formative components of skills, 249–50
  functions, 9
  Gandhian philosophical foundation, 277
  global definition, 207, 345
  history in the USA, 19
  IFSW, definition, 194
  Indian Conference of Social Work, 64
  Indic values, 283
  individualization, 209
  major goal, 298
  meaning, 5
  methods, 212
  NASW, Code of Ethics, 299
  national associations and promotion of core values, 183
  New Deal, 51
  non-judgemental attitude, 211
  objectives, 8, 79
  Pincus and Minahan's views, 206
  practice-based profession, 6
  practice-oriented subject, 168
  preaching of Buddha and Mahavira, 272–73
  primary objective, 142
  principles, 207
  professional education, 207
  profession/semi-profession, 167

Index

provision of resources, 9
relevance, 339
remedial model, 222–23
restoration, 9
roles, 8
scope of profession, 7
self-determination, 210
Shri Shankaracharya
    preaching, 274
skills, 248, 252–53
skills required by professional, 208
strengths perspective, 238–39
sustainable model, 225–26
value, 80
social work education, 190
    background and practice, 191–94
social workers, 8
    anti-oppressive practice, 238
    core skills required, 253–56
    documentation skills, 256
    human skills, 257
    International Federation, 64
    interviewing skills, 256
    levels, 7
    National Association, 64
    organization skills, 256
    prominent subsidiary skills, 256–57
    relationship skills, 256
    role in legal assistance, 112
    role in social security, 154
social work models, 220
social work practice
    community, 199
    criminal justice and correctional services, 198–99
    crisis intervention and disaster management, 198
    definition and ethical guiding principles, 194–95
    health, 196–97
    industrial sector, 200
    international level, 200–01
    scope, 196
    women and child welfare, 197–98

social work profession
    knowledge and training, 167
    mission, 283
    values, 283
social work research, 214
social work skills
    classification, 257
social work values
    concept, 283
    definitions, 284
    skill building, 285
Speenhamland System, 18
Sree Narayana Guru, 276
Sri Ramakrishna, 275
Statewide poverty relief, 81
statues of labourers, 223
strengths perspective, 238
    assumptions and principles, 239
    origin, 238
suffering, 286
    definitions, 286
Sustainable Development Goals (SDGs), 68, 195, 226
sustainable model, 225–26
Swami Dayanand Saraswati
    Arya Samaj, 38
Swami Vivekananda, 275
    Ramakrishna Mission, 35
Syed Ahmed, 42

task-centred model, 241
    builds on peoples strengths, 242
    clients, 242
    fundamental nature, 241
    partnership and empowerment, 241
    provide help, 242
Tata Institute of Social Sciences (TISS), 54
Textile Labour Association (TLA), 360
theory, 231
    significance in social work practice, 232
Theory of urban bias, 138
Theosophical Society, 35
The USA, history of social work
    Charity Organization Society, 20

Hull-house model, 20
poor relief, 19
private charity, 20
Settlement House Movement, 20
Third World, 138
Thirukkural, 271, 272
Thompson's PCS model, 237
    emphasises on social workers, 237
traditional practice, 289

unconscious suffering, 286
Universal Declaration of Human Rights (UDHR), 192
University Grants Commission
    review committees on social work education, 165
Upanishads
    role, 23
Upeksha, 284
utilitarianism, 321
    historical origins and development, 322
    social work practice, 322
utopianism, 318

values
    social work, 286
Vasudhaiva Kutumbakam, 63
Vidyadana, 270
visitors of the indigent, 20

wake-up term, 288
welfare
    defined by Webster's Encyclopedic Unabridged Dictionary, 61
Widow Remarriage Association, 40
wisdom
    practising, 282
Women's Association/Mahila Samitis, 336
Workmen's Compensation Act, 1923, 153

Yoga, 22
Young Bengal movement, 38